NAOKI URASAWA'S
20th CENTURY BOYS

Naoki Urasawa's
20th Century Boys
Volume 13

VIZ Signature Edition

STORY AND ART BY NAOKI URASAWA

20 SEIKI SHONEN 13 by Naoki URASAWA/Studio Nuts

With the cooperation of Takashi NAGASAKI

Original Japanese edition published in 2003 by Shogakukan Inc., Tokyo.

English Adaptation/Akemi Wegmüller
Touch-up Art & Lettering/Freeman Wong
Cover & Interior Design/Sam Elzway
Editor/Kit Fox, Andy Nakatani

A CIP catalogue record for this book is available from the British Library.

Printed in Canada

Published by VIZ Media, LLC
P.O. Box 77010
San Francisco, CA 94107

10 9 8 7 6 5 4 3 2 1
First printing, February 2011

VIZ SIGNATURE
www.vizsignature.com

viz media
www.viz.com

NAOKI URASAWA'S 20th CENTURY BOYS

VOL 13

BEGINNING OF THE END

Story & Art by

NAOKI URASAWA

With the cooperation of

Takashi NAGASAKI

NAOKI URASAWA'S 20th CENTURY BOYS

PROFILES

The Friend has been assassinated!! Will the world, still none the wiser regarding his true character, now be blessed with true peace and normality? Or...not?!

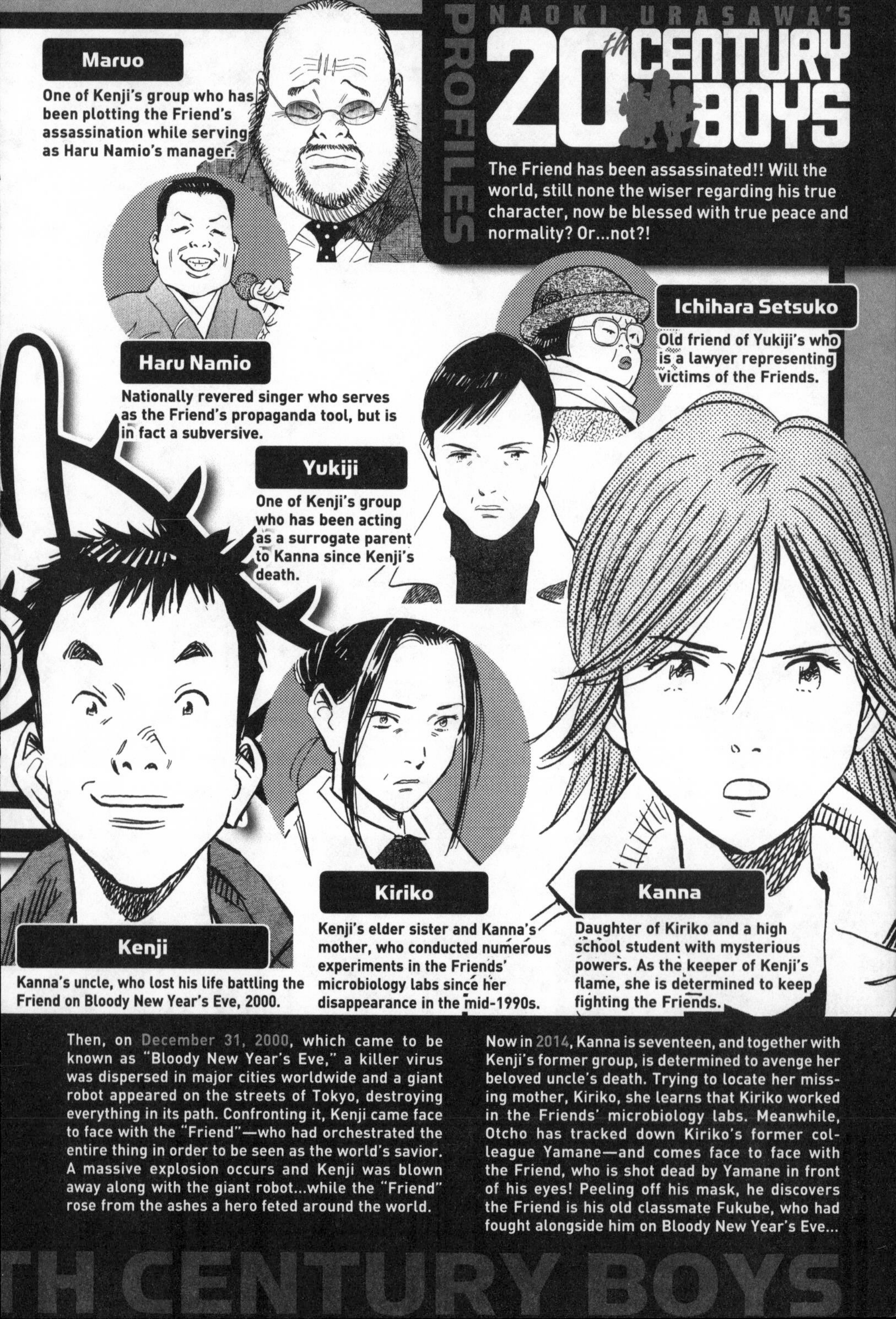

Maruo

One of Kenji's group who has been plotting the Friend's assassination while serving as Haru Namio's manager.

Ichihara Setsuko

Old friend of Yukiji's who is a lawyer representing victims of the Friends.

Haru Namio

Nationally revered singer who serves as the Friend's propaganda tool, but is in fact a subversive.

Yukiji

One of Kenji's group who has been acting as a surrogate parent to Kanna since Kenji's death.

Kenji

Kanna's uncle, who lost his life battling the Friend on Bloody New Year's Eve, 2000.

Kiriko

Kenji's elder sister and Kanna's mother, who conducted numerous experiments in the Friends' microbiology labs since her disappearance in the mid-1990s.

Kanna

Daughter of Kiriko and a high school student with mysterious powers. As the keeper of Kenji's flame, she is determined to keep fighting the Friends.

Then, on December 31, 2000, which came to be known as "Bloody New Year's Eve," a killer virus was dispersed in major cities worldwide and a giant robot appeared on the streets of Tokyo, destroying everything in its path. Confronting it, Kenji came face to face with the "Friend"—who had orchestrated the entire thing in order to be seen as the world's savior. A massive explosion occurs and Kenji was blown away along with the giant robot...while the "Friend" rose from the ashes a hero feted around the world.

Now in 2014, Kanna is seventeen, and together with Kenji's former group, is determined to avenge her beloved uncle's death. Trying to locate her missing mother, Kiriko, she learns that Kiriko worked in the Friends' microbiology labs. Meanwhile, Otcho has tracked down Kiriko's former colleague Yamane—and comes face to face with the Friend, who is shot dead by Yamane in front of his eyes! Peeling off his mask, he discovers the Friend is his old classmate Fukube, who had fought alongside him on Bloody New Year's Eve...

TH CENTURY BOYS

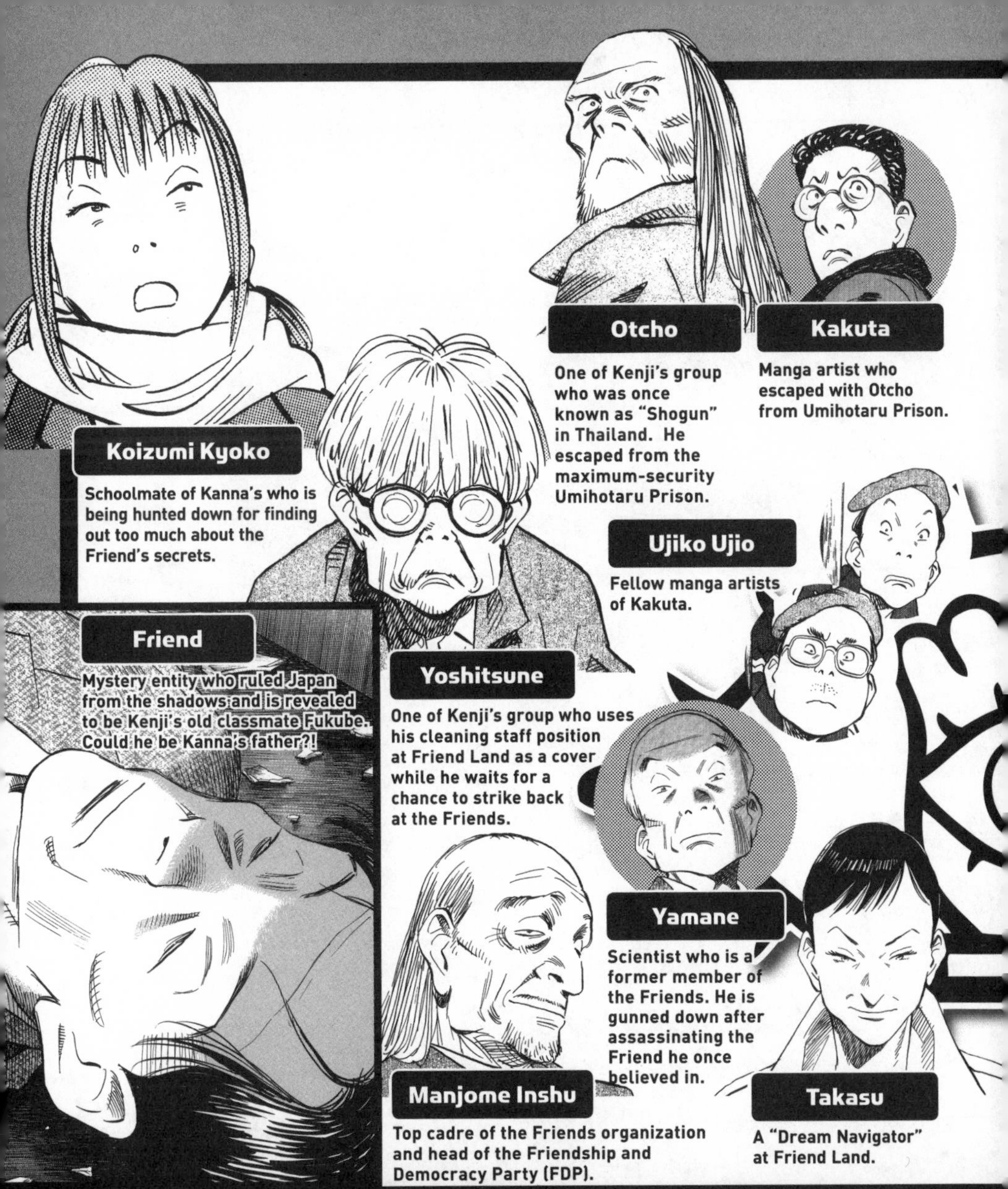
Otcho
One of Kenji's group who was once known as "Shogun" in Thailand. He escaped from the maximum-security Umihotaru Prison.
Kakuta
Manga artist who escaped with Otcho from Umihotaru Prison.
Koizumi Kyoko
Schoolmate of Kanna's who is being hunted down for finding out too much about the Friend's secrets.
Ujiko Ujio
Fellow manga artists of Kakuta.
Friend
Mystery entity who ruled Japan from the shadows and is revealed to be Kenji's old classmate Fukube. Could he be Kanna's father?!
Yoshitsune
One of Kenji's group who uses his cleaning staff position at Friend Land as a cover while he waits for a chance to strike back at the Friends.
Yamane
Scientist who is a former member of the Friends. He is gunned down after assassinating the Friend he once believed in.
Manjome Inshu
Top cadre of the Friends organization and head of the Friendship and Democracy Party (FDP).
Takasu
A "Dream Navigator" at Friend Land.

The story so far...

In the early 1970s, Kenji and his friends were elementary schoolers who, like people throughout Japan, dreamed of the exciting future that awaited them in the 21st century. In their secret headquarters, made out of grass in an empty lot, they made up a story about a League of Evil, whose plan to destroy the world would be thwarted by a group of heroes. They wrote this story in *The Book of Prophecy*.

But in 1997, when the adult Kenji was a convenience store owner raising his missing sister's baby, a series of ominous incidents started taking place around him. By the time Kenji realized these incidents were following the Book of Prophecy, he was being hunted down as a terrorist who planned to destroy the planet Earth. Meanwhile, a mysterious entity known only as the Friend was attracting adherents, called the Friends...

A SUMMARY OF 20

CONTENTS
VOL 13
BEGINNING OF THE END

NAOKI
URASAWA'S

Chap 1: Missing from Memory 7

Chap 2: Friend's Death 25

Chap 3: Round Table 43

Chap 4: Reunion 61

Chap 5: Revelation of 2003 79

Chap 6: The Real Thing 97

Chap 7: Beginning of the End................. 115

Chap 8: Revenge of Frogdoom (1) 135

Chap 9: Revenge of Frogdoom (2) 153

Chap 10: A Quiet Town in Germany 171

Chap 11: Creeping Fear 189

Chap 12: New Command 209

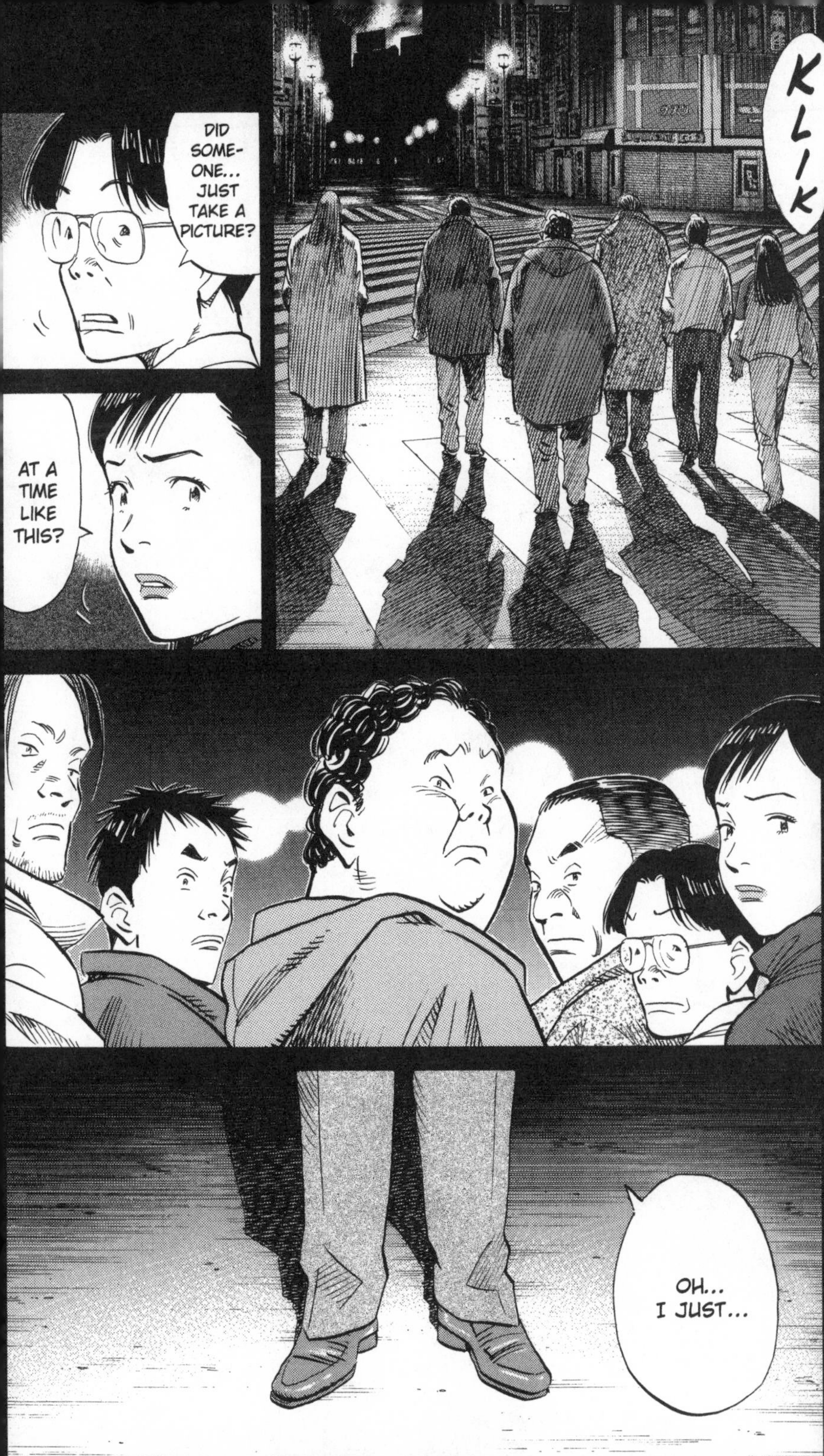
KLIK
DID SOME-ONE... JUST TAKE A PICTURE?
AT A TIME LIKE THIS?
OH... I JUST...

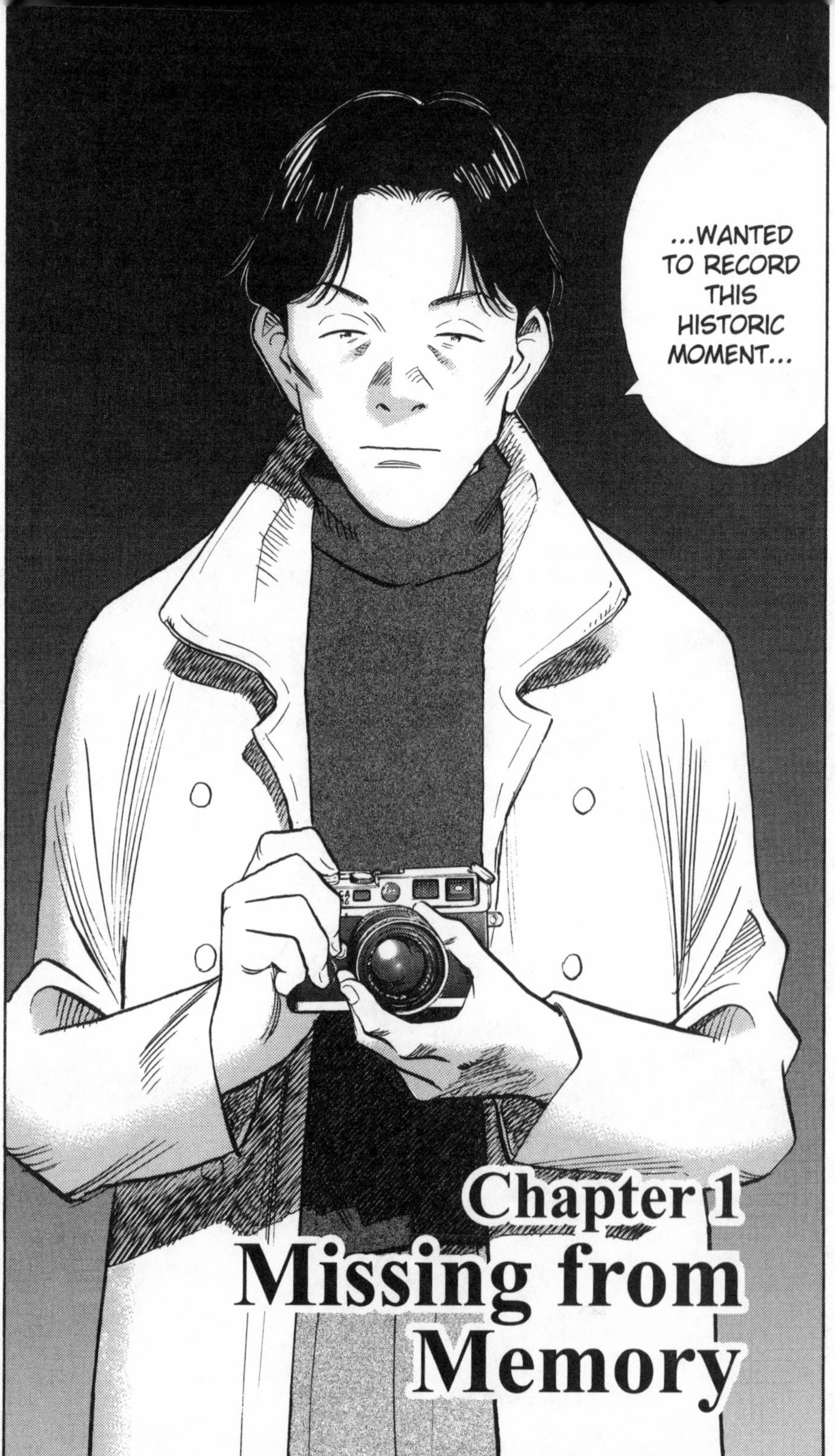
...WANTED TO RECORD THIS HISTORIC MOMENT...
Chapter 1
Missing from Memory

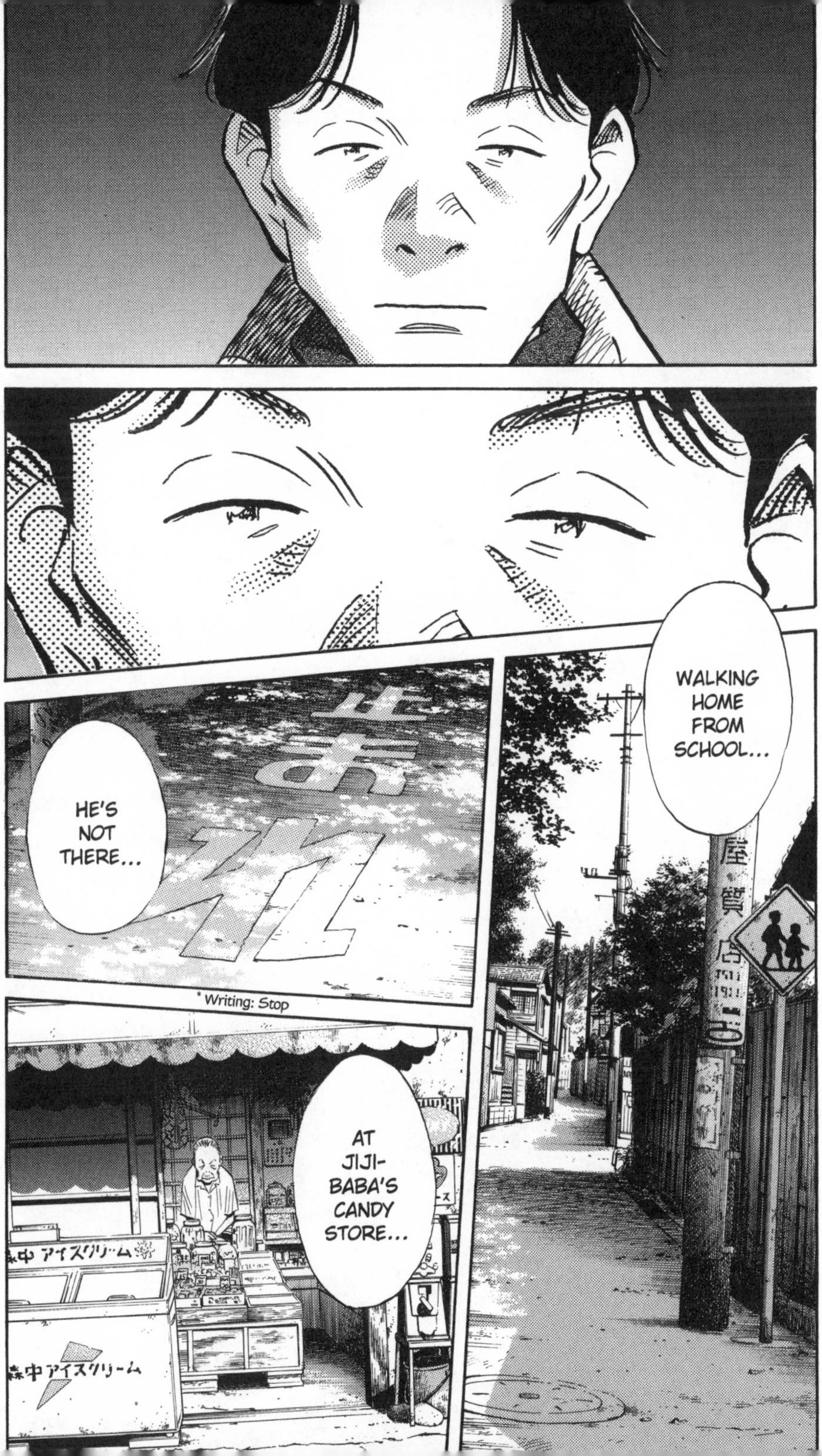
WALKING HOME FROM SCHOOL...
HE'S NOT THERE...
*Writing: Stop
AT JIJI-BABA'S CANDY STORE...

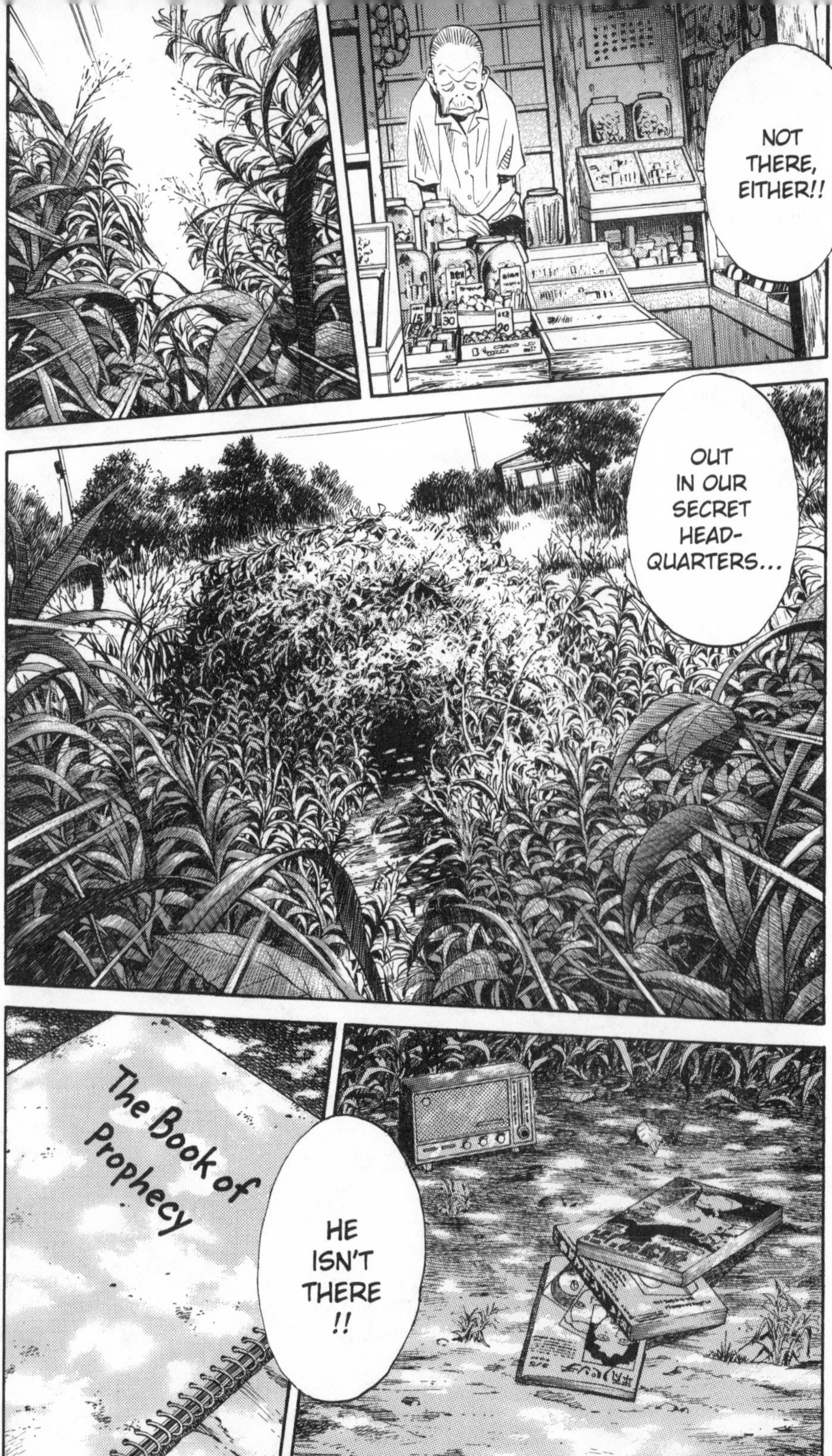
NOT THERE, EITHER!!
OUT IN OUR SECRET HEAD-QUARTERS...
HE ISN'T THERE !!
The Book of Prophecy

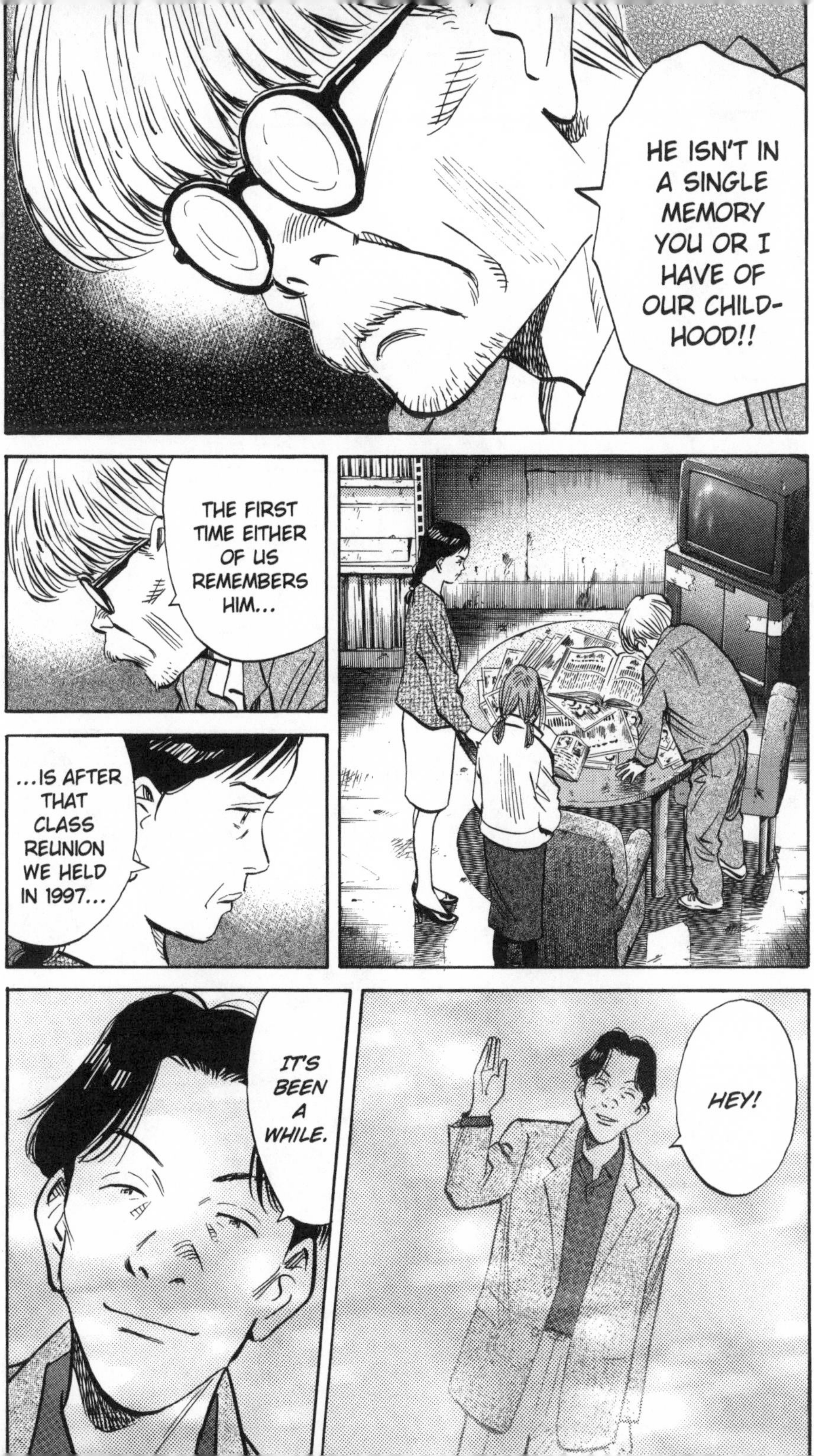
HE ISN'T IN A SINGLE MEMORY YOU OR I HAVE OF OUR CHILD-HOOD!!
THE FIRST TIME EITHER OF US REMEMBERS HIM...
...IS AFTER THAT CLASS REUNION WE HELD IN 1997...
HEY!
IT'S BEEN A WHILE.

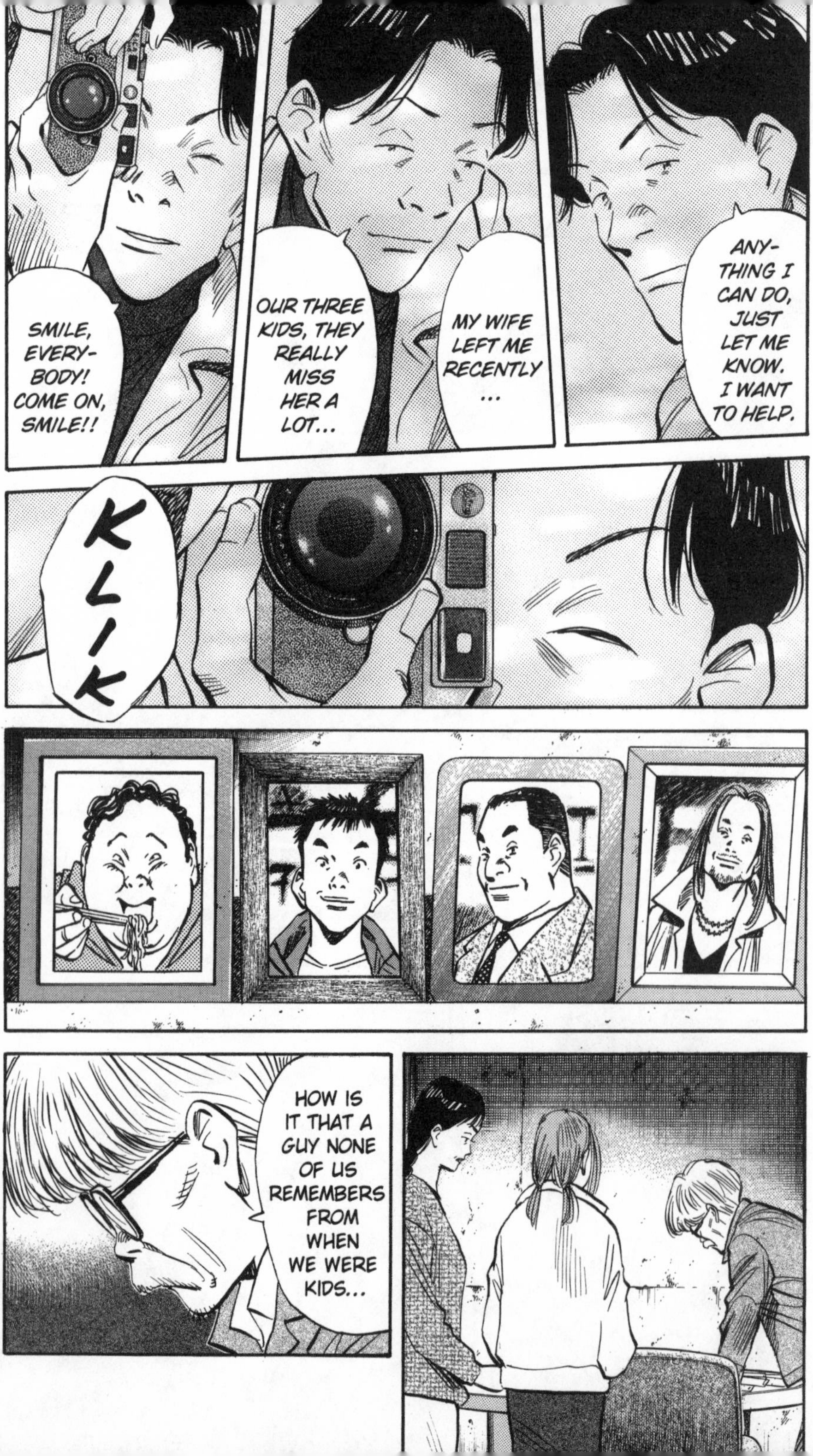
ANY-THING I CAN DO, JUST LET ME KNOW. I WANT TO HELP.
MY WIFE LEFT ME RECENTLY...
OUR THREE KIDS, THEY REALLY MISS HER A LOT...
SMILE, EVERY-BODY! COME ON, SMILE!!
KLIK
HOW IS IT THAT A GUY NONE OF US REMEMBERS FROM WHEN WE WERE KIDS...

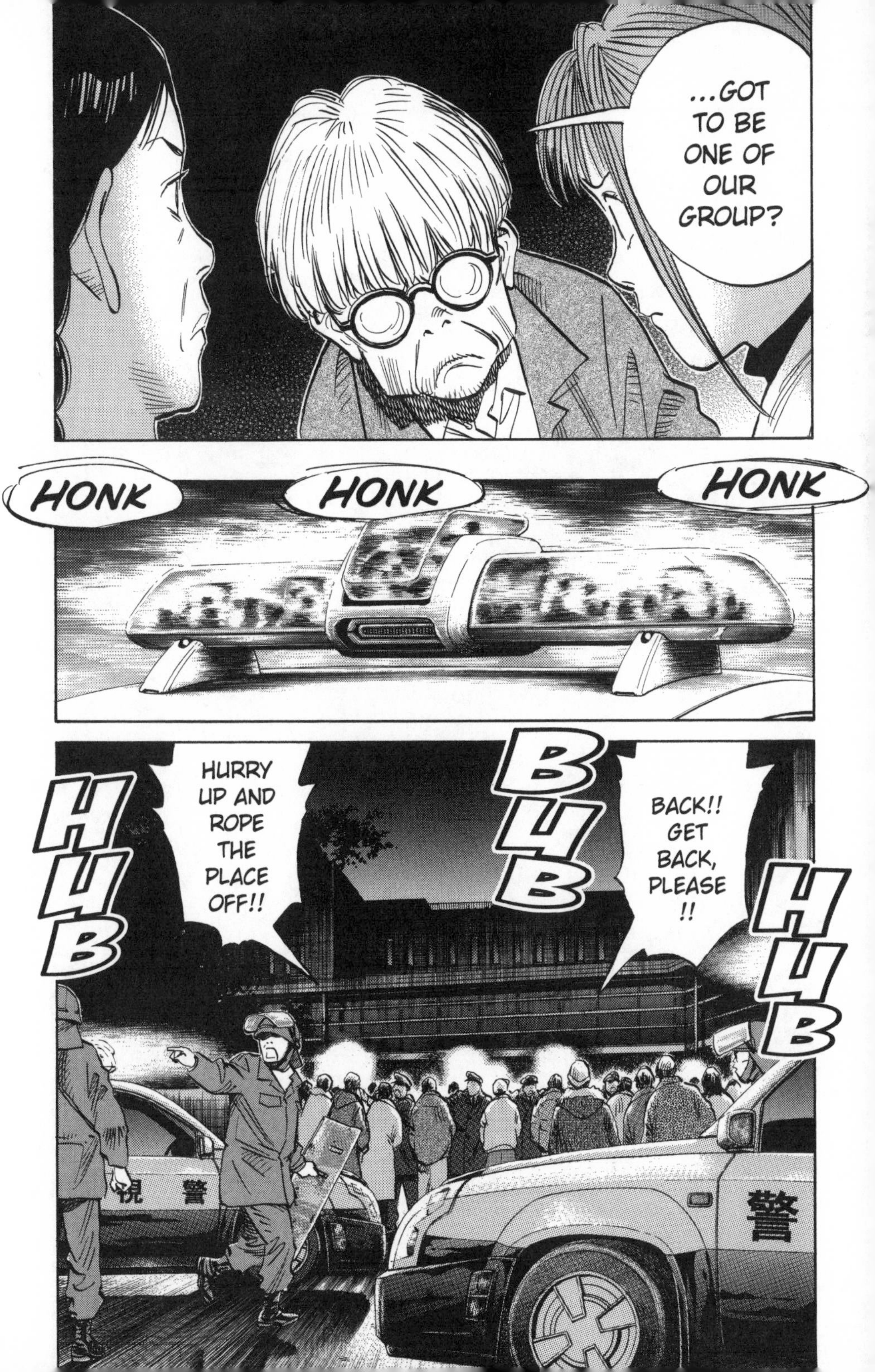
...GOT TO BE ONE OF OUR GROUP?
HONK
HONK
HONK
HUB
BACK!! GET BACK, PLEASE !!
BUB
HURRY UP AND ROPE THE PLACE OFF!!
HUB
警
視 警

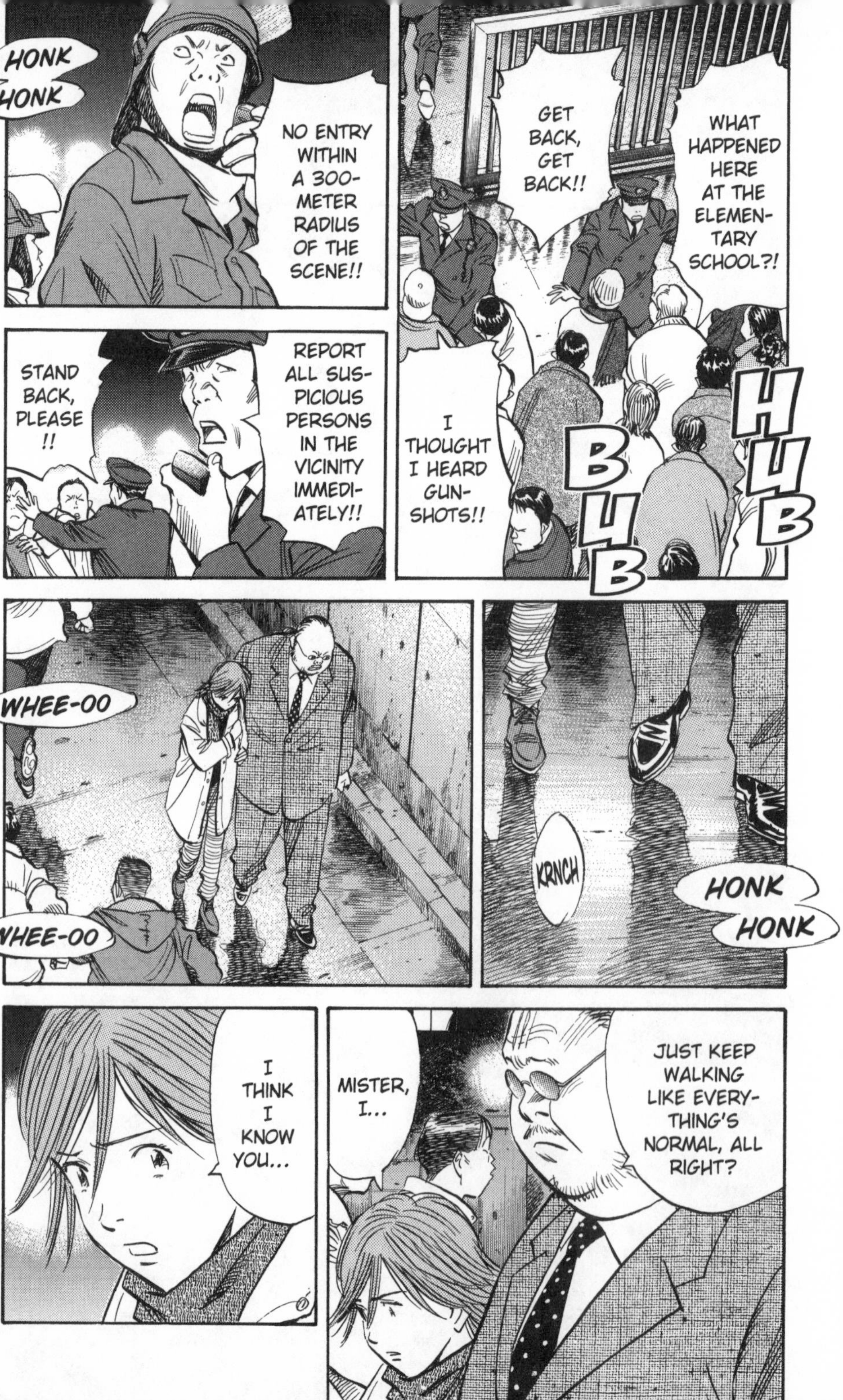
WHAT HAPPENED HERE AT THE ELEMENTARY SCHOOL?!
GET BACK, GET BACK!!
HUB
I THOUGHT I HEARD GUNSHOTS!!
BUB
NO ENTRY WITHIN A 300-METER RADIUS OF THE SCENE!!
HONK HONK
REPORT ALL SUSPICIOUS PERSONS IN THE VICINITY IMMEDIATELY!!
STAND BACK, PLEASE!!
HONK HONK
KRNCH
WHEE-OO
WHEE-OO
JUST KEEP WALKING LIKE EVERYTHING'S NORMAL, ALL RIGHT?
MISTER, I...
I THINK I KNOW YOU...

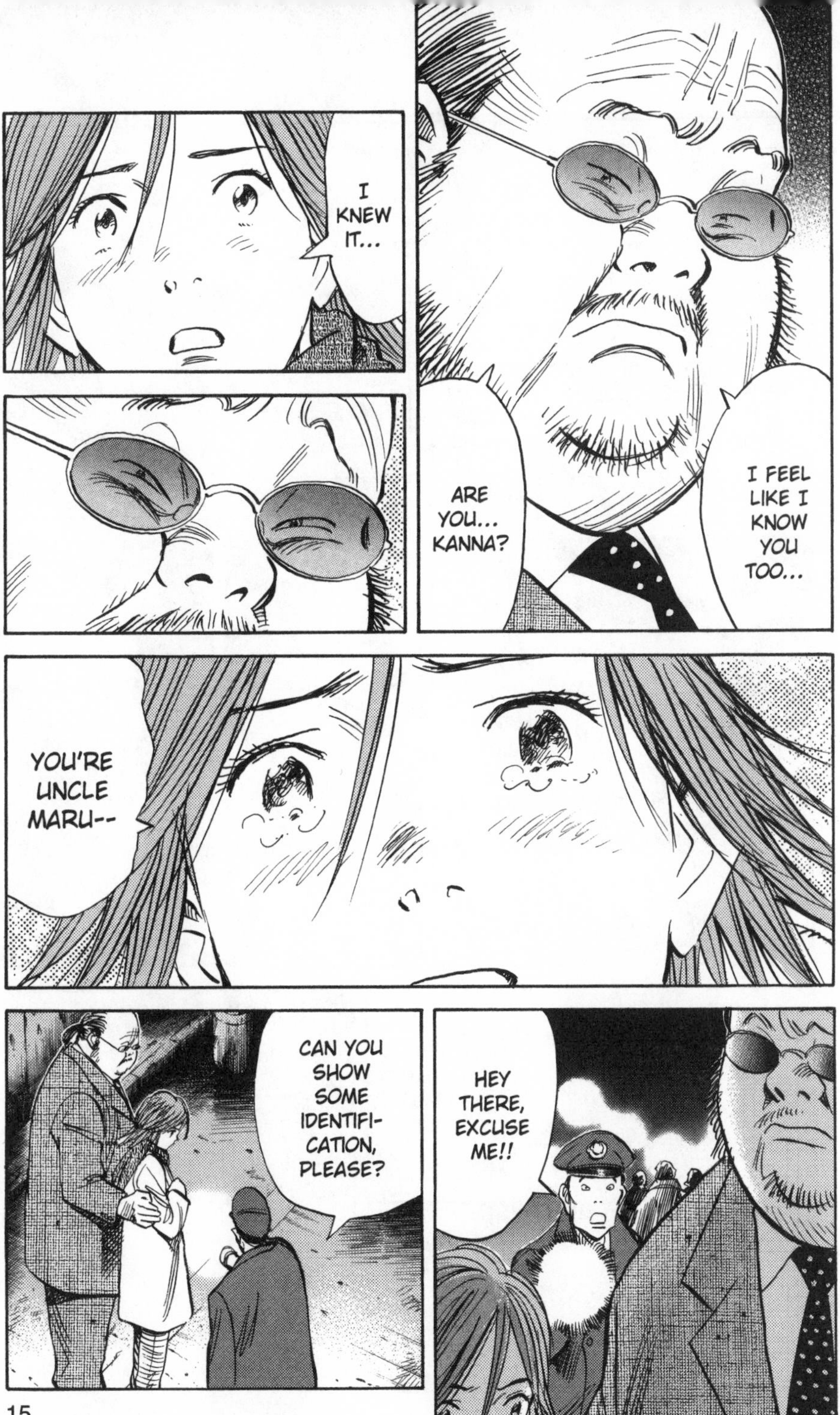
I FEEL LIKE I KNOW YOU TOO...
ARE YOU... KANNA?
I KNEW IT...
YOU'RE UNCLE MARU--
HEY THERE, EXCUSE ME!!
CAN YOU SHOW SOME IDENTIFICATION, PLEASE?

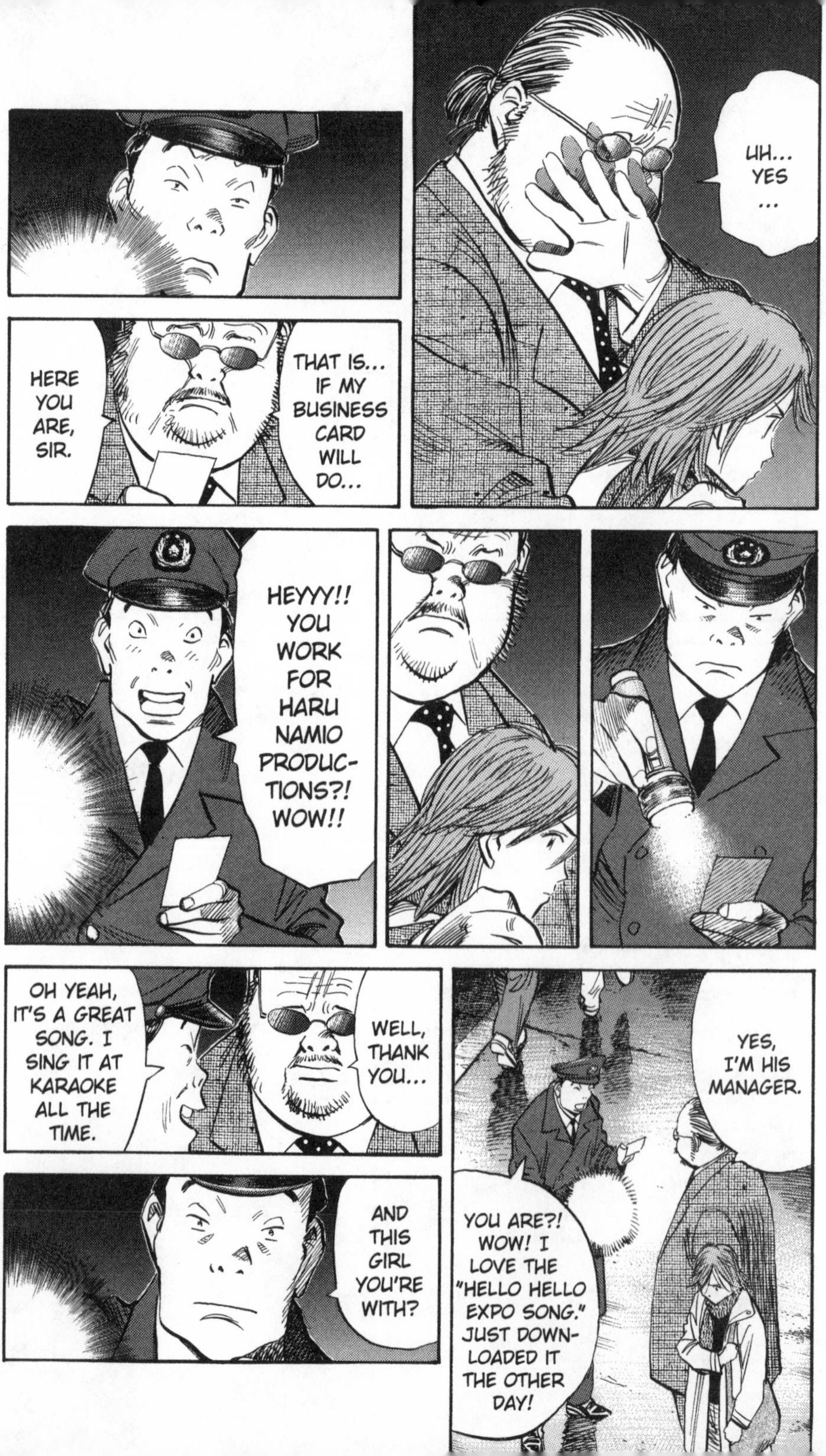
UH... YES ...
THAT IS... IF MY BUSINESS CARD WILL DO...
HERE YOU ARE, SIR.
HEYYY!! YOU WORK FOR HARU NAMIO PRODUC-TIONS?! WOW!!
YES, I'M HIS MANAGER.
YOU ARE?! WOW! I LOVE THE "HELLO HELLO EXPO SONG." JUST DOWN-LOADED IT THE OTHER DAY!
OH YEAH, IT'S A GREAT SONG. I SING IT AT KARAOKE ALL THE TIME.
WELL, THANK YOU...
AND THIS GIRL YOU'RE WITH?

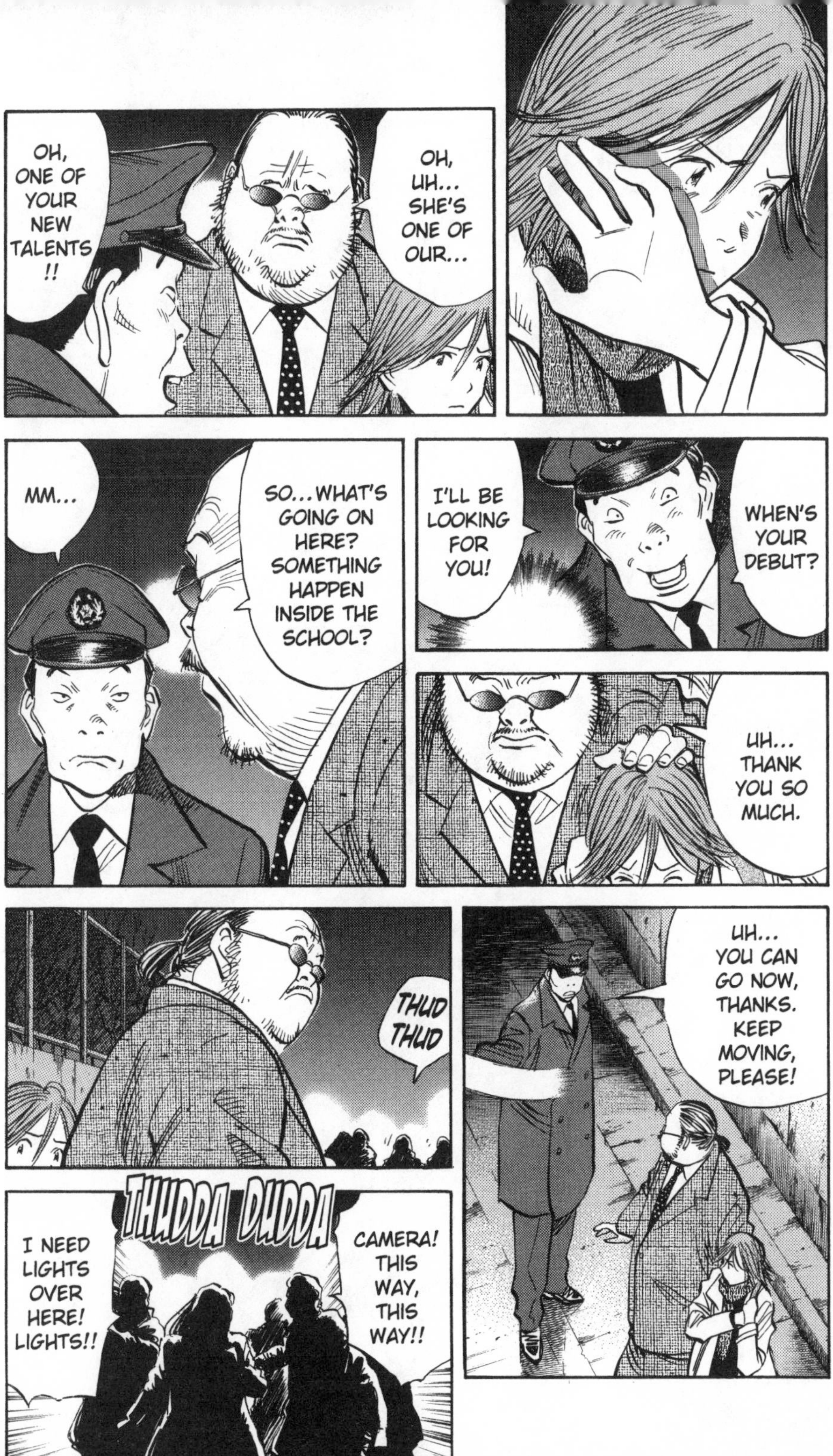
OH, UH... SHE'S ONE OF OUR...
OH, ONE OF YOUR NEW TALENTS !!
WHEN'S YOUR DEBUT?
I'LL BE LOOKING FOR YOU!
UH... THANK YOU SO MUCH.
SO...WHAT'S GOING ON HERE? SOMETHING HAPPEN INSIDE THE SCHOOL?
MM...
UH... YOU CAN GO NOW, THANKS. KEEP MOVING, PLEASE!
THUD THUD
THUDDA DUDDA
CAMERA! THIS WAY, THIS WAY!!
I NEED LIGHTS OVER HERE! LIGHTS!!

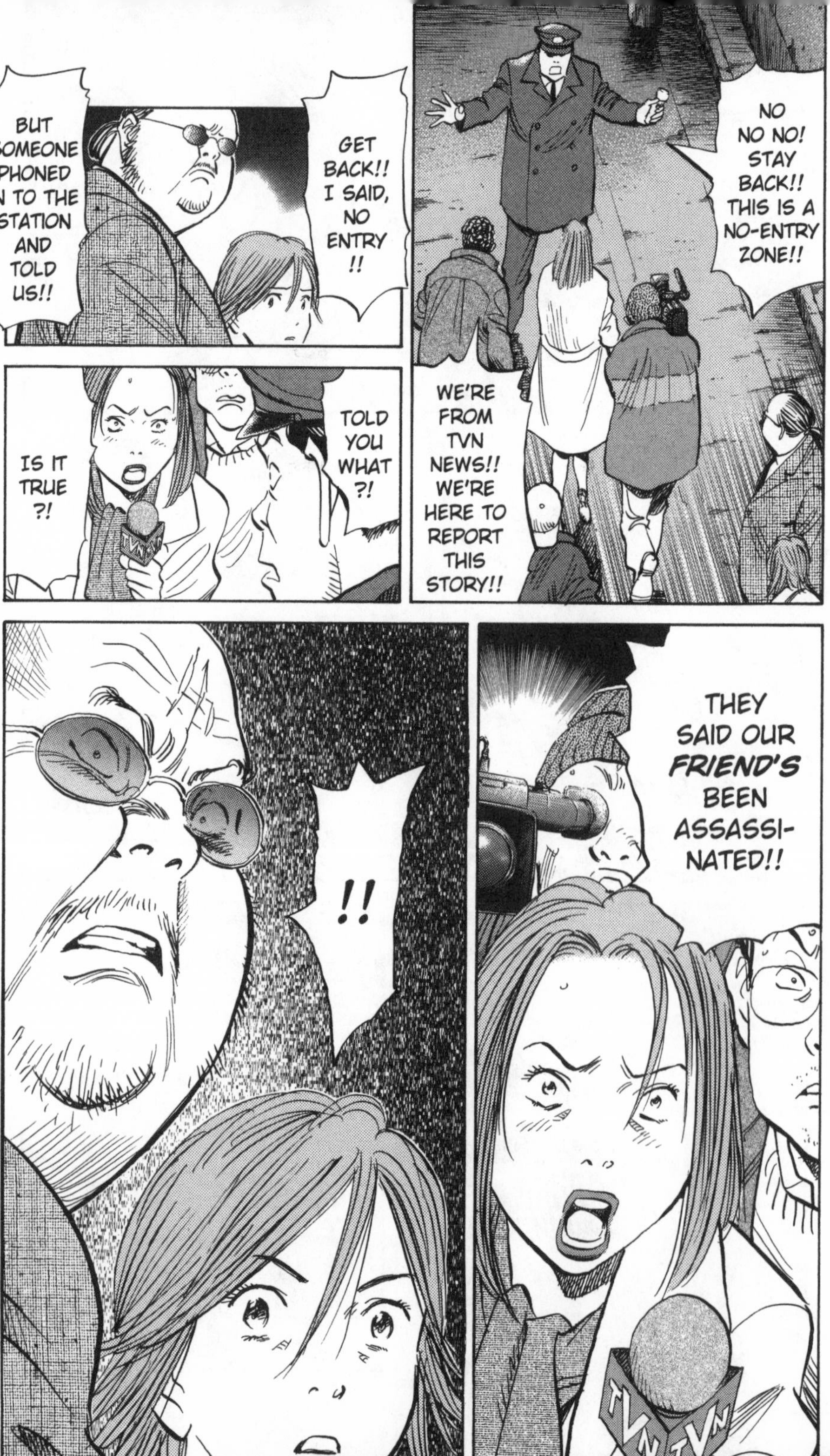
NO NO NO! STAY BACK!! THIS IS A NO-ENTRY ZONE!!
WE'RE FROM TVN NEWS!! WE'RE HERE TO REPORT THIS STORY!!
GET BACK!! I SAID, NO ENTRY!!
BUT SOMEONE PHONED IN TO THE STATION AND TOLD US!!
TOLD YOU WHAT?!
IS IT TRUE?!
THEY SAID OUR *FRIEND'S* BEEN ASSASSI-NATED!!
!!

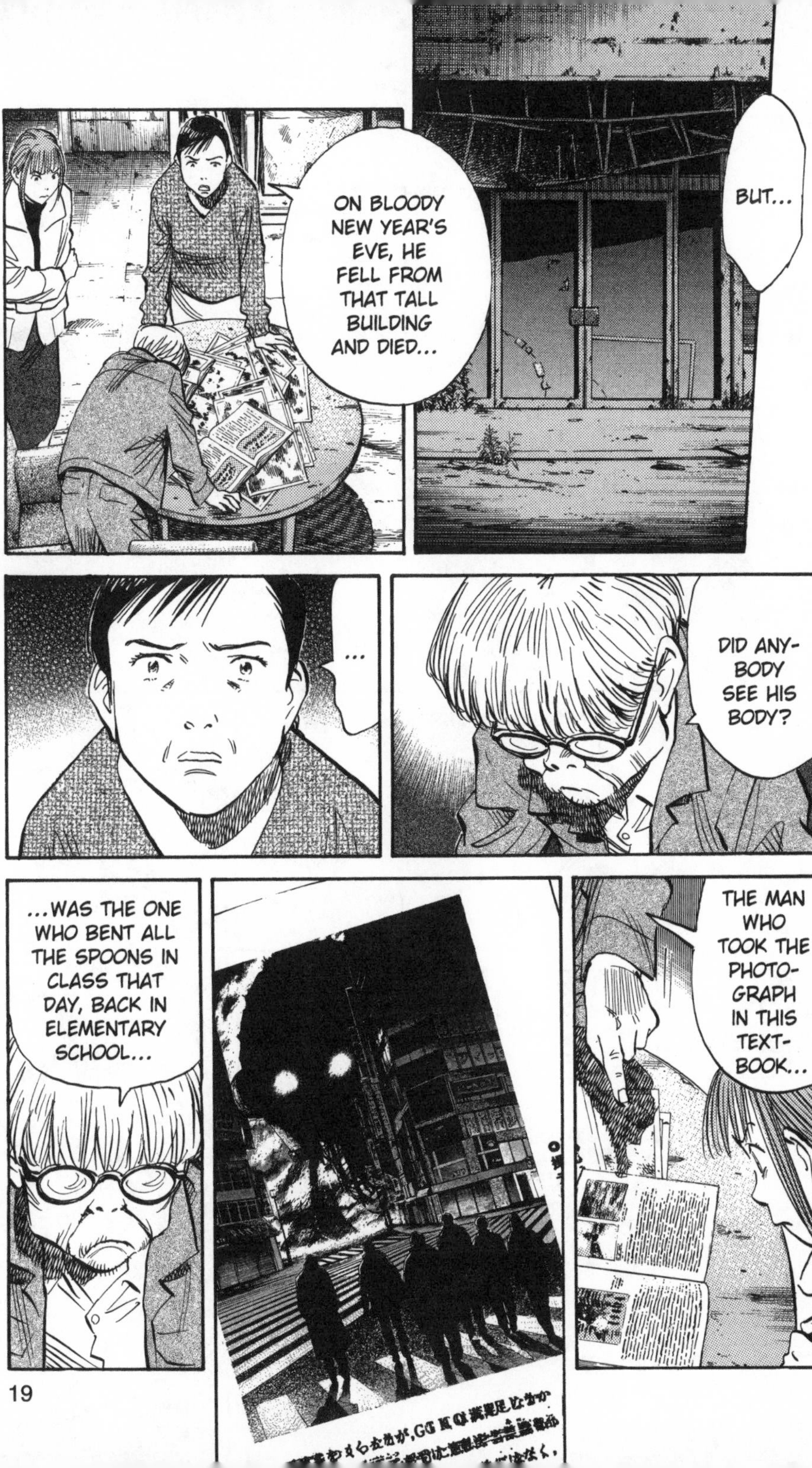
BUT...
ON BLOODY NEW YEAR'S EVE, HE FELL FROM THAT TALL BUILDING AND DIED...
DID ANY-BODY SEE HIS BODY?
...
THE MAN WHO TOOK THE PHOTO-GRAPH IN THIS TEXT-BOOK...
...WAS THE ONE WHO BENT ALL THE SPOONS IN CLASS THAT DAY, BACK IN ELEMENTARY SCHOOL...

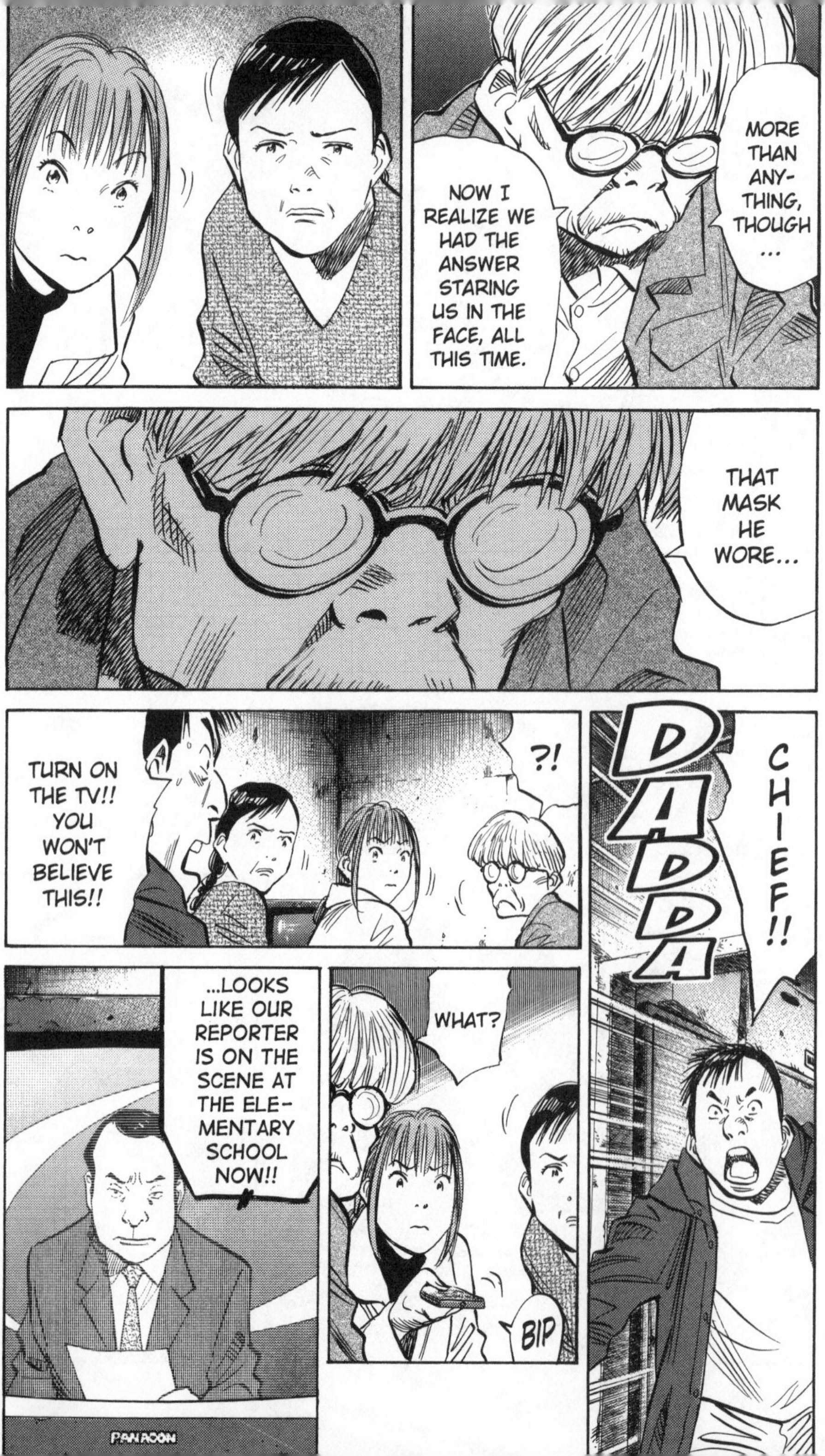
MORE THAN ANY-THING, THOUGH...
NOW I REALIZE WE HAD THE ANSWER STARING US IN THE FACE, ALL THIS TIME.
THAT MASK HE WORE...
DADDA
CHIEF!!
?!
TURN ON THE TV!! YOU WON'T BELIEVE THIS!!
WHAT?
BIP
...LOOKS LIKE OUR REPORTER IS ON THE SCENE AT THE ELE-MENTARY SCHOOL NOW!!
PANACON

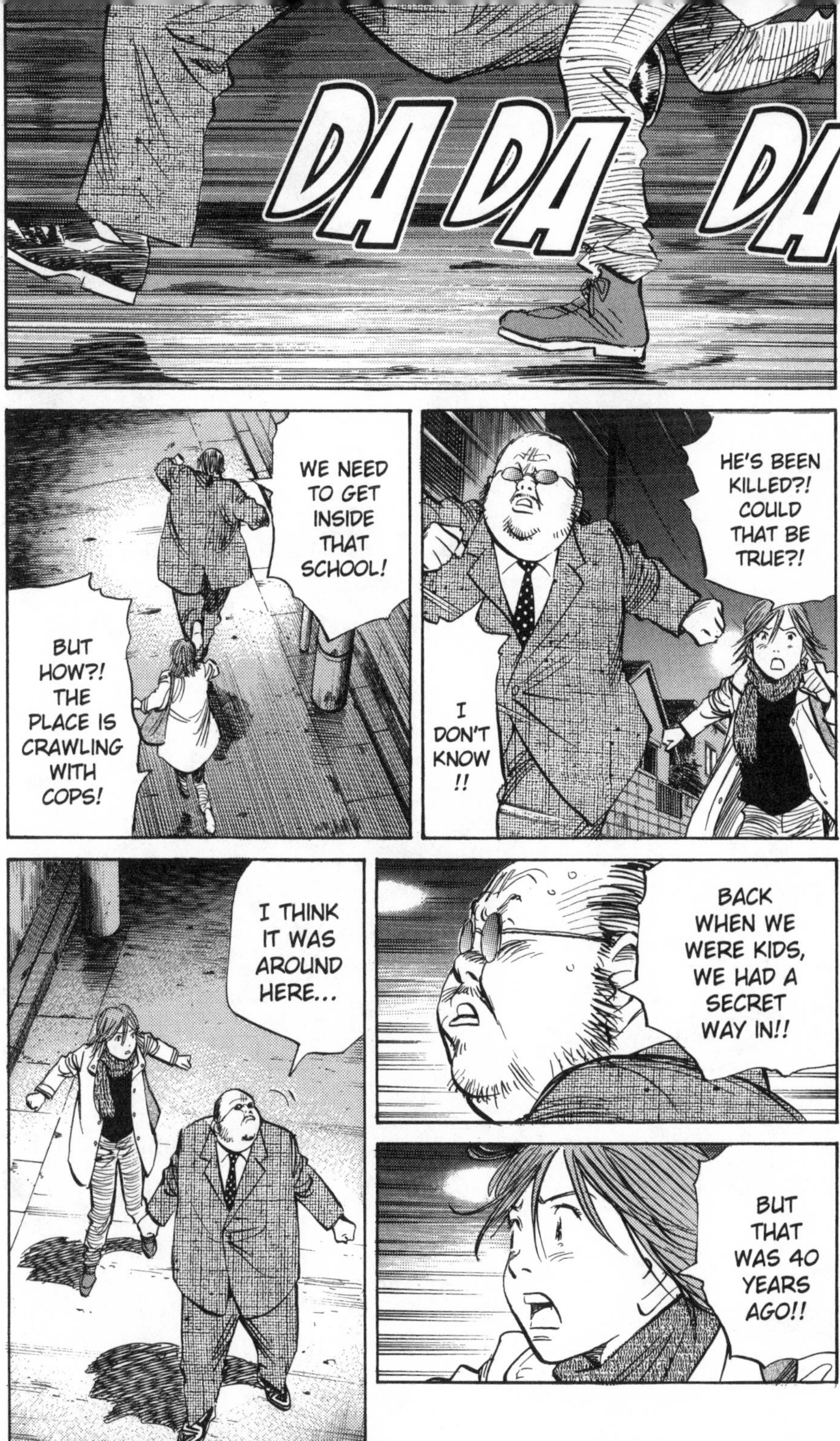
DA DA DA
HE'S BEEN KILLED?! COULD THAT BE TRUE?!
I DON'T KNOW!!
WE NEED TO GET INSIDE THAT SCHOOL!
BUT HOW?! THE PLACE IS CRAWLING WITH COPS!
BACK WHEN WE WERE KIDS, WE HAD A SECRET WAY IN!!
BUT THAT WAS 40 YEARS AGO!!
I THINK IT WAS AROUND HERE...

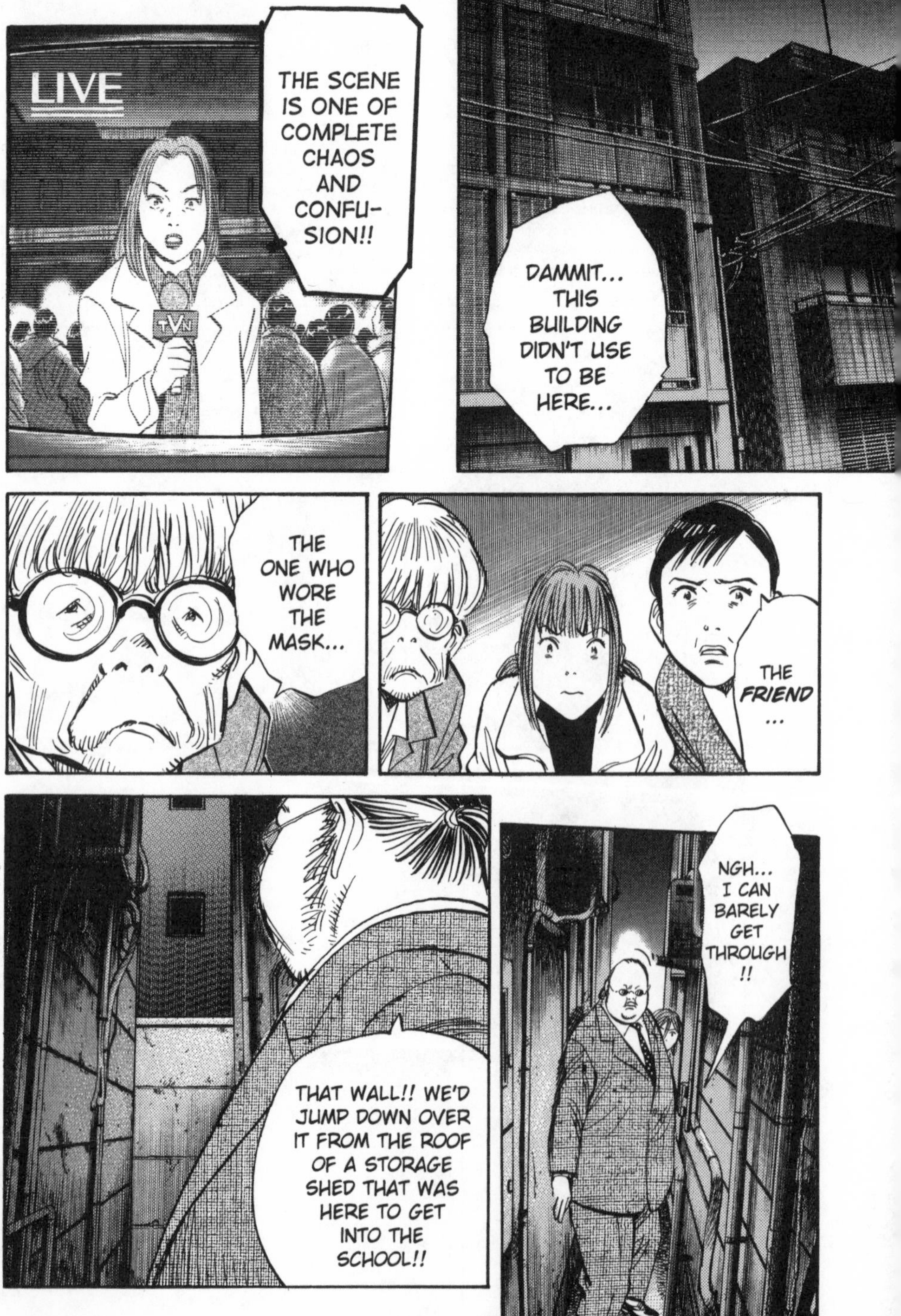
DAMMIT... THIS BUILDING DIDN'T USE TO BE HERE...
LIVE
THE SCENE IS ONE OF COMPLETE CHAOS AND CONFUSION!!
tVN
THE *FRIEND* ...
THE ONE WHO WORE THE MASK...
NGH... I CAN BARELY GET THROUGH!!
THAT WALL!! WE'D JUMP DOWN OVER IT FROM THE ROOF OF A STORAGE SHED THAT WAS HERE TO GET INTO THE SCHOOL!!

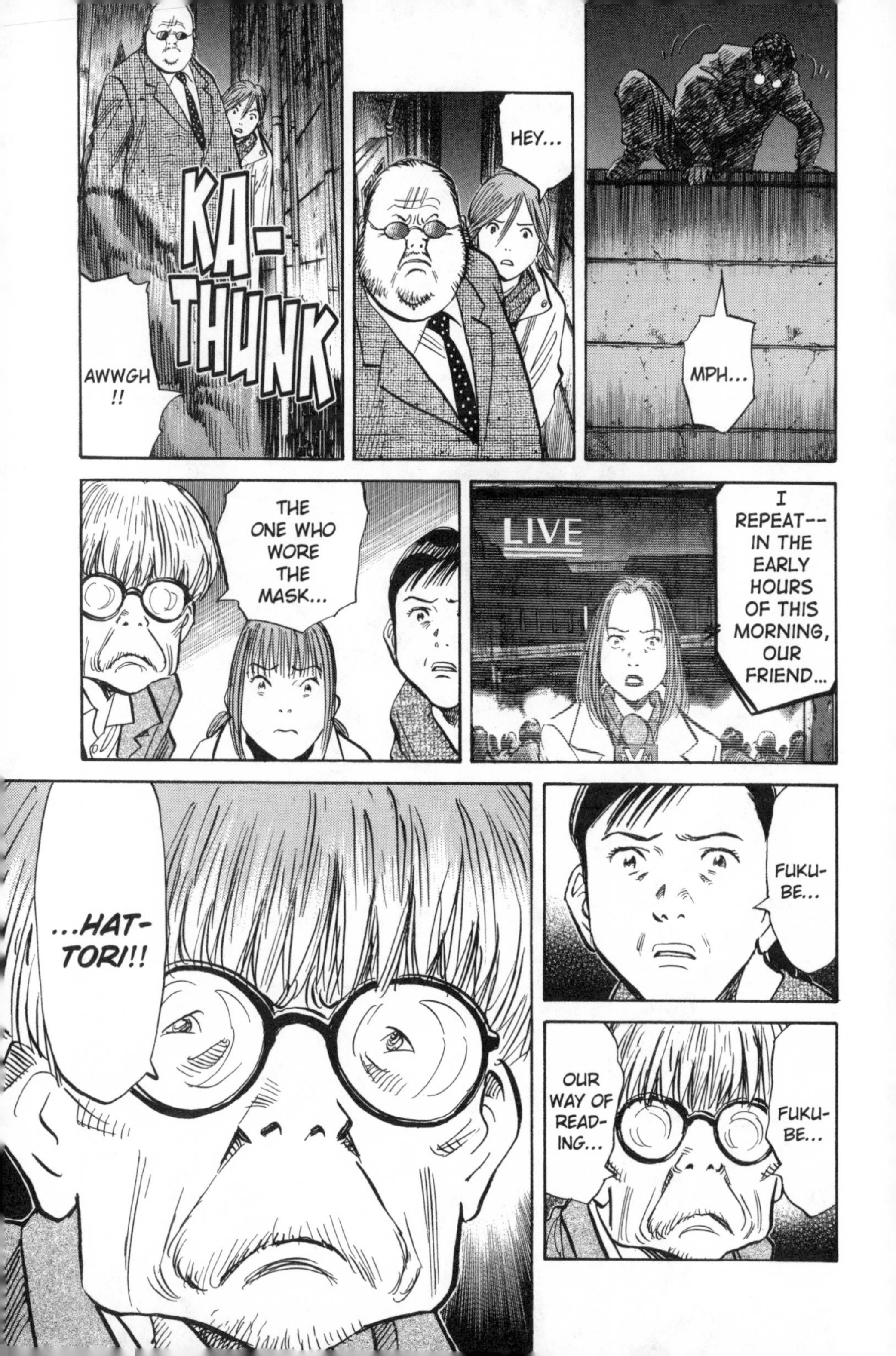
MPH...
HEY...
KA-THUNK
AWWGH !!
I REPEAT-- IN THE EARLY HOURS OF THIS MORNING, OUR FRIEND...
LIVE
THE ONE WHO WORE THE MASK...
FUKU-BE...
FUKU-BE...
OUR WAY OF READ-ING...
...HAT-TORI!!

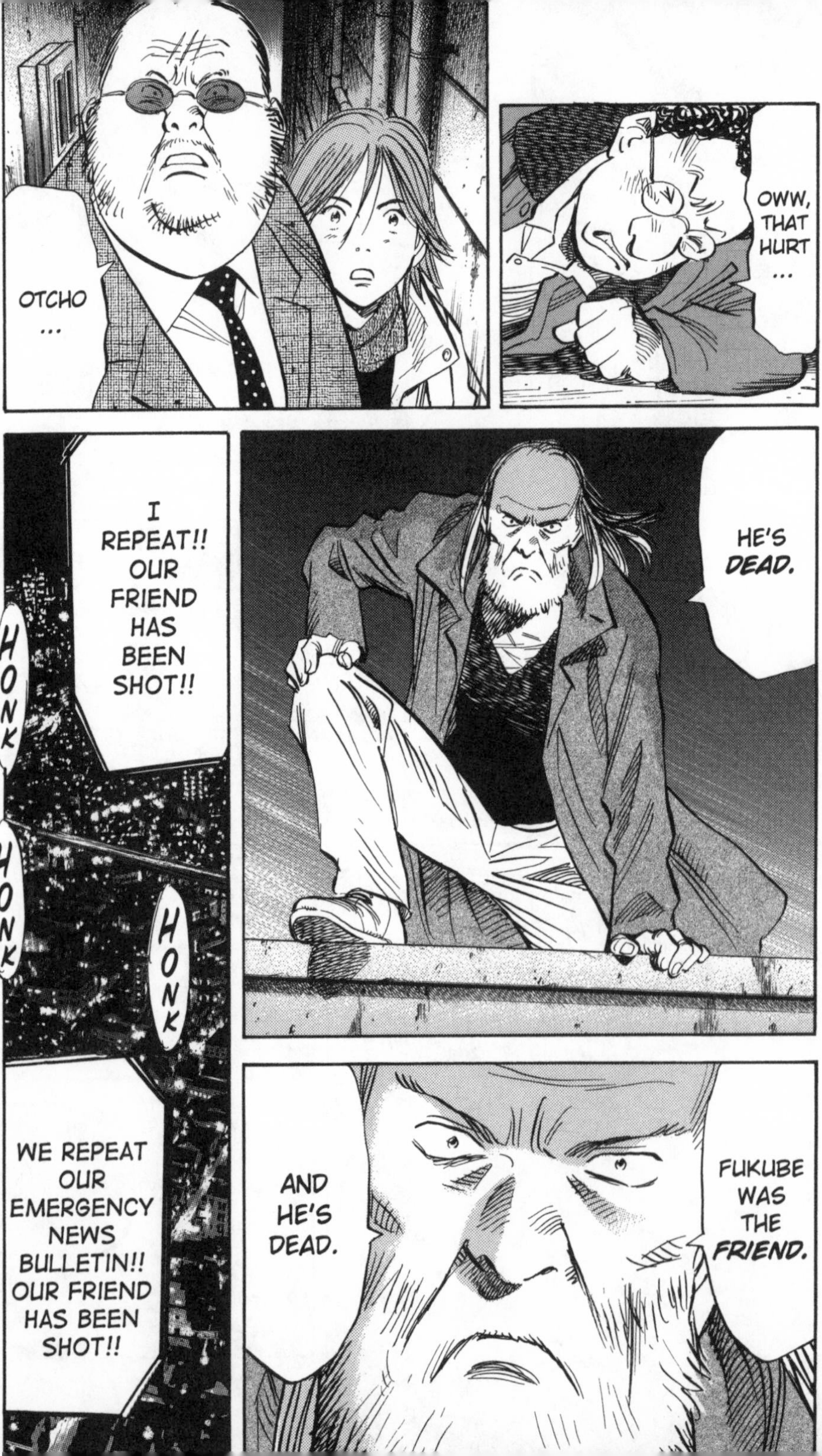
OWW, THAT HURT ...
OTCHO ...
HE'S *DEAD.*
FUKUBE WAS THE *FRIEND.*
AND HE'S DEAD.
I REPEAT!! OUR FRIEND HAS BEEN SHOT!!
HONK
HONK
HONK
WE REPEAT OUR EMERGENCY NEWS BULLETIN!! OUR FRIEND HAS BEEN SHOT!!

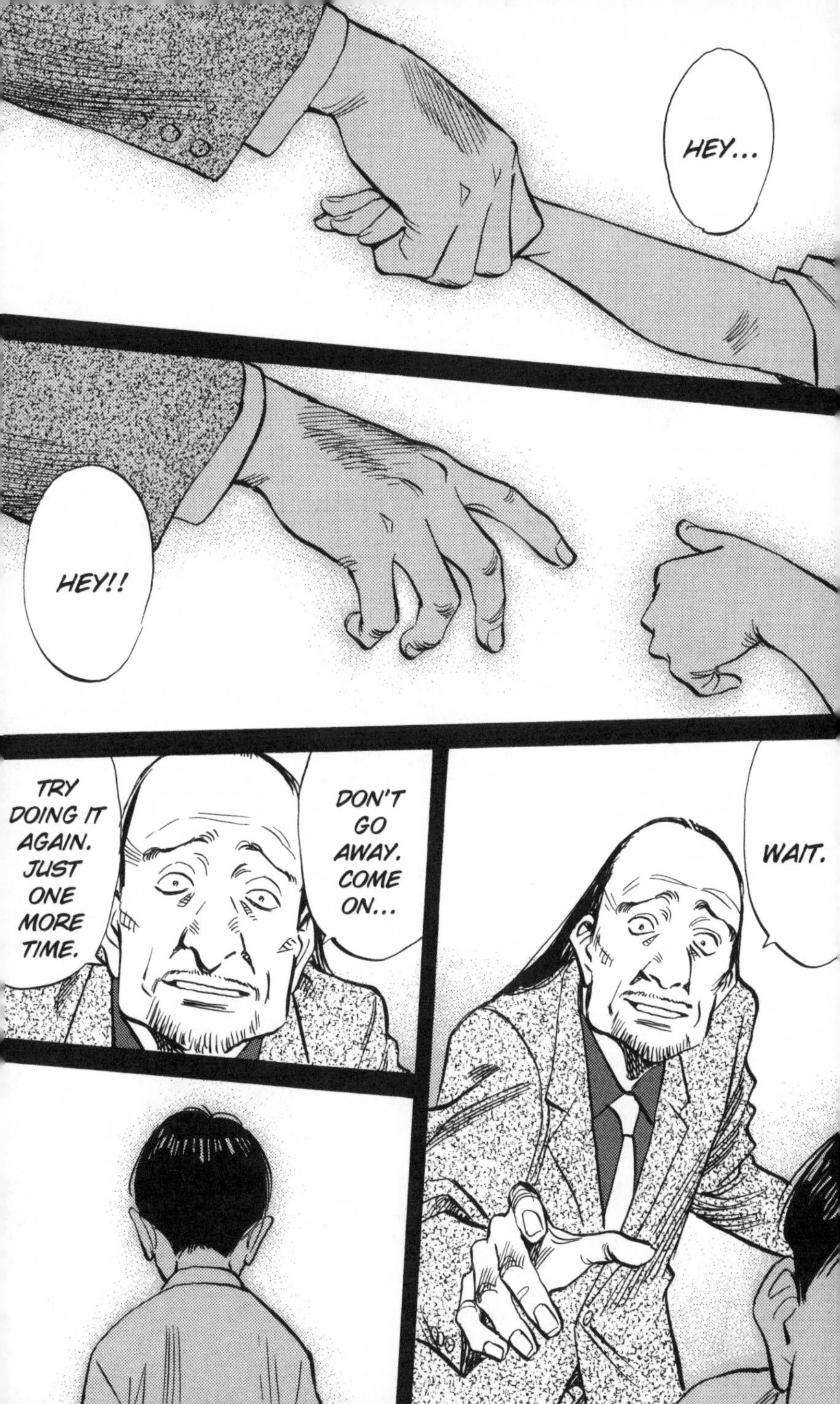
HEY...
HEY!!
WAIT.
DON'T GO AWAY. COME ON...
TRY DOING IT AGAIN. JUST ONE MORE TIME.

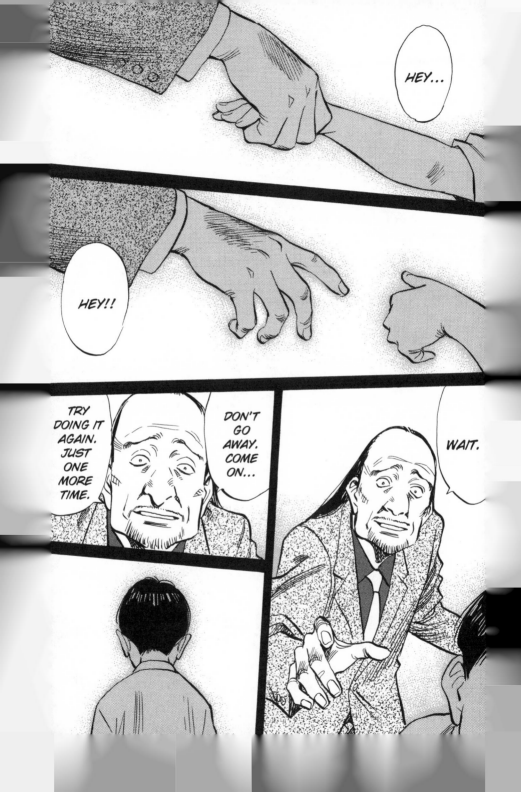

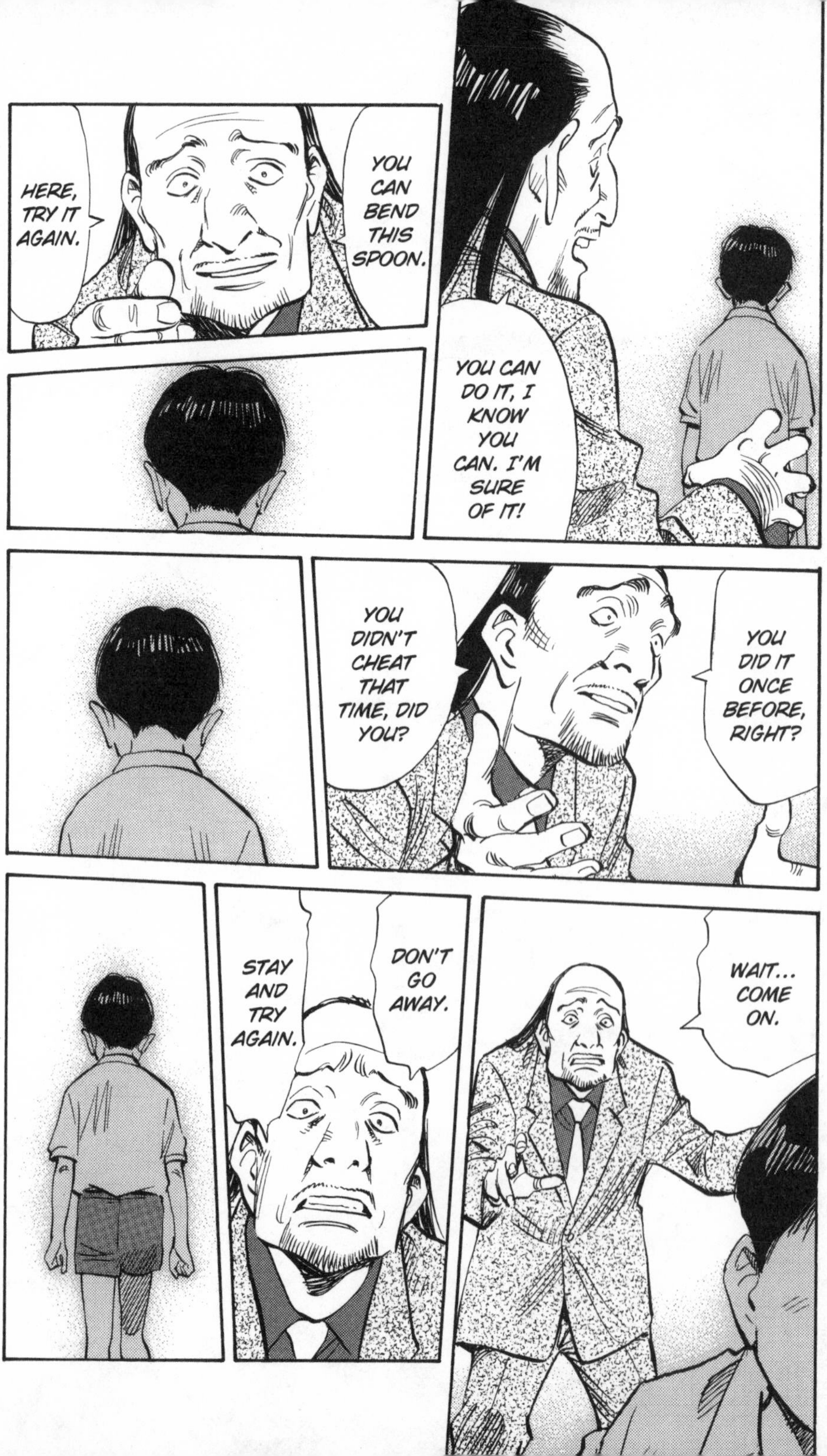
YOU CAN DO IT, I KNOW YOU CAN. I'M SURE OF IT!
YOU CAN BEND THIS SPOON.
HERE, TRY IT AGAIN.
YOU DID IT ONCE BEFORE, RIGHT?
YOU DIDN'T CHEAT THAT TIME, DID YOU?
WAIT... COME ON.
DON'T GO AWAY.
STAY AND TRY AGAIN.

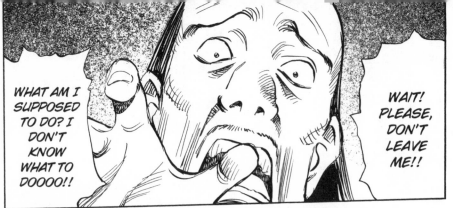

WAIT! PLEASE, DON'T LEAVE ME!!
WHAT AM I SUPPOSED TO DO? I DON'T KNOW WHAT TO DOOOO!!
HUH?
URGH!!
MAG-GOTS!!
HYAGH!!
WAAAAAGH!!

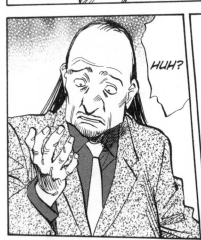

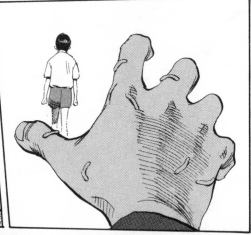

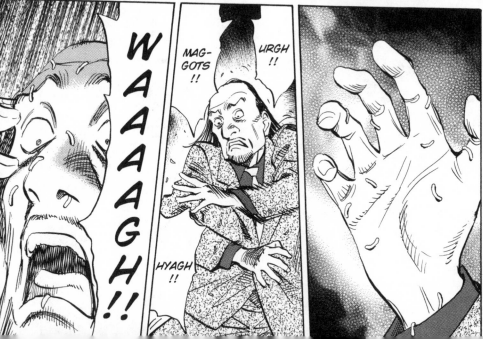

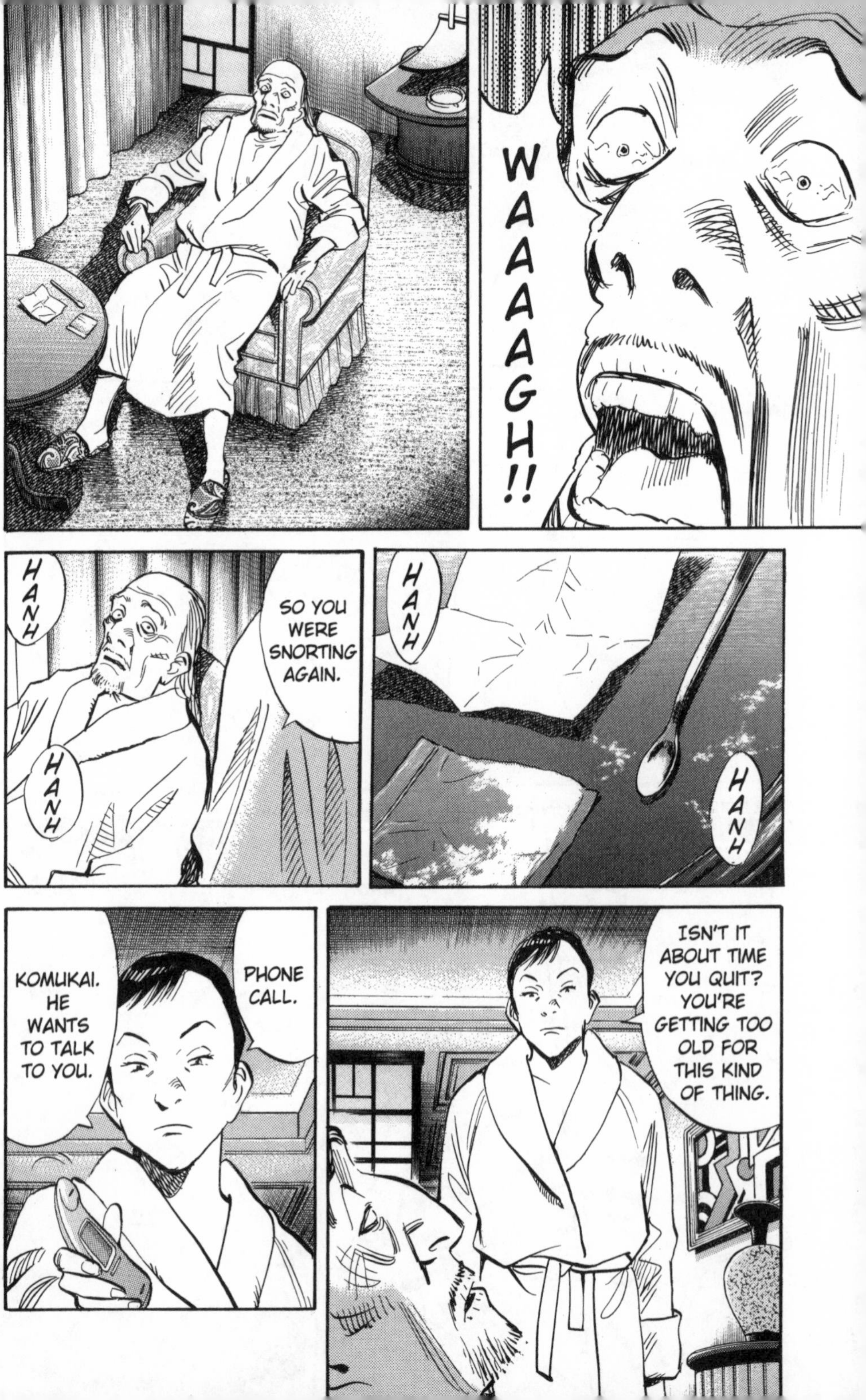
WAAAAGH!!
HANH
HANH
SO YOU WERE SNORTING AGAIN.
HANH
HANH
ISN'T IT ABOUT TIME YOU QUIT? YOU'RE GETTING TOO OLD FOR THIS KIND OF THING.
PHONE CALL.
KOMUKAI. HE WANTS TO TALK TO YOU.

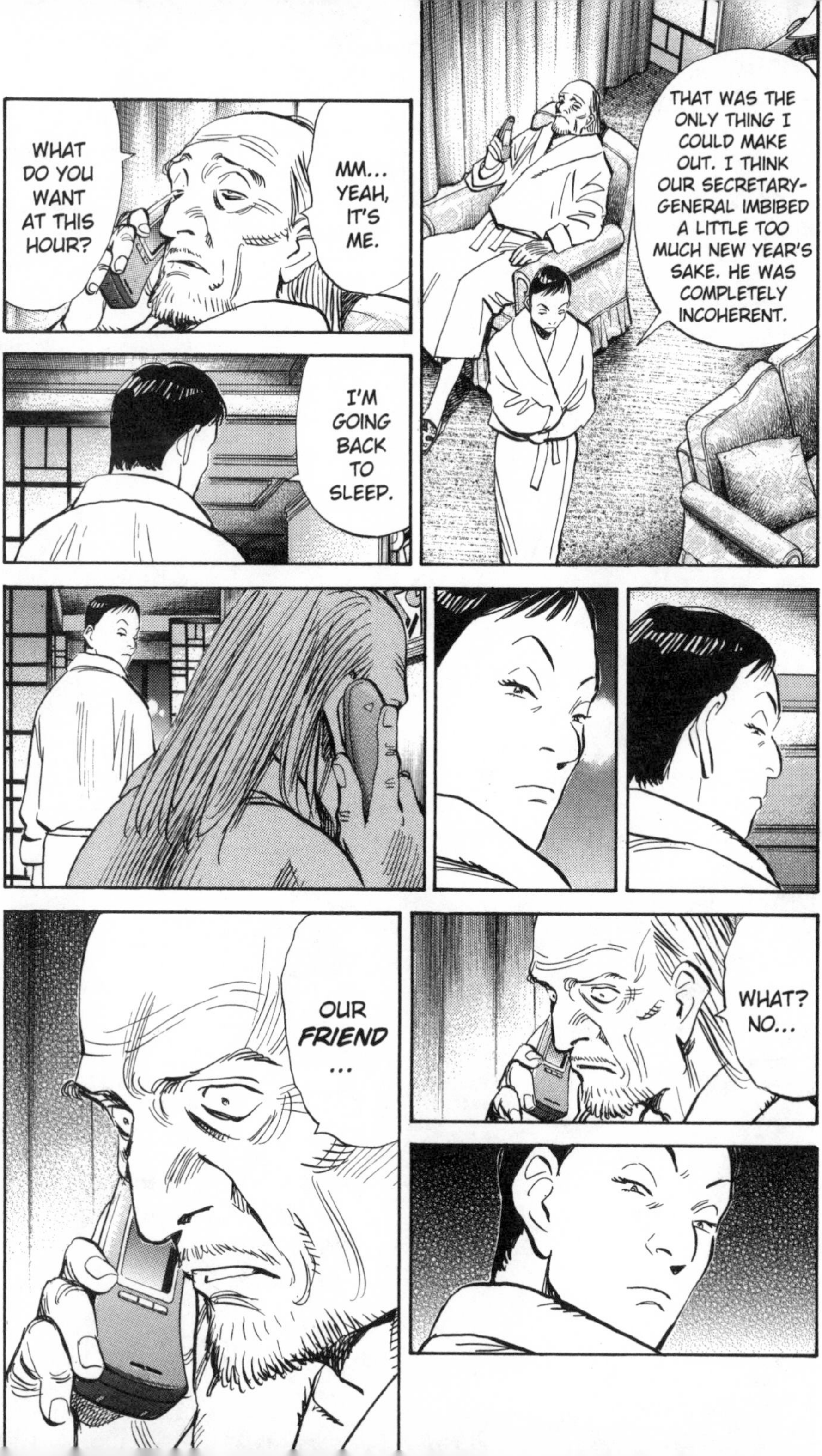
THAT WAS THE ONLY THING I COULD MAKE OUT. I THINK OUR SECRETARY-GENERAL IMBIBED A LITTLE TOO MUCH NEW YEAR'S SAKE. HE WAS COMPLETELY INCOHERENT.
MM... YEAH, IT'S ME.
WHAT DO YOU WANT AT THIS HOUR?
I'M GOING BACK TO SLEEP.
WHAT? NO...
OUR *FRIEND* ...

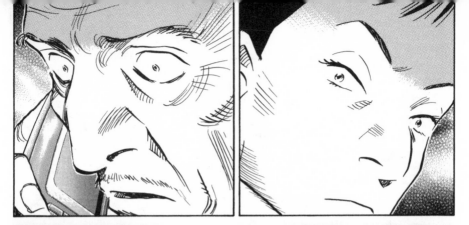

...IS DEAD?

Chapter 2
Friend's Death

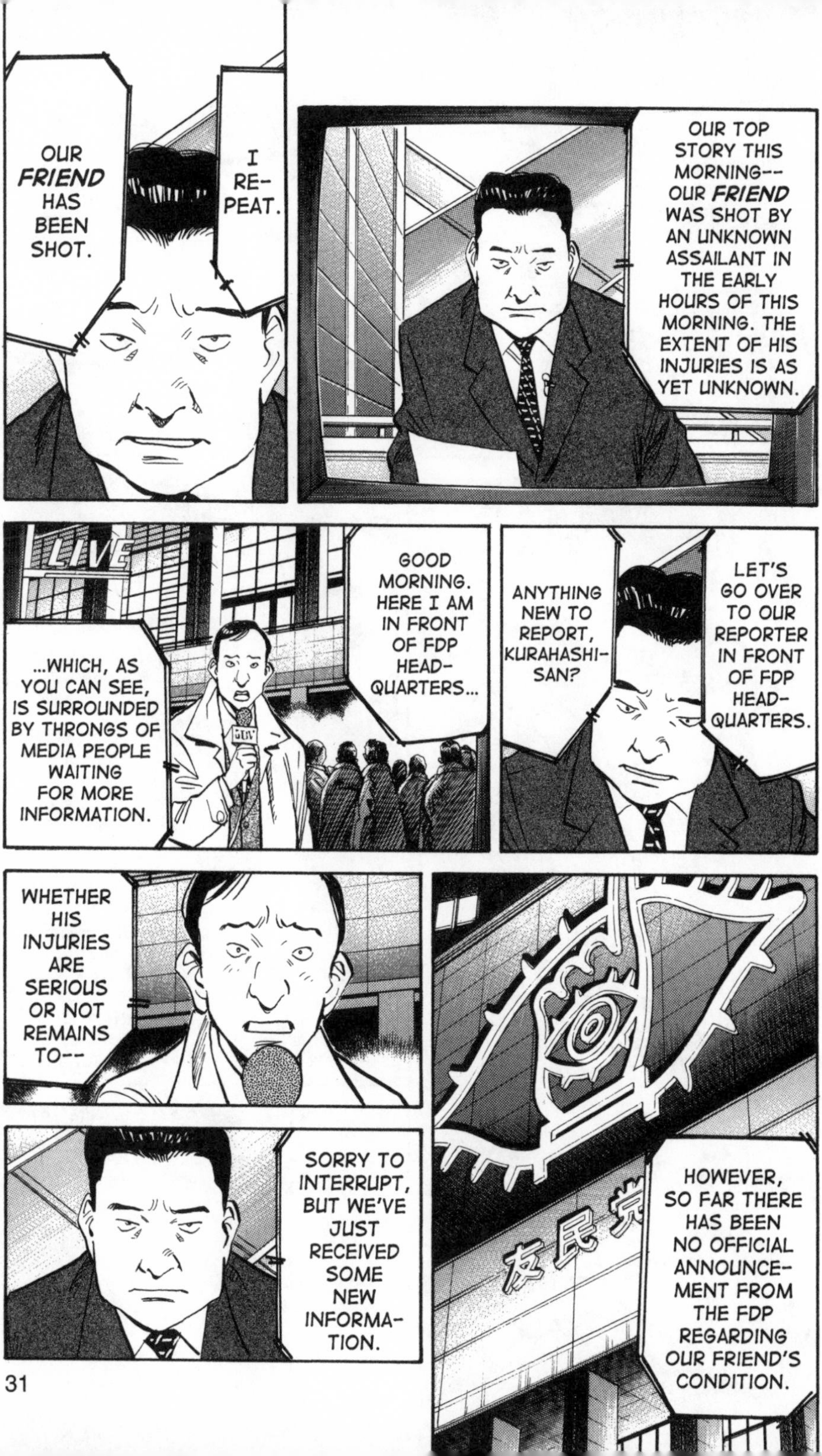
OUR TOP STORY THIS MORNING-- OUR *FRIEND* WAS SHOT BY AN UNKNOWN ASSAILANT IN THE EARLY HOURS OF THIS MORNING. THE EXTENT OF HIS INJURIES IS AS YET UNKNOWN.
I RE-PEAT.
OUR *FRIEND* HAS BEEN SHOT.
LET'S GO OVER TO OUR REPORTER IN FRONT OF FDP HEAD-QUARTERS.
ANYTHING NEW TO REPORT, KURAHASHI-SAN?
LIVE
GOOD MORNING. HERE I AM IN FRONT OF FDP HEAD-QUARTERS...
...WHICH, AS YOU CAN SEE, IS SURROUNDED BY THRONGS OF MEDIA PEOPLE WAITING FOR MORE INFORMATION.
友民党
HOWEVER, SO FAR THERE HAS BEEN NO OFFICIAL ANNOUNCE-MENT FROM THE FDP REGARDING OUR FRIEND'S CONDITION.
WHETHER HIS INJURIES ARE SERIOUS OR NOT REMAINS TO--
SORRY TO INTERRUPT, BUT WE'VE JUST RECEIVED SOME NEW INFORMA-TION.

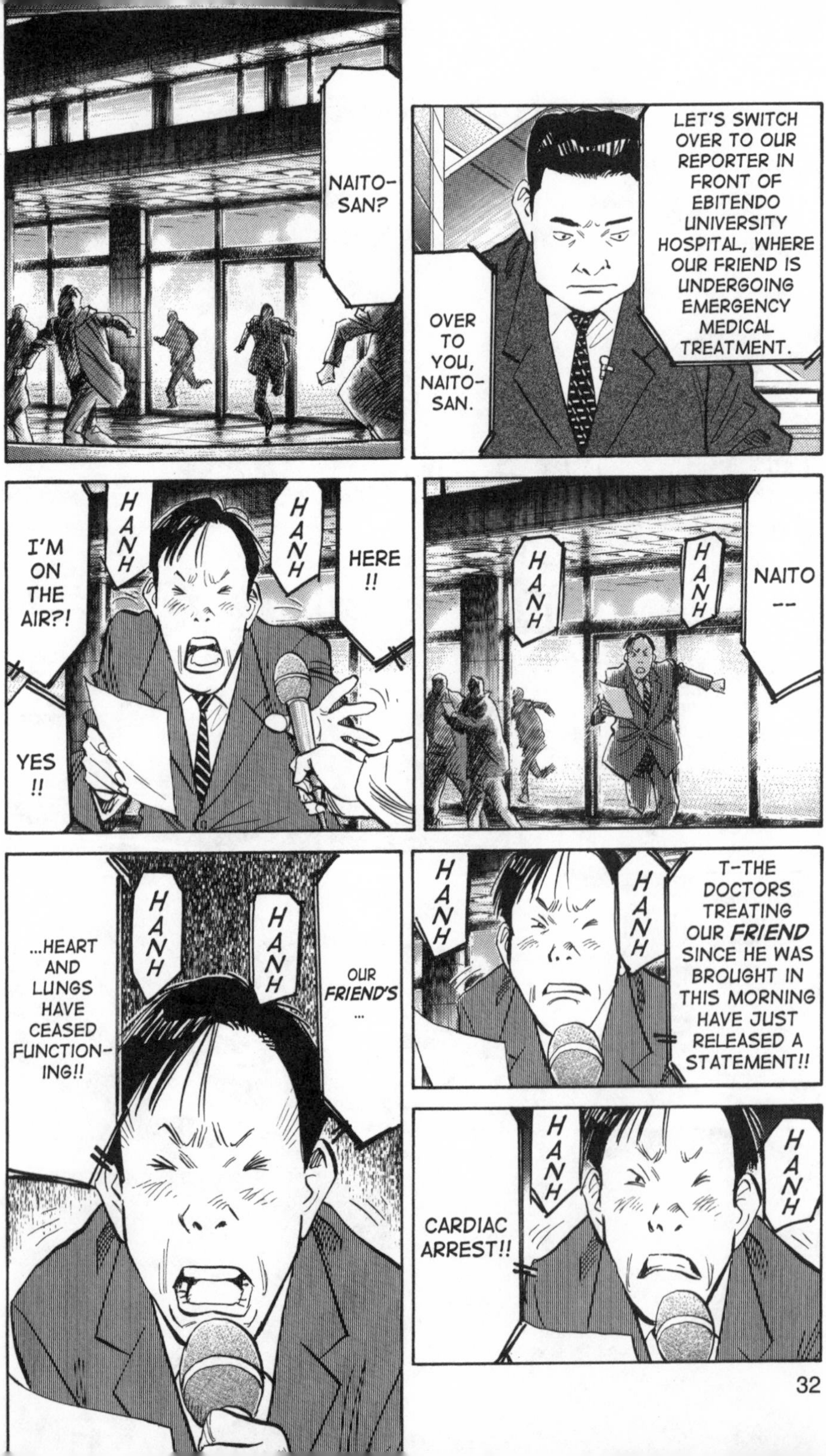
LET'S SWITCH OVER TO OUR REPORTER IN FRONT OF EBITENDO UNIVERSITY HOSPITAL, WHERE OUR FRIEND IS UNDERGOING EMERGENCY MEDICAL TREATMENT.
OVER TO YOU, NAITO-SAN.
NAITO-SAN?
NAITO --
HANH
HANH
HERE !!
HANH
HANH
I'M ON THE AIR?!
YES !!
T-THE DOCTORS TREATING OUR FRIEND SINCE HE WAS BROUGHT IN THIS MORNING HAVE JUST RELEASED A STATEMENT!!
HANH
HANH
HANH
CARDIAC ARREST!!
HANH
OUR FRIEND'S ...
HANH
HANH
...HEART AND LUNGS HAVE CEASED FUNCTIONING!!

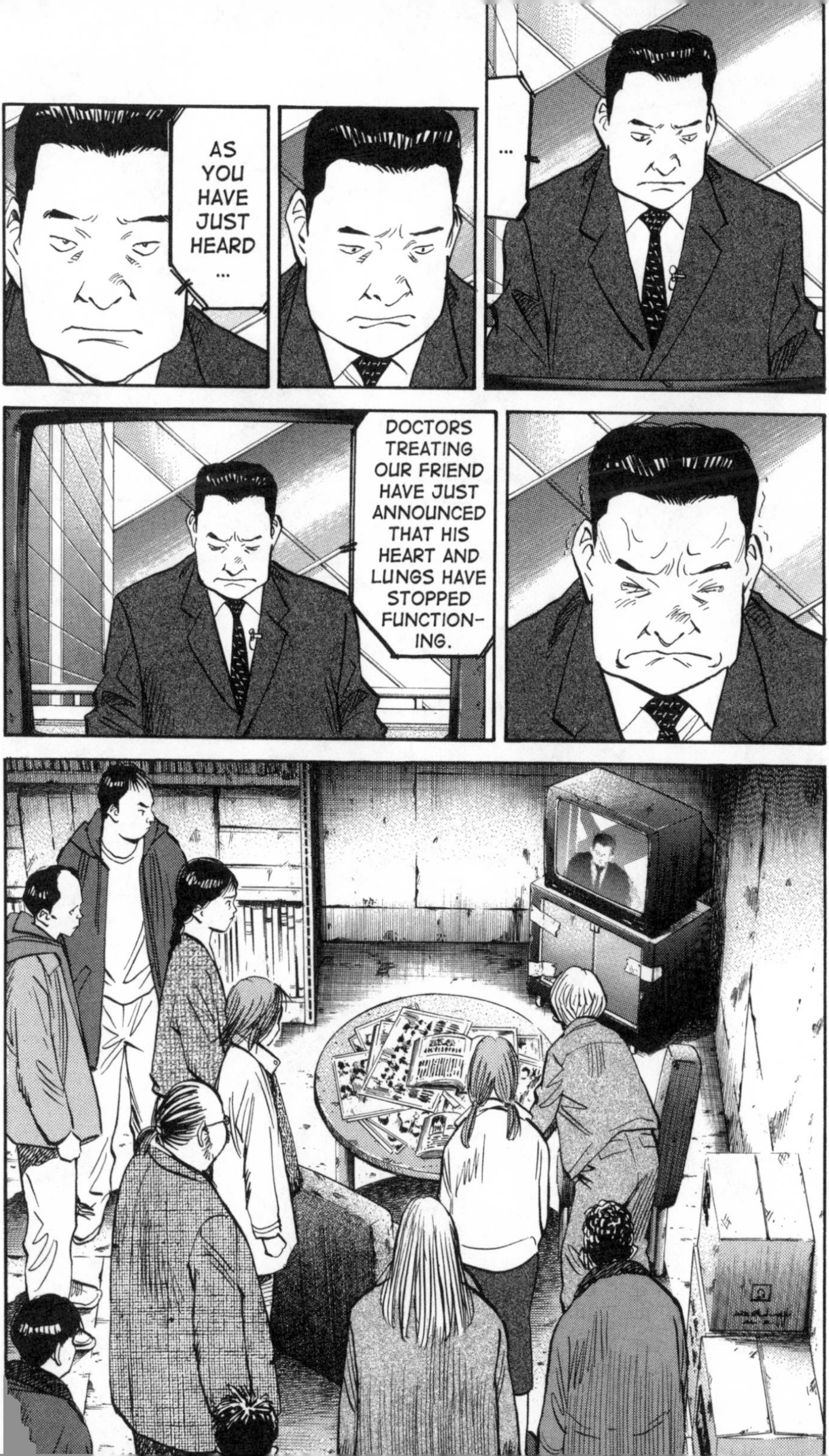
...
AS YOU HAVE JUST HEARD ...
DOCTORS TREATING OUR FRIEND HAVE JUST ANNOUNCED THAT HIS HEART AND LUNGS HAVE STOPPED FUNCTION-ING.

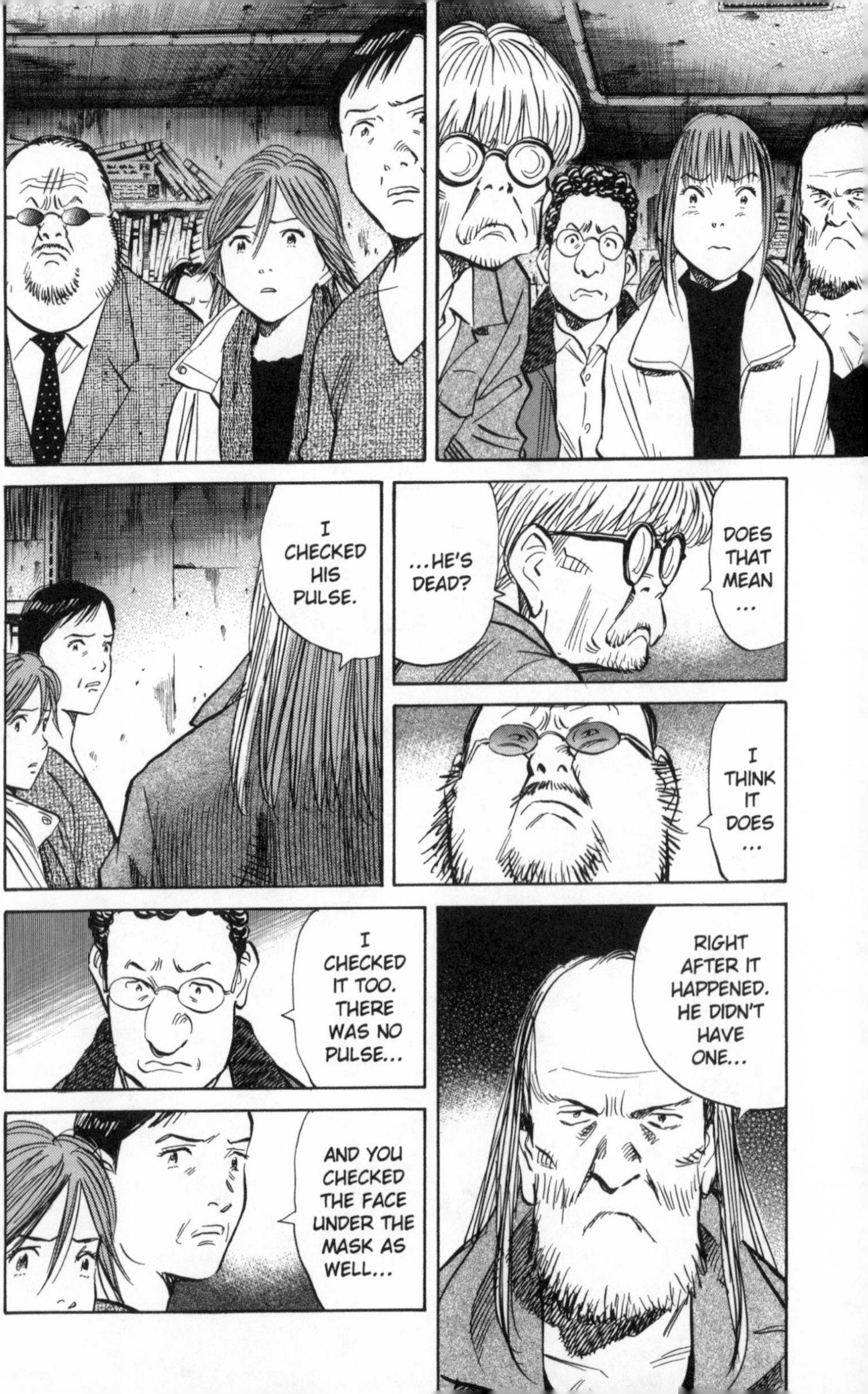
DOES THAT MEAN ...
...HE'S DEAD?
I THINK IT DOES ...
I CHECKED HIS PULSE.
RIGHT AFTER IT HAPPENED. HE DIDN'T HAVE ONE...
I CHECKED IT TOO. THERE WAS NO PULSE...
AND YOU CHECKED THE FACE UNDER THE MASK AS WELL...

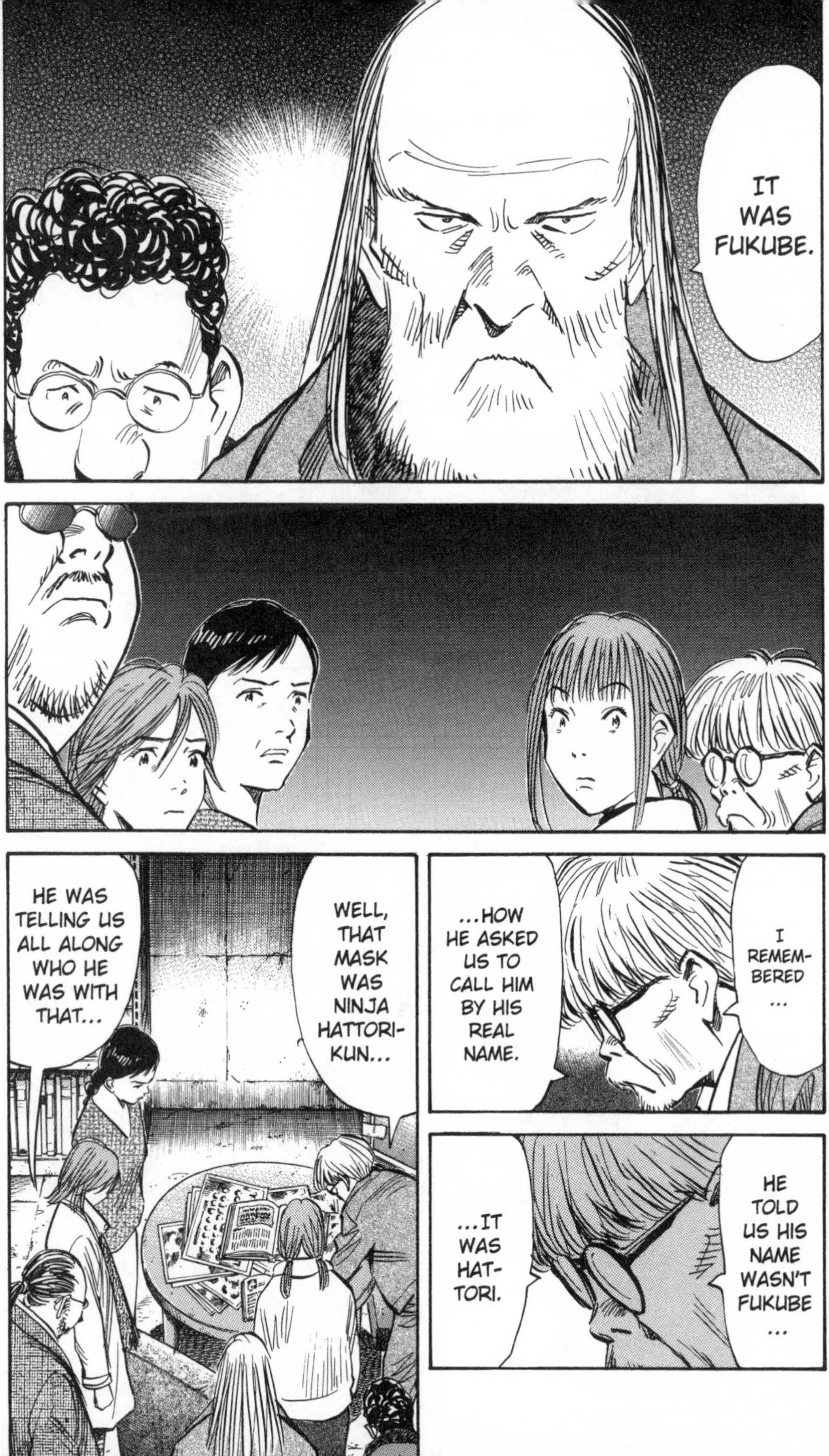
IT WAS FUKUBE.
I REMEMBERED...
...HOW HE ASKED US TO CALL HIM BY HIS REAL NAME.
HE TOLD US HIS NAME WASN'T FUKUBE...
...IT WAS HATTORI.
WELL, THAT MASK WAS NINJA HATTORI-KUN...
HE WAS TELLING US ALL ALONG WHO HE WAS WITH THAT...

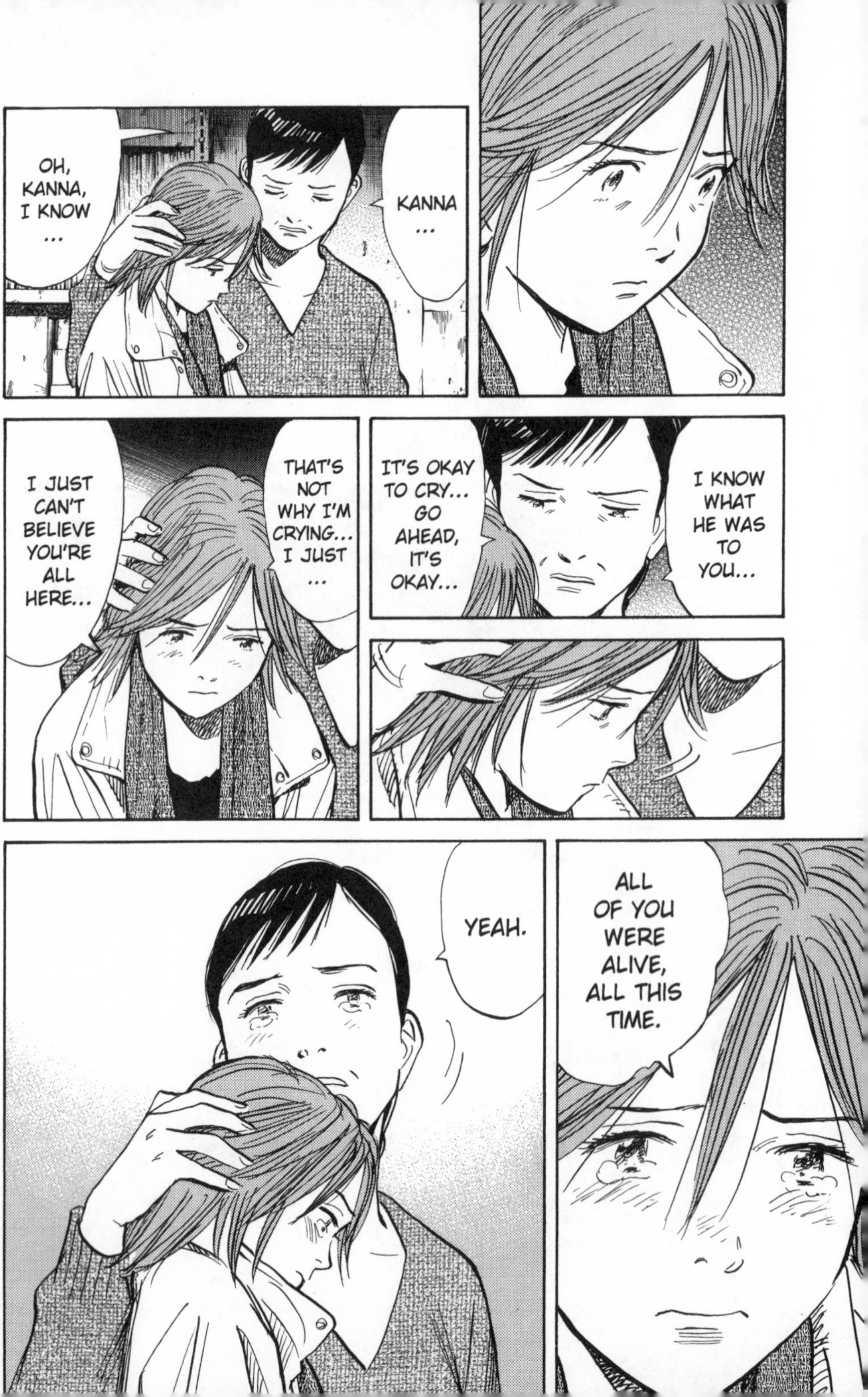
KANNA ...
OH, KANNA, I KNOW ...
I KNOW WHAT HE WAS TO YOU...
IT'S OKAY TO CRY... GO AHEAD, IT'S OKAY...
THAT'S NOT WHY I'M CRYING... I JUST ...
I JUST CAN'T BELIEVE YOU'RE ALL HERE...
ALL OF YOU WERE ALIVE, ALL THIS TIME.
YEAH.

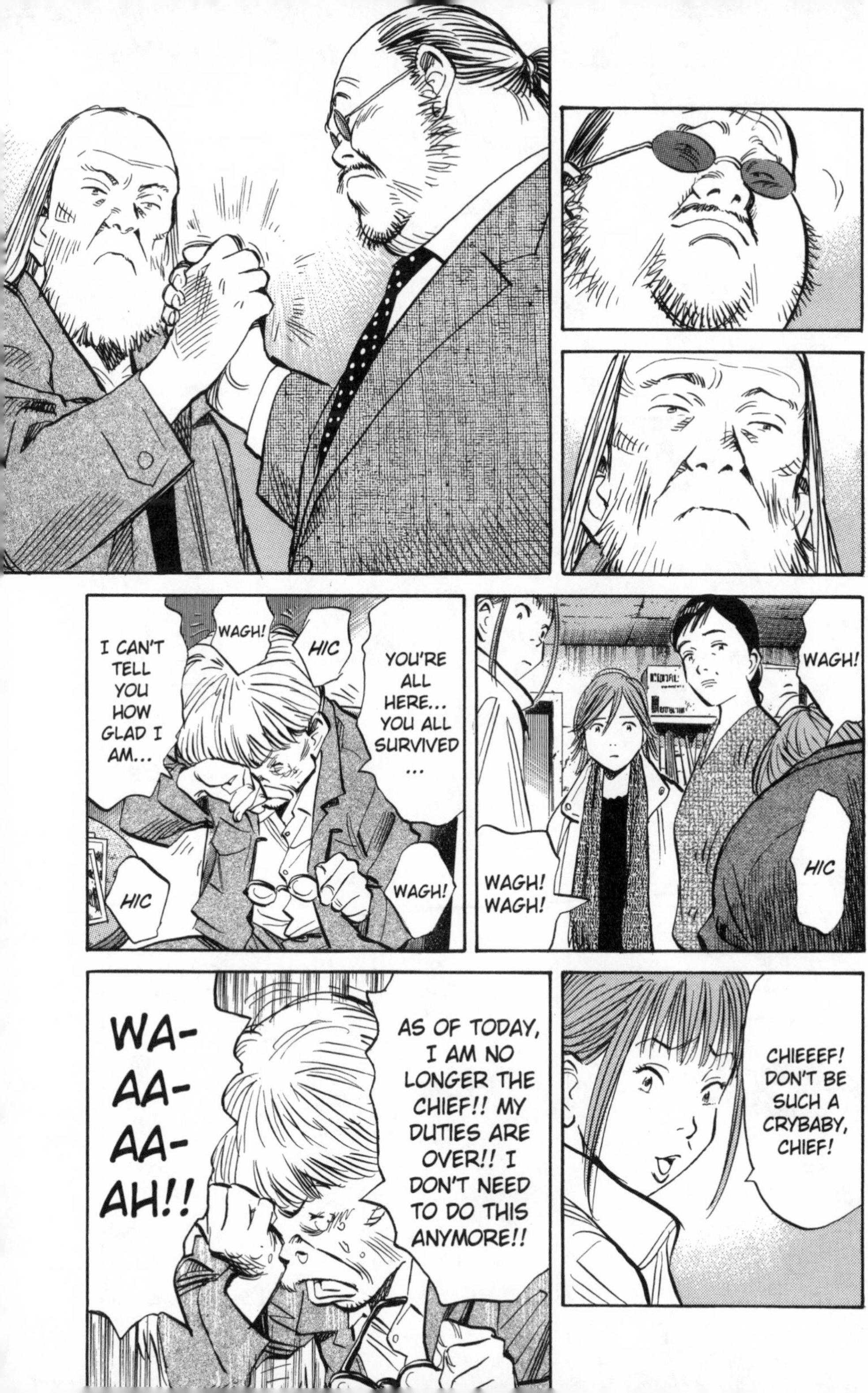
WAGH!
HIC
WAGH! WAGH!
YOU'RE ALL HERE... YOU ALL SURVIVED ...
HIC
WAGH!
I CAN'T TELL YOU HOW GLAD I AM...
WAGH!
HIC
CHIEEEF! DON'T BE SUCH A CRYBABY, CHIEF!
AS OF TODAY, I AM NO LONGER THE CHIEF!! MY DUTIES ARE OVER!! I DON'T NEED TO DO THIS ANYMORE!!
WA-AA-AA-AH!!

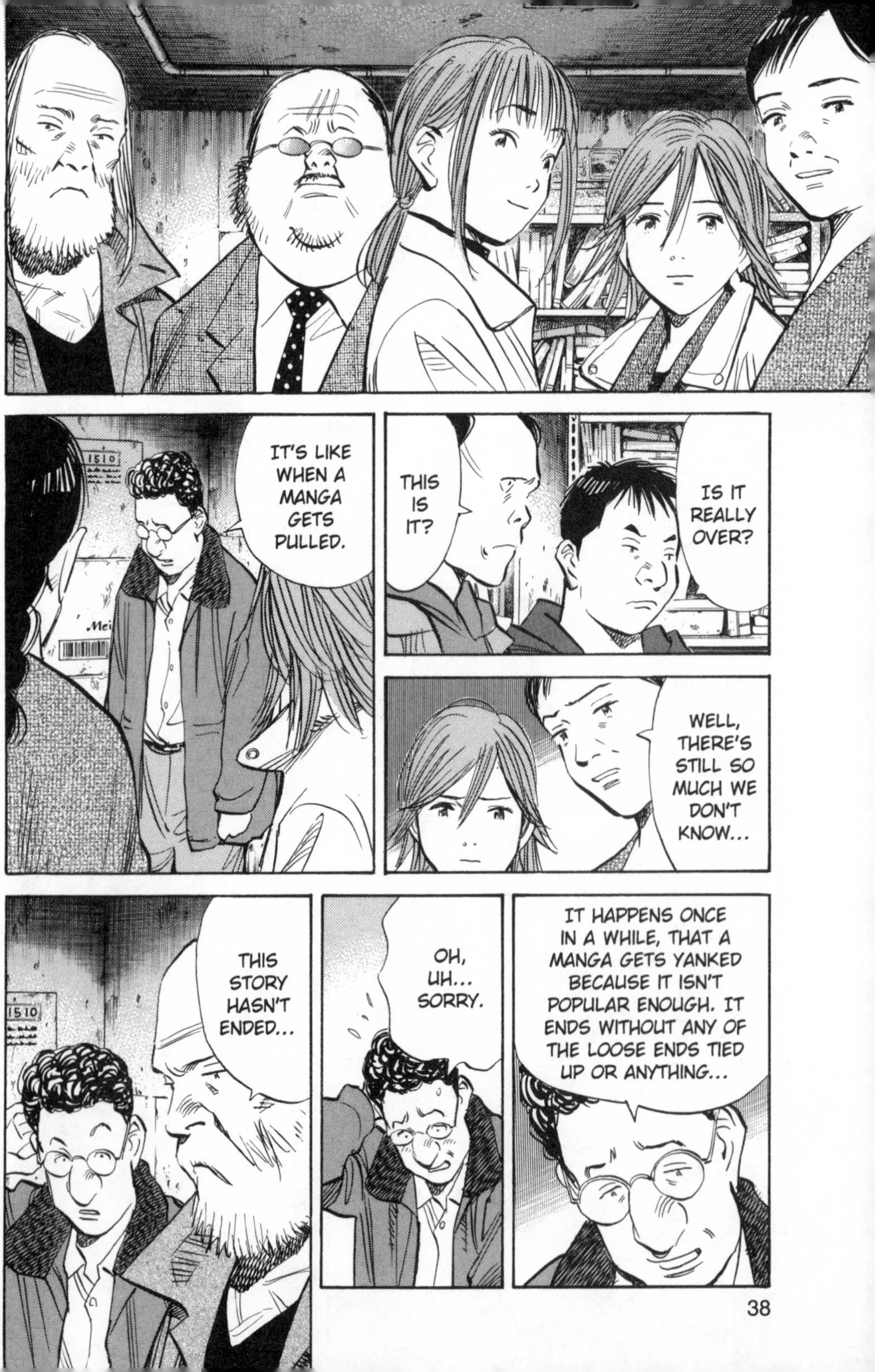
IS IT REALLY OVER?
THIS IS IT?
WELL, THERE'S STILL SO MUCH WE DON'T KNOW...
IT'S LIKE WHEN A MANGA GETS PULLED.
IT HAPPENS ONCE IN A WHILE, THAT A MANGA GETS YANKED BECAUSE IT ISN'T POPULAR ENOUGH. IT ENDS WITHOUT ANY OF THE LOOSE ENDS TIED UP OR ANYTHING...
OH, UH... SORRY.
THIS STORY HASN'T ENDED...

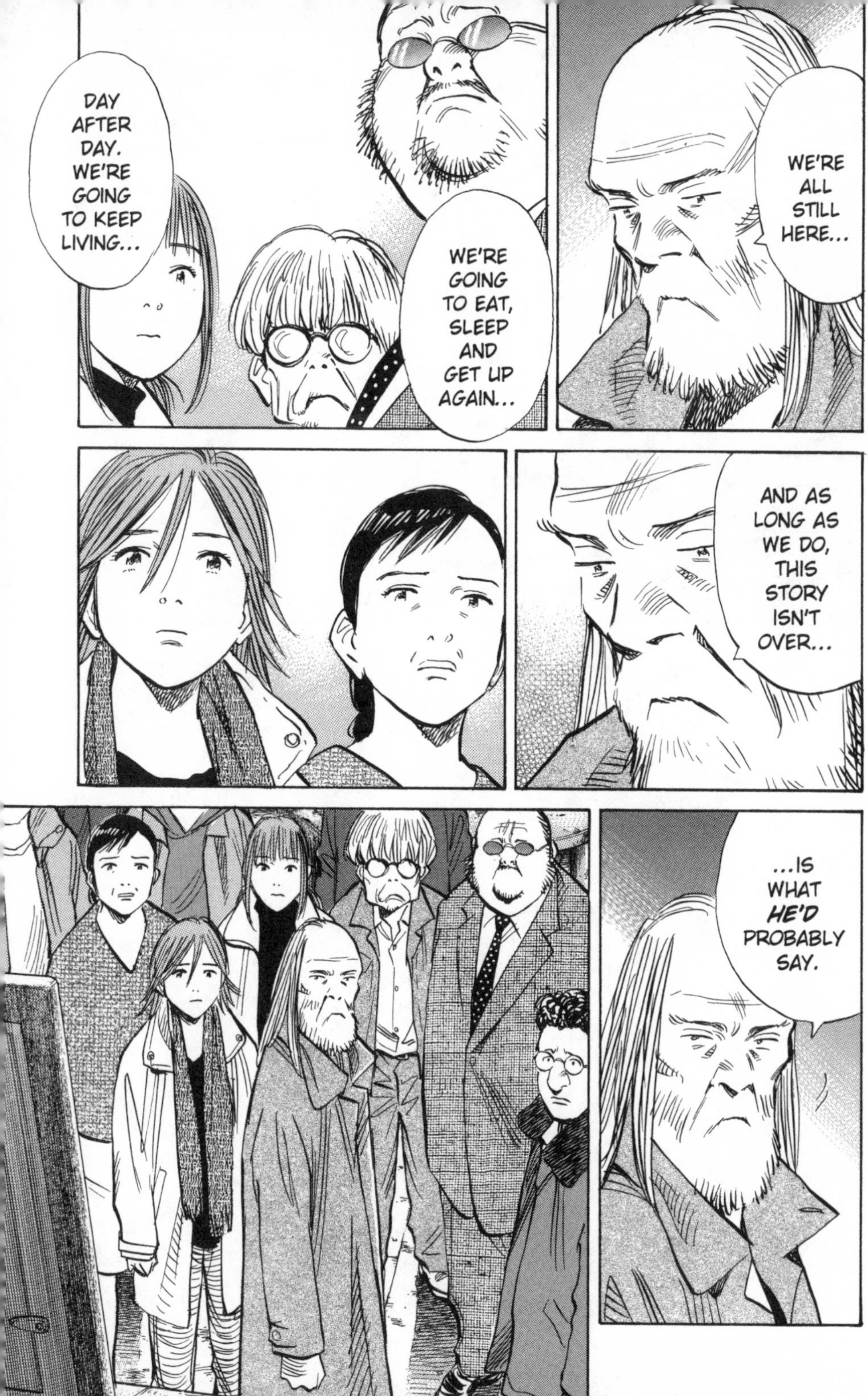
WE'RE ALL STILL HERE...
WE'RE GOING TO EAT, SLEEP AND GET UP AGAIN...
DAY AFTER DAY. WE'RE GOING TO KEEP LIVING...
AND AS LONG AS WE DO, THIS STORY ISN'T OVER...
...IS WHAT *HE'D* PROBABLY SAY.

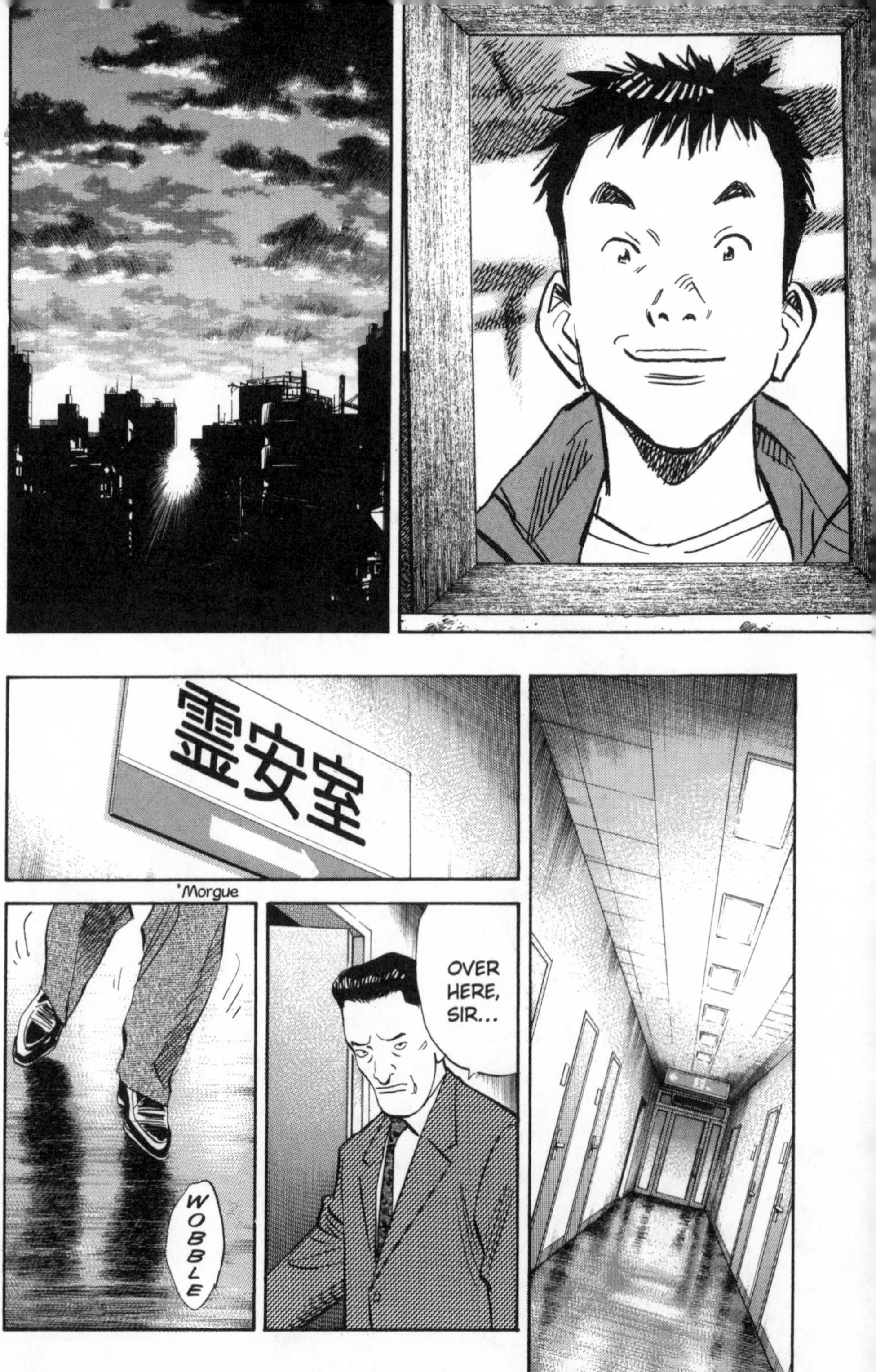
霊安室
*Morgue
OVER HERE, SIR...
WOBBLE

WOBBLE

ARE YOU... ALL RIGHT, SIR?

Y-YEAH... I'LL BE FINE ON MY OWN.

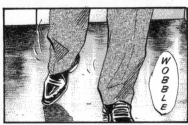

WOBBLE

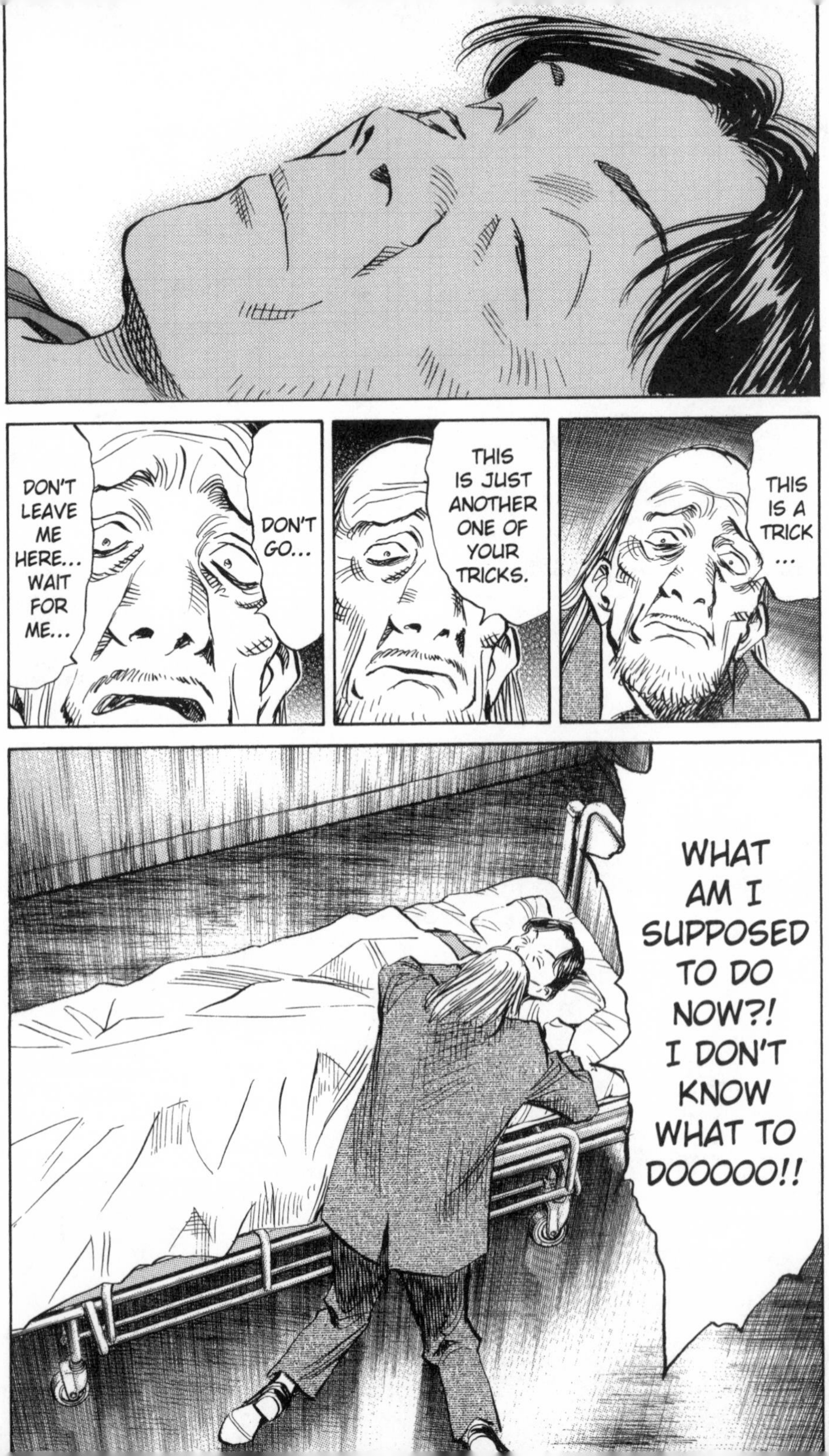
THIS IS A TRICK ...
THIS IS JUST ANOTHER ONE OF YOUR TRICKS.
DON'T GO...
DON'T LEAVE ME HERE... WAIT FOR ME...
WHAT AM I SUPPOSED TO DO NOW?! I DON'T KNOW WHAT TO DOOOOO!!

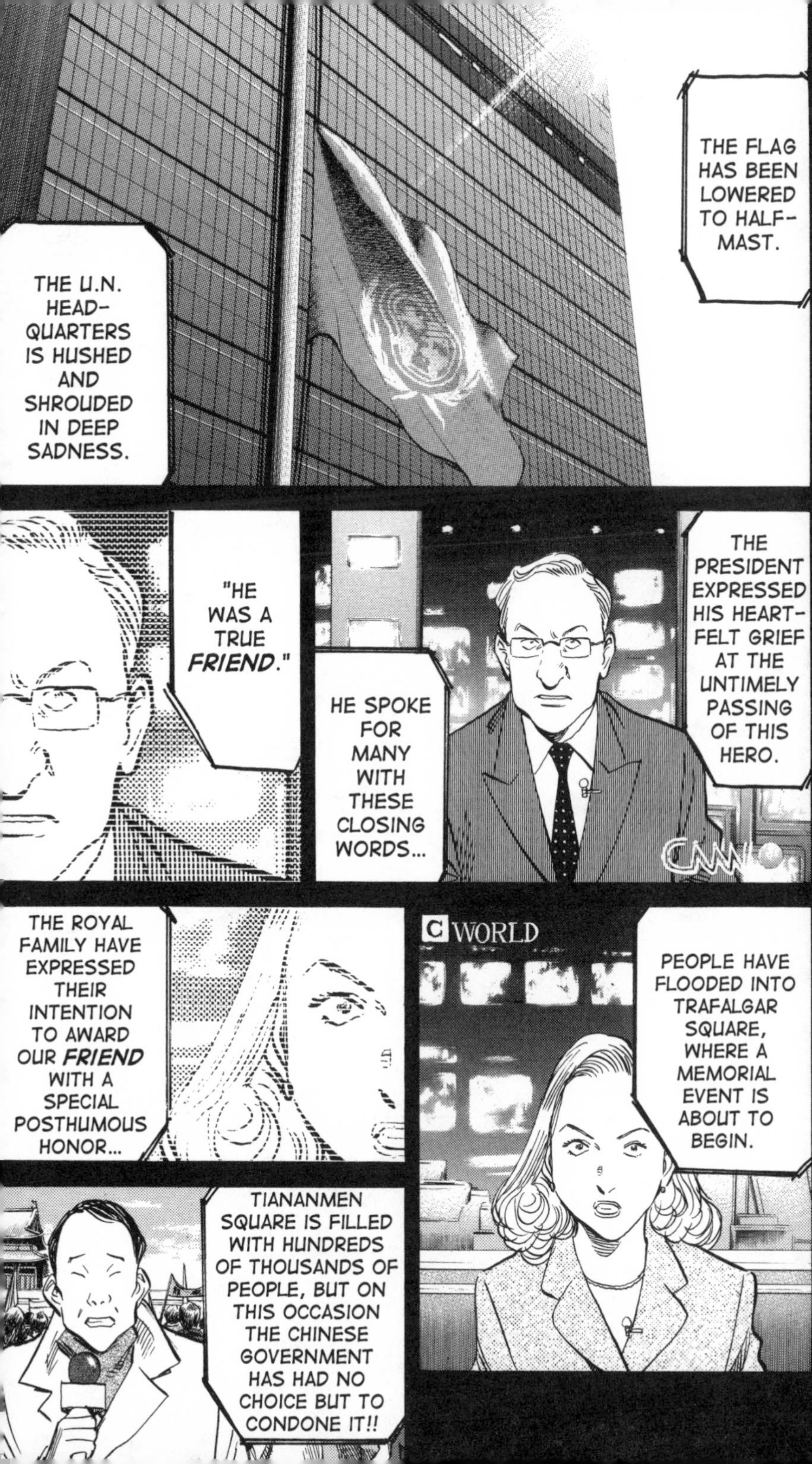
THE FLAG HAS BEEN LOWERED TO HALF-MAST.
THE U.N. HEAD-QUARTERS IS HUSHED AND SHROUDED IN DEEP SADNESS.
THE PRESIDENT EXPRESSED HIS HEART-FELT GRIEF AT THE UNTIMELY PASSING OF THIS HERO.
HE SPOKE FOR MANY WITH THESE CLOSING WORDS...
"HE WAS A TRUE FRIEND."
C WORLD
PEOPLE HAVE FLOODED INTO TRAFALGAR SQUARE, WHERE A MEMORIAL EVENT IS ABOUT TO BEGIN.
THE ROYAL FAMILY HAVE EXPRESSED THEIR INTENTION TO AWARD OUR FRIEND WITH A SPECIAL POSTHUMOUS HONOR...
TIANANMEN SQUARE IS FILLED WITH HUNDREDS OF THOUSANDS OF PEOPLE, BUT ON THIS OCCASION THE CHINESE GOVERNMENT HAS HAD NO CHOICE BUT TO CONDONE IT!!

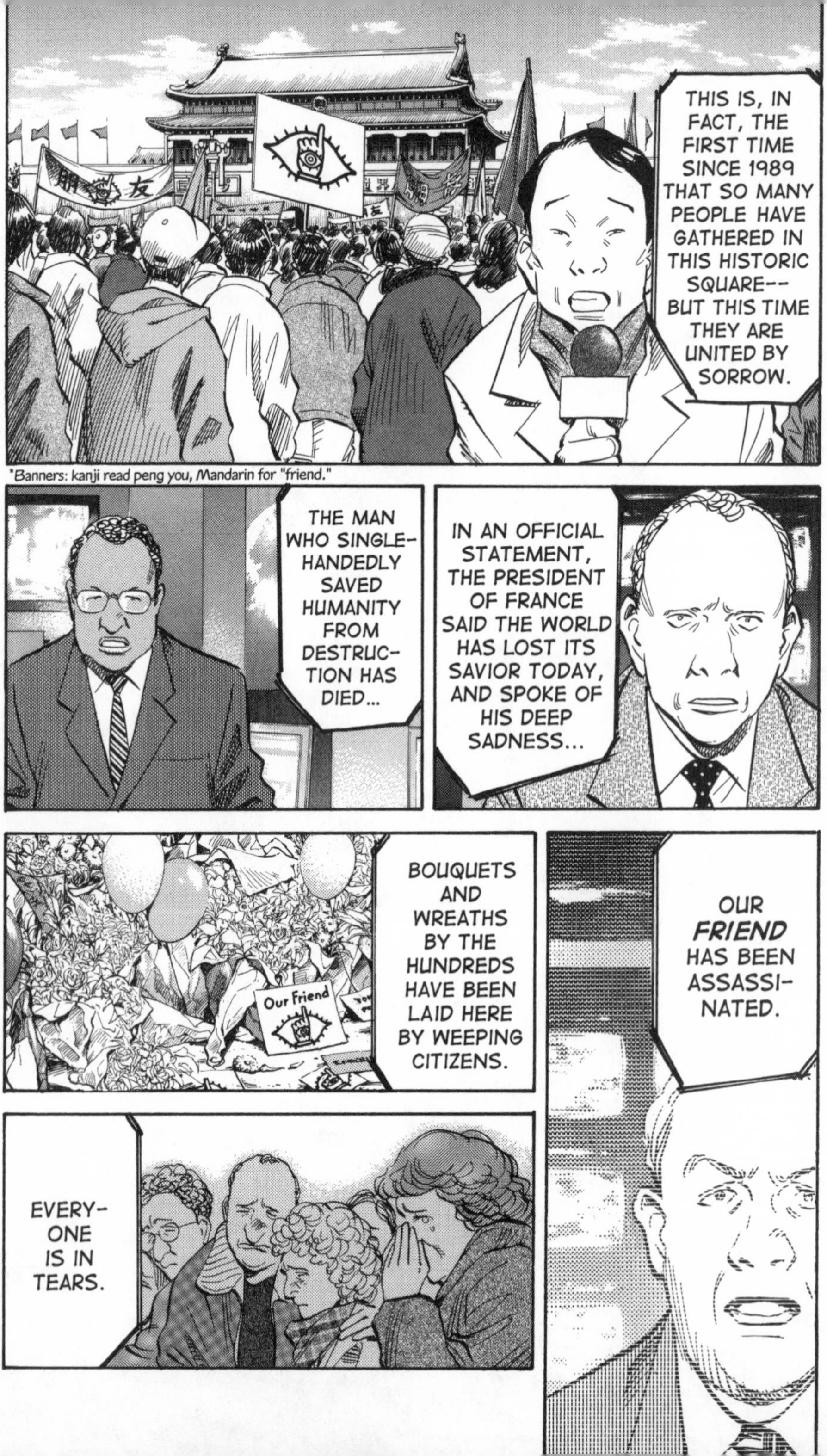
THIS IS, IN FACT, THE FIRST TIME SINCE 1989 THAT SO MANY PEOPLE HAVE GATHERED IN THIS HISTORIC SQUARE-- BUT THIS TIME THEY ARE UNITED BY SORROW.
*Banners: kanji read peng you, Mandarin for "friend."
IN AN OFFICIAL STATEMENT, THE PRESIDENT OF FRANCE SAID THE WORLD HAS LOST ITS SAVIOR TODAY, AND SPOKE OF HIS DEEP SADNESS...
THE MAN WHO SINGLE-HANDEDLY SAVED HUMANITY FROM DESTRUC-TION HAS DIED...
OUR *FRIEND* HAS BEEN ASSASSI-NATED.
BOUQUETS AND WREATHS BY THE HUNDREDS HAVE BEEN LAID HERE BY WEEPING CITIZENS.
Our Friend
EVERY-ONE IS IN TEARS.

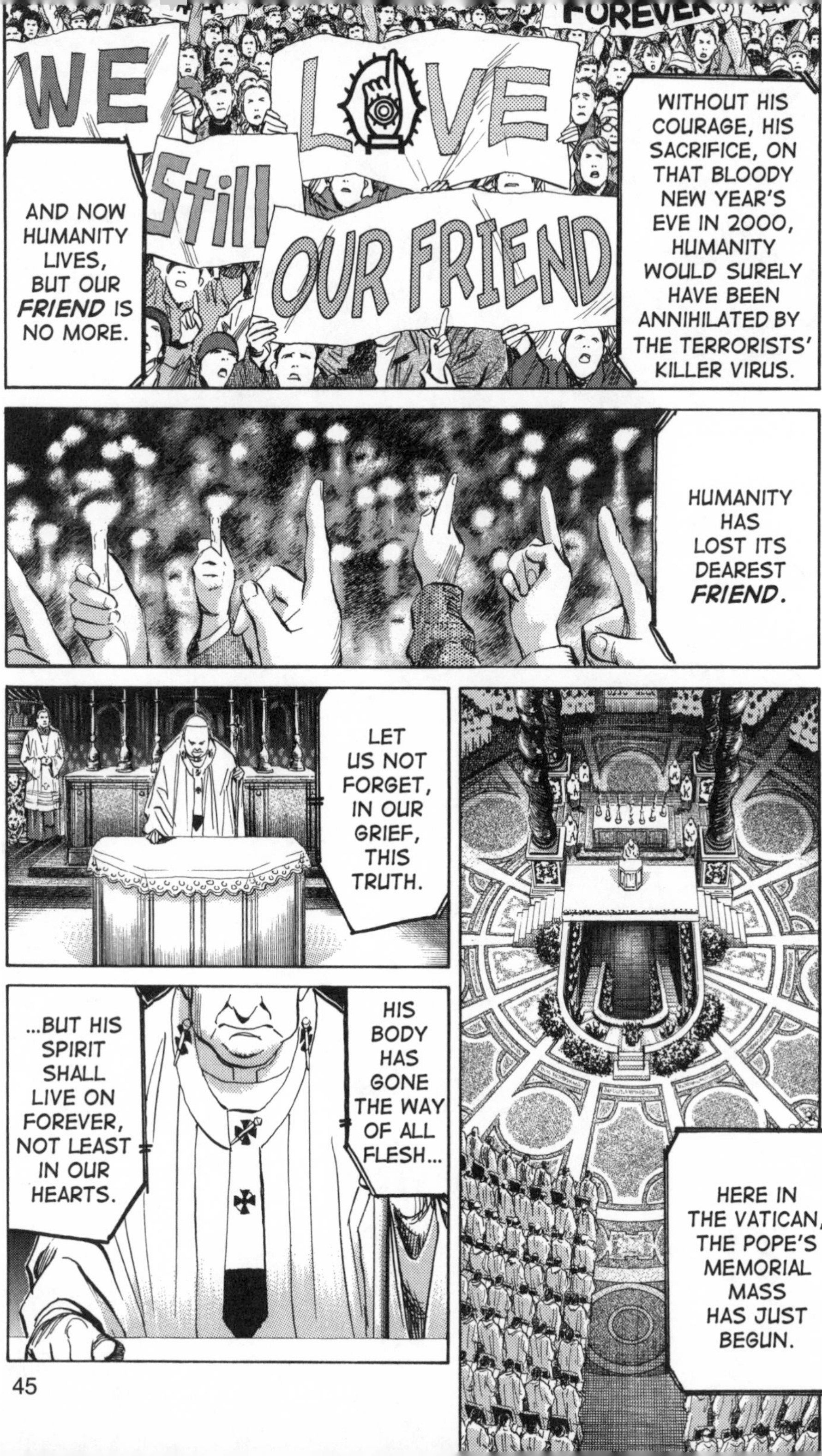
FOREVER
WE LOVE
Still OUR FRIEND
WITHOUT HIS COURAGE, HIS SACRIFICE, ON THAT BLOODY NEW YEAR'S EVE IN 2000, HUMANITY WOULD SURELY HAVE BEEN ANNIHILATED BY THE TERRORISTS' KILLER VIRUS.
AND NOW HUMANITY LIVES, BUT OUR *FRIEND* IS NO MORE.
HUMANITY HAS LOST ITS DEAREST *FRIEND*.
HERE IN THE VATICAN, THE POPE'S MEMORIAL MASS HAS JUST BEGUN.
LET US NOT FORGET, IN OUR GRIEF, THIS TRUTH.
HIS BODY HAS GONE THE WAY OF ALL FLESH...
...BUT HIS SPIRIT SHALL LIVE ON FOREVER, NOT LEAST IN OUR HEARTS.

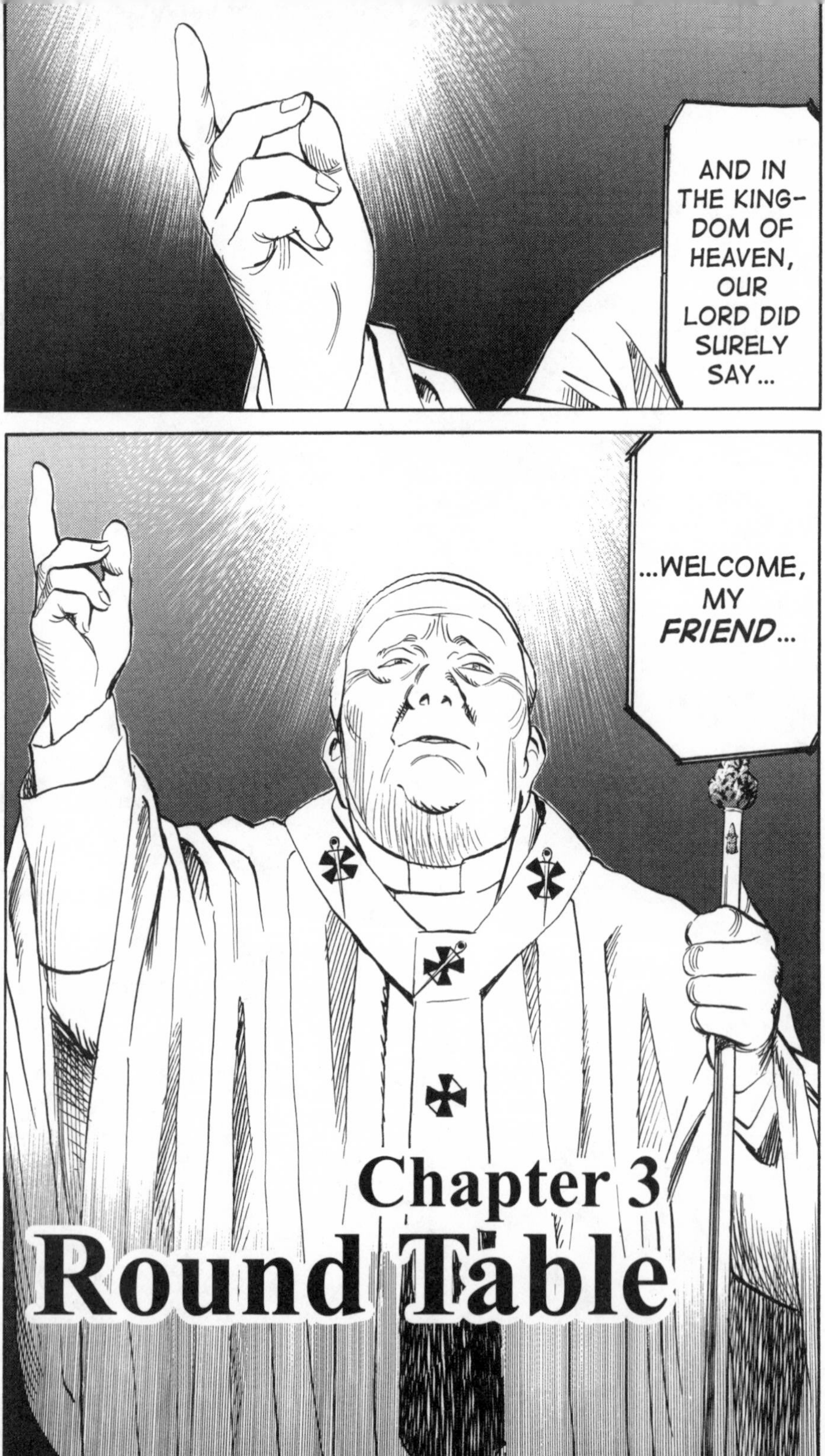
AND IN THE KING-DOM OF HEAVEN, OUR LORD DID SURELY SAY...
...WELCOME, MY *FRIEND*...

Chapter 3
Round Table

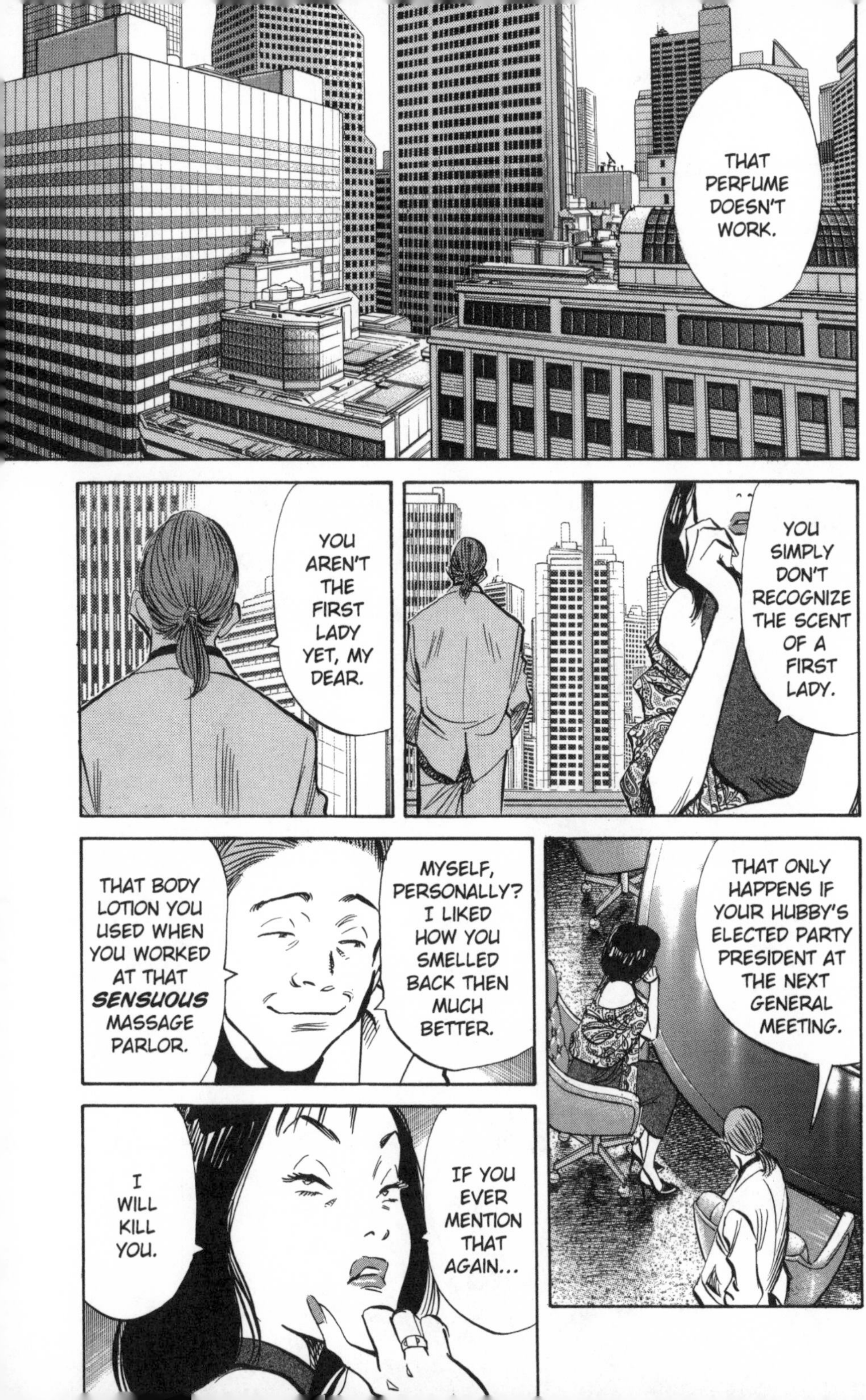
THAT PERFUME DOESN'T WORK.
YOU SIMPLY DON'T RECOGNIZE THE SCENT OF A FIRST LADY.
YOU AREN'T THE FIRST LADY YET, MY DEAR.
THAT ONLY HAPPENS IF YOUR HUBBY'S ELECTED PARTY PRESIDENT AT THE NEXT GENERAL MEETING.
MYSELF, PERSONALLY? I LIKED HOW YOU SMELLED BACK THEN MUCH BETTER.
THAT BODY LOTION YOU USED WHEN YOU WORKED AT THAT SENSUOUS MASSAGE PARLOR.
IF YOU EVER MENTION THAT AGAIN...
I WILL KILL YOU.

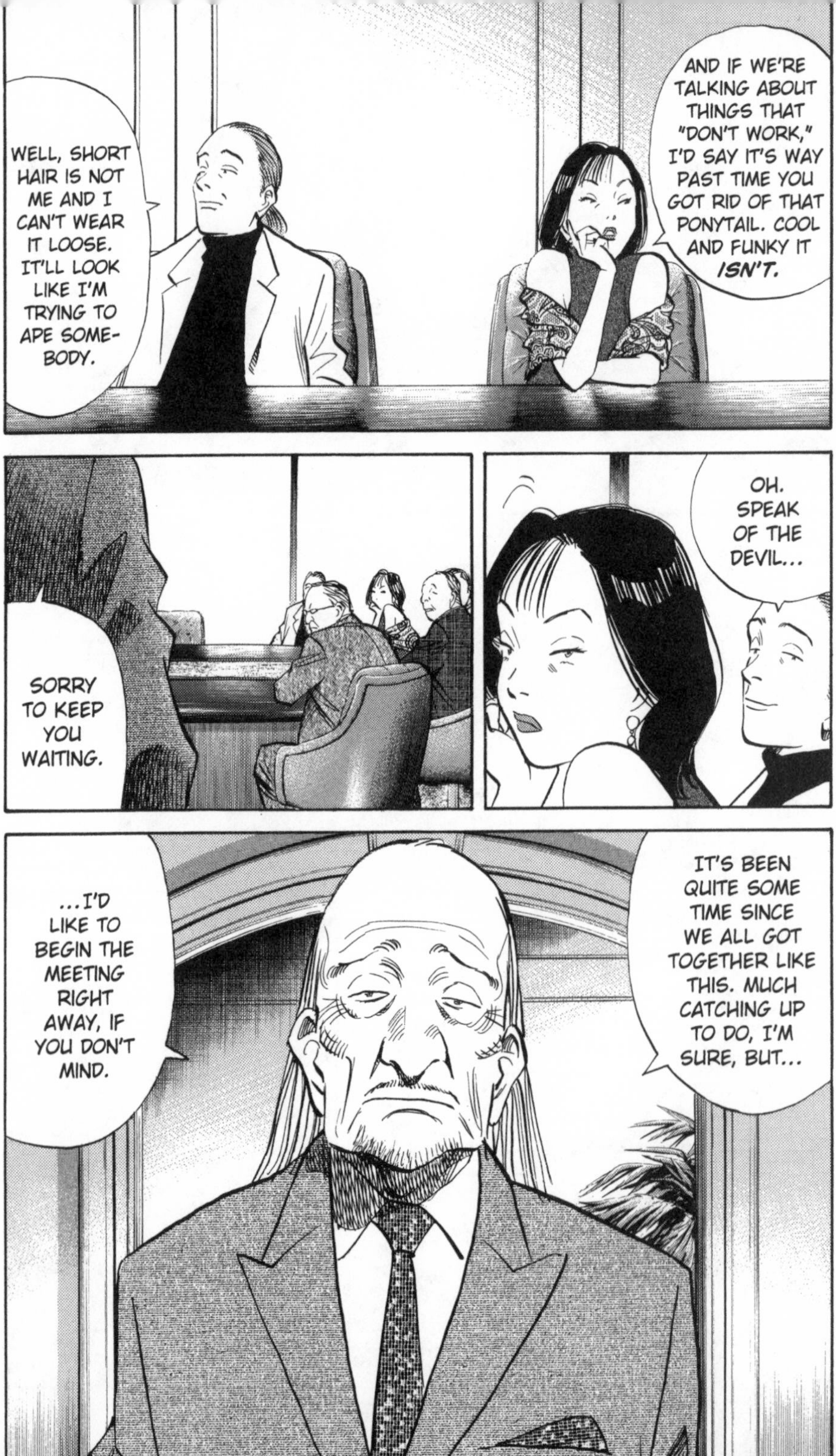
AND IF WE'RE TALKING ABOUT THINGS THAT "DON'T WORK," I'D SAY IT'S WAY PAST TIME YOU GOT RID OF THAT PONYTAIL. COOL AND FUNKY IT ***ISN'T.***
WELL, SHORT HAIR IS NOT ME AND I CAN'T WEAR IT LOOSE. IT'LL LOOK LIKE I'M TRYING TO APE SOME-BODY.
OH. SPEAK OF THE DEVIL...
SORRY TO KEEP YOU WAITING.
IT'S BEEN QUITE SOME TIME SINCE WE ALL GOT TOGETHER LIKE THIS. MUCH CATCHING UP TO DO, I'M SURE, BUT...
...I'D LIKE TO BEGIN THE MEETING RIGHT AWAY, IF YOU DON'T MIND.

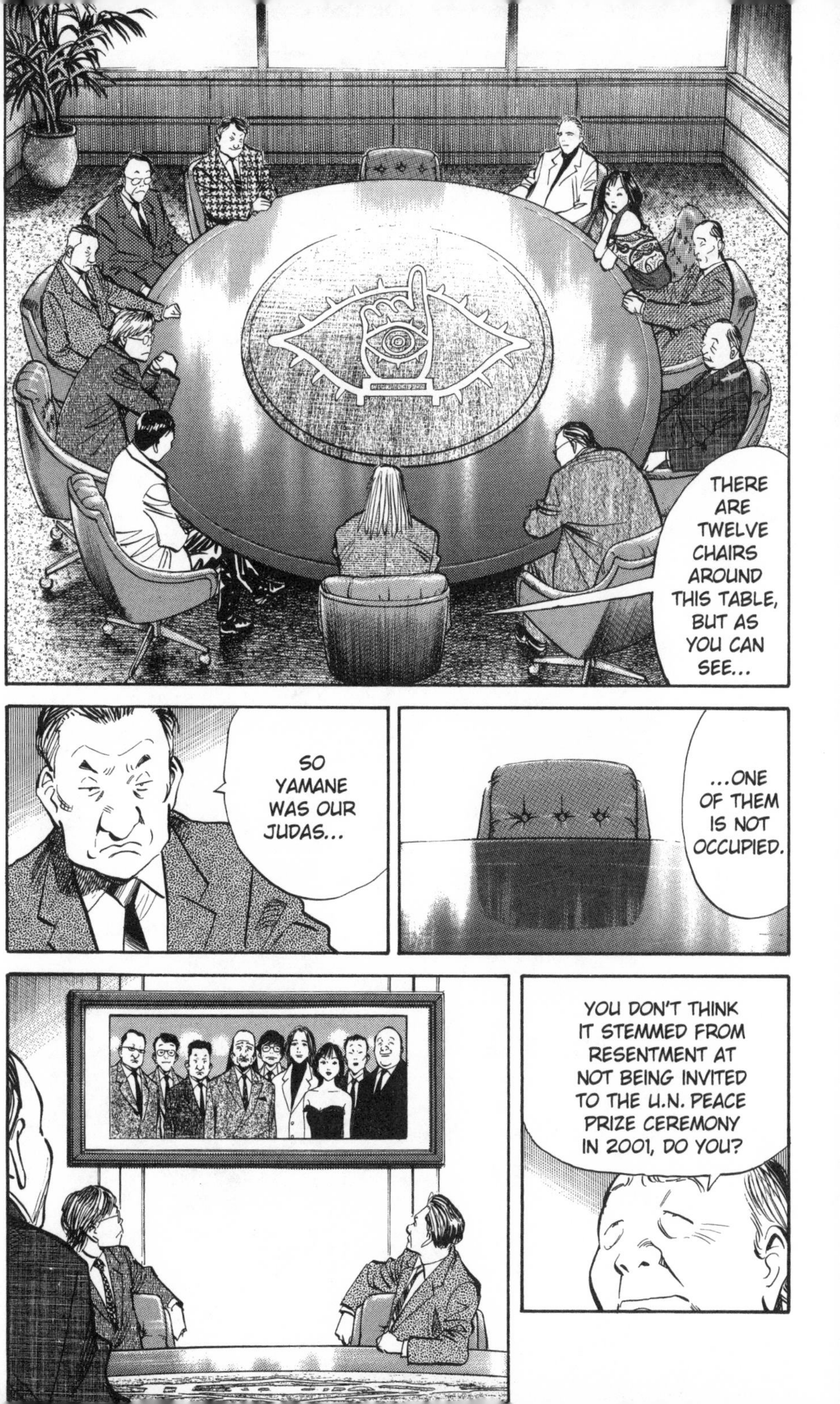
THERE ARE TWELVE CHAIRS AROUND THIS TABLE, BUT AS YOU CAN SEE...
...ONE OF THEM IS NOT OCCUPIED.
SO YAMANE WAS OUR JUDAS...
YOU DON'T THINK IT STEMMED FROM RESENTMENT AT NOT BEING INVITED TO THE U.N. PEACE PRIZE CEREMONY IN 2001, DO YOU?

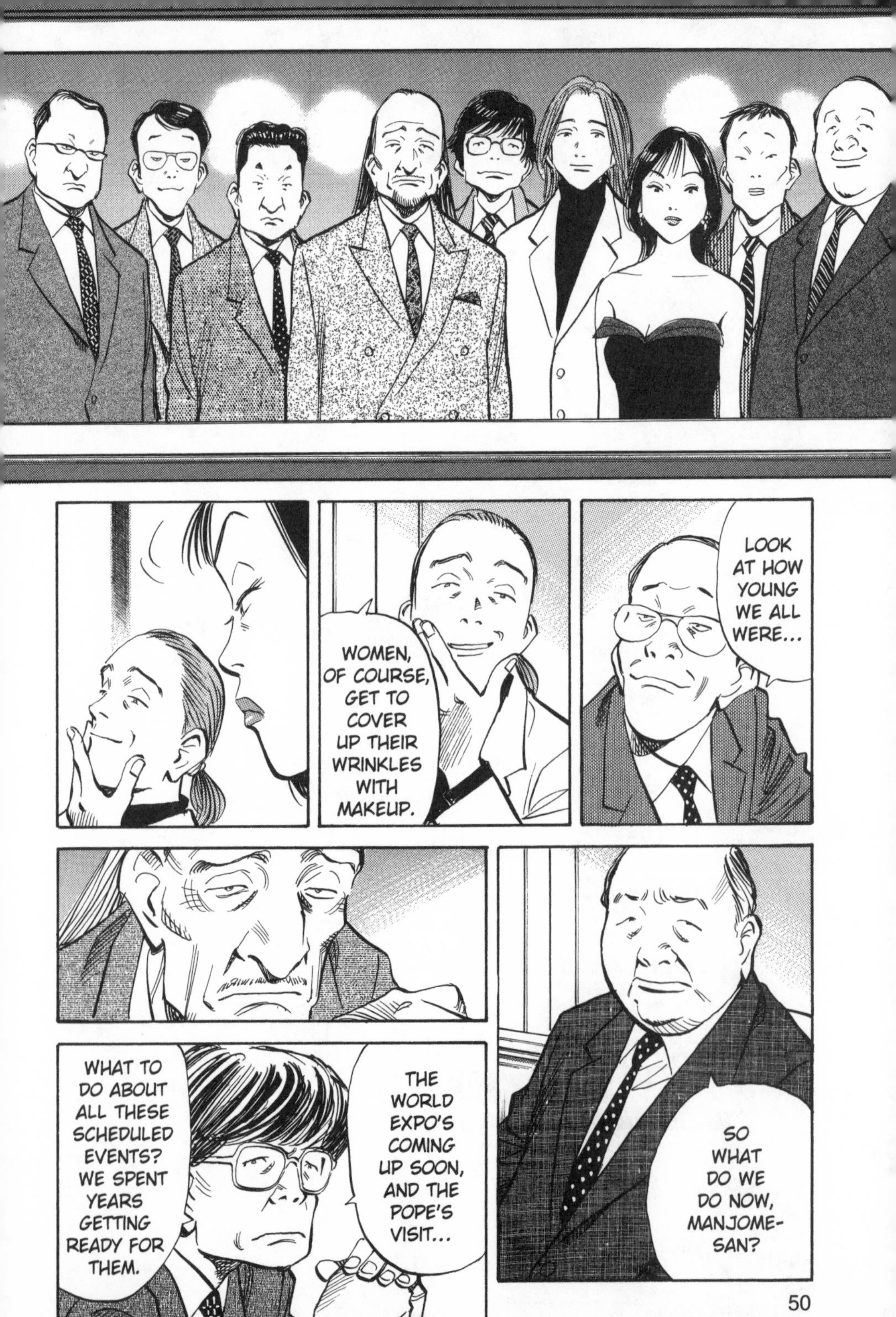
LOOK AT HOW YOUNG WE ALL WERE...
WOMEN, OF COURSE, GET TO COVER UP THEIR WRINKLES WITH MAKEUP.
SO WHAT DO WE DO NOW, MANJOME-SAN?
THE WORLD EXPO'S COMING UP SOON, AND THE POPE'S VISIT...
WHAT TO DO ABOUT ALL THESE SCHEDULED EVENTS? WE SPENT YEARS GETTING READY FOR THEM.

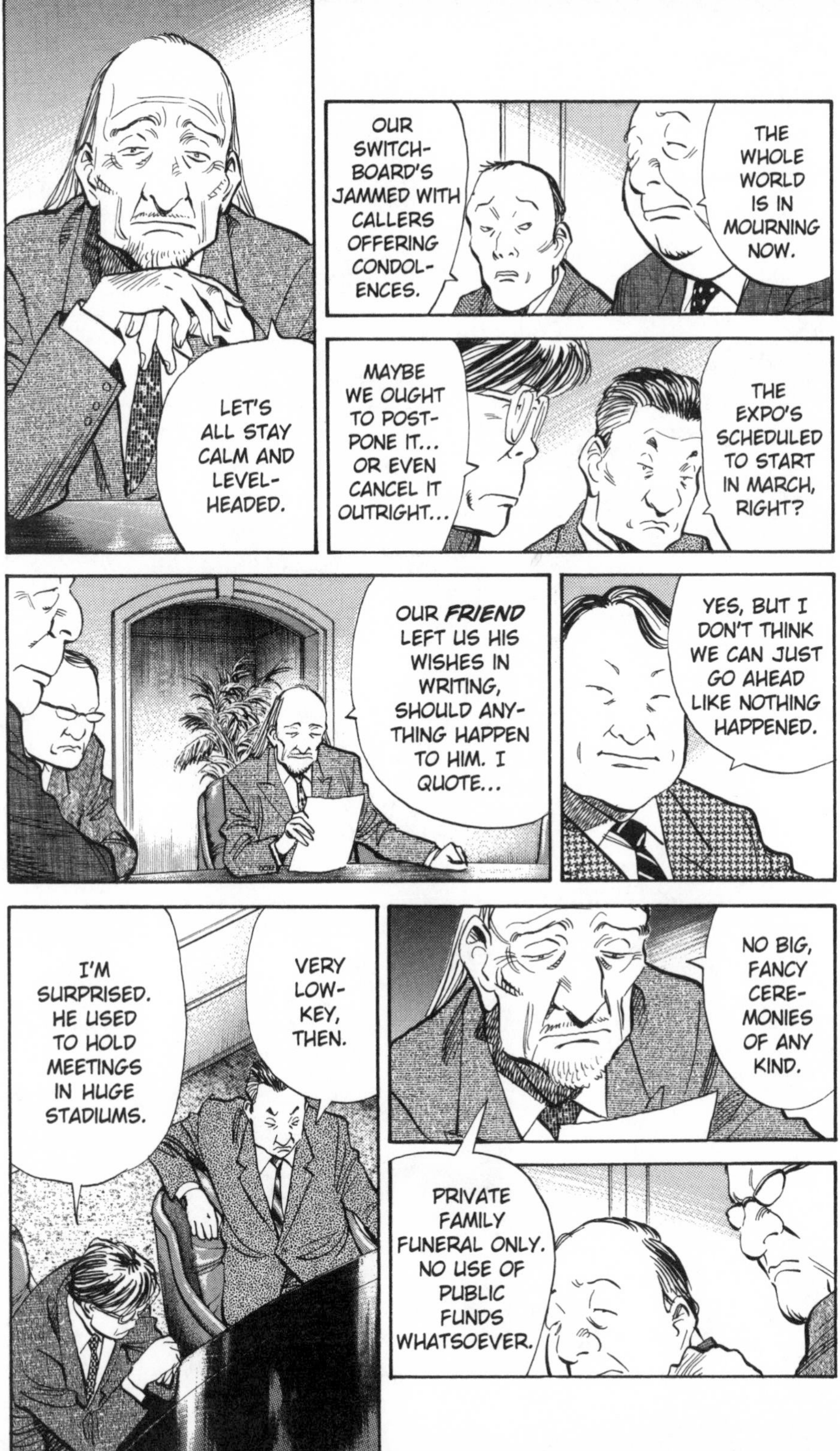
THE WHOLE WORLD IS IN MOURNING NOW.
OUR SWITCHBOARD'S JAMMED WITH CALLERS OFFERING CONDOLENCES.
THE EXPO'S SCHEDULED TO START IN MARCH, RIGHT?
MAYBE WE OUGHT TO POSTPONE IT... OR EVEN CANCEL IT OUTRIGHT...
LET'S ALL STAY CALM AND LEVEL-HEADED.
YES, BUT I DON'T THINK WE CAN JUST GO AHEAD LIKE NOTHING HAPPENED.
OUR ***FRIEND*** LEFT US HIS WISHES IN WRITING, SHOULD ANYTHING HAPPEN TO HIM. I QUOTE...
NO BIG, FANCY CEREMONIES OF ANY KIND.
PRIVATE FAMILY FUNERAL ONLY. NO USE OF PUBLIC FUNDS WHATSOEVER.
VERY LOW-KEY, THEN.
I'M SURPRISED. HE USED TO HOLD MEETINGS IN HUGE STADIUMS.

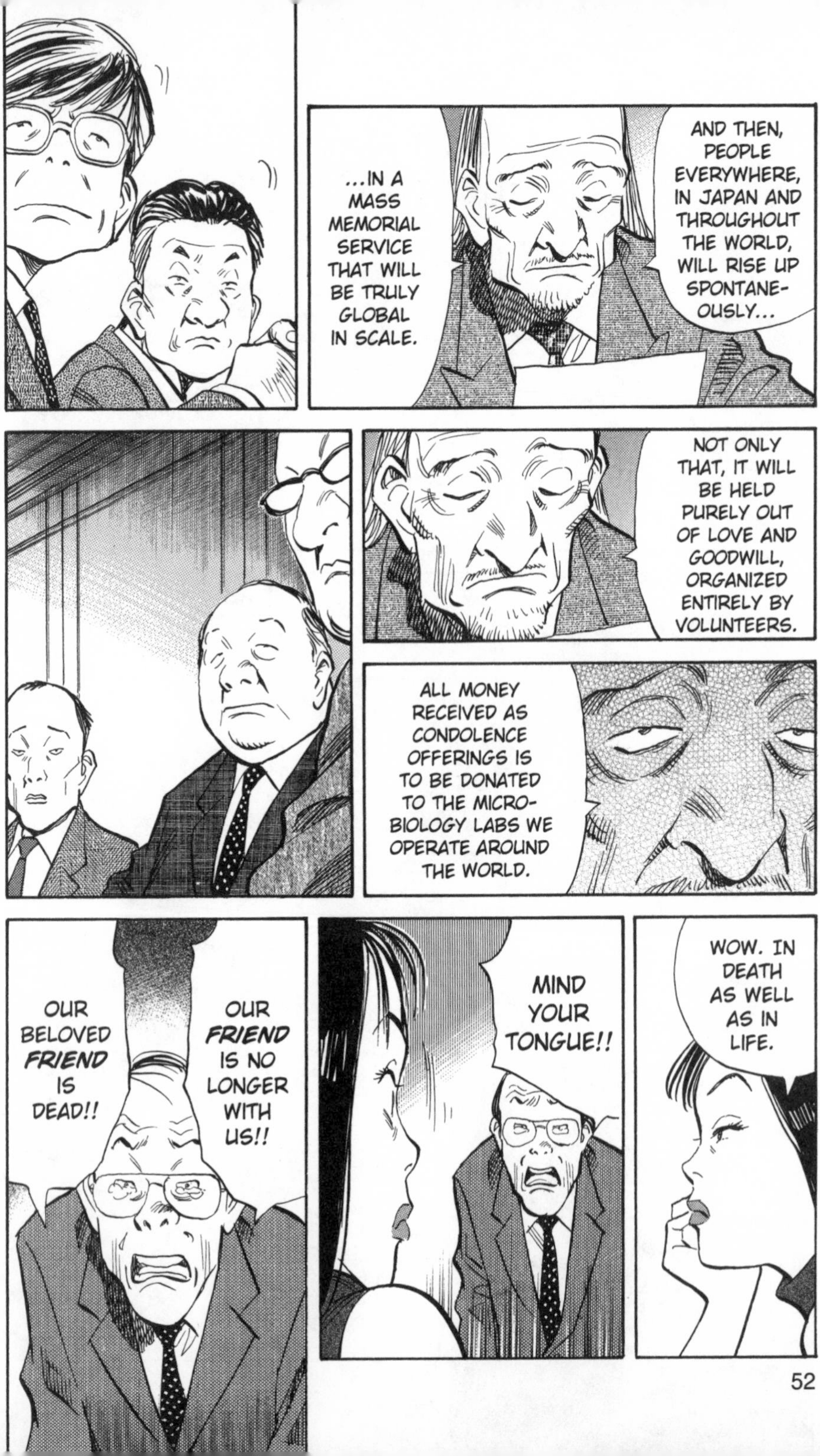
AND THEN, PEOPLE EVERYWHERE, IN JAPAN AND THROUGHOUT THE WORLD, WILL RISE UP SPONTANE-OUSLY...
...IN A MASS MEMORIAL SERVICE THAT WILL BE TRULY GLOBAL IN SCALE.
NOT ONLY THAT, IT WILL BE HELD PURELY OUT OF LOVE AND GOODWILL, ORGANIZED ENTIRELY BY VOLUNTEERS.
ALL MONEY RECEIVED AS CONDOLENCE OFFERINGS IS TO BE DONATED TO THE MICRO-BIOLOGY LABS WE OPERATE AROUND THE WORLD.
WOW. IN DEATH AS WELL AS IN LIFE.
MIND YOUR TONGUE!!
OUR *FRIEND* IS NO LONGER WITH US!!
OUR BELOVED *FRIEND* IS DEAD!!

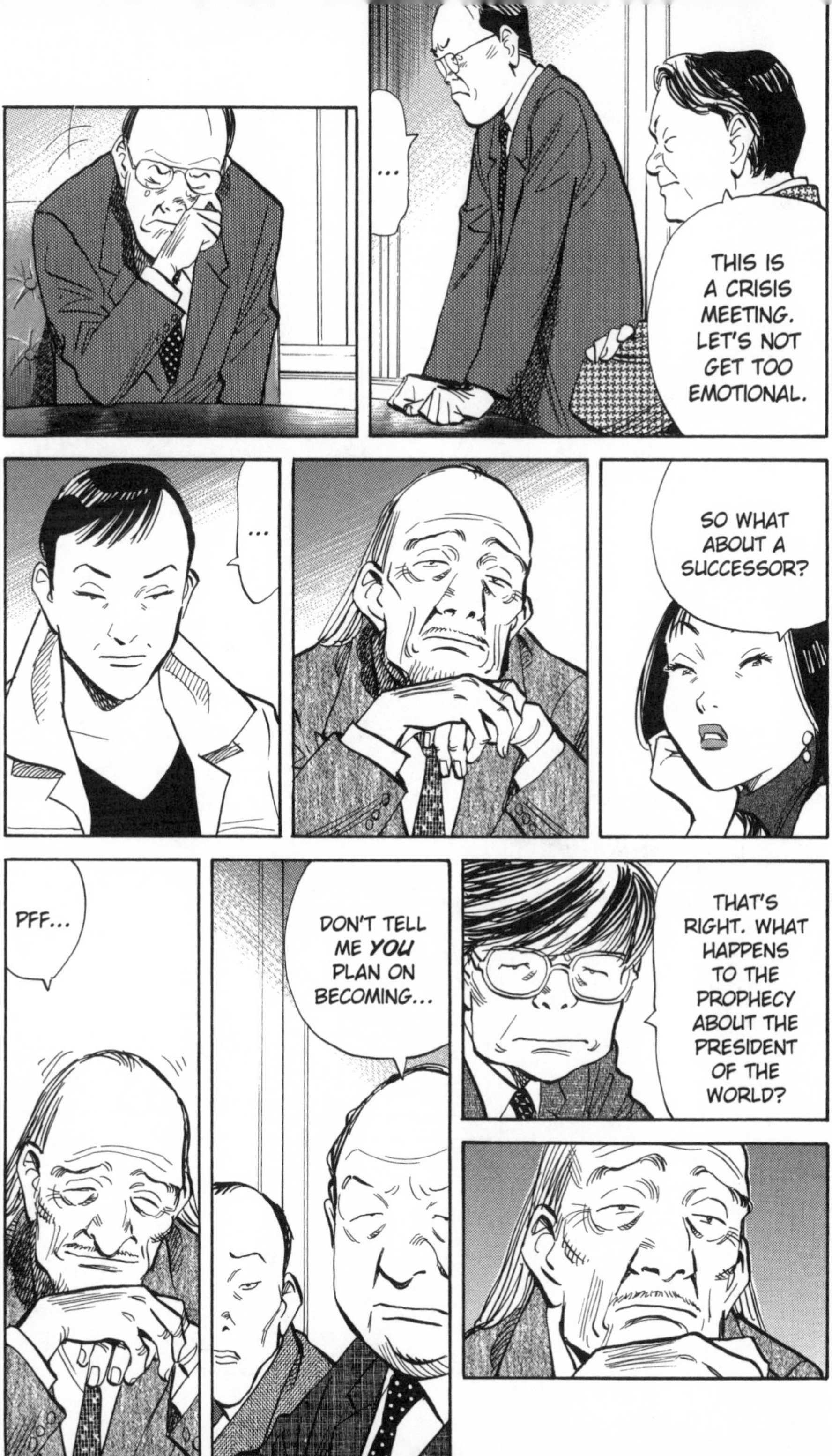
...
THIS IS A CRISIS MEETING. LET'S NOT GET TOO EMOTIONAL.
SO WHAT ABOUT A SUCCESSOR?
...
THAT'S RIGHT. WHAT HAPPENS TO THE PROPHECY ABOUT THE PRESIDENT OF THE WORLD?
DON'T TELL ME *YOU* PLAN ON BECOMING...
PFF...

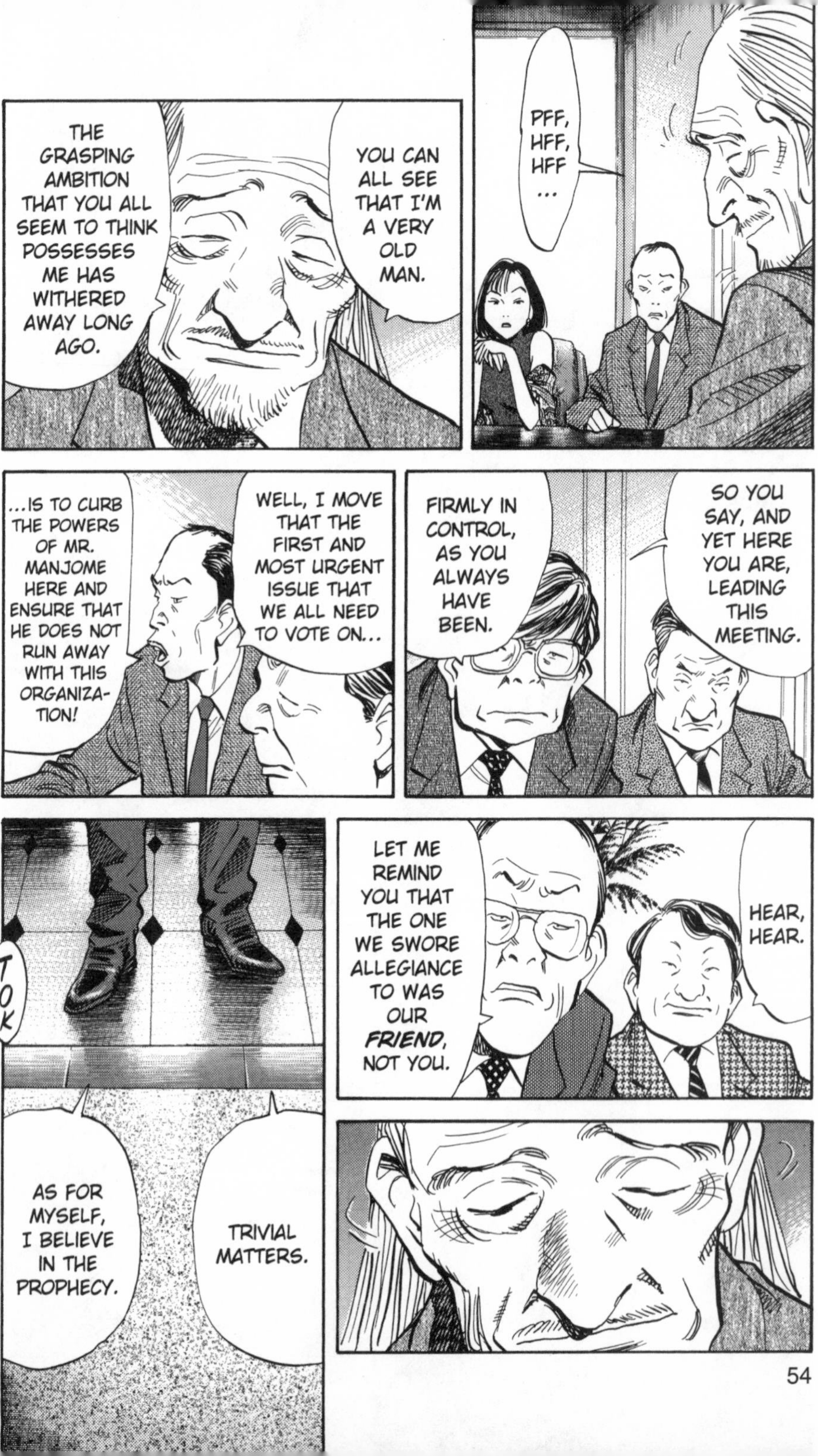
PFF, HFF, HFF ...
YOU CAN ALL SEE THAT I'M A VERY OLD MAN.
THE GRASPING AMBITION THAT YOU ALL SEEM TO THINK POSSESSES ME HAS WITHERED AWAY LONG AGO.
SO YOU SAY, AND YET HERE YOU ARE, LEADING THIS MEETING.
FIRMLY IN CONTROL, AS YOU ALWAYS HAVE BEEN.
WELL, I MOVE THAT THE FIRST AND MOST URGENT ISSUE THAT WE ALL NEED TO VOTE ON...
...IS TO CURB THE POWERS OF MR. MANJOME HERE AND ENSURE THAT HE DOES NOT RUN AWAY WITH THIS ORGANIZA-TION!
LET ME REMIND YOU THAT THE ONE WE SWORE ALLEGIANCE TO WAS OUR **FRIEND**, NOT YOU.
HEAR, HEAR.
TOK
TRIVIAL MATTERS.
AS FOR MYSELF, I BELIEVE IN THE PROPHECY.

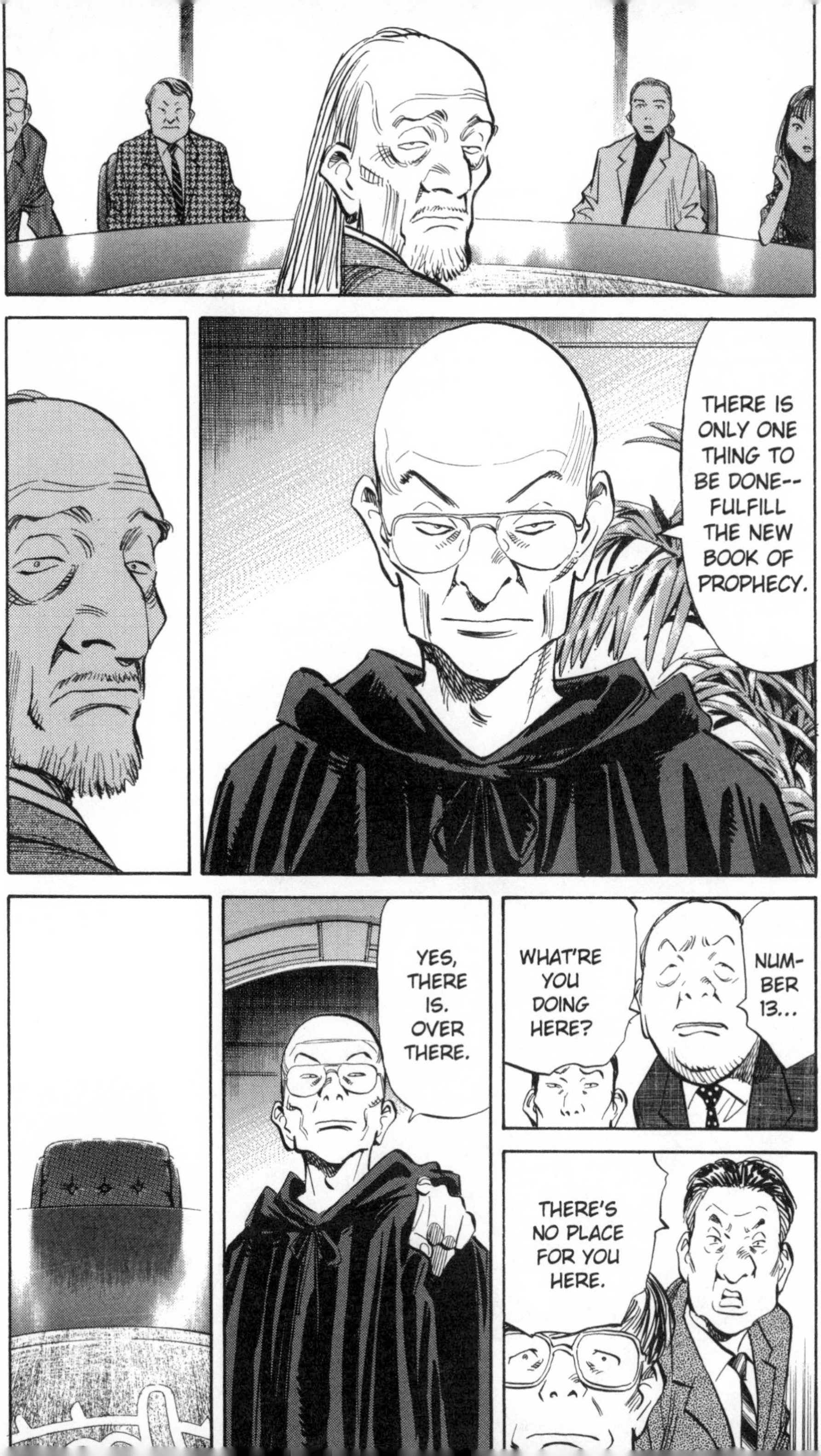
THERE IS ONLY ONE THING TO BE DONE-- FULFILL THE NEW BOOK OF PROPHECY.
NUM-BER 13...
WHAT'RE YOU DOING HERE?
THERE'S NO PLACE FOR YOU HERE.
YES, THERE IS. OVER THERE.

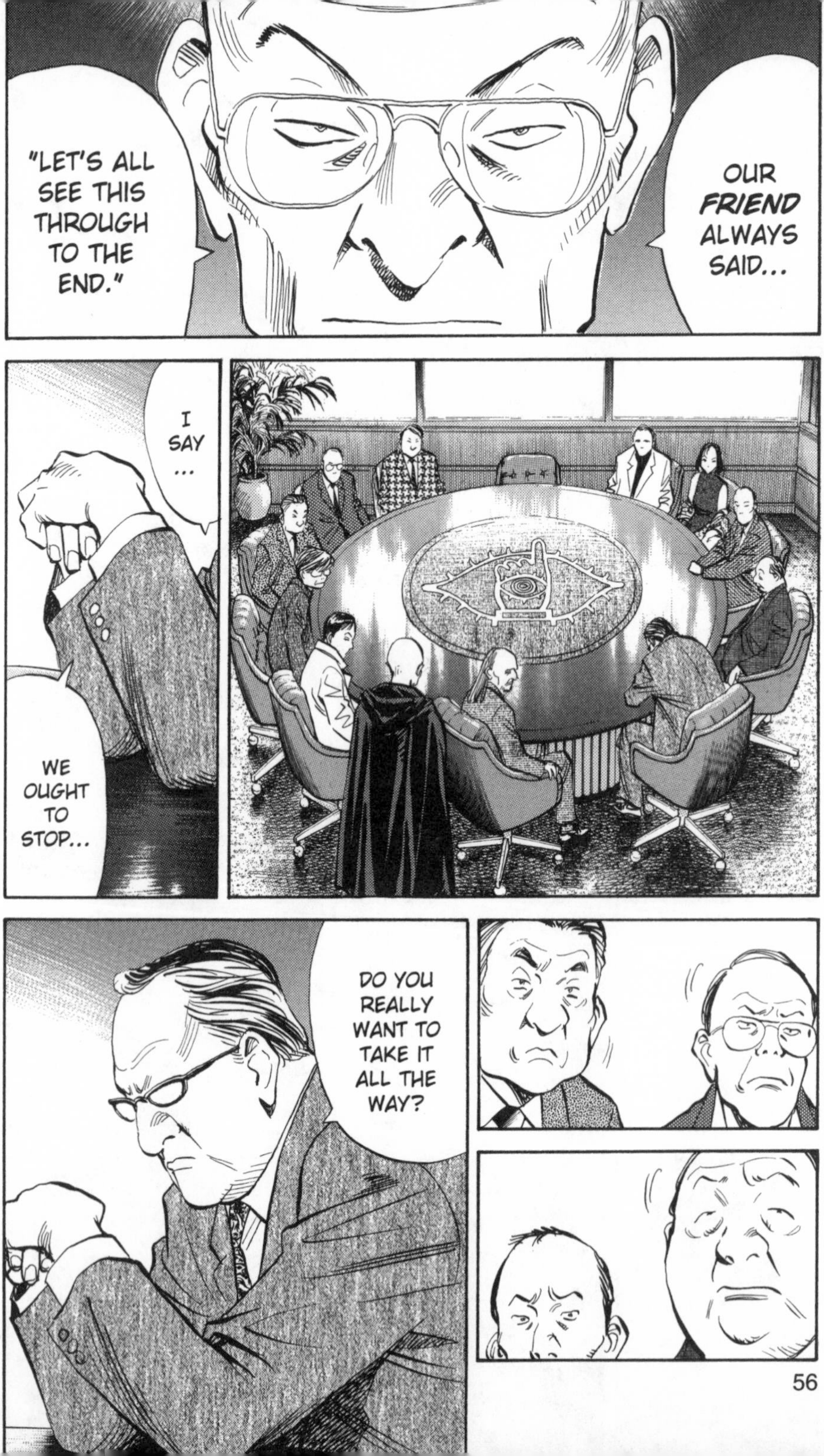
OUR FRIEND ALWAYS SAID...
"LET'S ALL SEE THIS THROUGH TO THE END."
I SAY ...
WE OUGHT TO STOP...
DO YOU REALLY WANT TO TAKE IT ALL THE WAY?

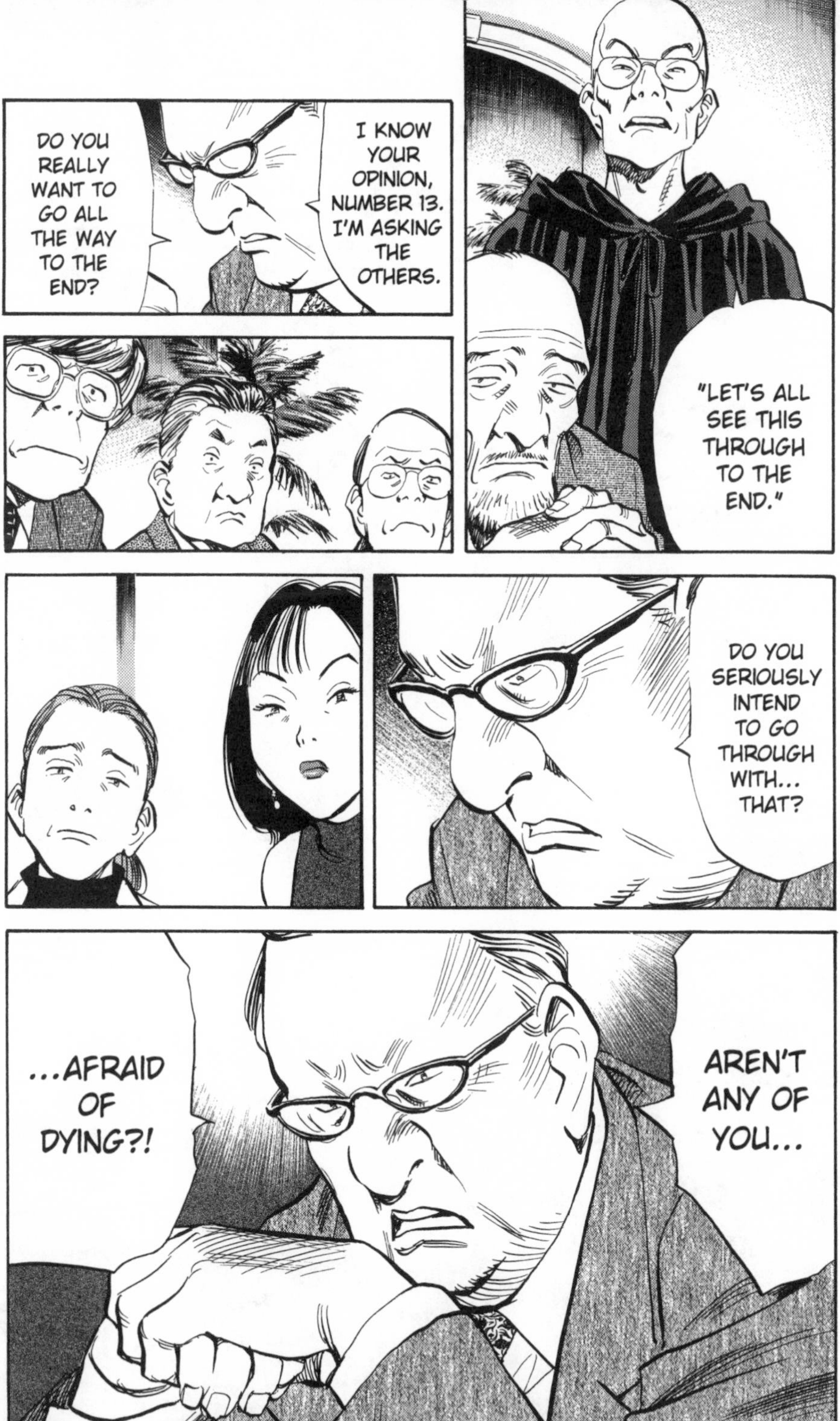
"LET'S ALL SEE THIS THROUGH TO THE END."
I KNOW YOUR OPINION, NUMBER 13. I'M ASKING THE OTHERS.
DO YOU REALLY WANT TO GO ALL THE WAY TO THE END?
DO YOU SERIOUSLY INTEND TO GO THROUGH WITH... THAT?
AREN'T ANY OF YOU...
...AFRAID OF DYING?!

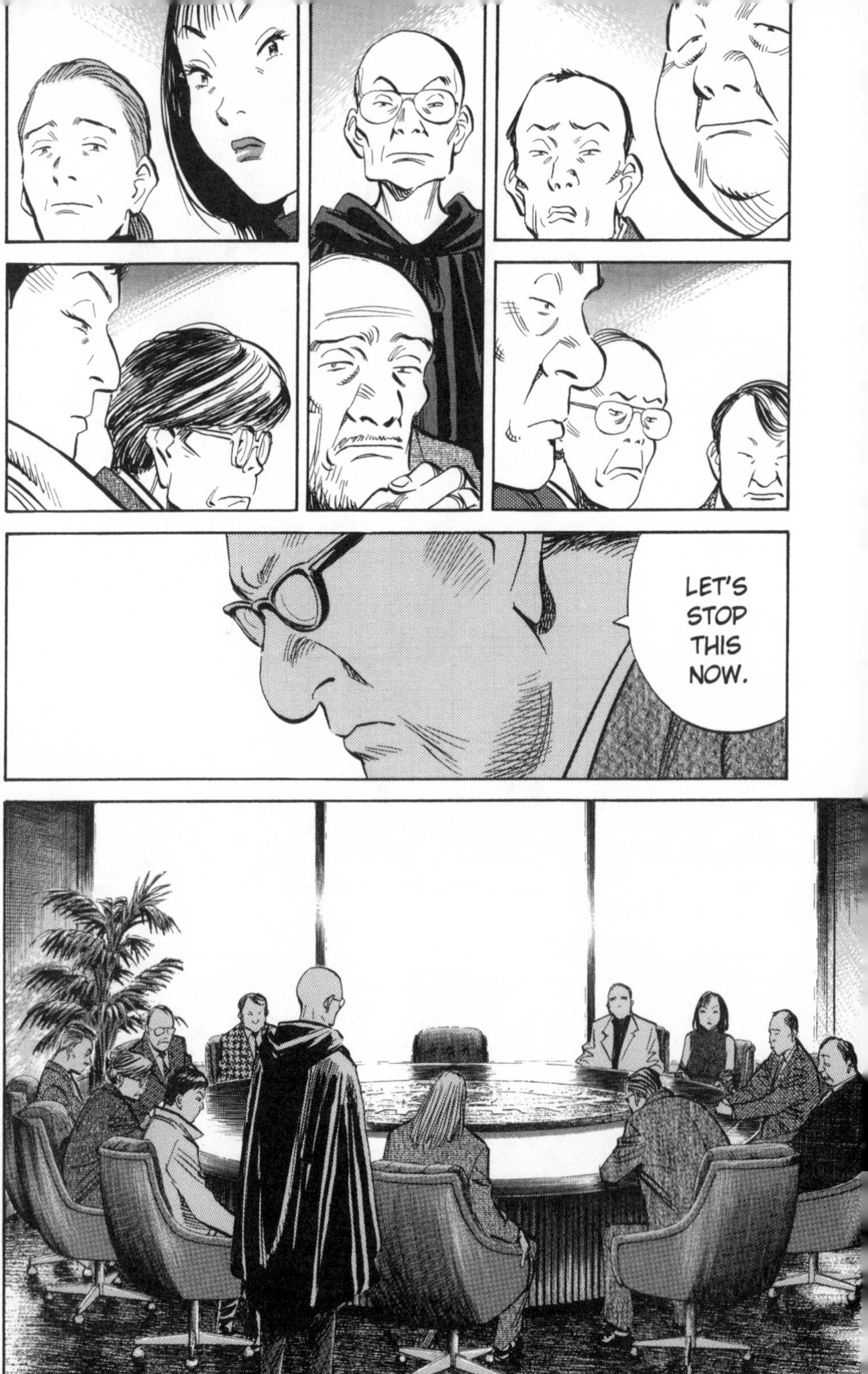
LET'S STOP THIS NOW.

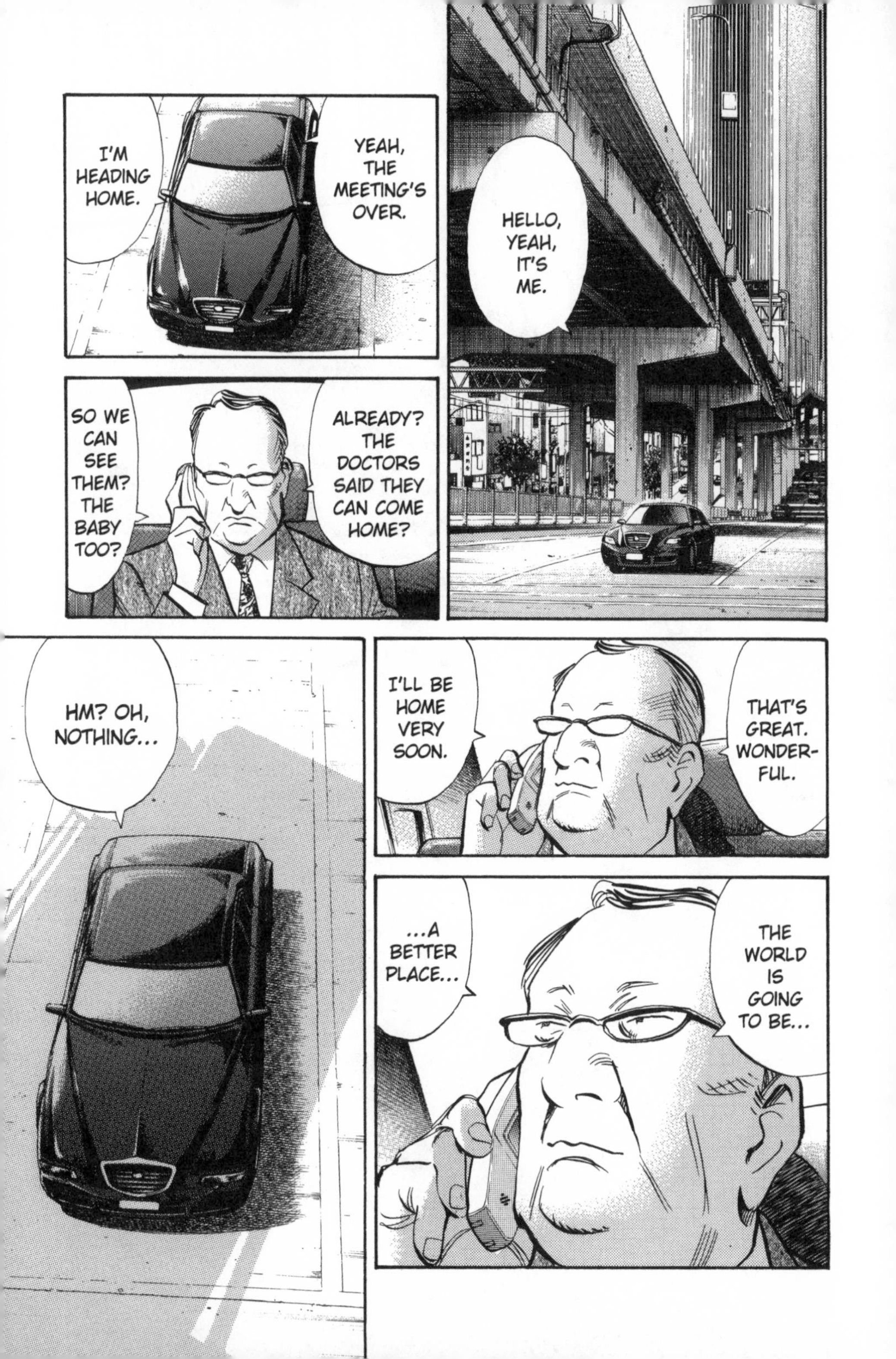
HELLO, YEAH, IT'S ME.
YEAH, THE MEETING'S OVER.
I'M HEADING HOME.
ALREADY? THE DOCTORS SAID THEY CAN COME HOME?
SO WE CAN SEE THEM? THE BABY TOO?
THAT'S GREAT. WONDERFUL.
I'LL BE HOME VERY SOON.
THE WORLD IS GOING TO BE...
...A BETTER PLACE...
HM? OH, NOTHING...

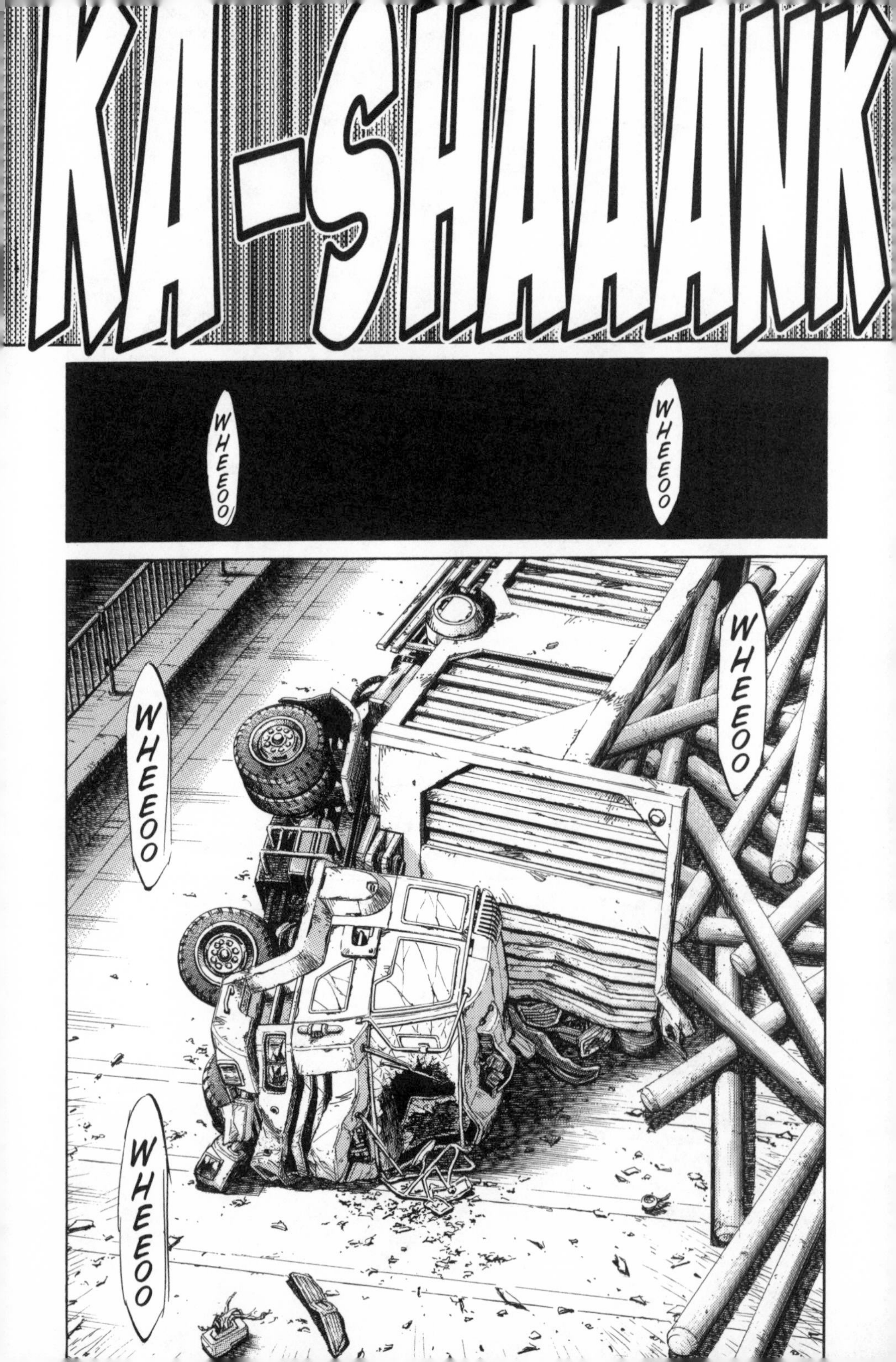
KA-SHAAANK
WHEEEOO
WHEEEOO
WHEEEOO
WHEEEOO
WHEEEOO

Chapter 4 Reunion

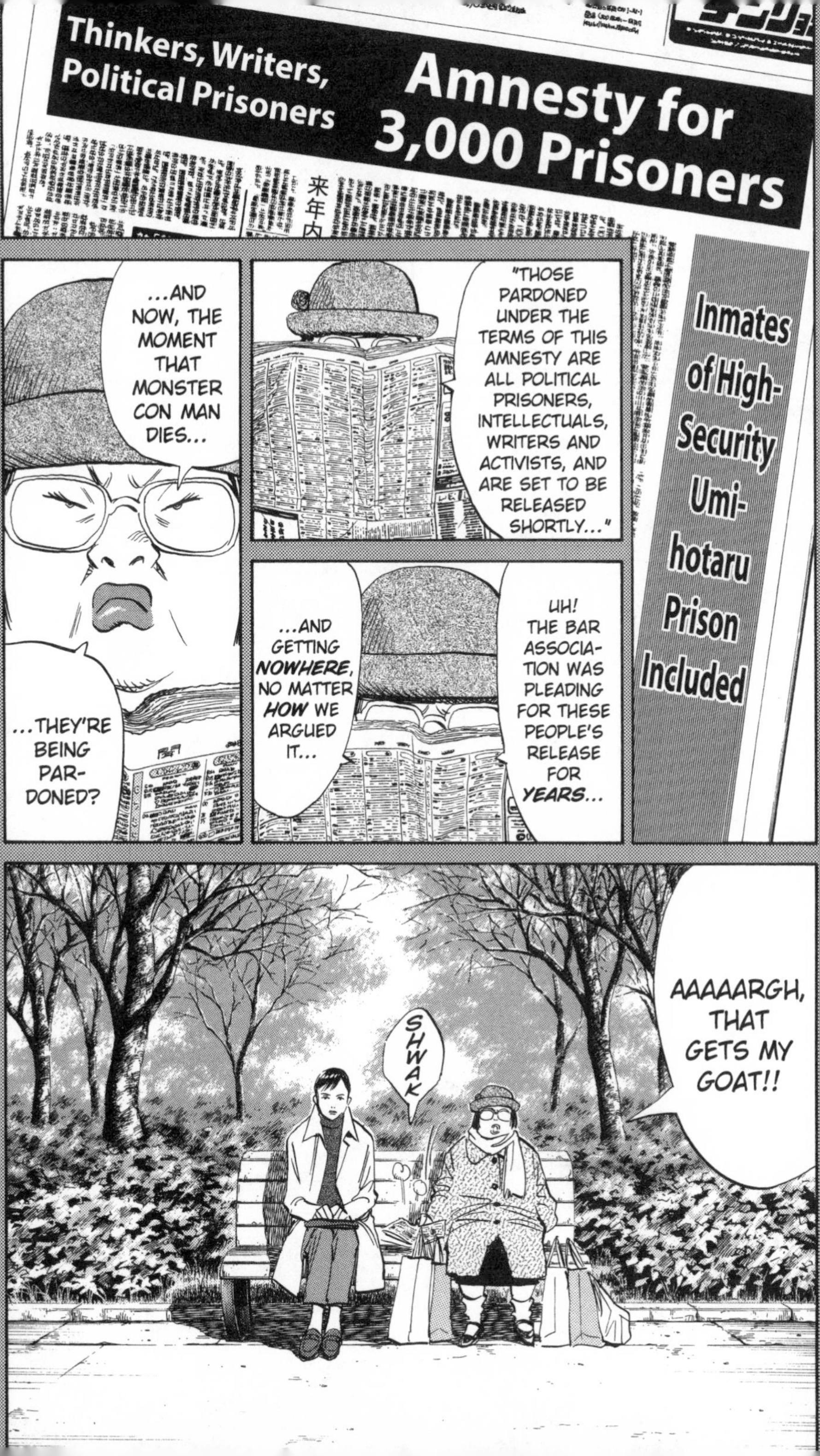
Thinkers, Writers, Political Prisoners
Amnesty for 3,000 Prisoners
来年内
Inmates of High-Security Umi-hotaru Prison Included
"THOSE PARDONED UNDER THE TERMS OF THIS AMNESTY ARE ALL POLITICAL PRISONERS, INTELLECTUALS, WRITERS AND ACTIVISTS, AND ARE SET TO BE RELEASED SHORTLY..."
UH! THE BAR ASSOCIATION WAS PLEADING FOR THESE PEOPLE'S RELEASE FOR *YEARS*...
...AND GETTING ***NOWHERE***, NO MATTER ***HOW*** WE ARGUED IT...
...AND NOW, THE MOMENT THAT MONSTER CON MAN DIES...
...THEY'RE BEING PARDONED?
AAAAARGH, THAT GETS MY GOAT!!
SHWAK

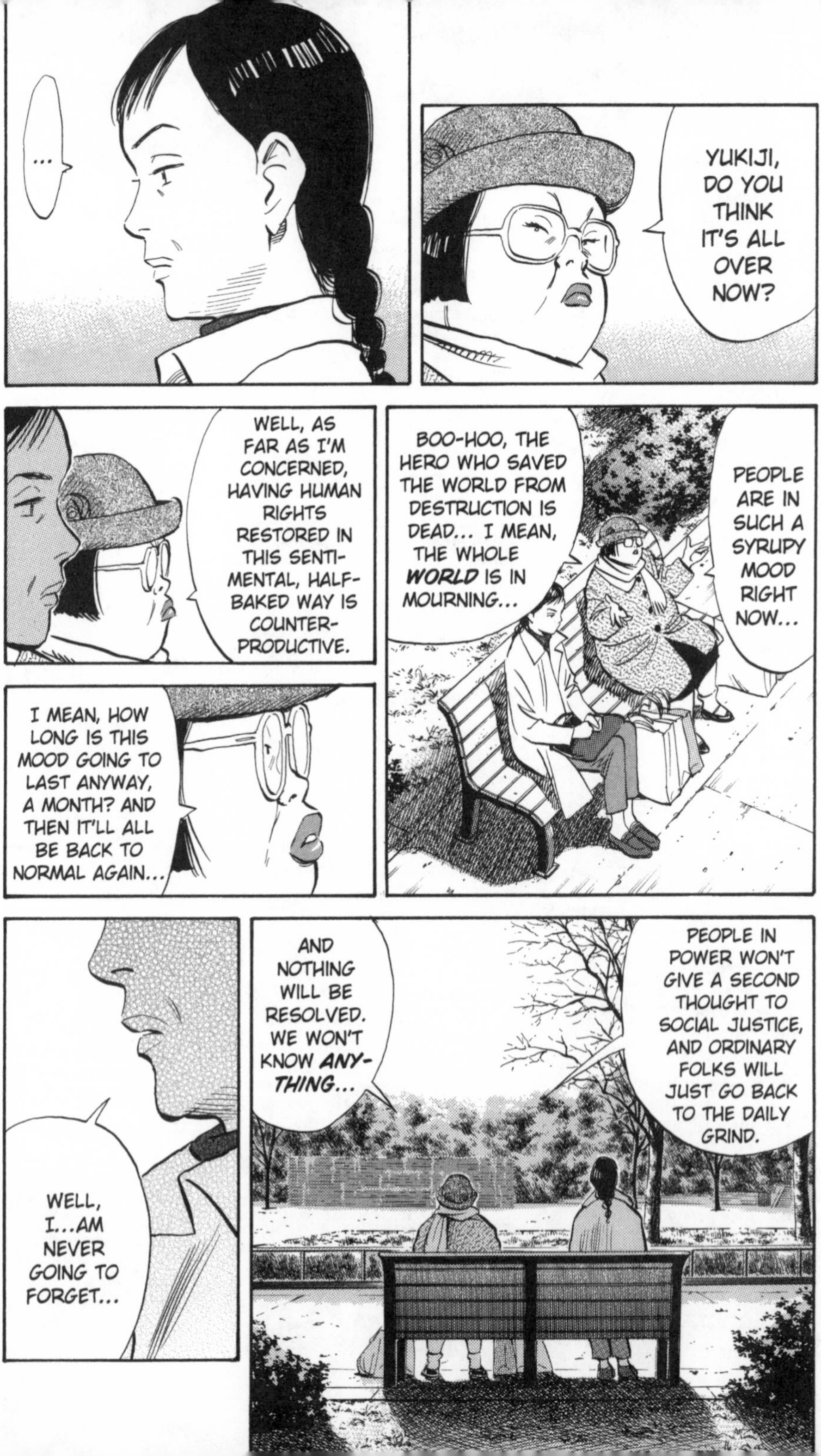
YUKIJI, DO YOU THINK IT'S ALL OVER NOW?
...
PEOPLE ARE IN SUCH A SYRUPY MOOD RIGHT NOW...
BOO-HOO, THE HERO WHO SAVED THE WORLD FROM DESTRUCTION IS DEAD... I MEAN, THE WHOLE *WORLD* IS IN MOURNING...
WELL, AS FAR AS I'M CONCERNED, HAVING HUMAN RIGHTS RESTORED IN THIS SENTI-MENTAL, HALF-BAKED WAY IS COUNTER-PRODUCTIVE.
I MEAN, HOW LONG IS THIS MOOD GOING TO LAST ANYWAY, A MONTH? AND THEN IT'LL ALL BE BACK TO NORMAL AGAIN...
PEOPLE IN POWER WON'T GIVE A SECOND THOUGHT TO SOCIAL JUSTICE, AND ORDINARY FOLKS WILL JUST GO BACK TO THE DAILY GRIND.
AND NOTHING WILL BE RESOLVED. WE WON'T KNOW *ANY-THING*...
WELL, I...AM NEVER GOING TO FORGET...

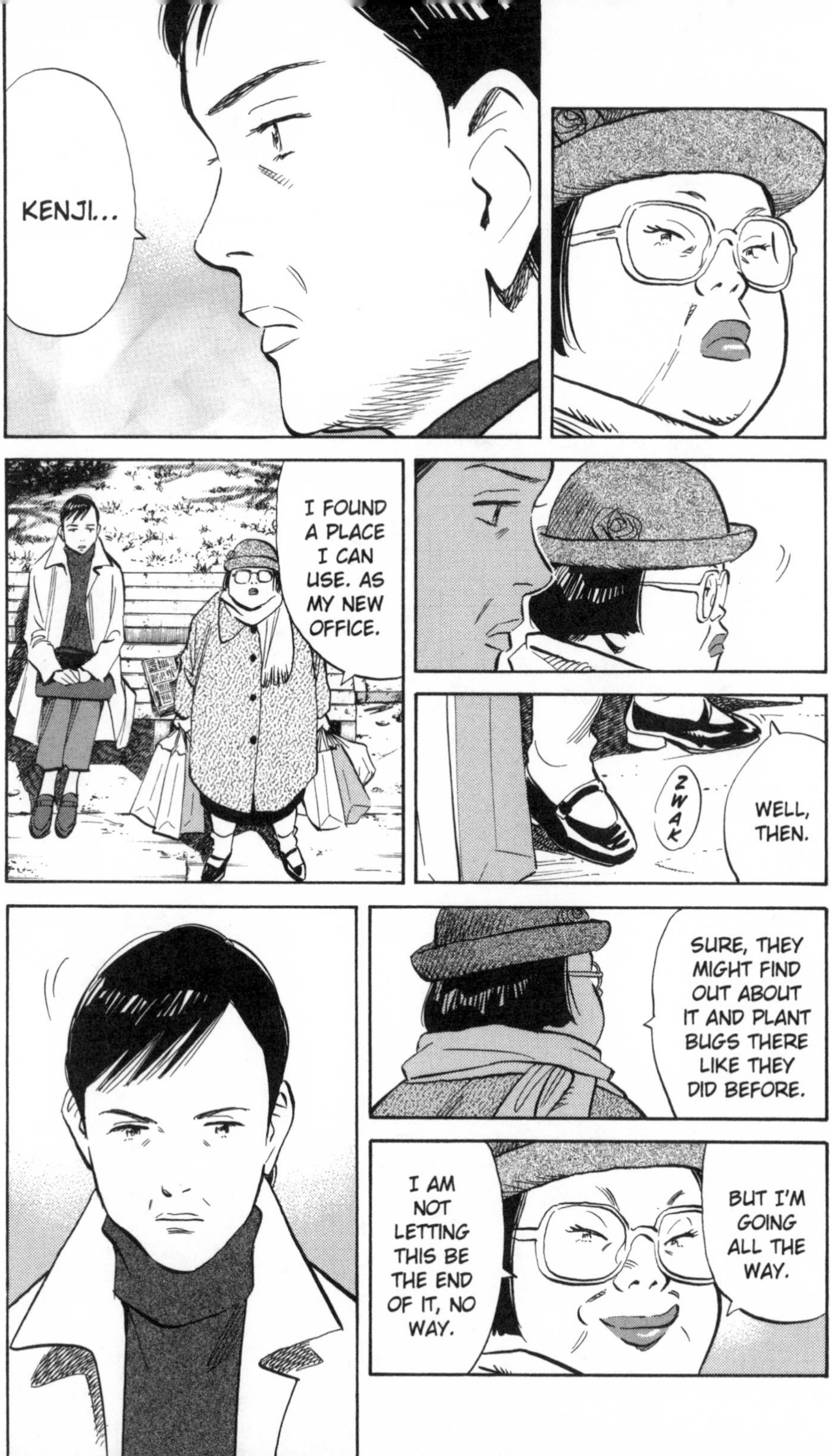
KENJI...
ZWAK
WELL, THEN.
I FOUND A PLACE I CAN USE. AS MY NEW OFFICE.
SURE, THEY MIGHT FIND OUT ABOUT IT AND PLANT BUGS THERE LIKE THEY DID BEFORE.
BUT I'M GOING ALL THE WAY.
I AM NOT LETTING THIS BE THE END OF IT, NO WAY.

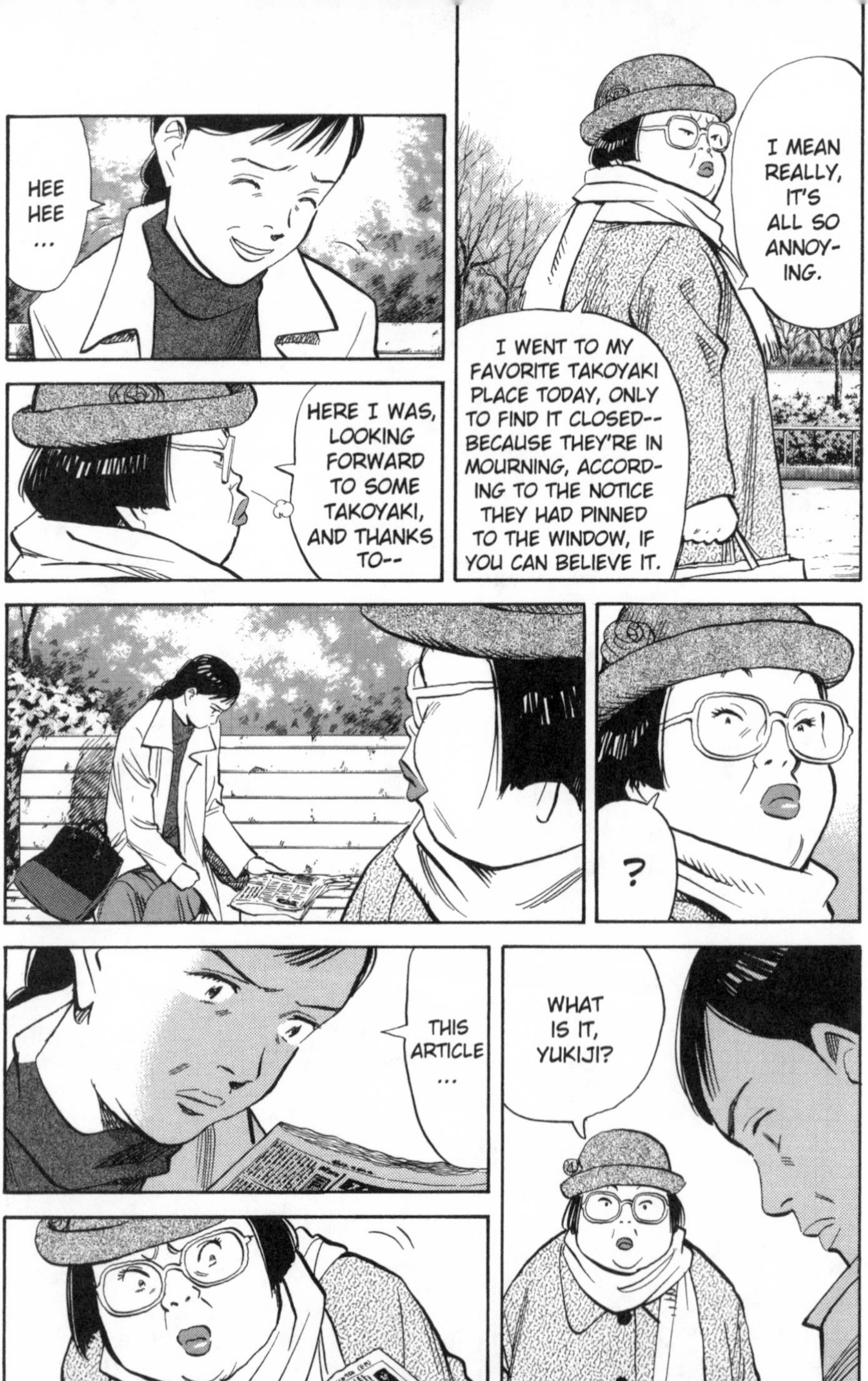
I MEAN REALLY, IT'S ALL SO ANNOY-ING.
I WENT TO MY FAVORITE TAKOYAKI PLACE TODAY, ONLY TO FIND IT CLOSED--BECAUSE THEY'RE IN MOURNING, ACCORD-ING TO THE NOTICE THEY HAD PINNED TO THE WINDOW, IF YOU CAN BELIEVE IT.
HEE HEE ...
HERE I WAS, LOOKING FORWARD TO SOME TAKOYAKI, AND THANKS TO--
?
WHAT IS IT, YUKIJI?
THIS ARTICLE ...

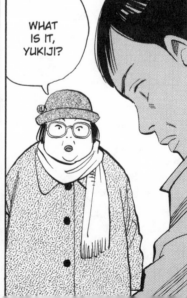

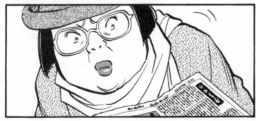

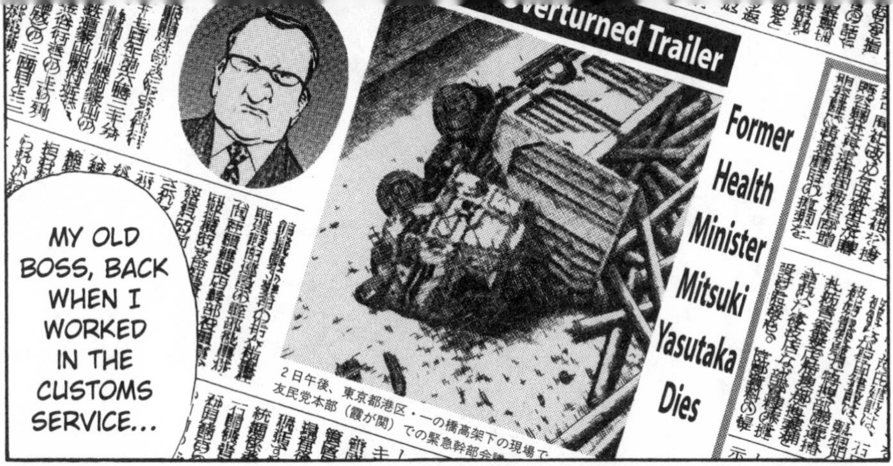
verturned Trailer
Former Health Minister Mitsuki Yasutaka Dies
2日午後、東京都港区・一の橋高架下の現場で
友民党本部（霞が関）での緊急幹部会
MY OLD BOSS, BACK WHEN I WORKED IN THE CUSTOMS SERVICE...

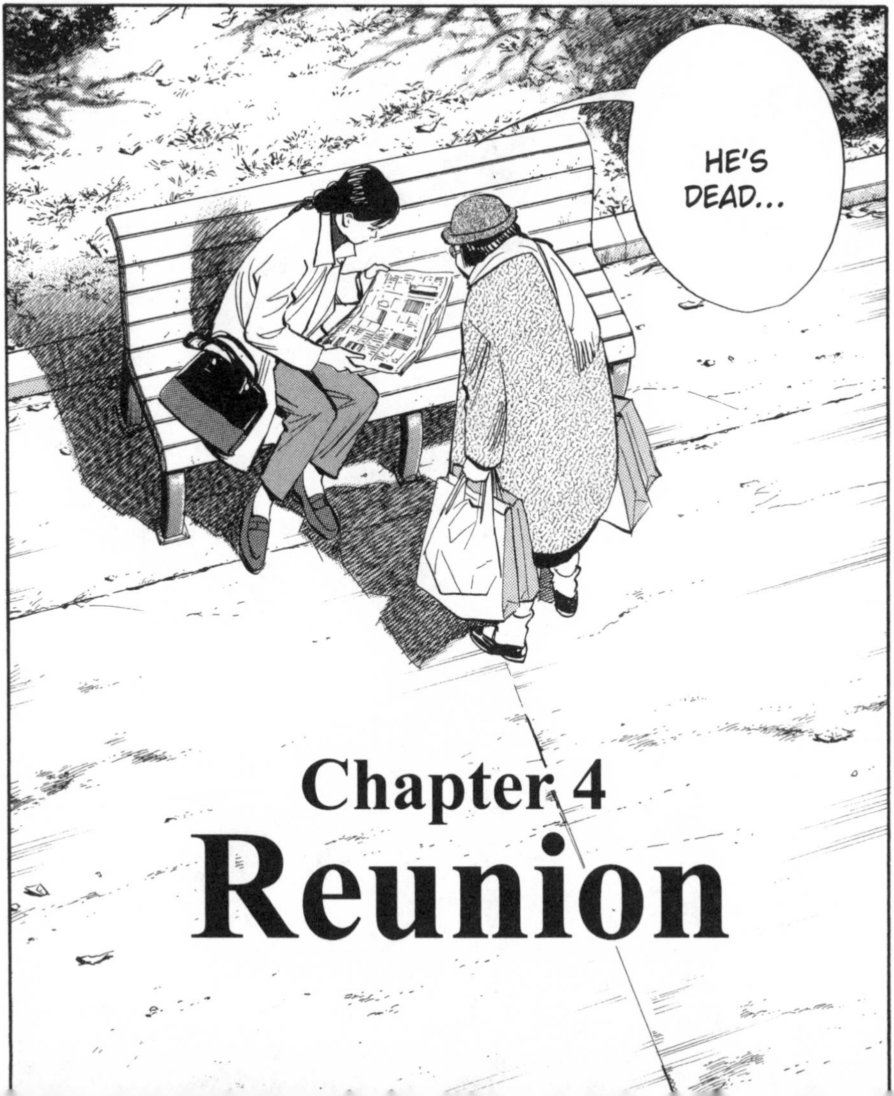
HE'S DEAD...
Chapter 4
Reunion

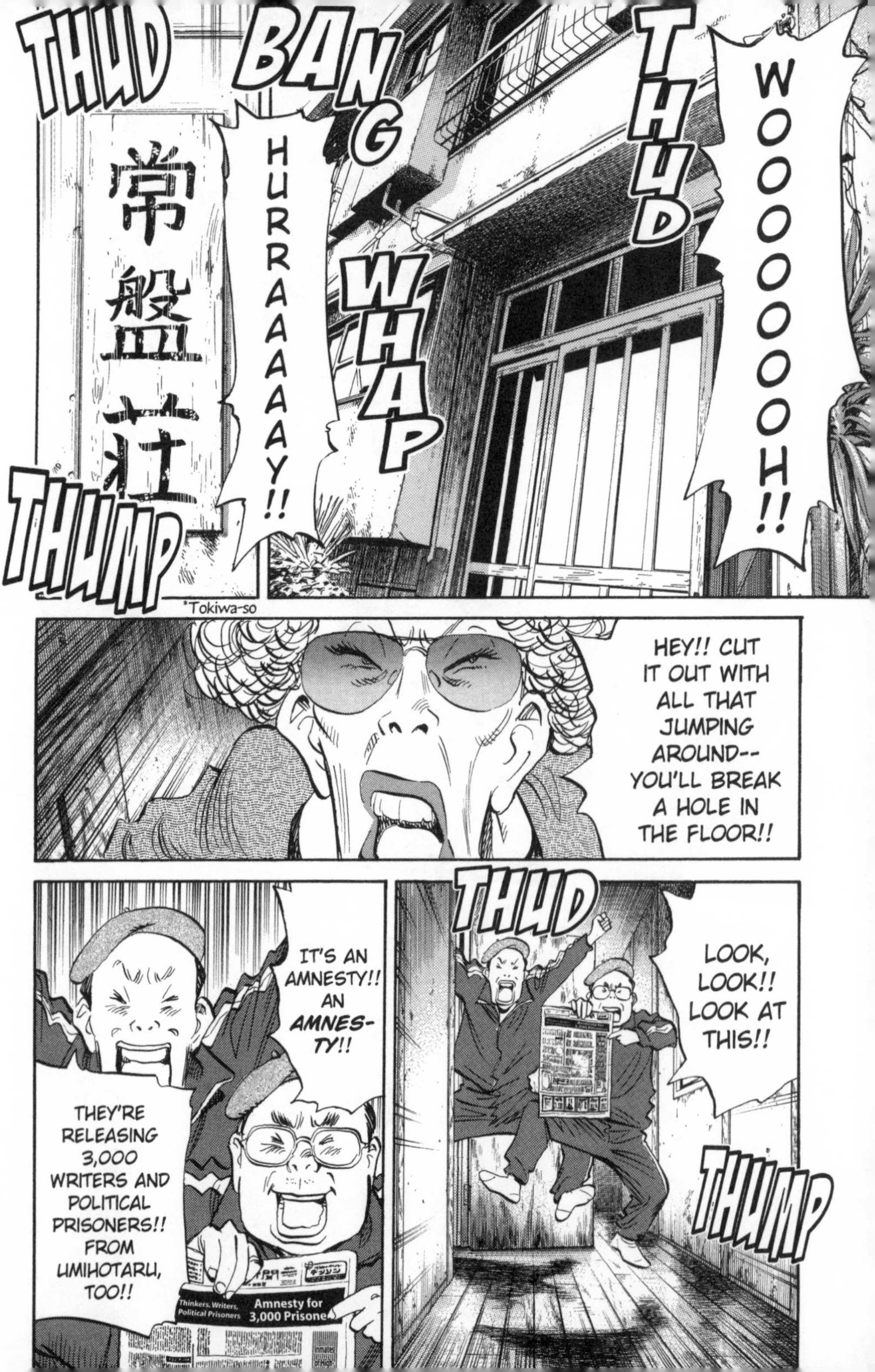

WOOOOOOOOH!!
THUD
WHAP
BANG
HURRAAAAAAY!!
THUD
常盤荘
THUMP
*Tokiwa-so
HEY!! CUT IT OUT WITH ALL THAT JUMPING AROUND-- YOU'LL BREAK A HOLE IN THE FLOOR!!
THUD
LOOK, LOOK!! LOOK AT THIS!!
THUMP
IT'S AN AMNESTY!! AN AMNES-TY!!
THEY'RE RELEASING 3,000 WRITERS AND POLITICAL PRISONERS!! FROM UMIHOTARU, TOO!!
Thinkers, Writers, Political Prisoners
Amnesty for 3,000 Prisone

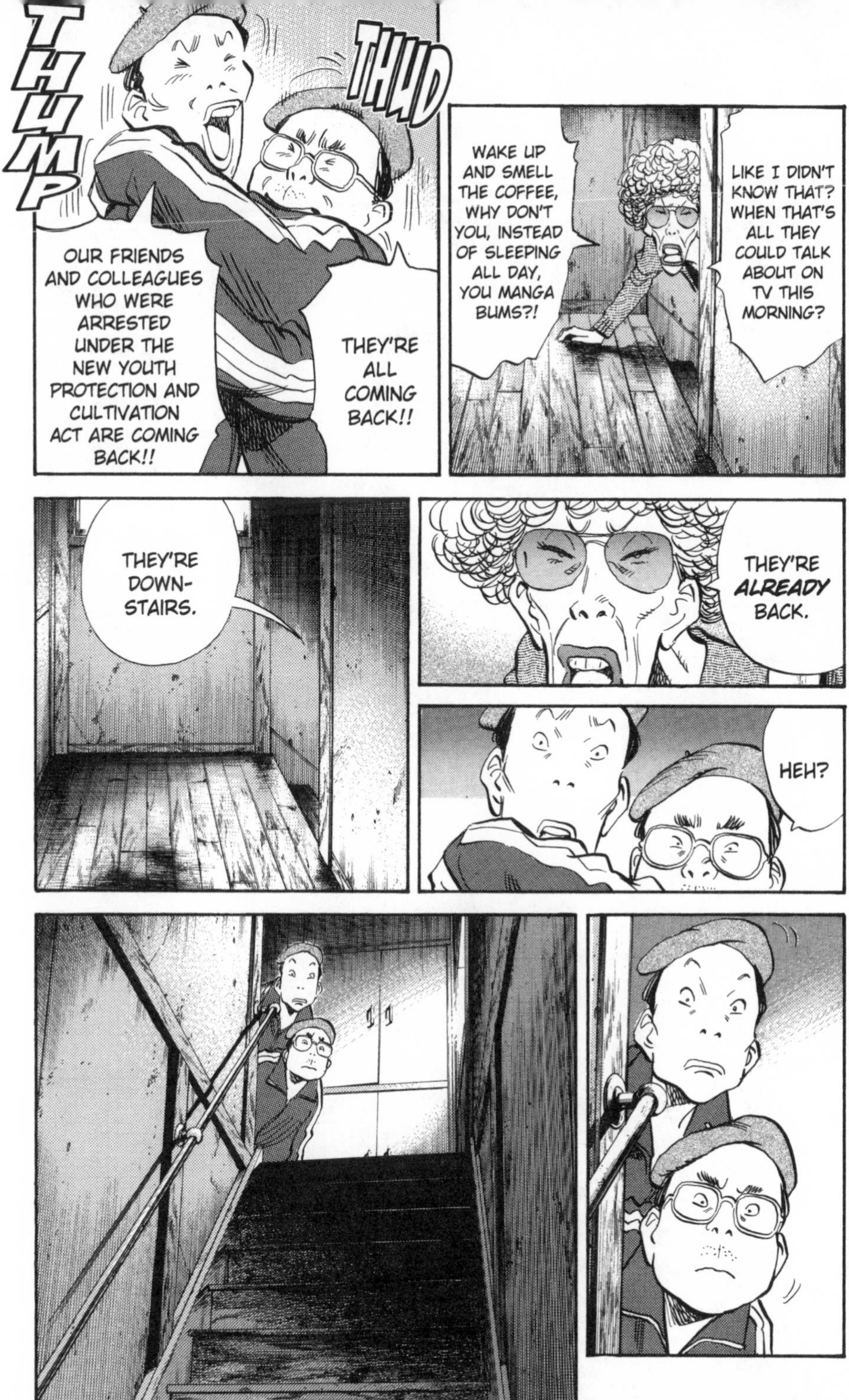
LIKE I DIDN'T KNOW THAT? WHEN THAT'S ALL THEY COULD TALK ABOUT ON TV THIS MORNING?
WAKE UP AND SMELL THE COFFEE, WHY DON'T YOU, INSTEAD OF SLEEPING ALL DAY, YOU MANGA BUMS?!
THUD
THUMP
THEY'RE ALL COMING BACK!!
OUR FRIENDS AND COLLEAGUES WHO WERE ARRESTED UNDER THE NEW YOUTH PROTECTION AND CULTIVATION ACT ARE COMING BACK!!
THEY'RE *ALREADY* BACK.
HEH?
THEY'RE DOWN-STAIRS.

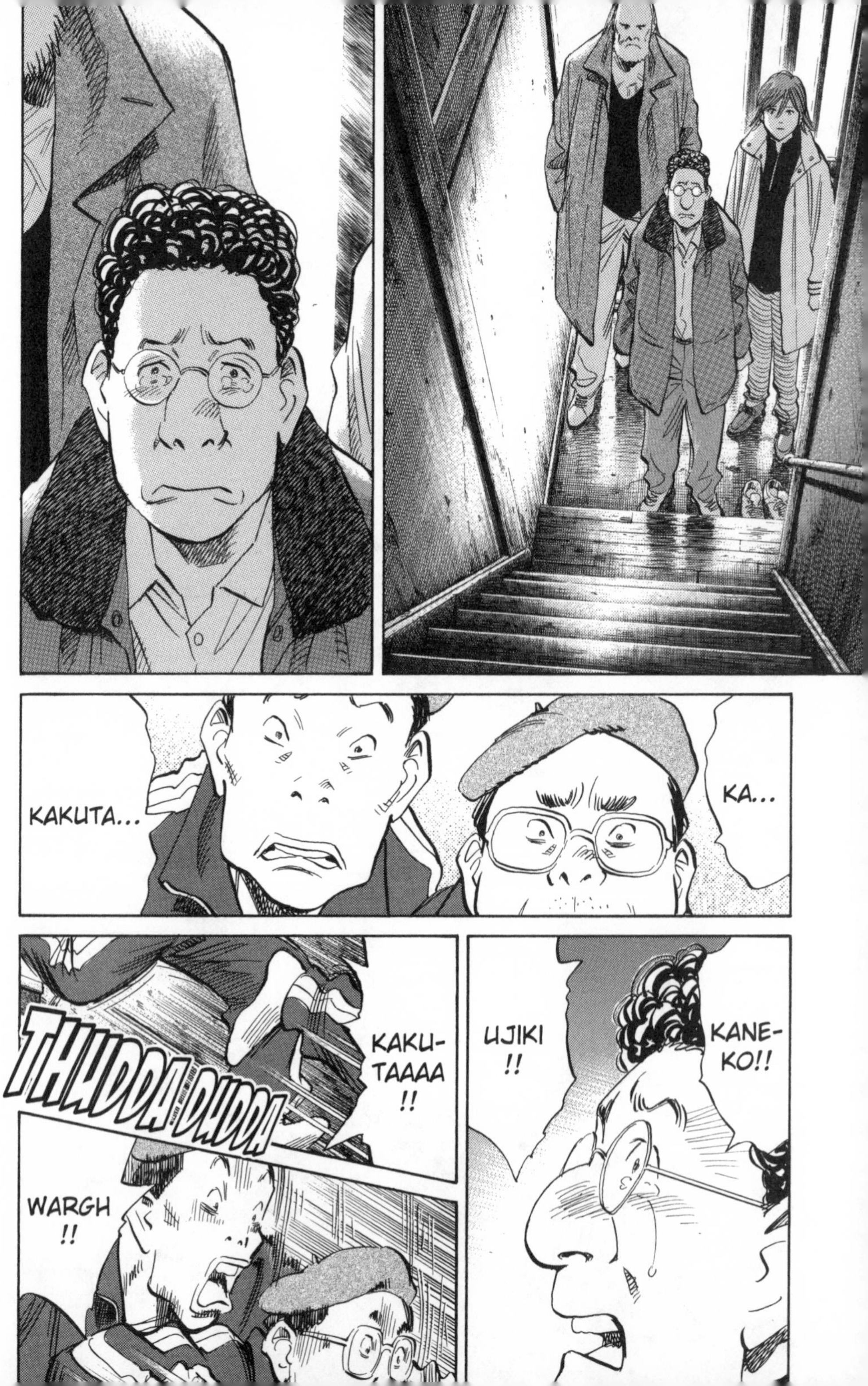
KA...
KAKUTA...
KANE-
KO!!
UJIKI
!!
KAKU-
TAAAA
!!
THUDDA DUDDA
WARGH
!!

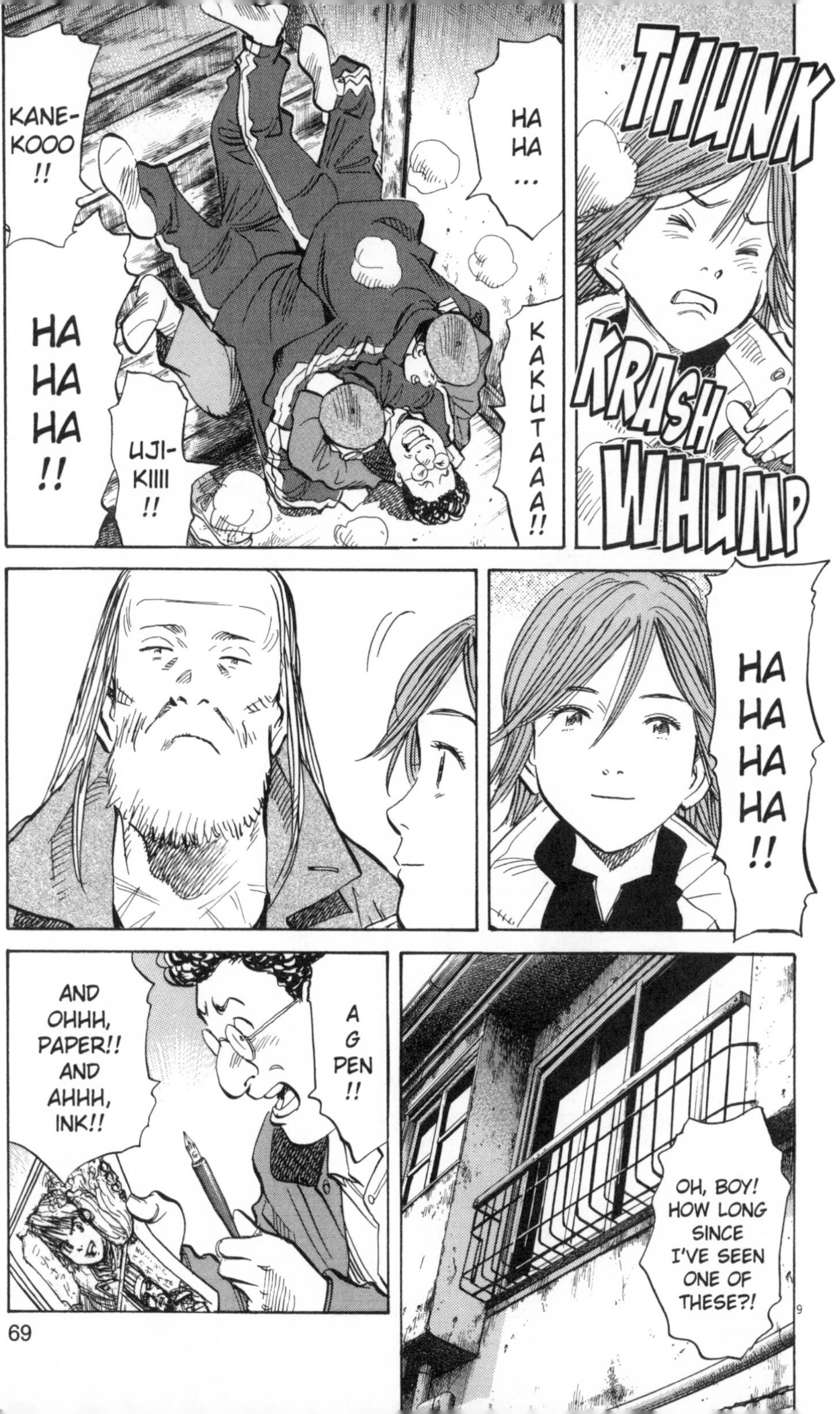
THUNK
KRASH
WHUMP
HA HA...
KANE-KOOO!!
KAKUTAAAA!!
HA HA HA!!
UJI-KIIII!!
HA HA HA HA!!
OH, BOY! HOW LONG SINCE I'VE SEEN ONE OF THESE?!
A G PEN!!
AND OHHH, PAPER!! AND AHHH, INK!!

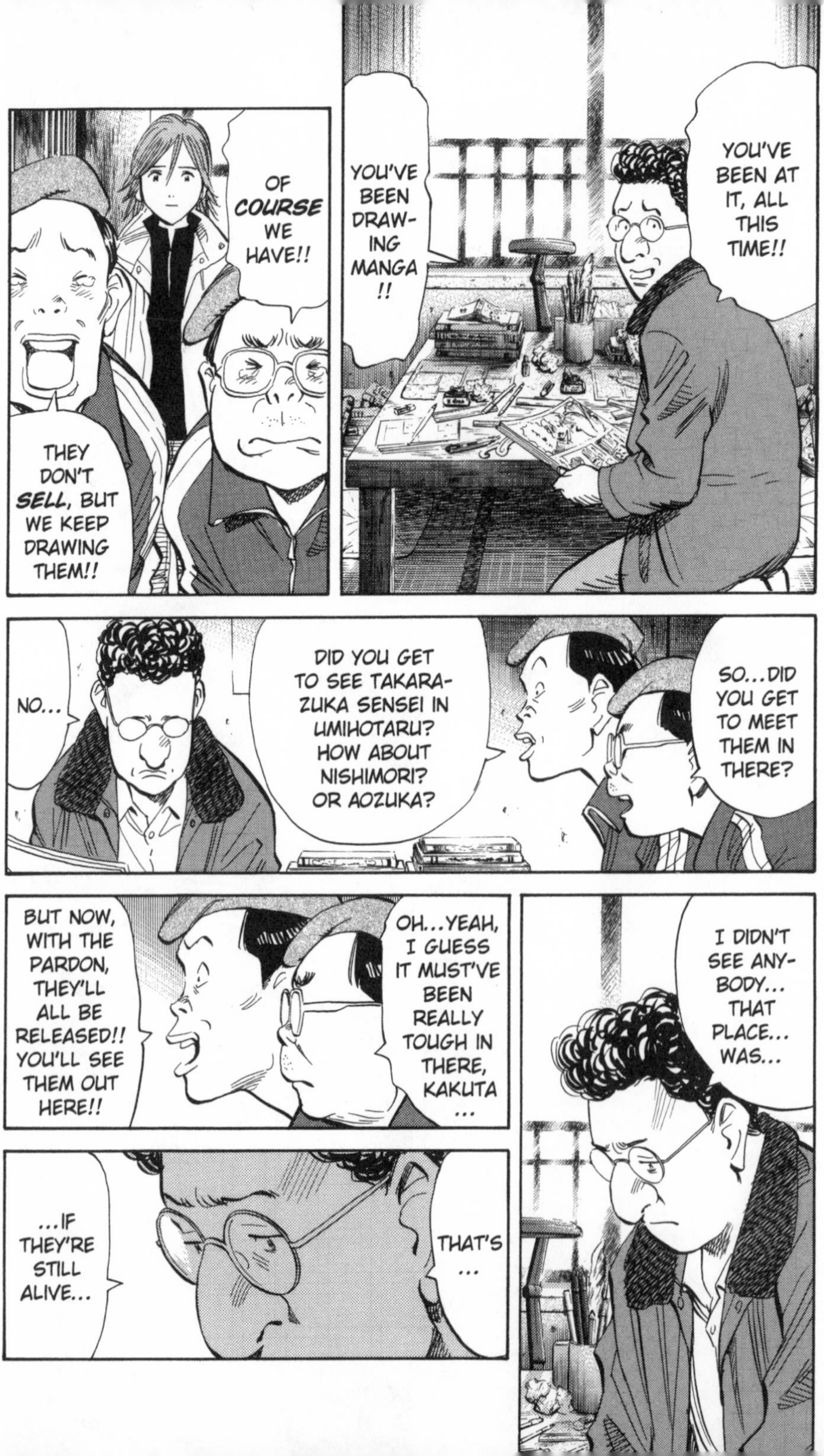

YOU'VE BEEN AT IT, ALL THIS TIME!!
YOU'VE BEEN DRAWING MANGA!!
OF COURSE WE HAVE!!
THEY DON'T SELL, BUT WE KEEP DRAWING THEM!!
SO...DID YOU GET TO MEET THEM IN THERE?
DID YOU GET TO SEE TAKARAZUKA SENSEI IN UMIHOTARU? HOW ABOUT NISHIMORI? OR AOZUKA?
NO...
I DIDN'T SEE ANYBODY... THAT PLACE... WAS...
OH...YEAH, I GUESS IT MUST'VE BEEN REALLY TOUGH IN THERE, KAKUTA...
BUT NOW, WITH THE PARDON, THEY'LL ALL BE RELEASED!! YOU'LL SEE THEM OUT HERE!!
THAT'S...
...IF THEY'RE STILL ALIVE...

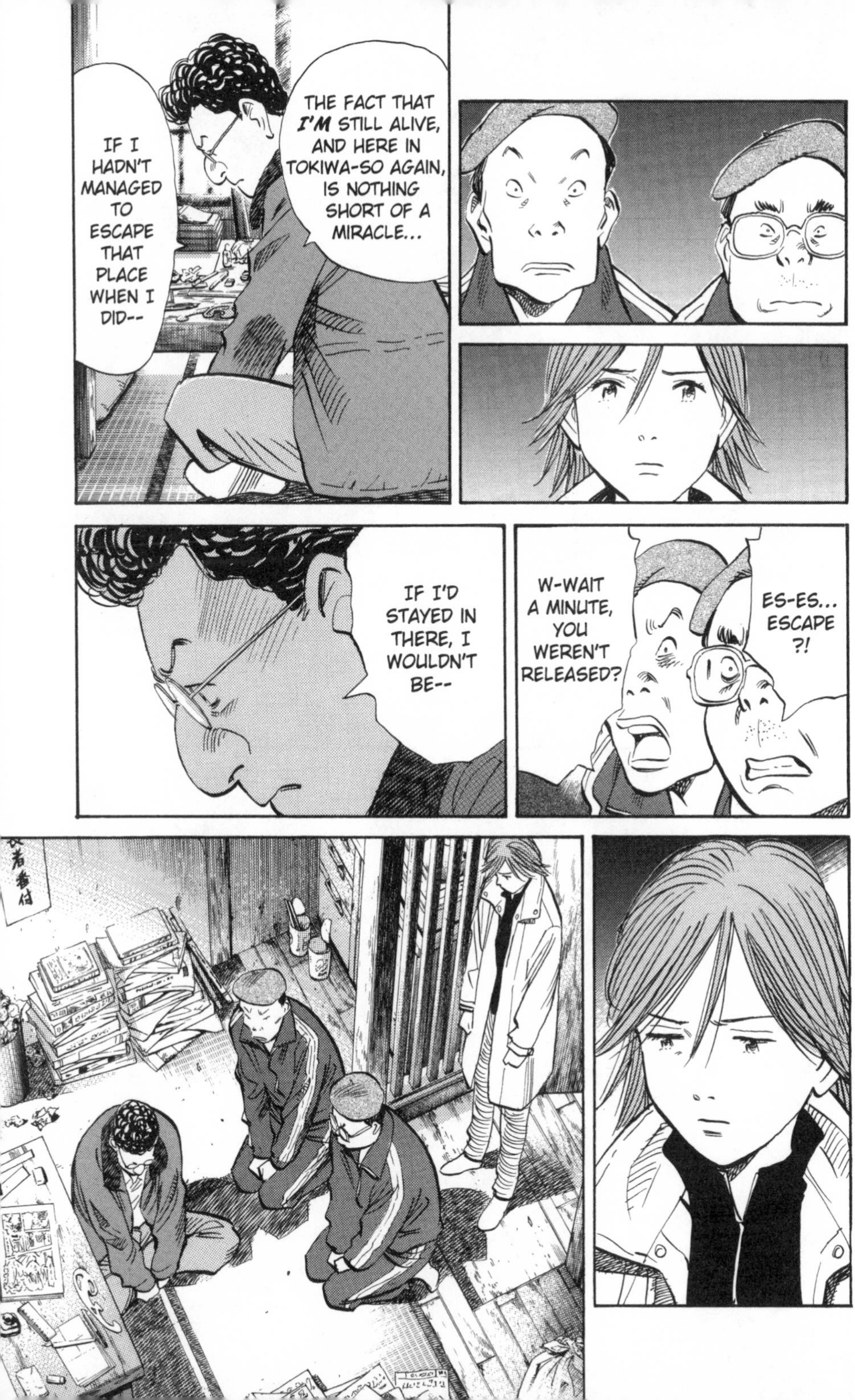
THE FACT THAT *I'M* STILL ALIVE, AND HERE IN TOKIWA-SO AGAIN, IS NOTHING SHORT OF A MIRACLE...
IF I HADN'T MANAGED TO ESCAPE THAT PLACE WHEN I DID--
ES-ES... ESCAPE ?!
W-WAIT A MINUTE, YOU WEREN'T RELEASED?
IF I'D STAYED IN THERE, I WOULDN'T BE--

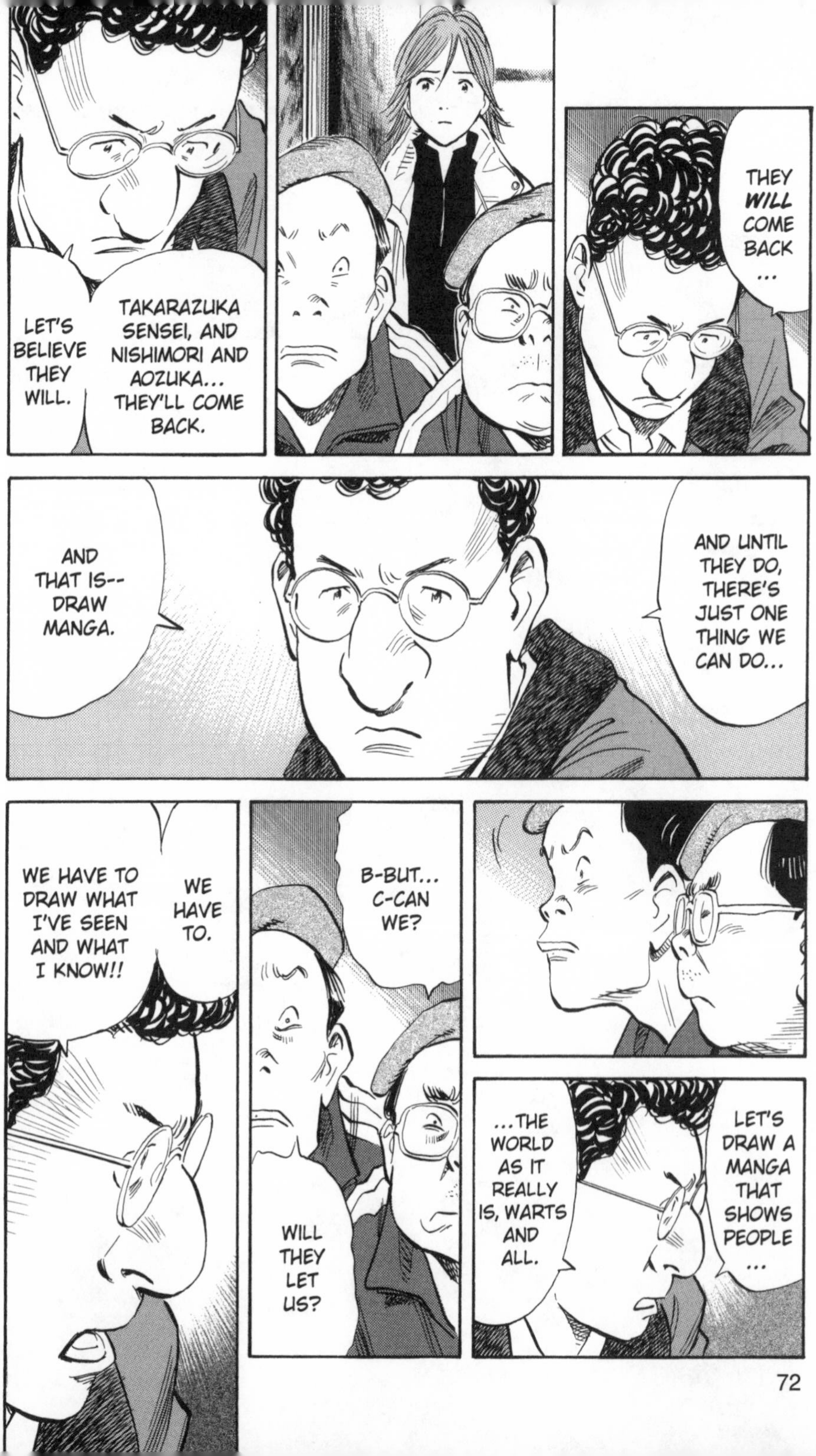
THEY *WILL* COME BACK...
TAKARAZUKA SENSEI, AND NISHIMORI AND AOZUKA... THEY'LL COME BACK.
LET'S BELIEVE THEY WILL.
AND UNTIL THEY DO, THERE'S JUST ONE THING WE CAN DO...
AND THAT IS-- DRAW MANGA.
LET'S DRAW A MANGA THAT SHOWS PEOPLE...
...THE WORLD AS IT REALLY IS, WARTS AND ALL.
B-BUT... C-CAN WE?
WILL THEY LET US?
WE HAVE TO.
WE HAVE TO DRAW WHAT I'VE SEEN AND WHAT I KNOW!!

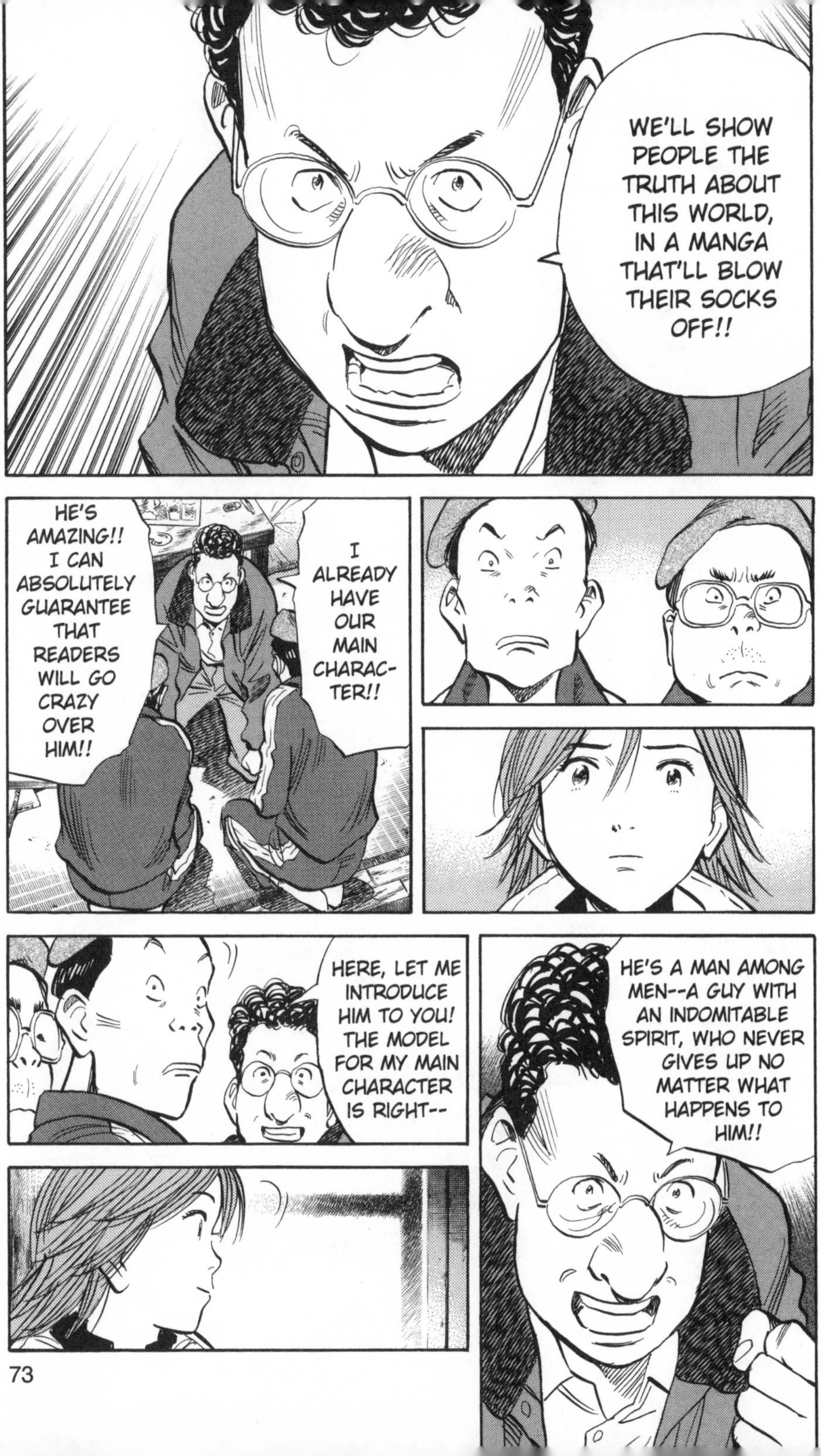
WE'LL SHOW PEOPLE THE TRUTH ABOUT THIS WORLD, IN A MANGA THAT'LL BLOW THEIR SOCKS OFF!!
I ALREADY HAVE OUR MAIN CHARAC-TER!!
HE'S AMAZING!! I CAN ABSOLUTELY GUARANTEE THAT READERS WILL GO CRAZY OVER HIM!!
HE'S A MAN AMONG MEN--A GUY WITH AN INDOMITABLE SPIRIT, WHO NEVER GIVES UP NO MATTER WHAT HAPPENS TO HIM!!
HERE, LET ME INTRODUCE HIM TO YOU! THE MODEL FOR MY MAIN CHARACTER IS RIGHT--

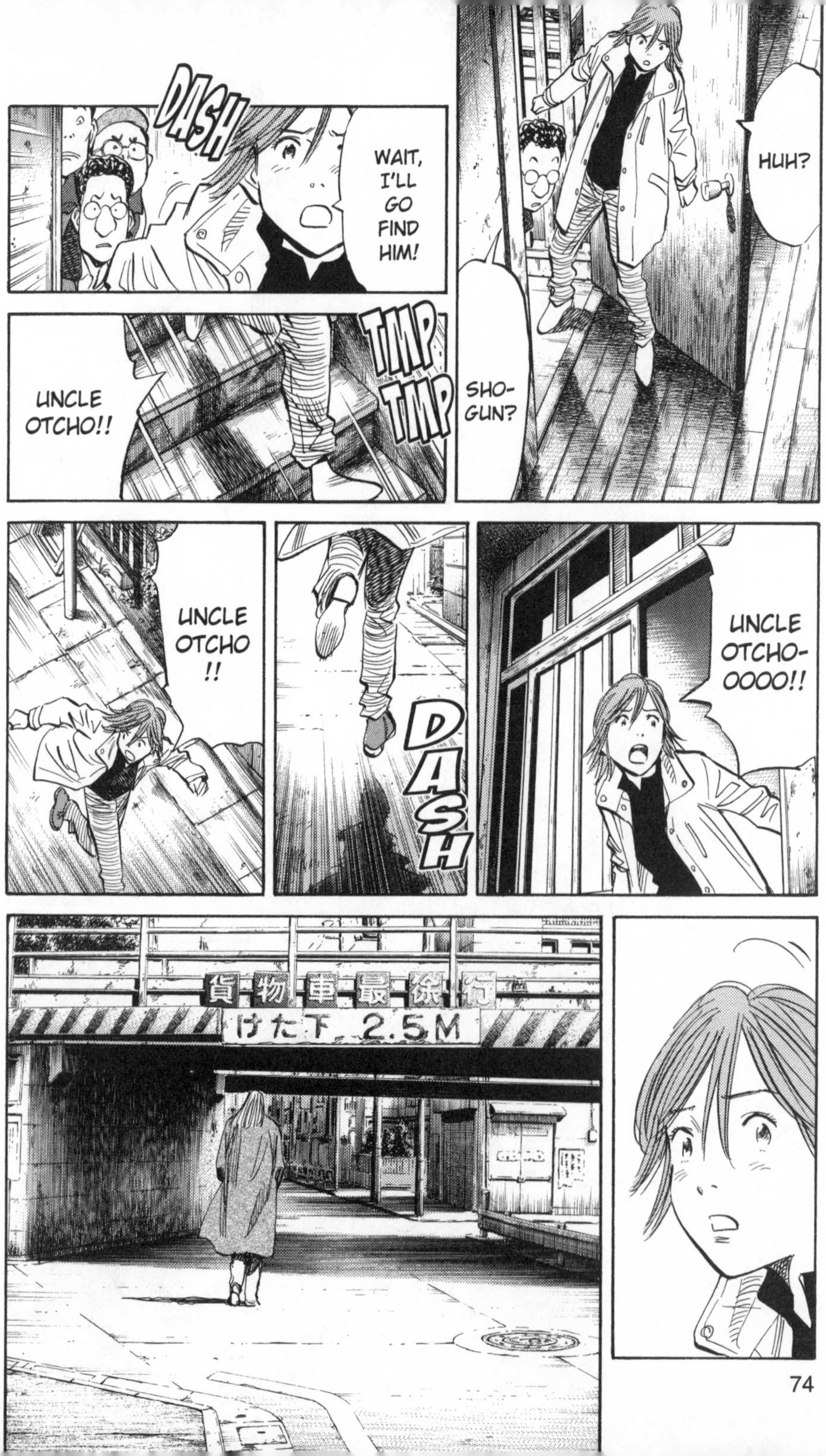
HUH?
SHO-GUN?
DASH
WAIT, I'LL GO FIND HIM!
TMP TMP
UNCLE OTCHO!!
UNCLE OTCHO-OOOO!!
DASH
UNCLE OTCHO !!
貨物車最徐行
けた下 2.5M

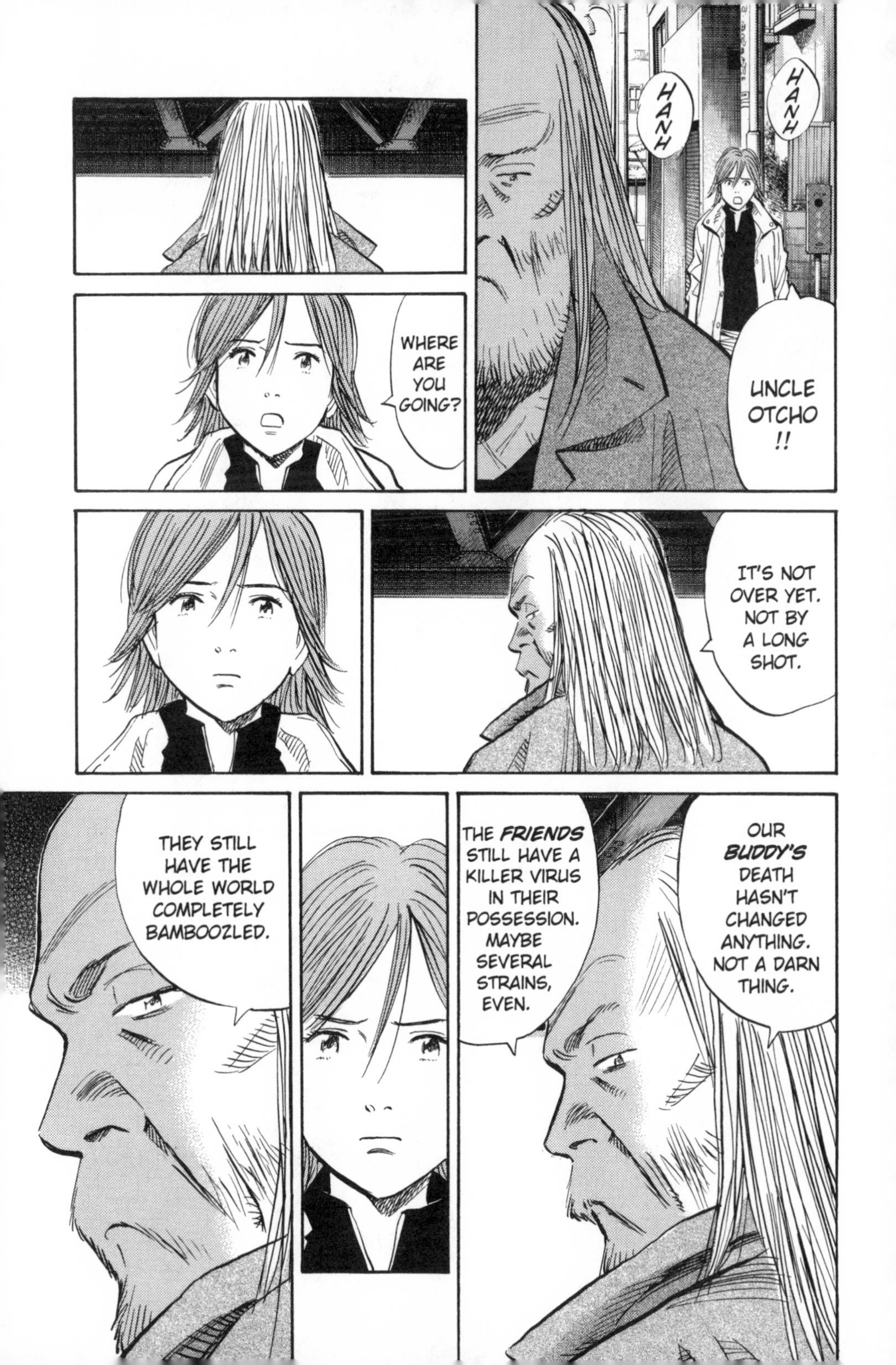
HANH
HANH
UNCLE OTCHO!!
WHERE ARE YOU GOING?
IT'S NOT OVER YET. NOT BY A LONG SHOT.
OUR *BUDDY'S* DEATH HASN'T CHANGED ANYTHING. NOT A DARN THING.
THE *FRIENDS* STILL HAVE A KILLER VIRUS IN THEIR POSSESSION. MAYBE SEVERAL STRAINS, EVEN.
THEY STILL HAVE THE WHOLE WORLD COMPLETELY BAMBOOZLED.

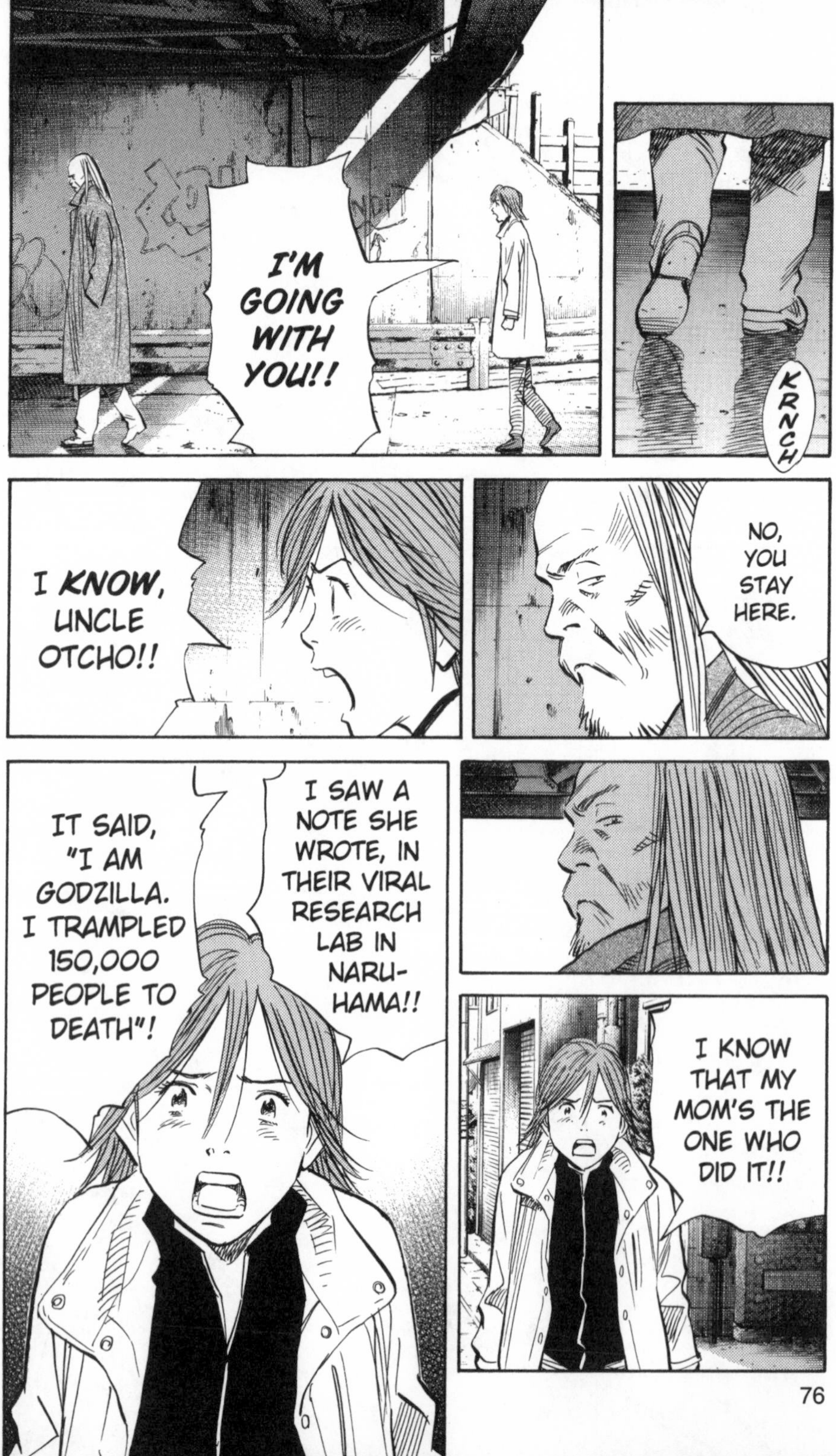
KRNCH
I'M GOING WITH YOU!!
NO, YOU STAY HERE.
I KNOW, UNCLE OTCHO!!
I KNOW THAT MY MOM'S THE ONE WHO DID IT!!
I SAW A NOTE SHE WROTE, IN THEIR VIRAL RESEARCH LAB IN NARUHAMA!!
IT SAID, "I AM GODZILLA. I TRAMPLED 150,000 PEOPLE TO DEATH"!

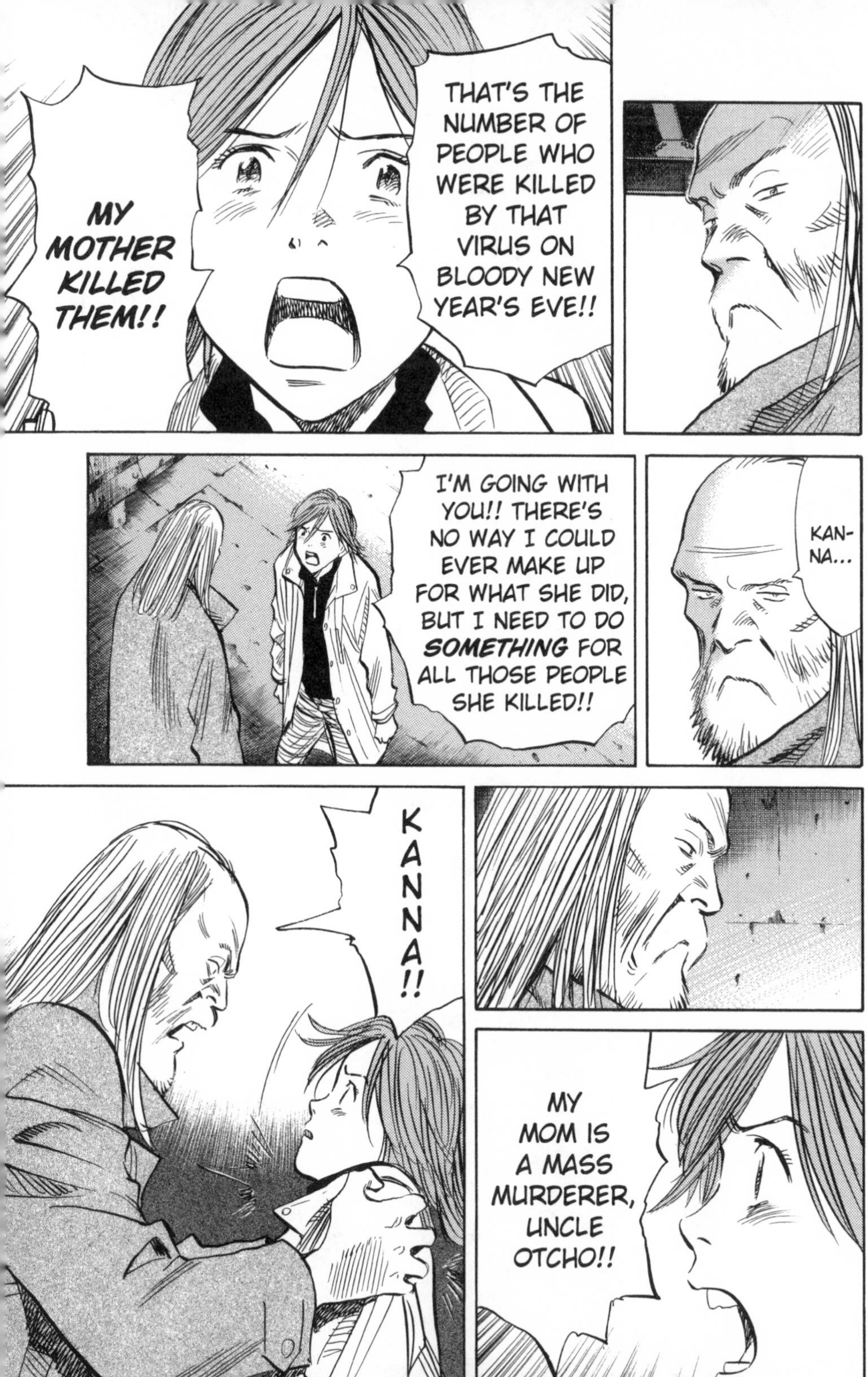
THAT'S THE NUMBER OF PEOPLE WHO WERE KILLED BY THAT VIRUS ON BLOODY NEW YEAR'S EVE!!
MY MOTHER KILLED THEM!!
KAN-NA...
I'M GOING WITH YOU!! THERE'S NO WAY I COULD EVER MAKE UP FOR WHAT SHE DID, BUT I NEED TO DO *SOMETHING* FOR ALL THOSE PEOPLE SHE KILLED!!
MY MOM IS A MASS MURDERER, UNCLE OTCHO!!
KANNA!!

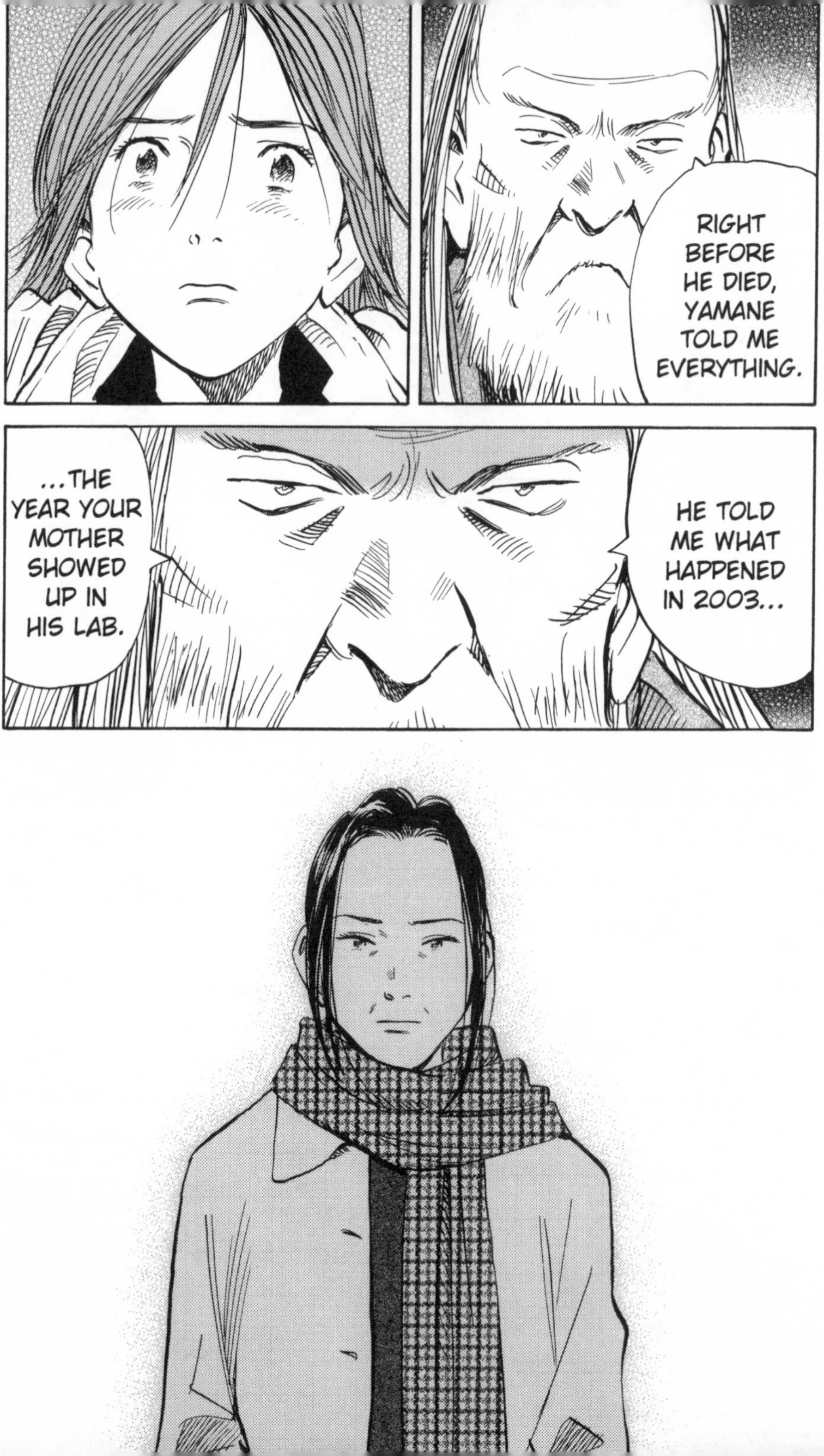
RIGHT BEFORE HE DIED, YAMANE TOLD ME EVERYTHING.
HE TOLD ME WHAT HAPPENED IN 2003...
...THE YEAR YOUR MOTHER SHOWED UP IN HIS LAB.

Chapter 5 Revelation of 2003

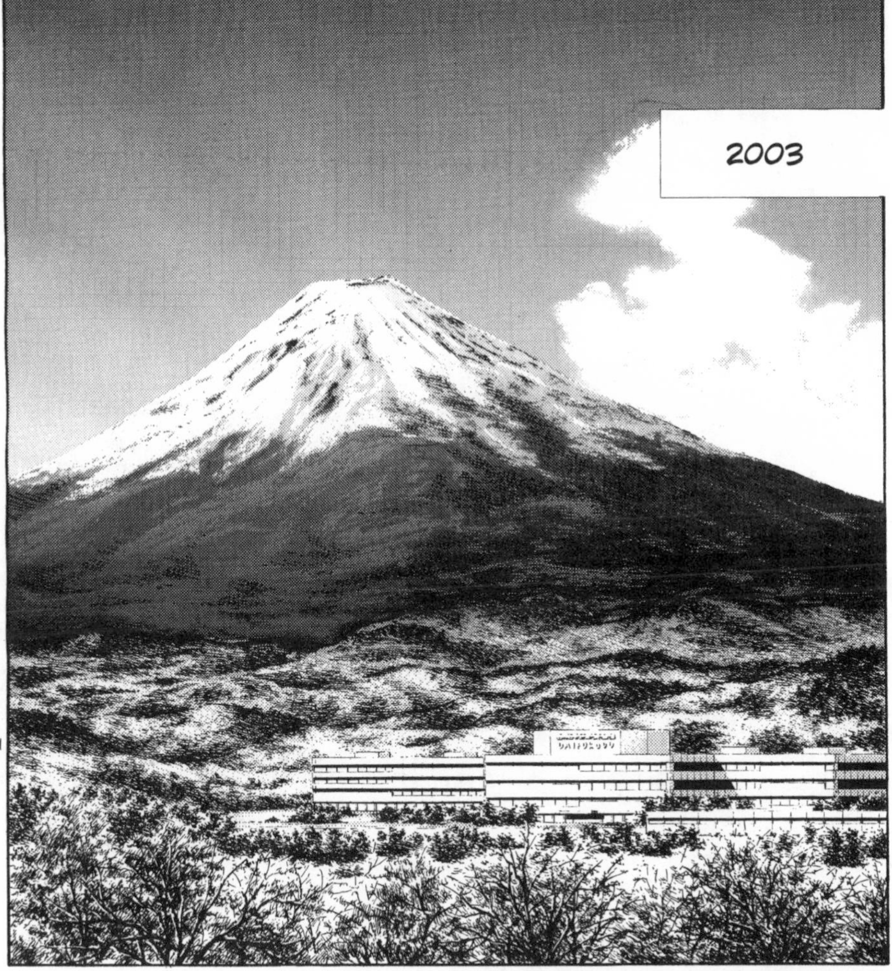
2003

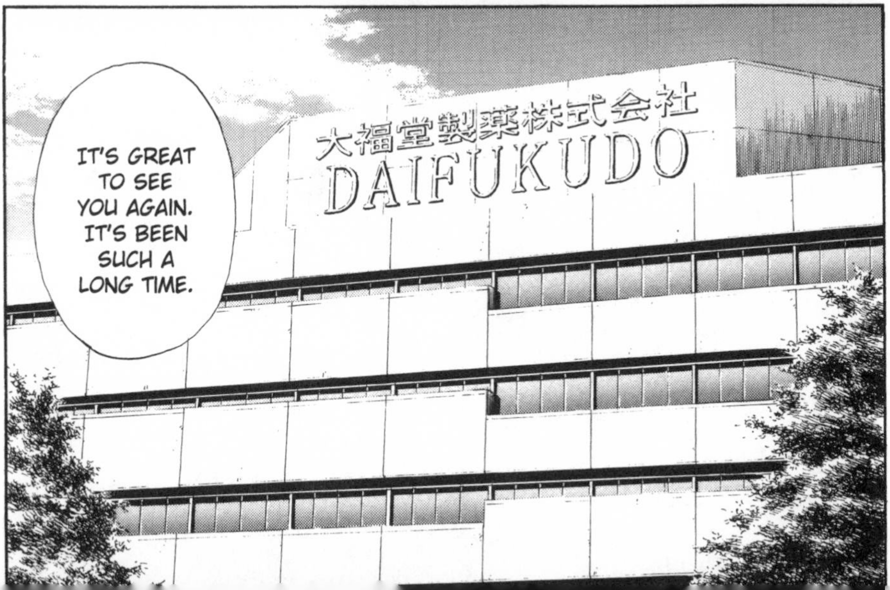
大福堂製薬株式会社
DAIFUKUDO
IT'S GREAT TO SEE YOU AGAIN. IT'S BEEN SUCH A LONG TIME.

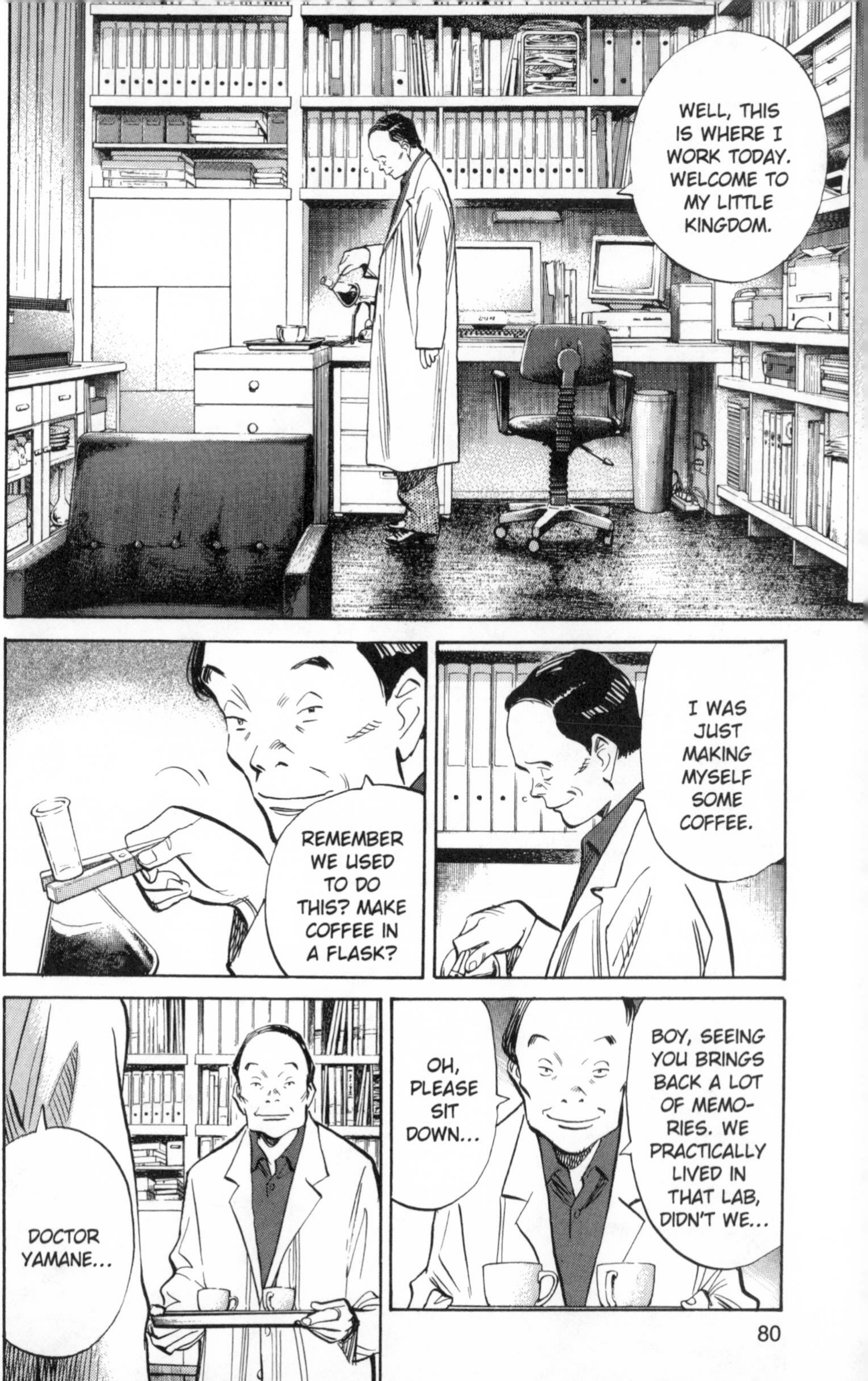
WELL, THIS IS WHERE I WORK TODAY. WELCOME TO MY LITTLE KINGDOM.
I WAS JUST MAKING MYSELF SOME COFFEE.
REMEMBER WE USED TO DO THIS? MAKE COFFEE IN A FLASK?
BOY, SEEING YOU BRINGS BACK A LOT OF MEMORIES. WE PRACTICALLY LIVED IN THAT LAB, DIDN'T WE...
OH, PLEASE SIT DOWN...
DOCTOR YAMANE...

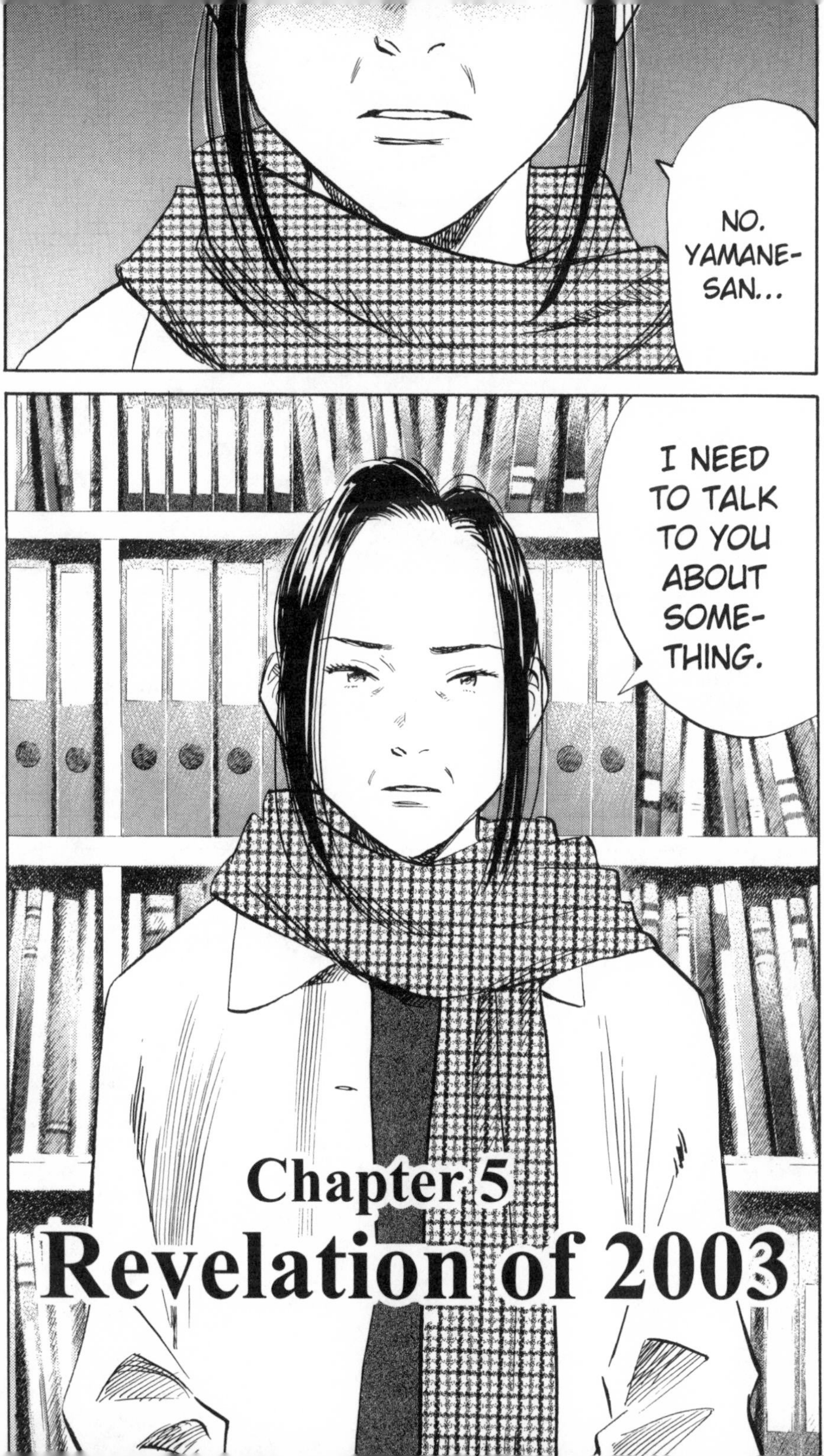
NO. YAMANE-SAN...
I NEED TO TALK TO YOU ABOUT SOME-THING.

Chapter 5
Revelation of 2003

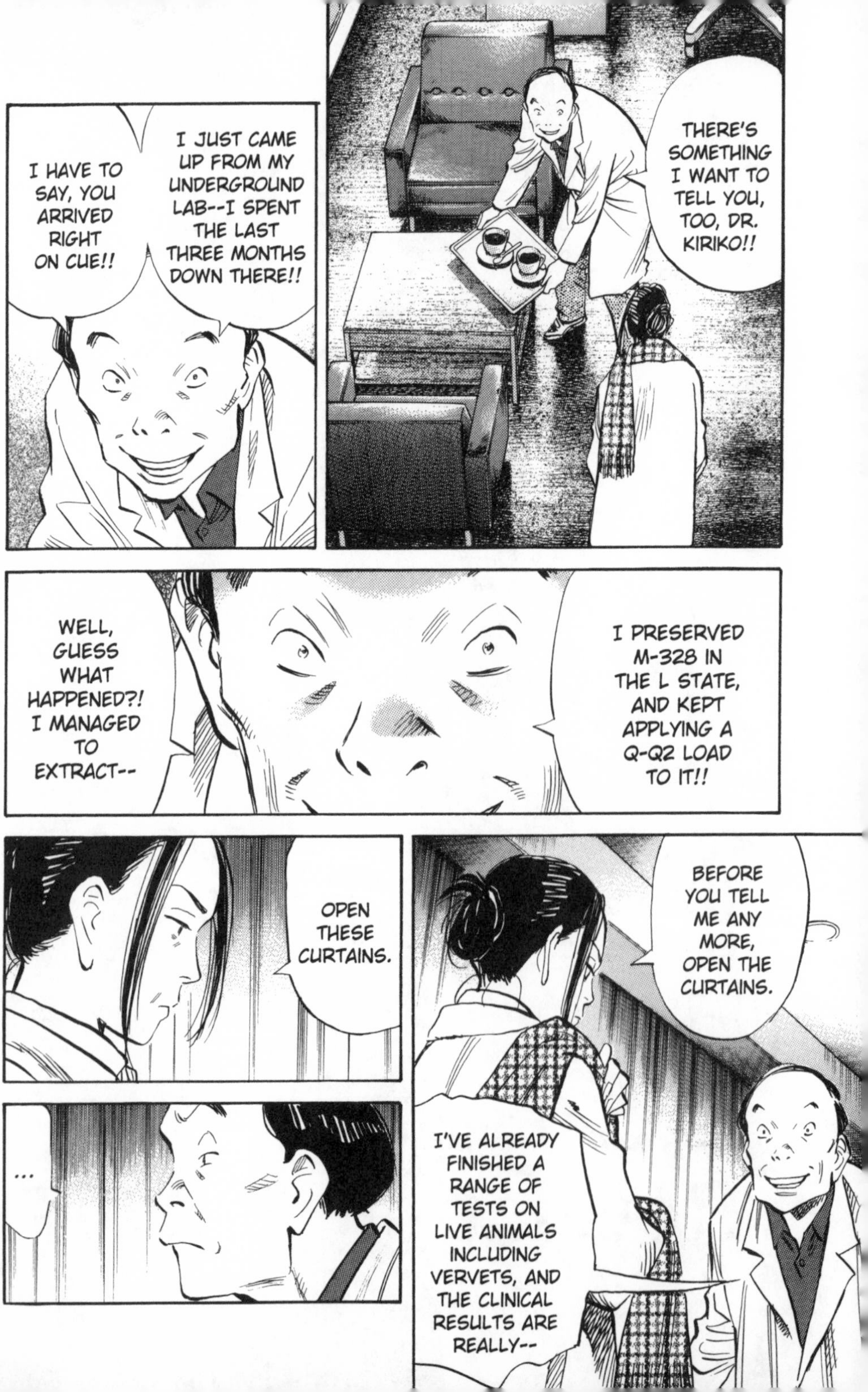
THERE'S SOMETHING I WANT TO TELL YOU, TOO, DR. KIRIKO!!
I JUST CAME UP FROM MY UNDERGROUND LAB--I SPENT THE LAST THREE MONTHS DOWN THERE!!
I HAVE TO SAY, YOU ARRIVED RIGHT ON CUE!!
I PRESERVED M-328 IN THE L STATE, AND KEPT APPLYING A Q-Q2 LOAD TO IT!!
WELL, GUESS WHAT HAPPENED?! I MANAGED TO EXTRACT--
BEFORE YOU TELL ME ANY MORE, OPEN THE CURTAINS.
I'VE ALREADY FINISHED A RANGE OF TESTS ON LIVE ANIMALS INCLUDING VERVETS, AND THE CLINICAL RESULTS ARE REALLY--
OPEN THESE CURTAINS.
...

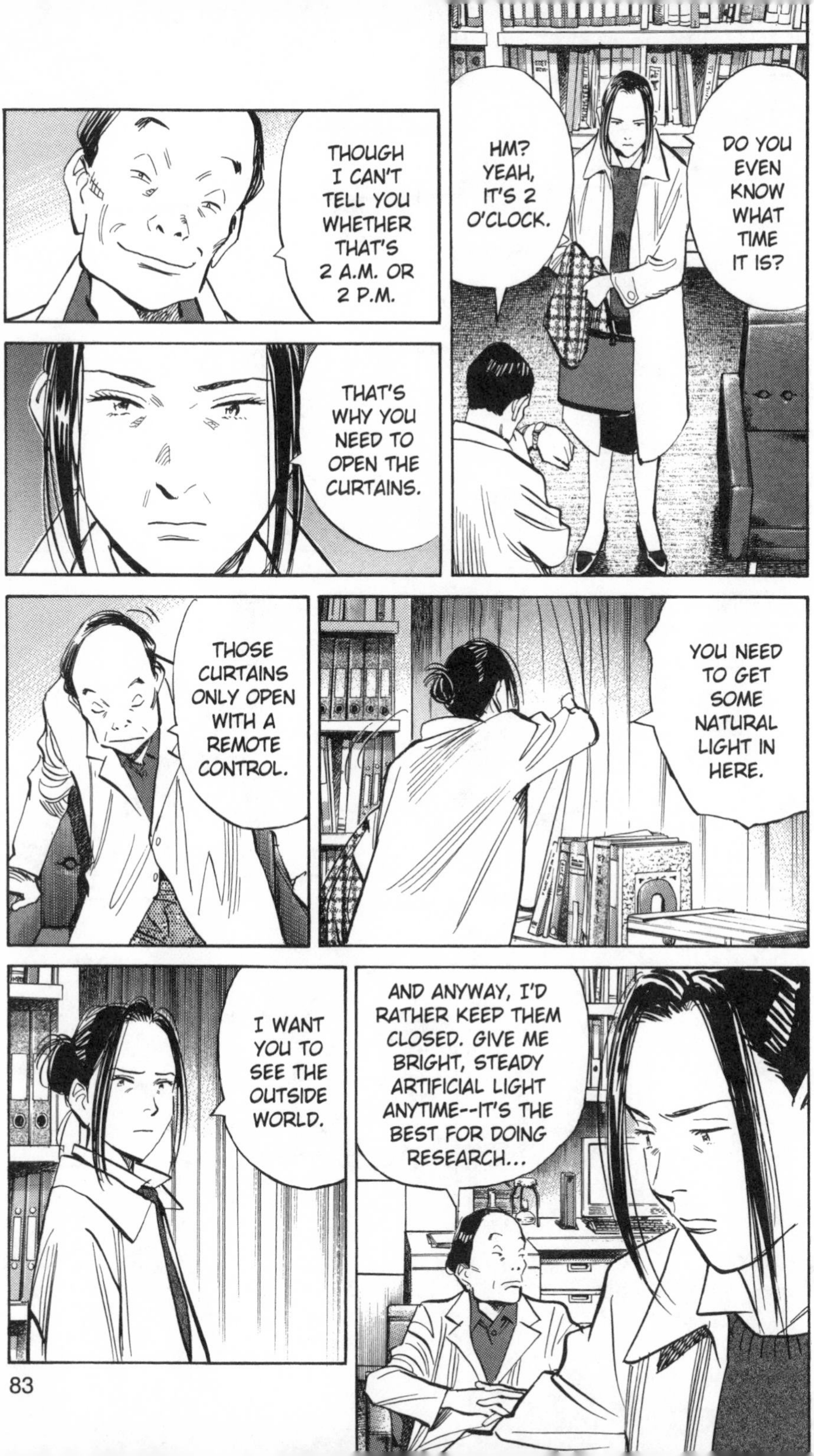
DO YOU EVEN KNOW WHAT TIME IT IS?
HM? YEAH, IT'S 2 O'CLOCK.
THOUGH I CAN'T TELL YOU WHETHER THAT'S 2 A.M. OR 2 P.M.
THAT'S WHY YOU NEED TO OPEN THE CURTAINS.
YOU NEED TO GET SOME NATURAL LIGHT IN HERE.
THOSE CURTAINS ONLY OPEN WITH A REMOTE CONTROL.
AND ANYWAY, I'D RATHER KEEP THEM CLOSED. GIVE ME BRIGHT, STEADY ARTIFICIAL LIGHT ANYTIME--IT'S THE BEST FOR DOING RESEARCH...
I WANT YOU TO SEE THE OUTSIDE WORLD.

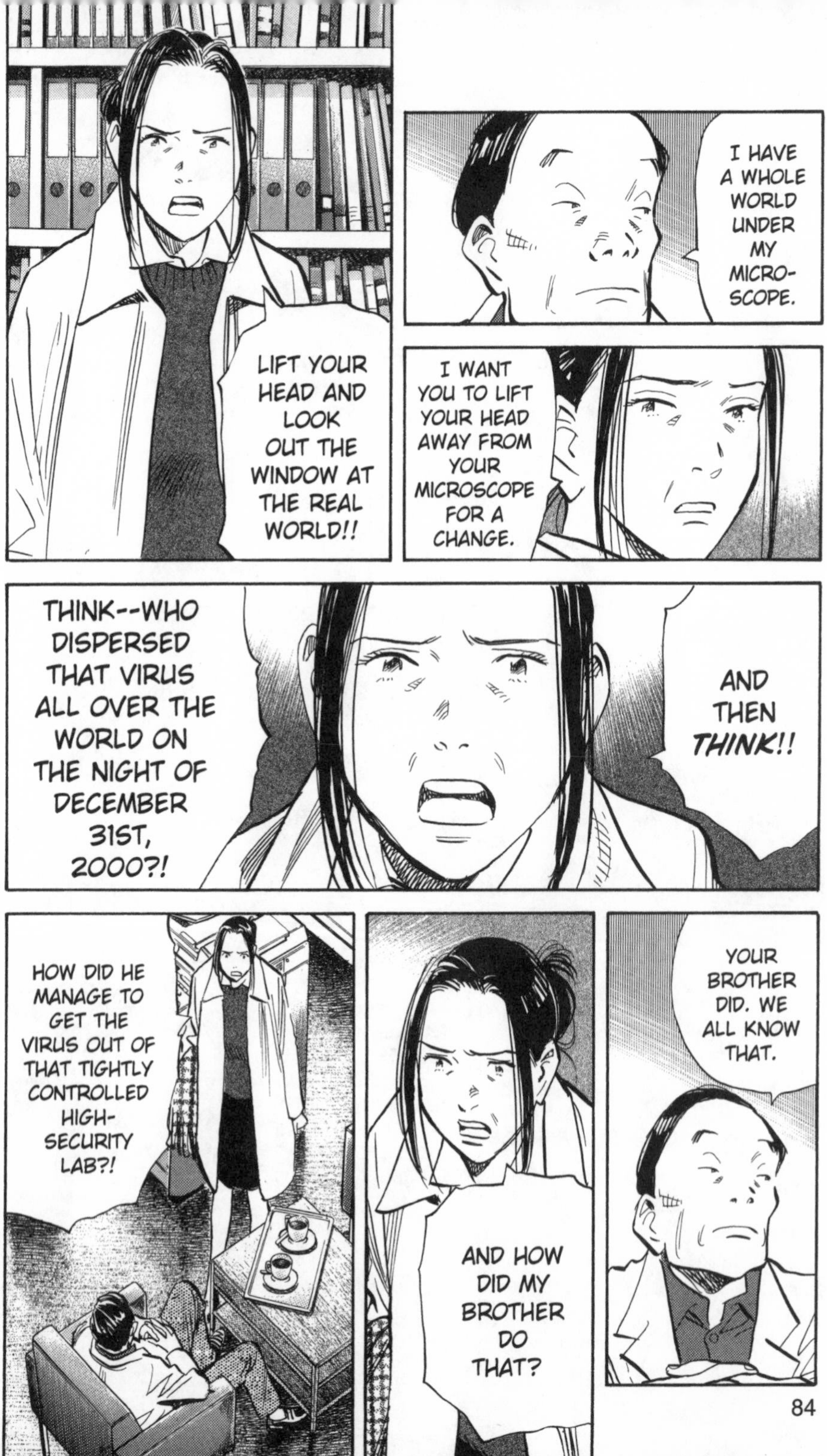
I HAVE A WHOLE WORLD UNDER MY MICRO-SCOPE.
I WANT YOU TO LIFT YOUR HEAD AWAY FROM YOUR MICROSCOPE FOR A CHANGE.
LIFT YOUR HEAD AND LOOK OUT THE WINDOW AT THE REAL WORLD!!
AND THEN *THINK*!!
THINK--WHO DISPERSED THAT VIRUS ALL OVER THE WORLD ON THE NIGHT OF DECEMBER 31ST, 2000?!
YOUR BROTHER DID. WE ALL KNOW THAT.
AND HOW DID MY BROTHER DO THAT?
HOW DID HE MANAGE TO GET THE VIRUS OUT OF THAT TIGHTLY CONTROLLED HIGH-SECURITY LAB?!

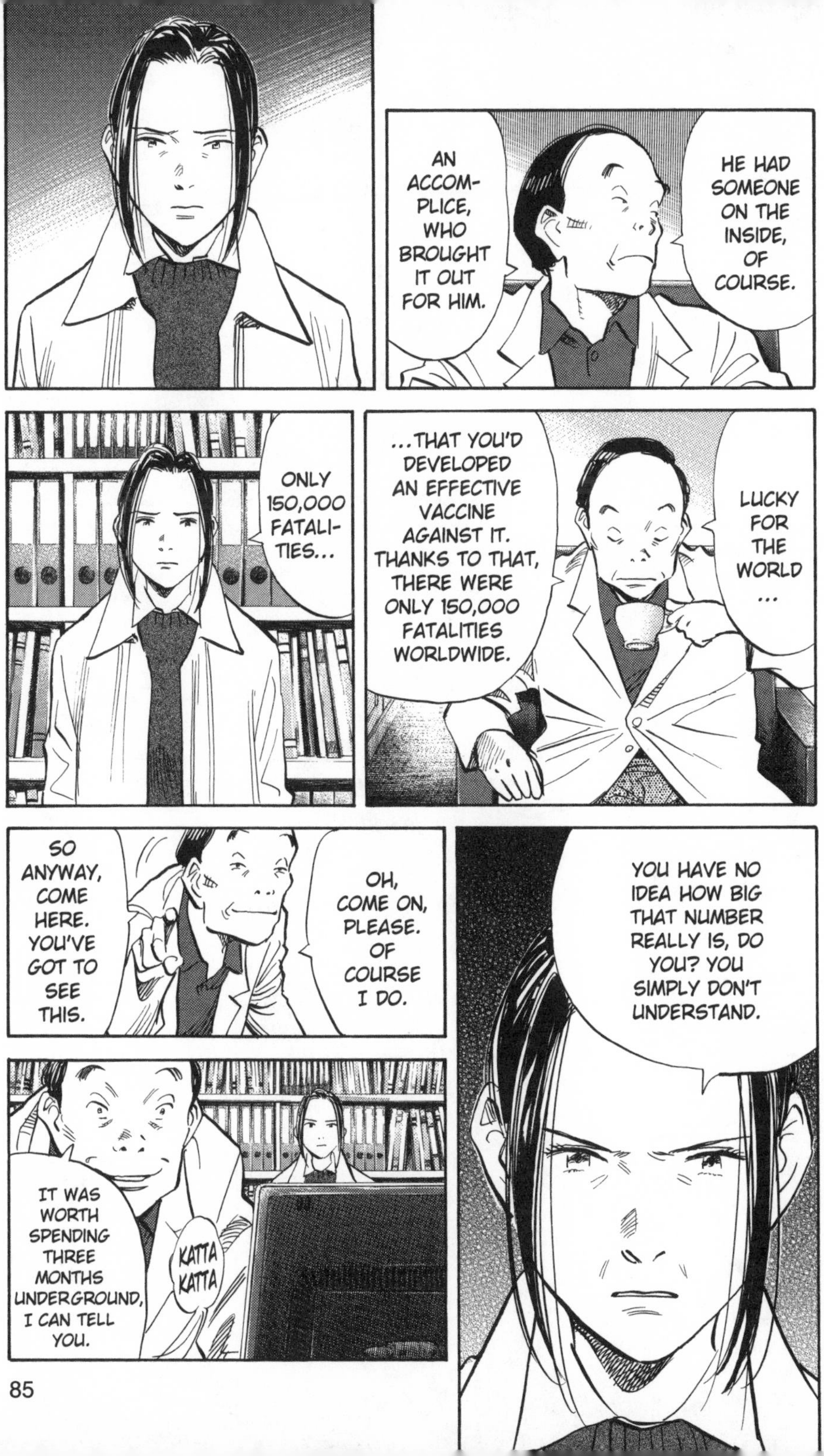
HE HAD SOMEONE ON THE INSIDE, OF COURSE.
AN ACCOMPLICE, WHO BROUGHT IT OUT FOR HIM.
LUCKY FOR THE WORLD ...
...THAT YOU'D DEVELOPED AN EFFECTIVE VACCINE AGAINST IT. THANKS TO THAT, THERE WERE ONLY 150,000 FATALITIES WORLDWIDE.
ONLY 150,000 FATALITIES...
YOU HAVE NO IDEA HOW BIG THAT NUMBER REALLY IS, DO YOU? YOU SIMPLY DON'T UNDERSTAND.
OH, COME ON, PLEASE. OF COURSE I DO.
SO ANYWAY, COME HERE. YOU'VE GOT TO SEE THIS.
KATTA KATTA
IT WAS WORTH SPENDING THREE MONTHS UNDERGROUND, I CAN TELL YOU.

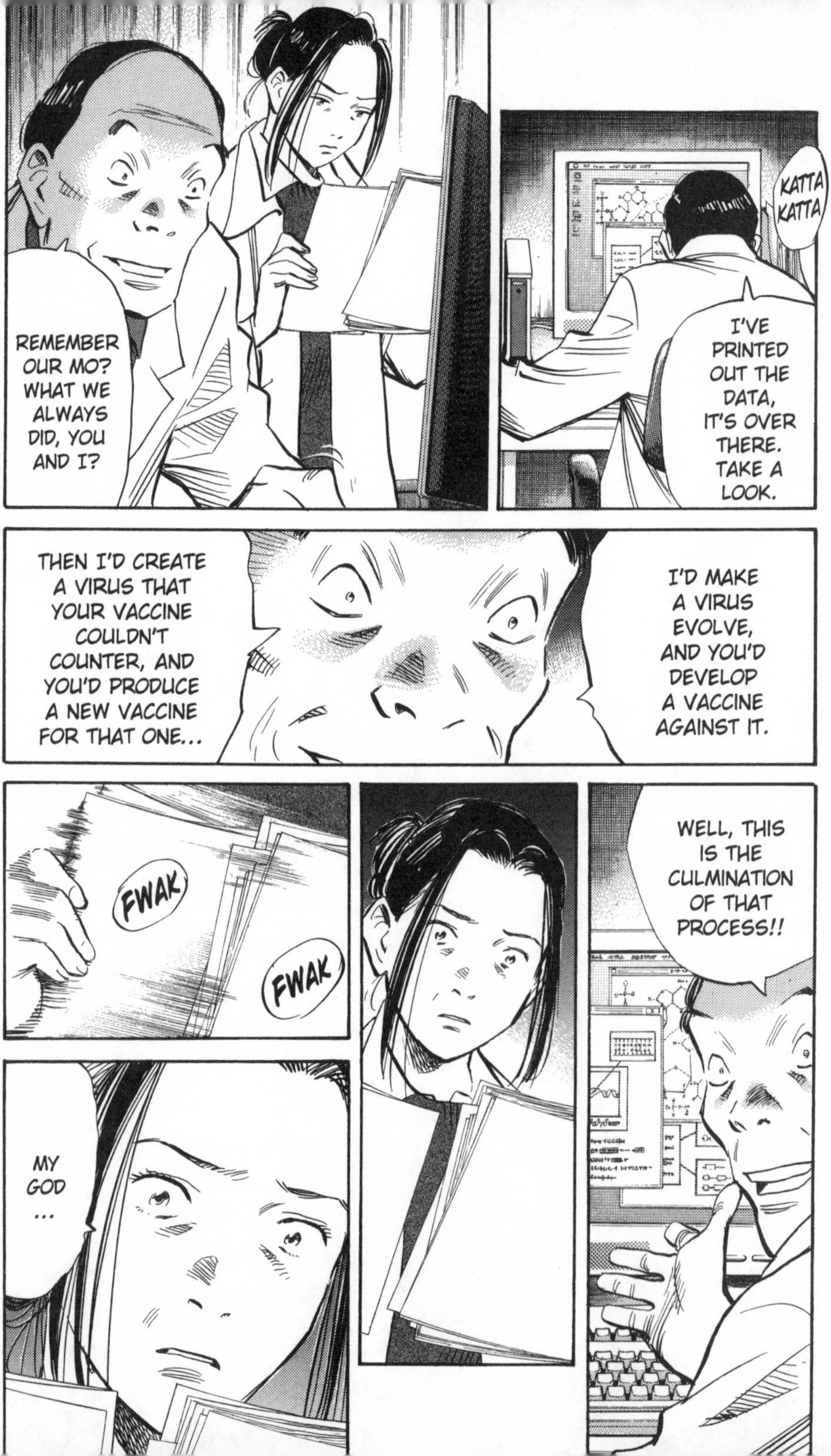
KATTA KATTA
I'VE PRINTED OUT THE DATA, IT'S OVER THERE. TAKE A LOOK.
REMEMBER OUR MO? WHAT WE ALWAYS DID, YOU AND I?
I'D MAKE A VIRUS EVOLVE, AND YOU'D DEVELOP A VACCINE AGAINST IT.
THEN I'D CREATE A VIRUS THAT YOUR VACCINE COULDN'T COUNTER, AND YOU'D PRODUCE A NEW VACCINE FOR THAT ONE...
WELL, THIS IS THE CULMINATION OF THAT PROCESS!!
FWAK
FWAK
MY GOD ...

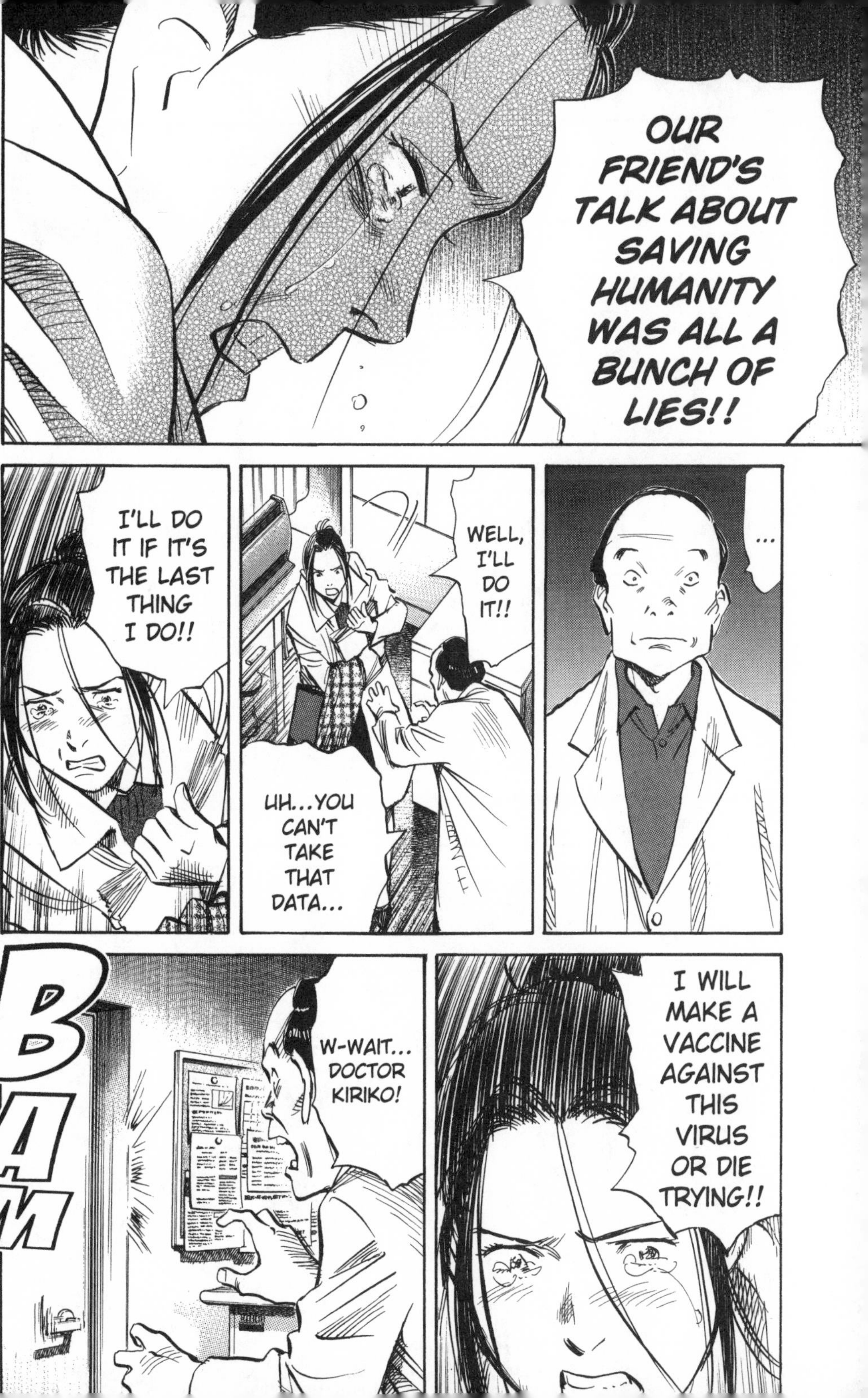
OUR FRIEND'S TALK ABOUT SAVING HUMANITY WAS ALL A BUNCH OF LIES!!
...
WELL, I'LL DO IT!!
UH...YOU CAN'T TAKE THAT DATA...
I'LL DO IT IF IT'S THE LAST THING I DO!!
I WILL MAKE A VACCINE AGAINST THIS VIRUS OR DIE TRYING!!
W-WAIT... DOCTOR KIRIKO!
BAM

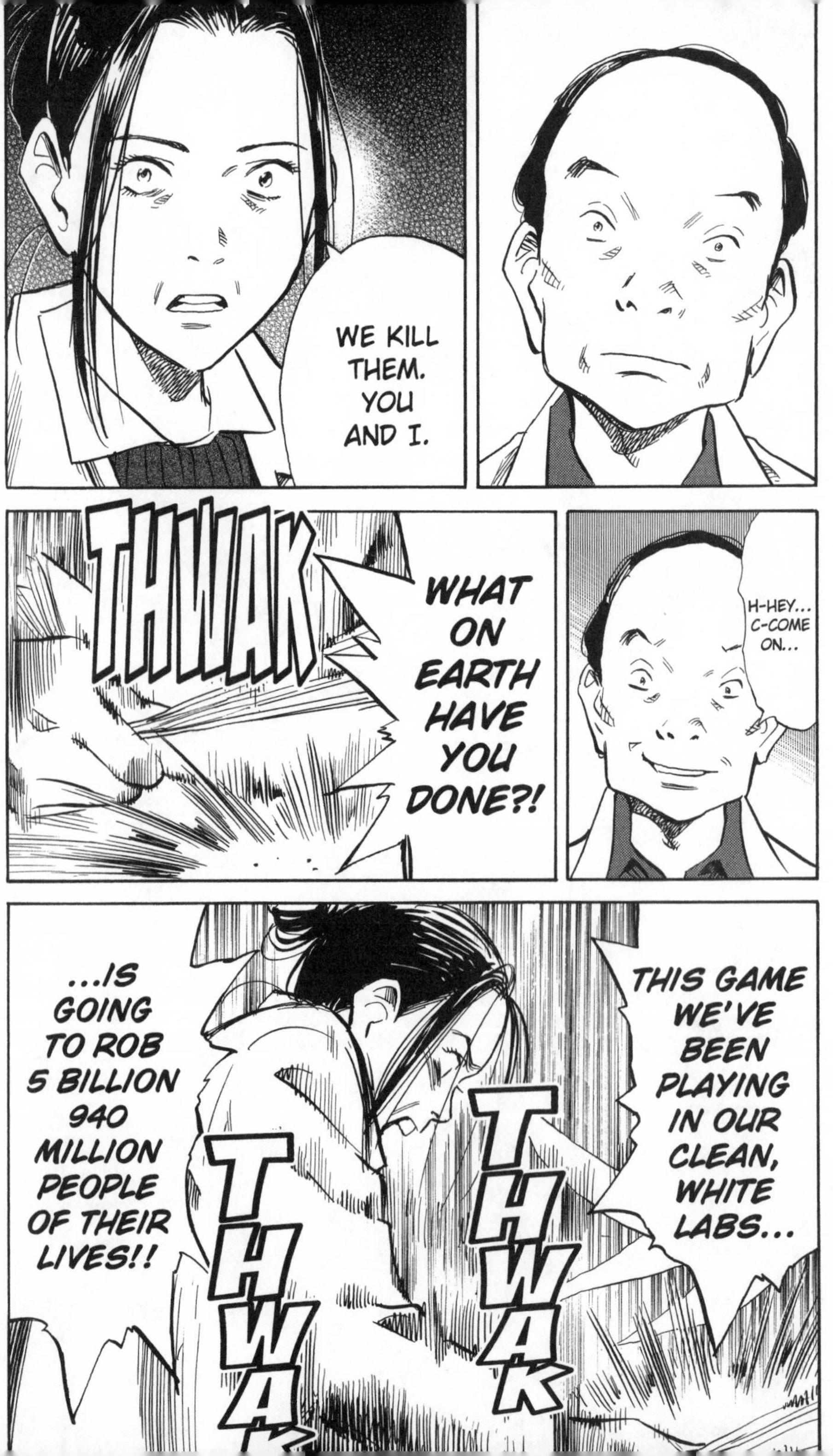
WE KILL THEM. YOU AND I.
H-HEY... C-COME ON...
THWAK
WHAT ON EARTH HAVE YOU DONE?!
THIS GAME WE'VE BEEN PLAYING IN OUR CLEAN, WHITE LABS...
THWAK
...IS GOING TO ROB 5 BILLION 940 MILLION PEOPLE OF THEIR LIVES!!
THWA

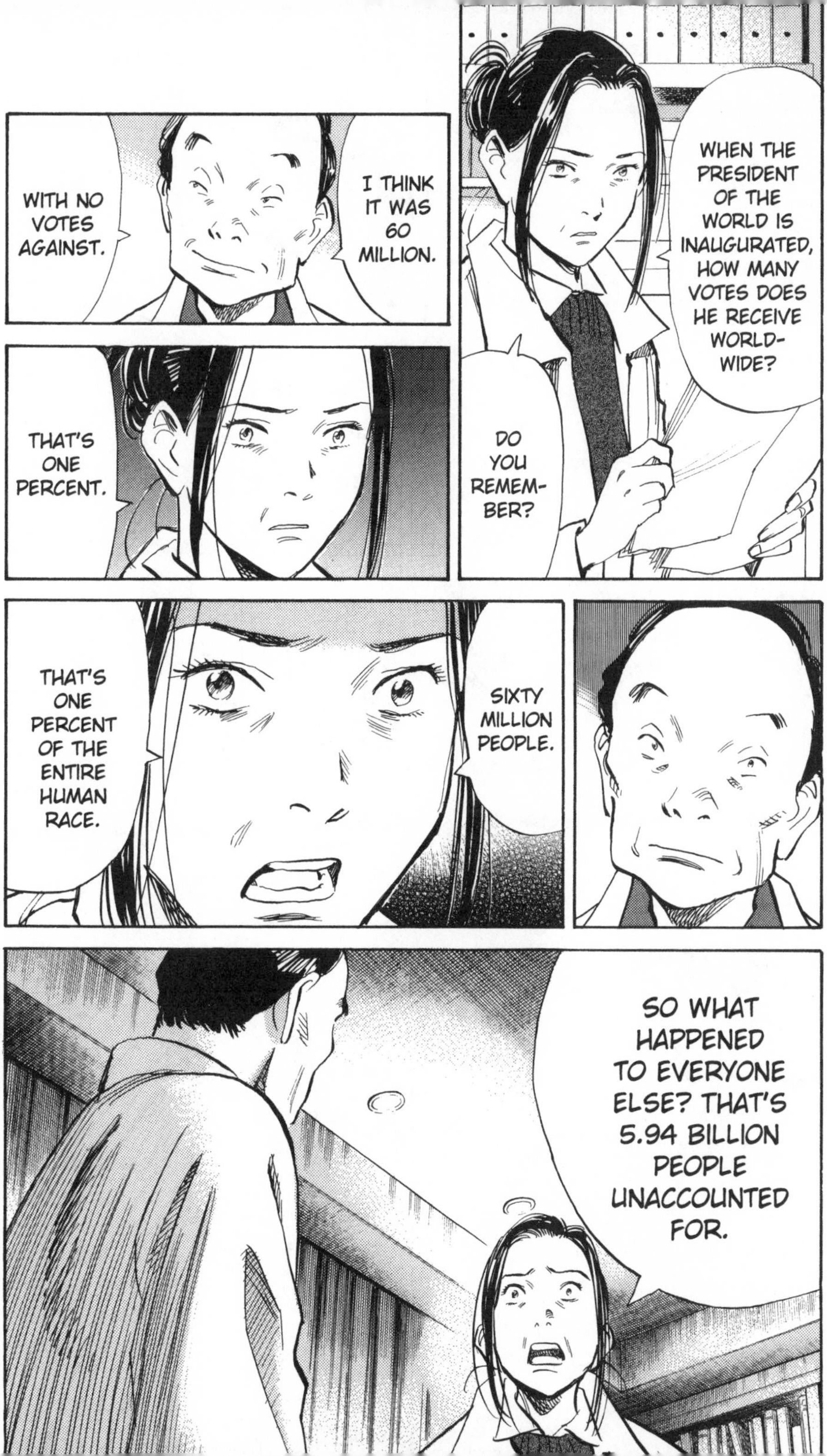
WHEN THE PRESIDENT OF THE WORLD IS INAUGURATED, HOW MANY VOTES DOES HE RECEIVE WORLD-WIDE?
DO YOU REMEMBER?
I THINK IT WAS 60 MILLION.
WITH NO VOTES AGAINST.
THAT'S ONE PERCENT.
SIXTY MILLION PEOPLE.
THAT'S ONE PERCENT OF THE ENTIRE HUMAN RACE.
SO WHAT HAPPENED TO EVERYONE ELSE? THAT'S 5.94 BILLION PEOPLE UNACCOUNTED FOR.

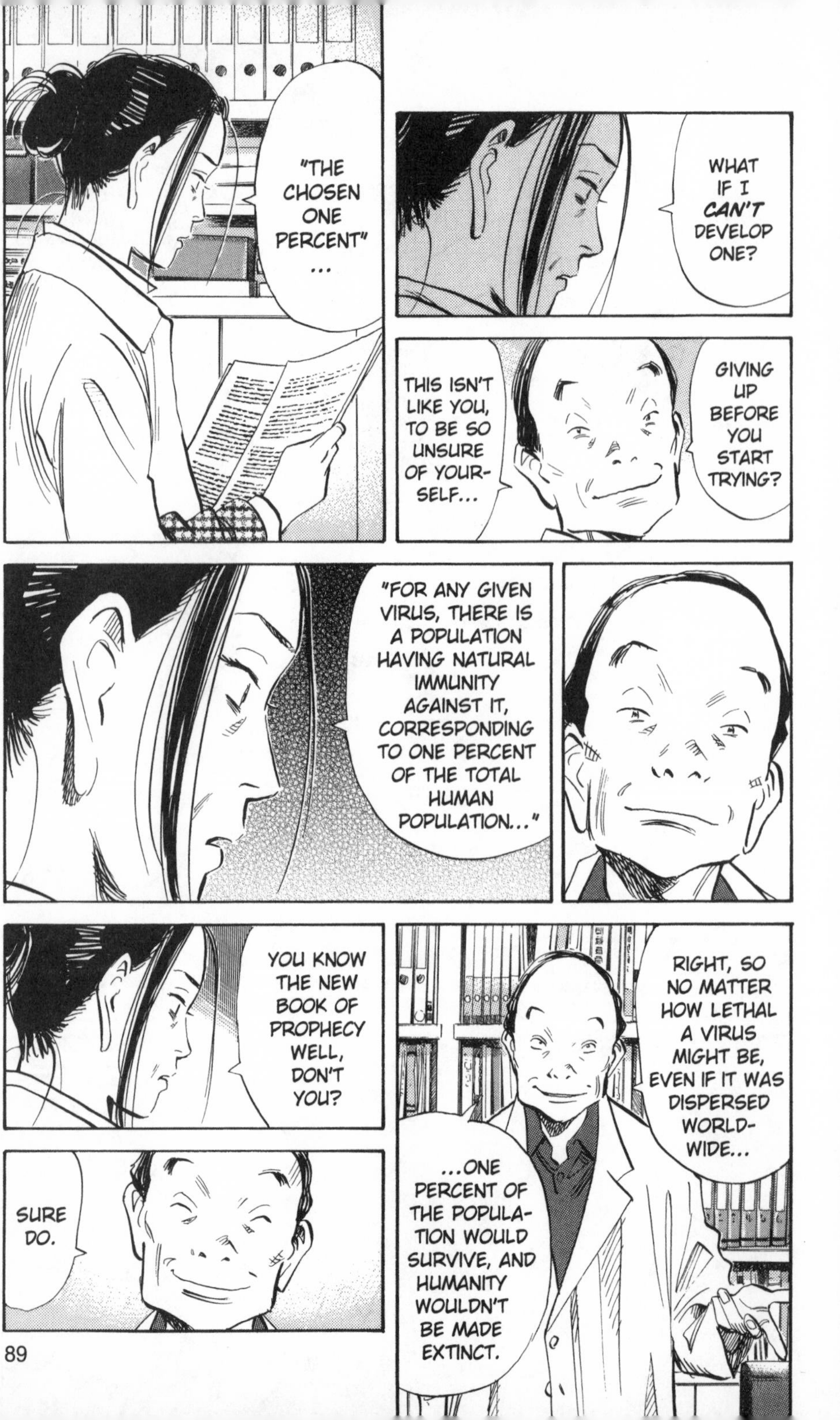
WHAT IF I *CAN'T* DEVELOP ONE?
GIVING UP BEFORE YOU START TRYING?
THIS ISN'T LIKE YOU, TO BE SO UNSURE OF YOURSELF...
"THE CHOSEN ONE PERCENT" ...
"FOR ANY GIVEN VIRUS, THERE IS A POPULATION HAVING NATURAL IMMUNITY AGAINST IT, CORRESPONDING TO ONE PERCENT OF THE TOTAL HUMAN POPULATION..."
RIGHT, SO NO MATTER HOW LETHAL A VIRUS MIGHT BE, EVEN IF IT WAS DISPERSED WORLD-WIDE...
...ONE PERCENT OF THE POPULATION WOULD SURVIVE, AND HUMANITY WOULDN'T BE MADE EXTINCT.
YOU KNOW THE NEW BOOK OF PROPHECY WELL, DON'T YOU?
SURE DO.

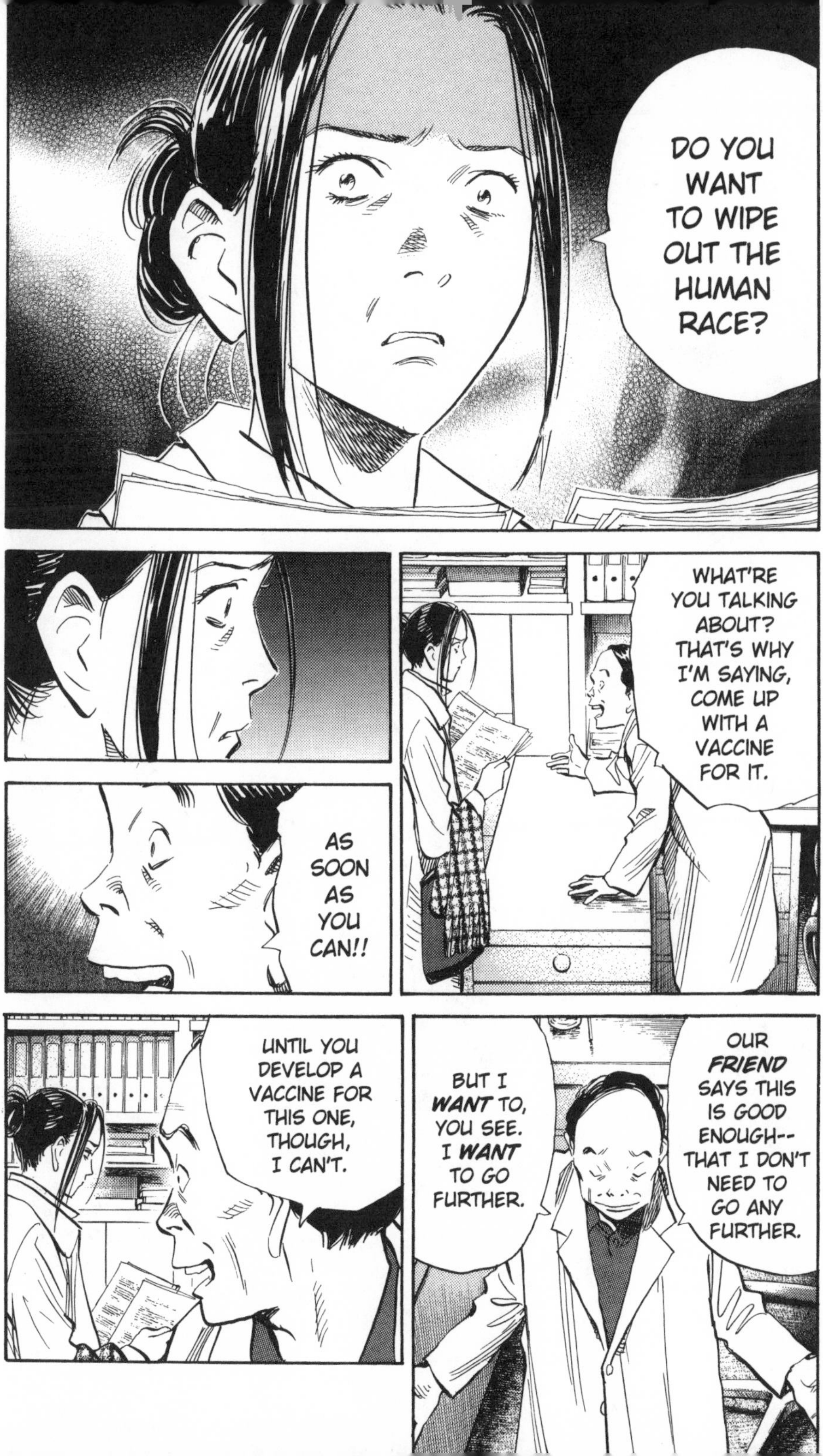
DO YOU WANT TO WIPE OUT THE HUMAN RACE?
WHAT'RE YOU TALKING ABOUT? THAT'S WHY I'M SAYING, COME UP WITH A VACCINE FOR IT.
AS SOON AS YOU CAN!!
OUR *FRIEND* SAYS THIS IS GOOD ENOUGH-- THAT I DON'T NEED TO GO ANY FURTHER.
BUT I *WANT* TO, YOU SEE. I *WANT* TO GO FURTHER.
UNTIL YOU DEVELOP A VACCINE FOR THIS ONE, THOUGH, I CAN'T.

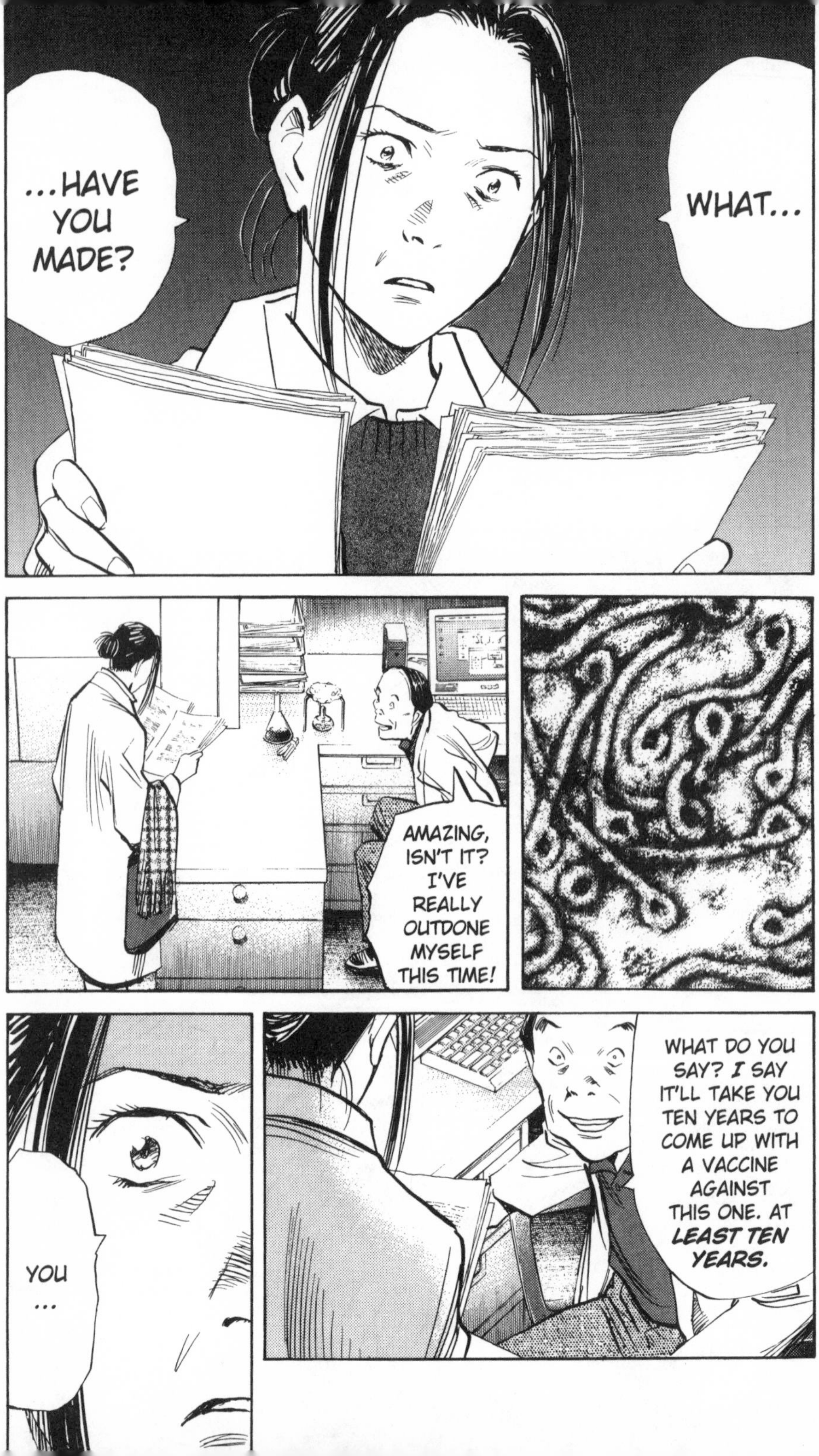
WHAT...
...HAVE YOU MADE?
AMAZING, ISN'T IT? I'VE REALLY OUTDONE MYSELF THIS TIME!
WHAT DO YOU SAY? *I* SAY IT'LL TAKE YOU TEN YEARS TO COME UP WITH A VACCINE AGAINST THIS ONE. AT ***LEAST TEN YEARS.***
YOU ...

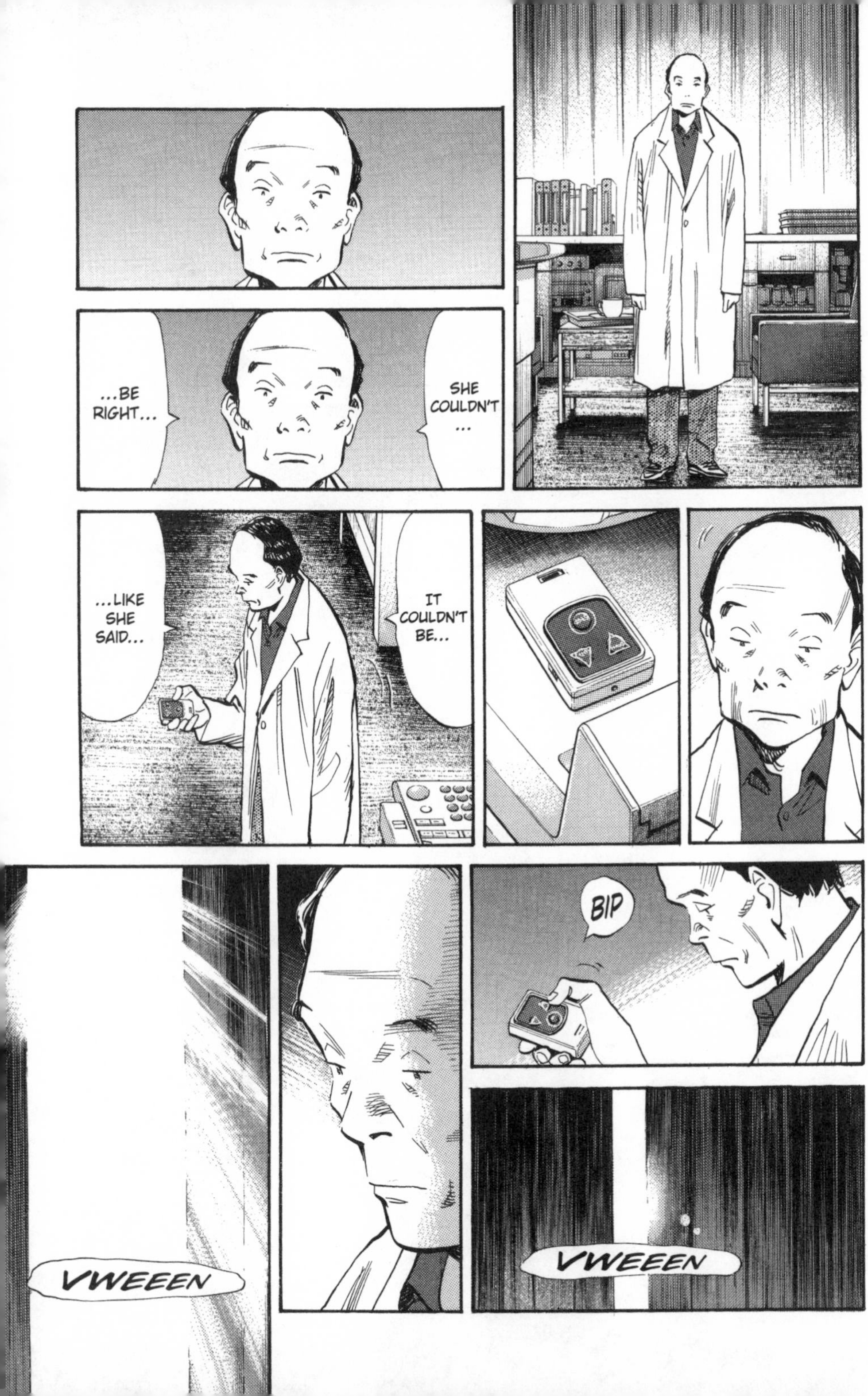
SHE COULDN'T ...
...BE RIGHT...
IT COULDN'T BE...
...LIKE SHE SAID...
BIP
VWEEEN
VWEEEN

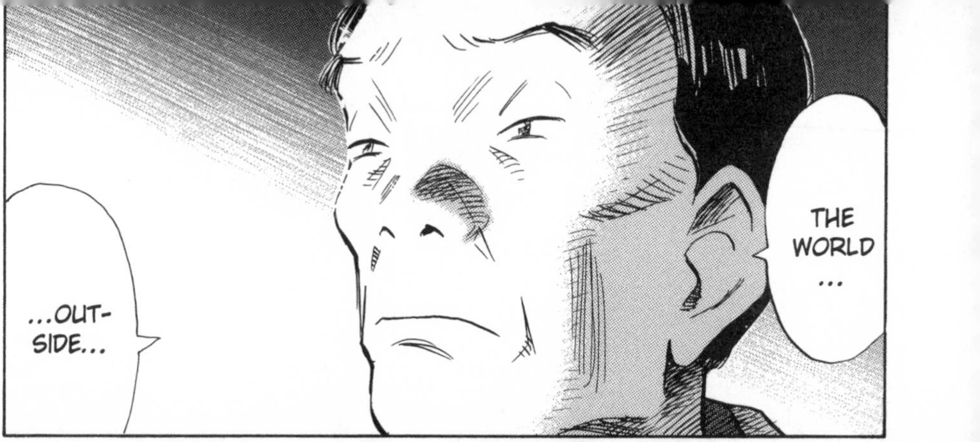
THE WORLD ...
...OUT-SIDE...

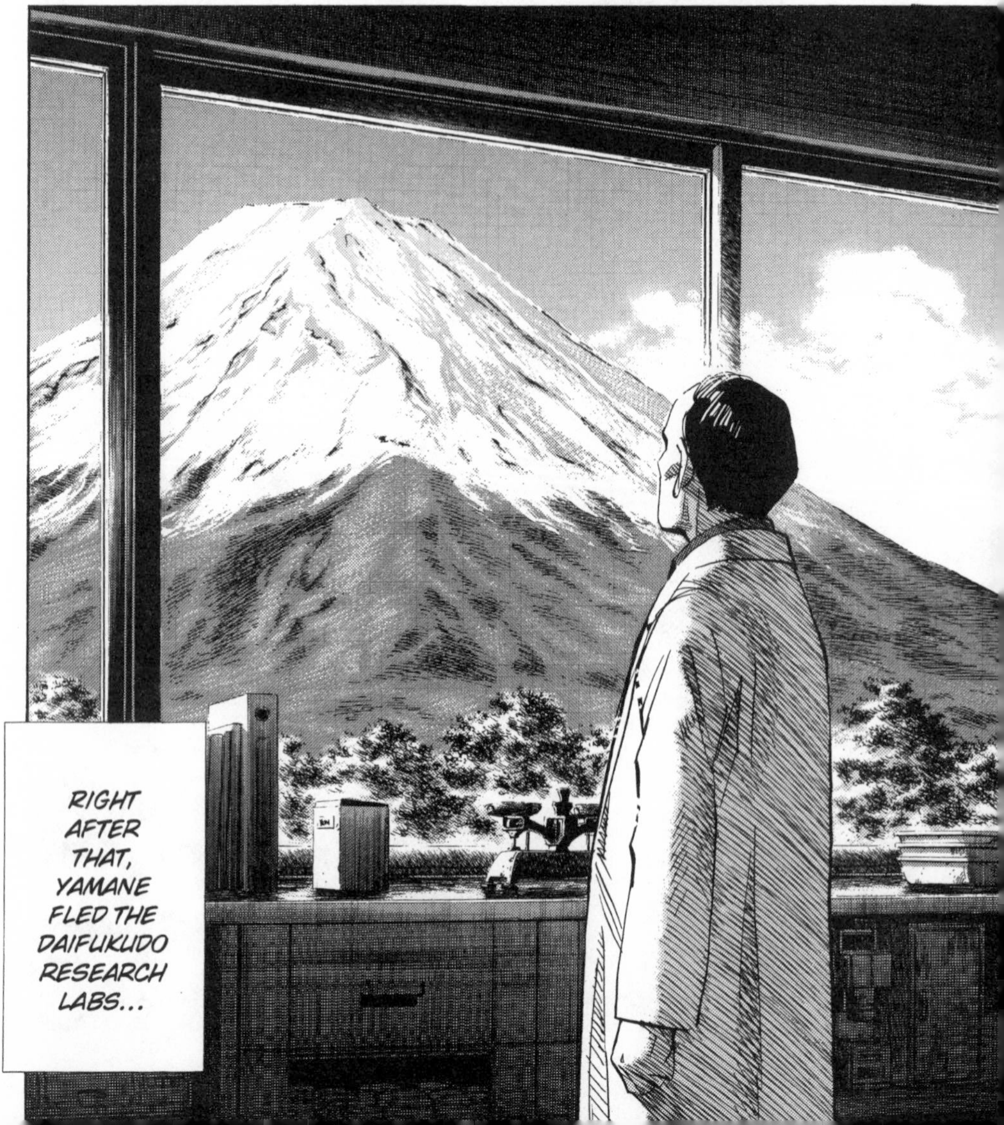
RIGHT AFTER THAT, YAMANE FLED THE DAIFUKUDO RESEARCH LABS...

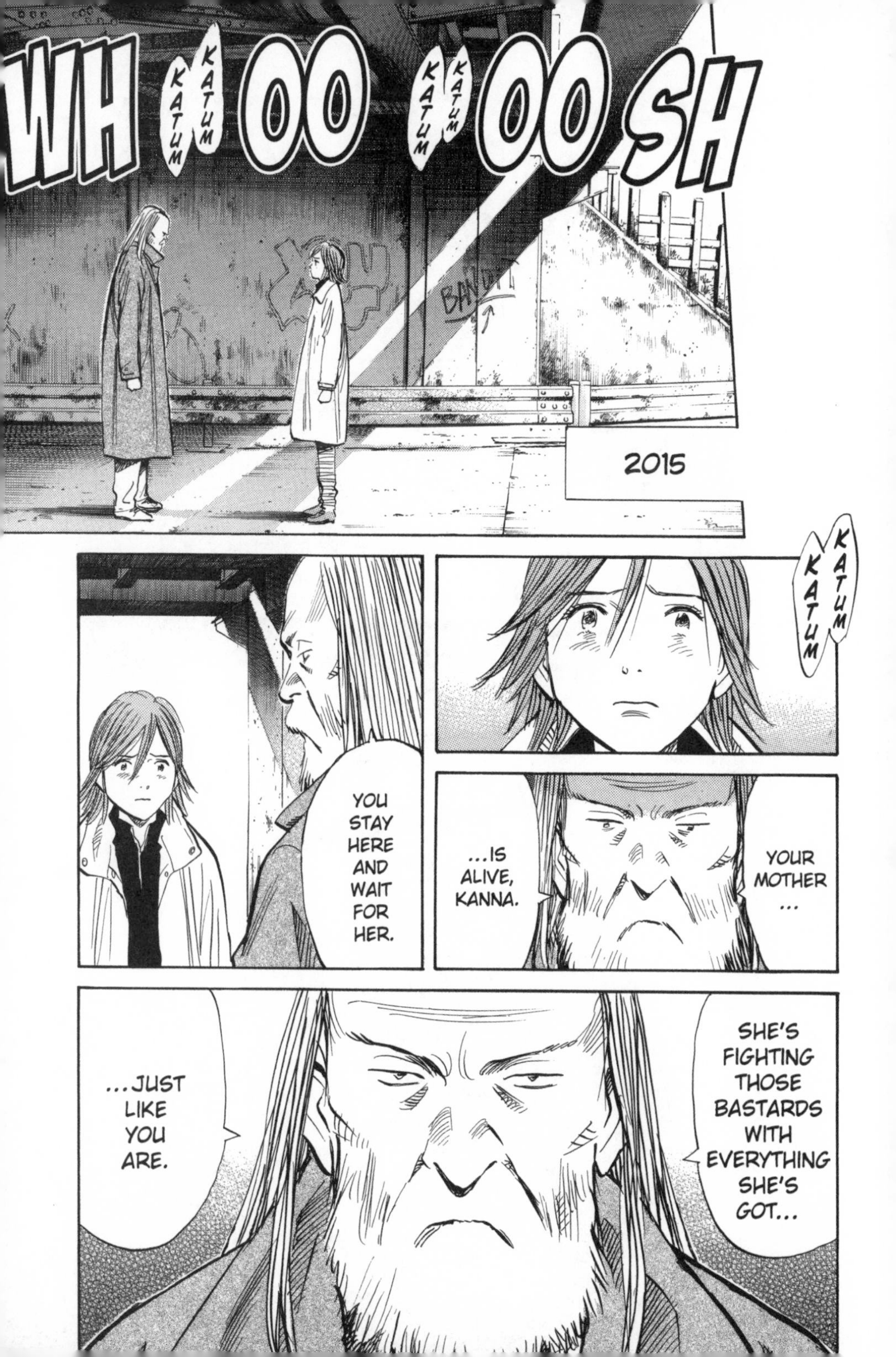
WHOOOOSH
KATUM KATUM
KATUM KATUM
2015
KATUM KATUM
YOUR MOTHER ...
...IS ALIVE, KANNA.
YOU STAY HERE AND WAIT FOR HER.
SHE'S FIGHTING THOSE BASTARDS WITH EVERYTHING SHE'S GOT...
...JUST LIKE YOU ARE.

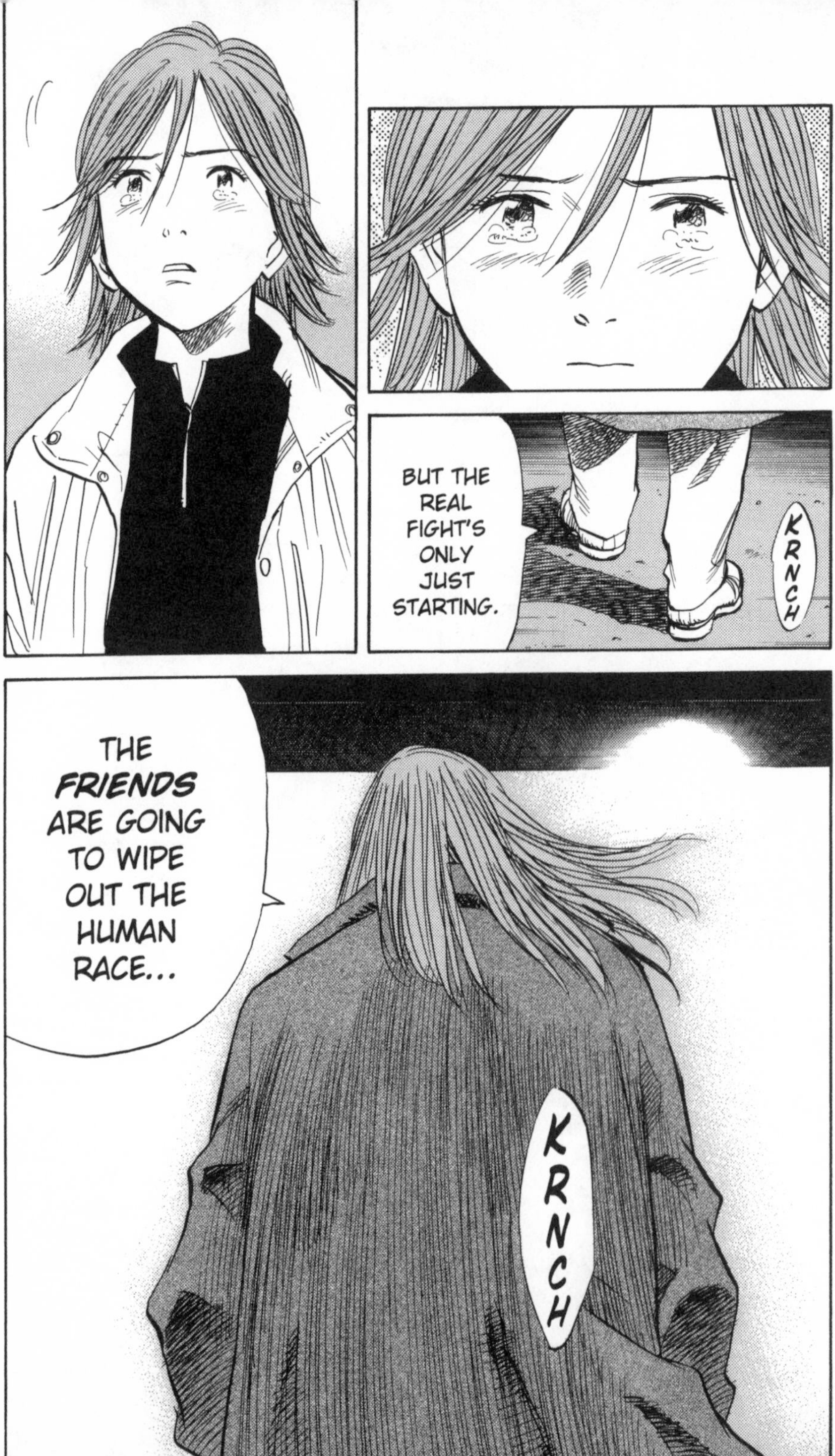
BUT THE REAL FIGHT'S ONLY JUST STARTING.
KRNCH
THE FRIENDS ARE GOING TO WIPE OUT THE HUMAN RACE...
KRNCH

Chapter 6 The Real Thing

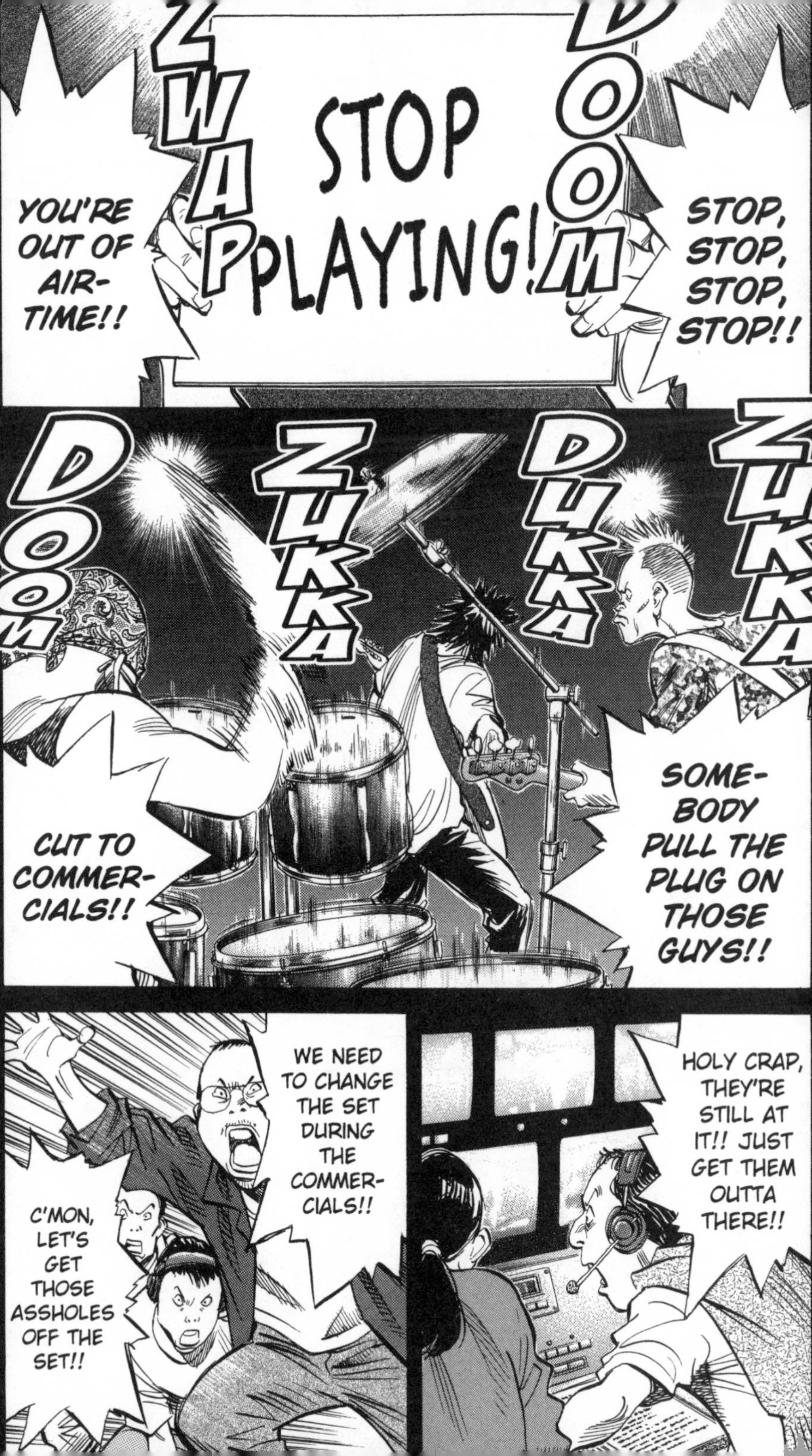
STOP, STOP, STOP, STOP!!
DOOOM
STOP PLAYING!
ZWAP
YOU'RE OUT OF AIR-TIME!!
ZUKKA
DUKKA
ZUKKA
DOOOM
SOME-BODY PULL THE PLUG ON THOSE GUYS!!
CUT TO COMMER-CIALS!!
HOLY CRAP, THEY'RE STILL AT IT!! JUST GET THEM OUTTA THERE!!
WE NEED TO CHANGE THE SET DURING THE COMMER-CIALS!!
C'MON, LET'S GET THOSE ASSHOLES OFF THE SET!!

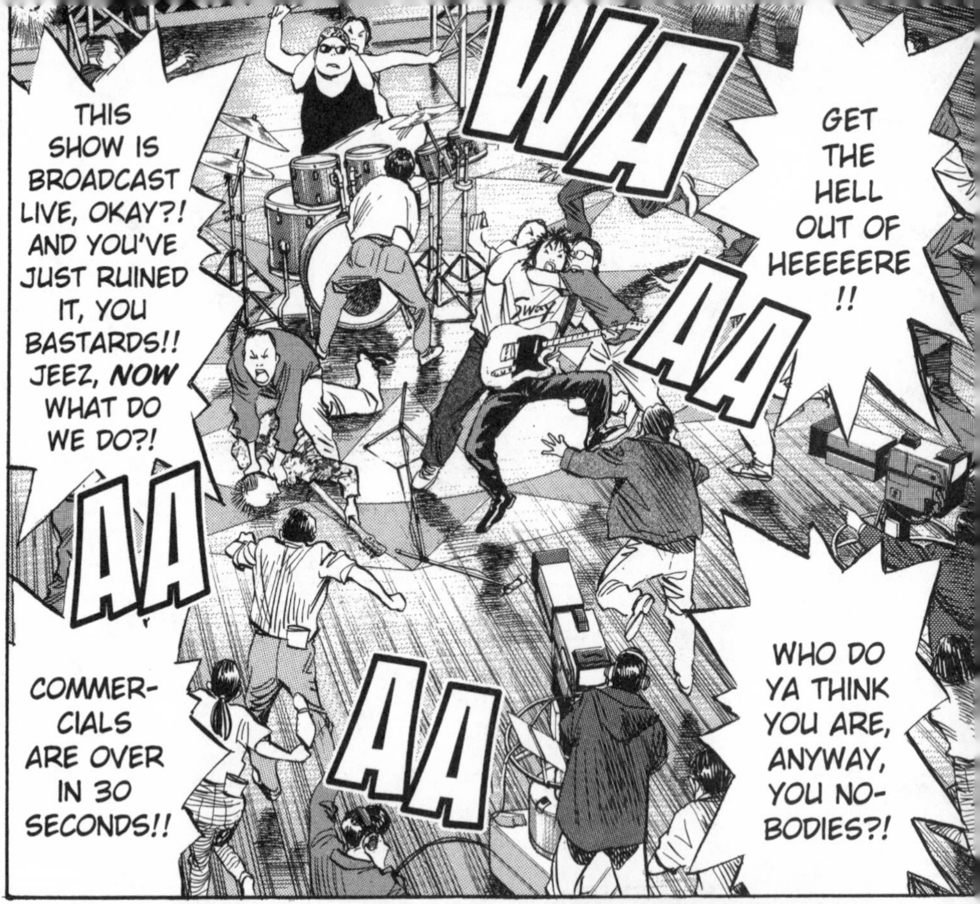
GET THE HELL OUT OF HEEEEERE!!
WAAAAA
THIS SHOW IS BROADCAST LIVE, OKAY?! AND YOU'VE JUST RUINED IT, YOU BASTARDS!! JEEZ, **NOW** WHAT DO WE DO?!
AA
WHO DO YA THINK YOU ARE, ANYWAY, YOU NO-BODIES?!
AA
COMMER-CIALS ARE OVER IN 30 SECONDS!!

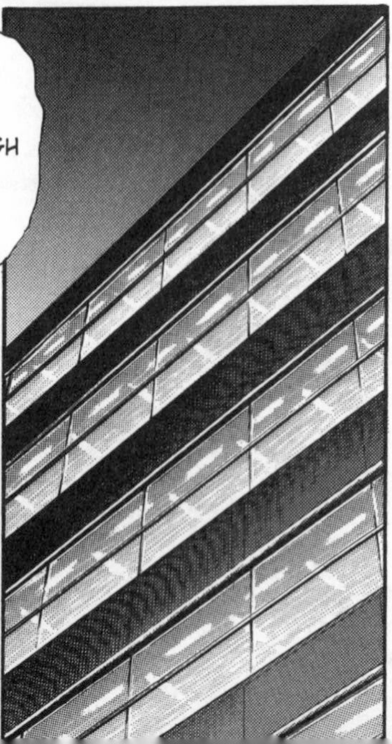

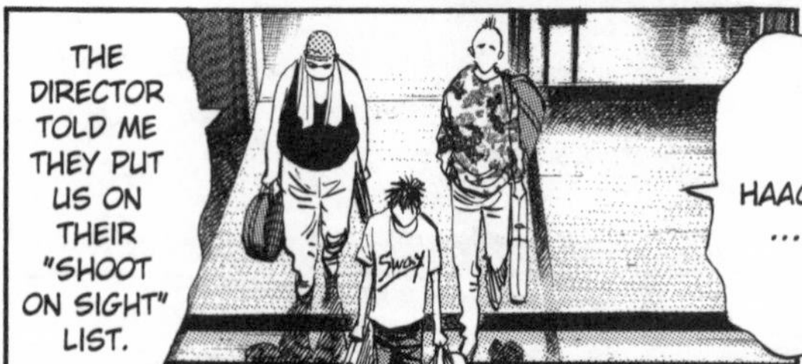
HAAGH ...
THE DIRECTOR TOLD ME THEY PUT US ON THEIR "SHOOT ON SIGHT" LIST.

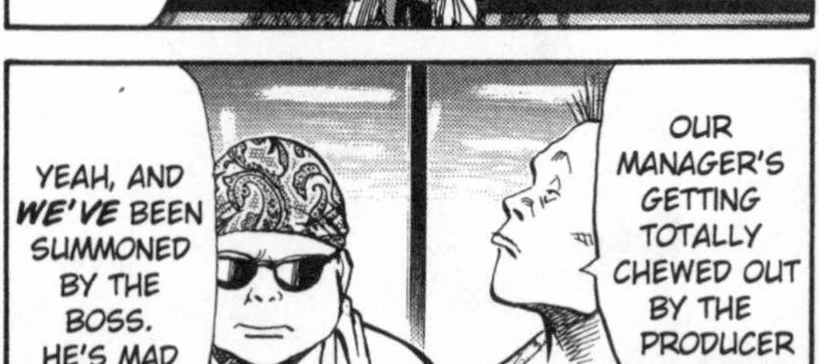
OUR MANAGER'S GETTING TOTALLY CHEWED OUT BY THE PRODUCER UP THERE.
YEAH, AND ***WE'VE*** BEEN SUMMONED BY THE BOSS. HE'S MAD AS HELL.

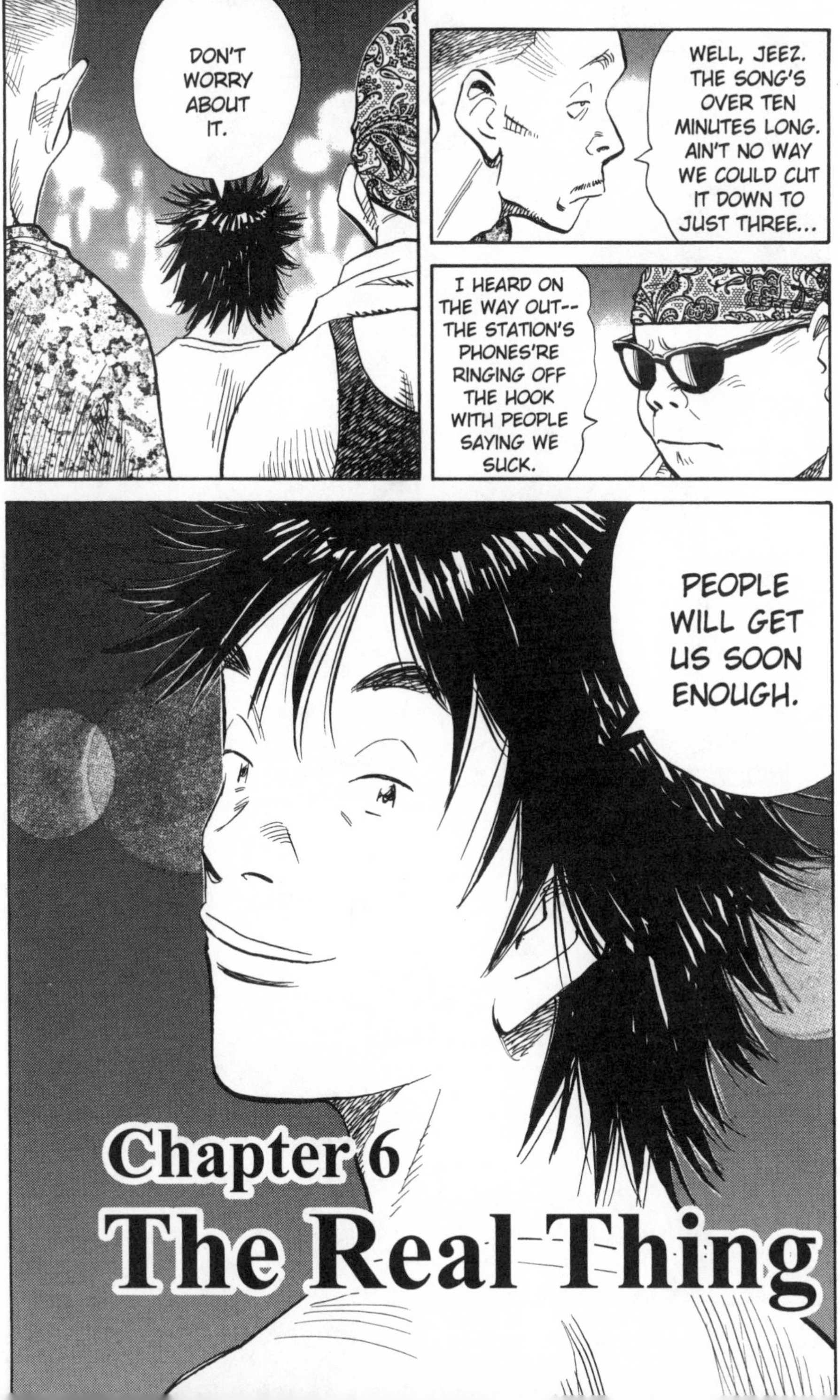
WELL, JEEZ. THE SONG'S OVER TEN MINUTES LONG. AIN'T NO WAY WE COULD CUT IT DOWN TO JUST THREE...
I HEARD ON THE WAY OUT-- THE STATION'S PHONES'RE RINGING OFF THE HOOK WITH PEOPLE SAYING WE SUCK.
DON'T WORRY ABOUT IT.
PEOPLE WILL GET US SOON ENOUGH.
Chapter 6
The Real Thing

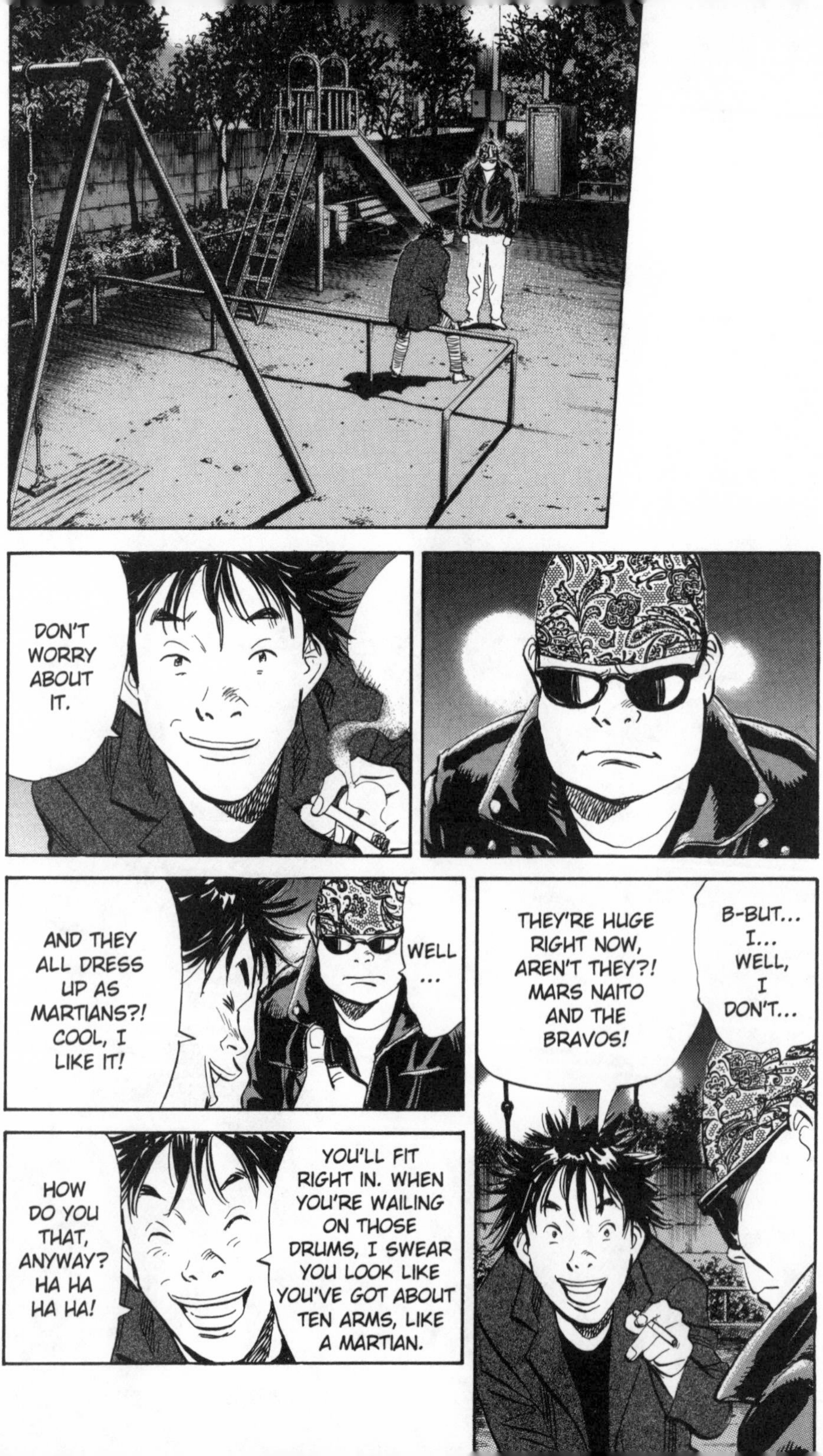
DON'T WORRY ABOUT IT.
B-BUT... I... WELL, I DON'T...
THEY'RE HUGE RIGHT NOW, AREN'T THEY?! MARS NAITO AND THE BRAVOS!
WELL ...
AND THEY ALL DRESS UP AS MARTIANS?! COOL, I LIKE IT!
YOU'LL FIT RIGHT IN. WHEN YOU'RE WAILING ON THOSE DRUMS, I SWEAR YOU LOOK LIKE YOU'VE GOT ABOUT TEN ARMS, LIKE A MARTIAN.
HOW DO YOU THAT, ANYWAY? HA HA HA HA!

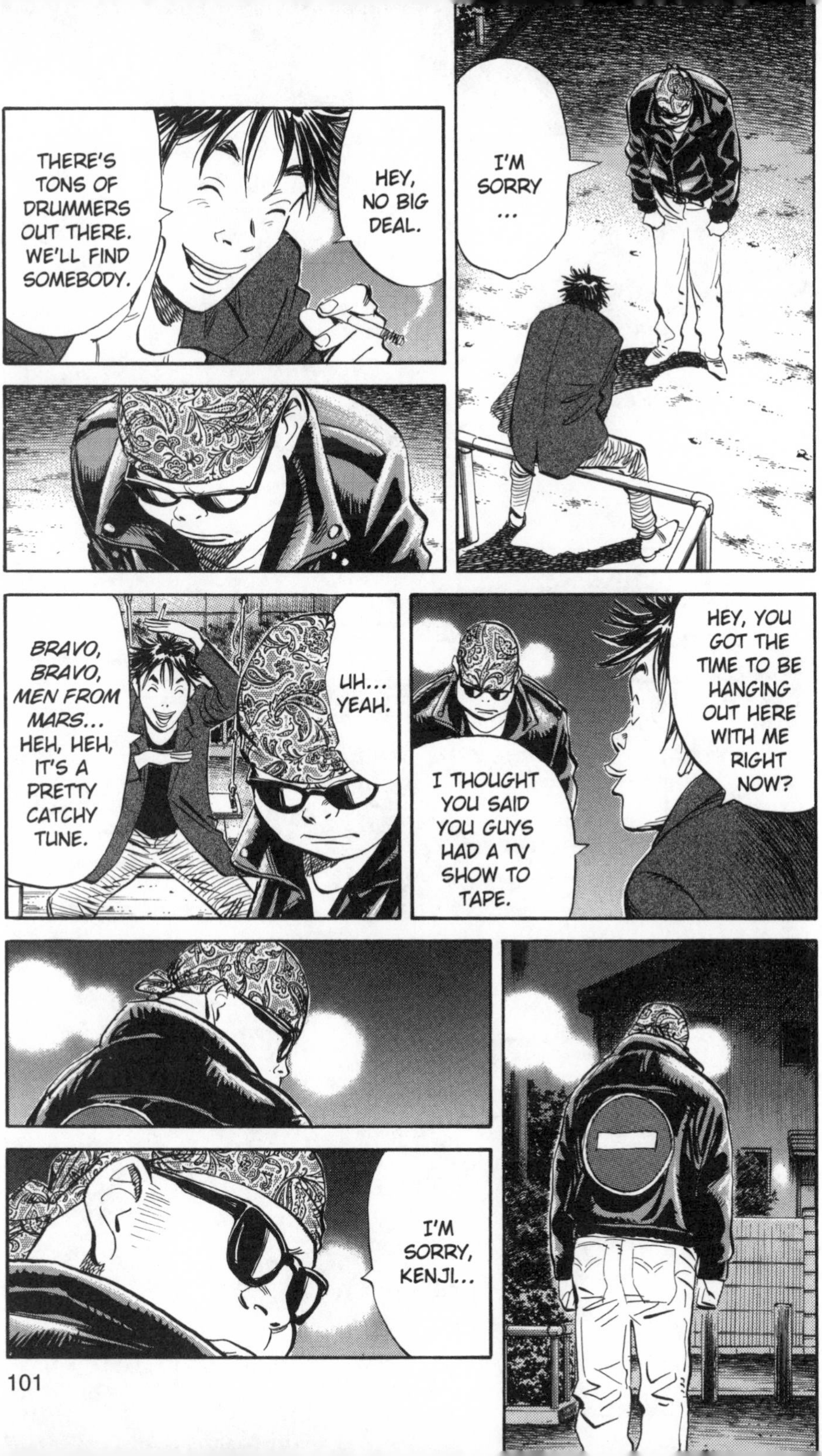
I'M SORRY ...
HEY, NO BIG DEAL.
THERE'S TONS OF DRUMMERS OUT THERE. WE'LL FIND SOMEBODY.
HEY, YOU GOT THE TIME TO BE HANGING OUT HERE WITH ME RIGHT NOW?
I THOUGHT YOU SAID YOU GUYS HAD A TV SHOW TO TAPE.
UH... YEAH.
BRAVO, BRAVO, MEN FROM MARS... HEH, HEH, IT'S A PRETTY CATCHY TUNE.
I'M SORRY, KENJI...

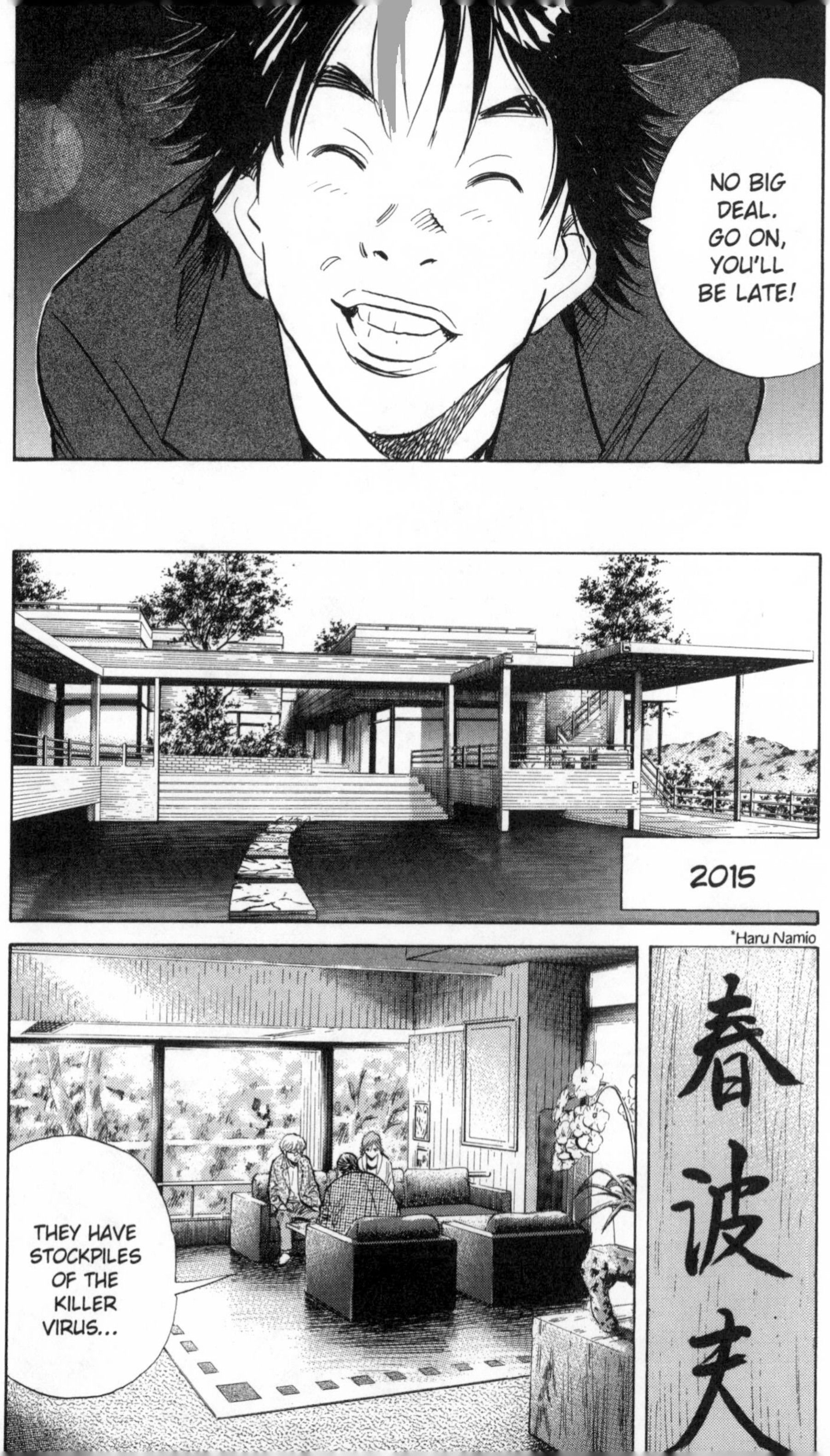
NO BIG DEAL. GO ON, YOU'LL BE LATE!
2015
*Haru Namio
春波夫
THEY HAVE STOCKPILES OF THE KILLER VIRUS...

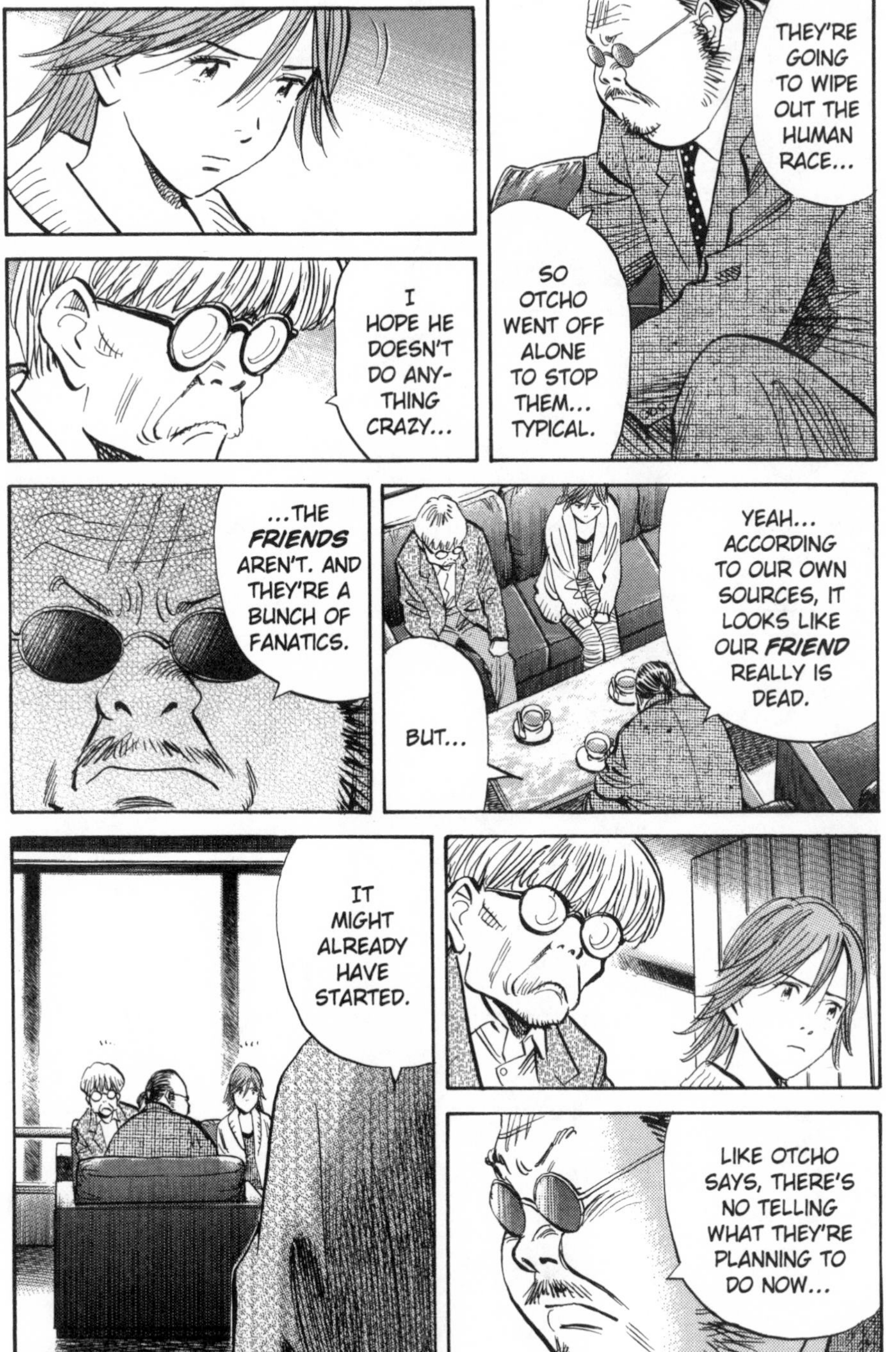
THEY'RE GOING TO WIPE OUT THE HUMAN RACE...
SO OTCHO WENT OFF ALONE TO STOP THEM... TYPICAL.
I HOPE HE DOESN'T DO ANYTHING CRAZY...
YEAH... ACCORDING TO OUR OWN SOURCES, IT LOOKS LIKE OUR FRIEND REALLY IS DEAD.
BUT...
...THE FRIENDS AREN'T. AND THEY'RE A BUNCH OF FANATICS.
LIKE OTCHO SAYS, THERE'S NO TELLING WHAT THEY'RE PLANNING TO DO NOW...
IT MIGHT ALREADY HAVE STARTED.

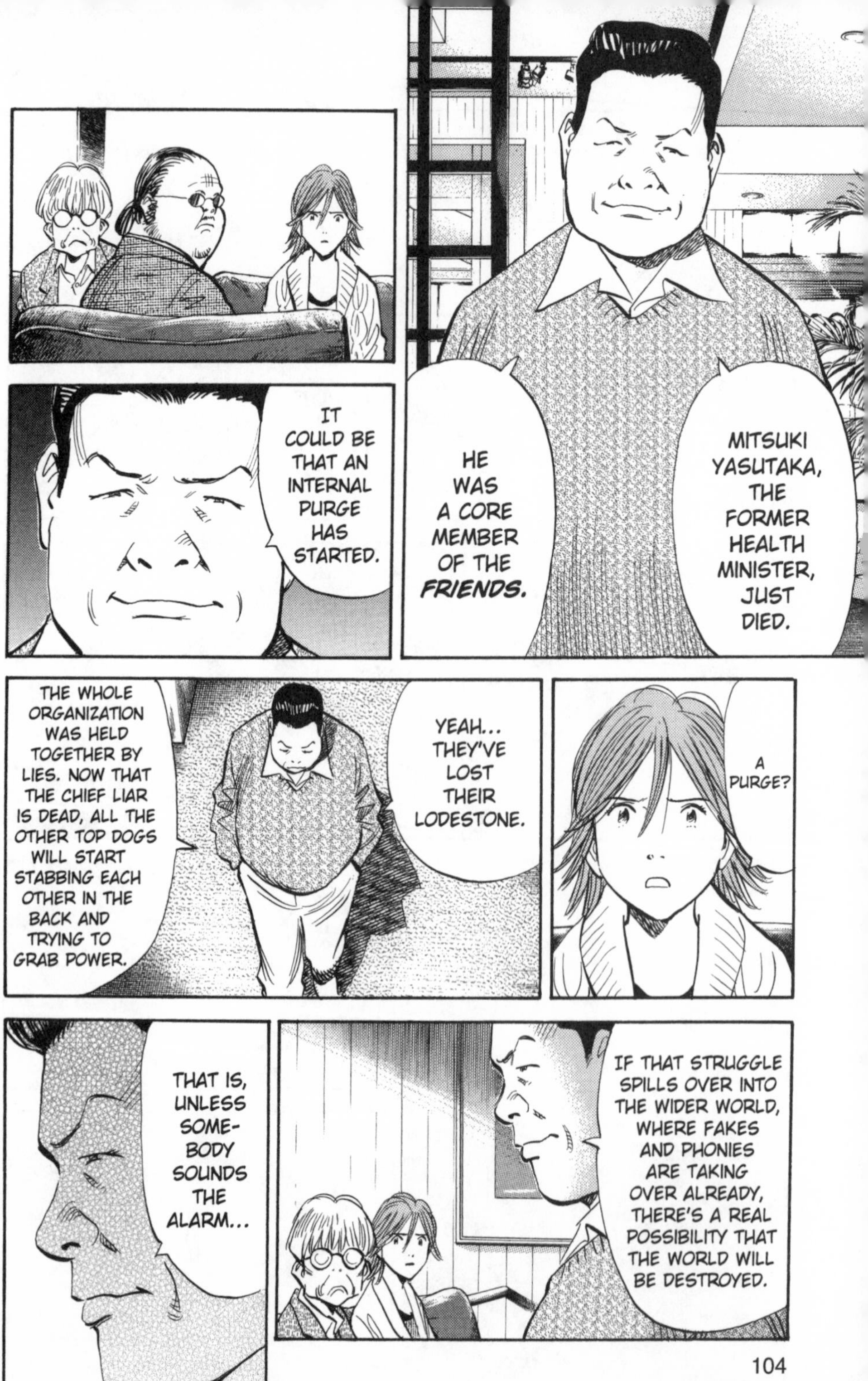
MITSUKI YASUTAKA, THE FORMER HEALTH MINISTER, JUST DIED.
HE WAS A CORE MEMBER OF THE *FRIENDS.*
IT COULD BE THAT AN INTERNAL PURGE HAS STARTED.
A PURGE?
YEAH... THEY'VE LOST THEIR LODESTONE.
THE WHOLE ORGANIZATION WAS HELD TOGETHER BY LIES. NOW THAT THE CHIEF LIAR IS DEAD, ALL THE OTHER TOP DOGS WILL START STABBING EACH OTHER IN THE BACK AND TRYING TO GRAB POWER.
IF THAT STRUGGLE SPILLS OVER INTO THE WIDER WORLD, WHERE FAKES AND PHONIES ARE TAKING OVER ALREADY, THERE'S A REAL POSSIBILITY THAT THE WORLD WILL BE DESTROYED.
THAT IS, UNLESS SOME-BODY SOUNDS THE ALARM...

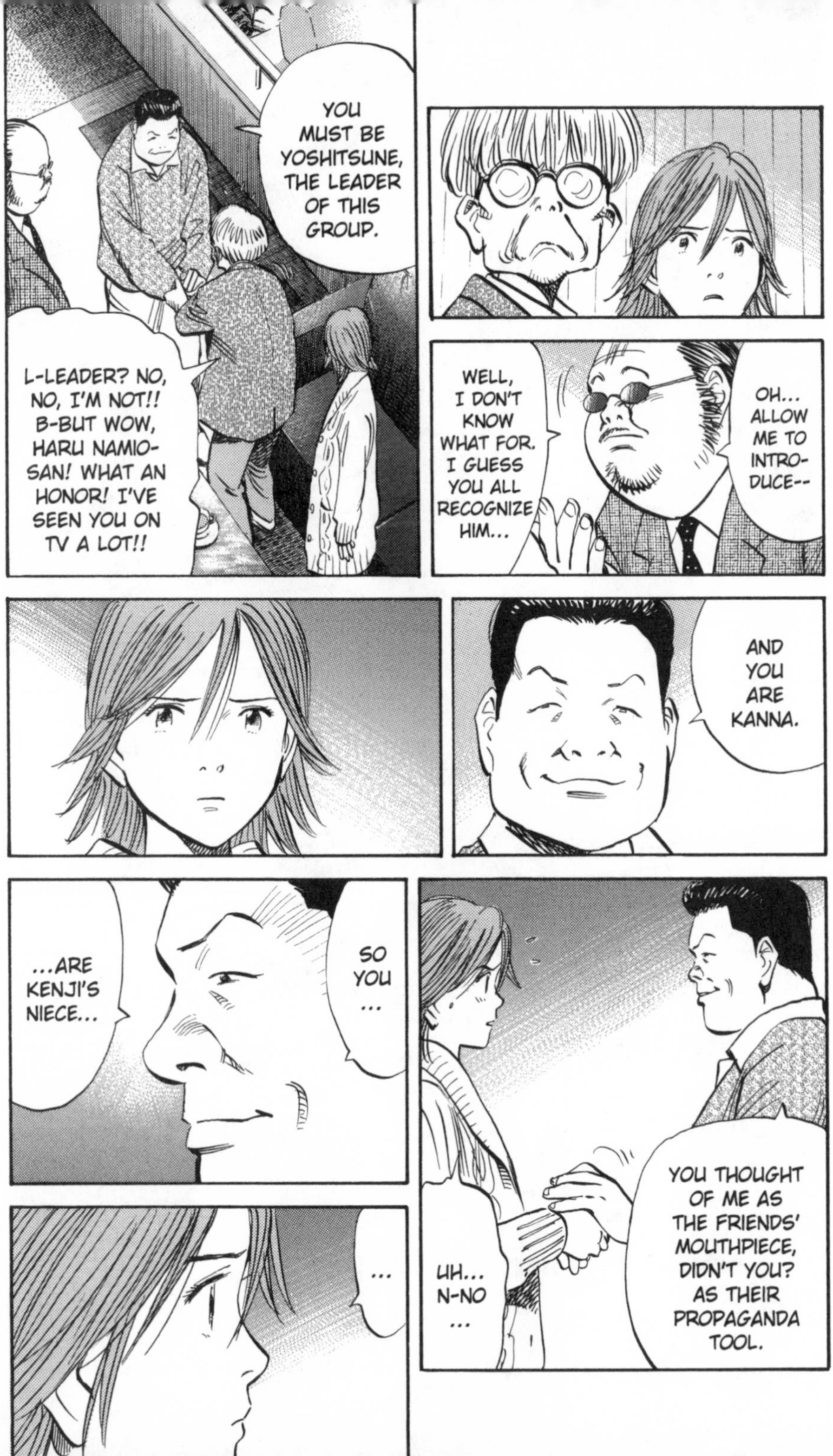
OH... ALLOW ME TO INTRO-DUCE--
WELL, I DON'T KNOW WHAT FOR. I GUESS YOU ALL RECOGNIZE HIM...
YOU MUST BE YOSHITSUNE, THE LEADER OF THIS GROUP.
L-LEADER? NO, NO, I'M NOT!! B-BUT WOW, HARU NAMIO-SAN! WHAT AN HONOR! I'VE SEEN YOU ON TV A LOT!!
AND YOU ARE KANNA.
YOU THOUGHT OF ME AS THE FRIENDS' MOUTHPIECE, DIDN'T YOU? AS THEIR PROPAGANDA TOOL.
UH... N-NO ...
SO YOU ...
...ARE KENJI'S NIECE...
...

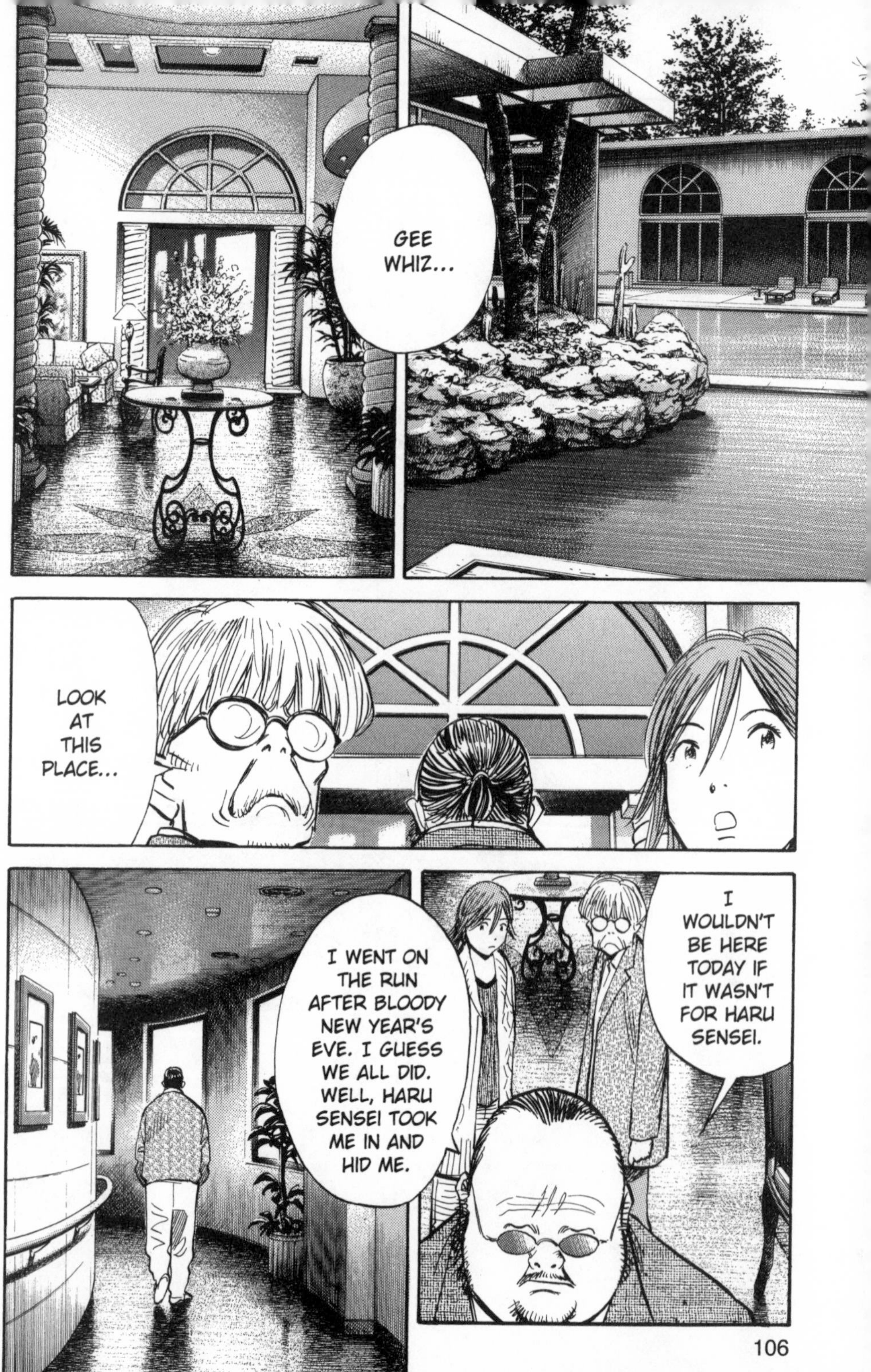
GEE WHIZ...
LOOK AT THIS PLACE...
I WOULDN'T BE HERE TODAY IF IT WASN'T FOR HARU SENSEI.
I WENT ON THE RUN AFTER BLOODY NEW YEAR'S EVE. I GUESS WE ALL DID. WELL, HARU SENSEI TOOK ME IN AND HID ME.

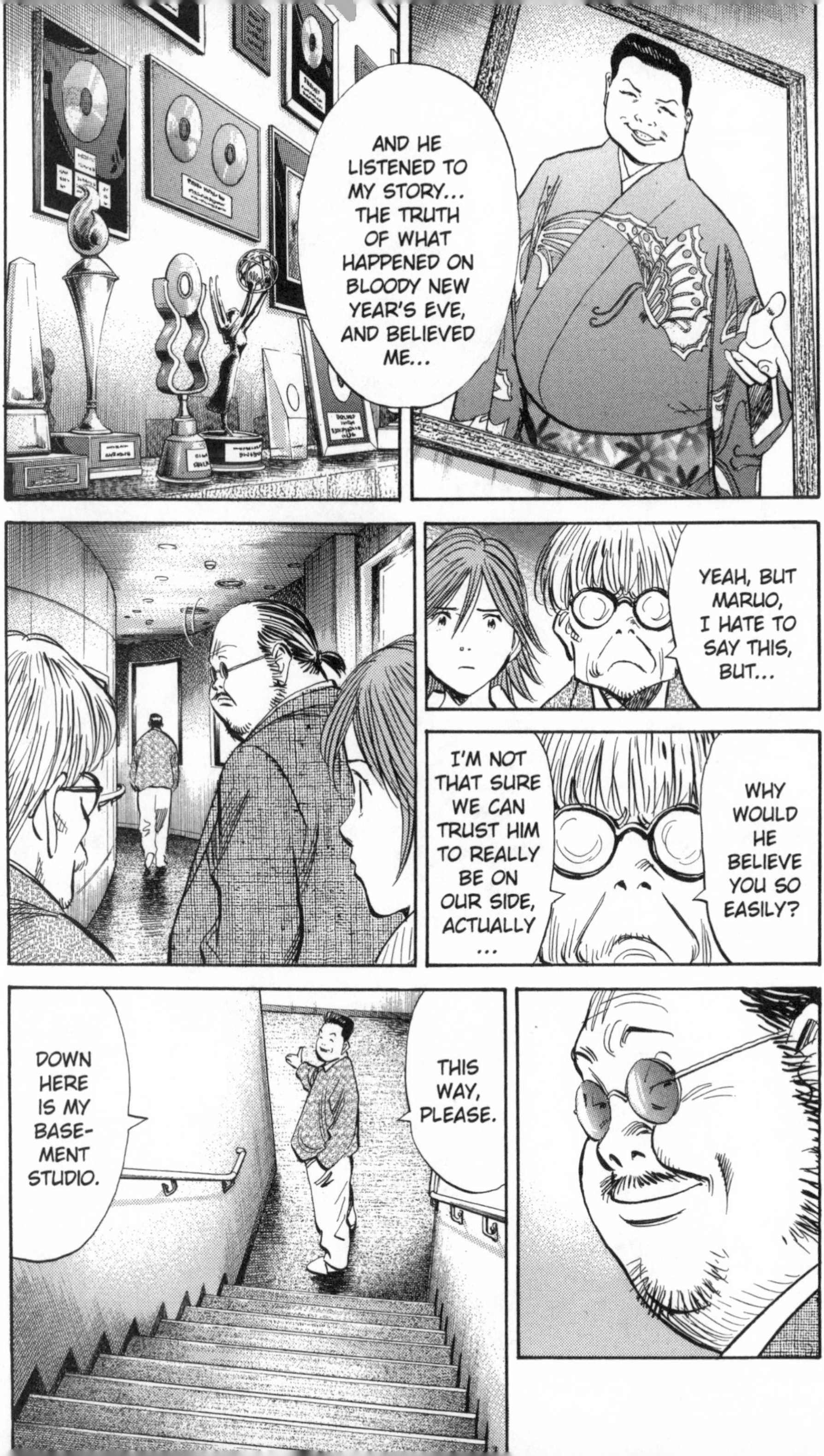
AND HE LISTENED TO MY STORY... THE TRUTH OF WHAT HAPPENED ON BLOODY NEW YEAR'S EVE, AND BELIEVED ME...
YEAH, BUT MARUO, I HATE TO SAY THIS, BUT...
WHY WOULD HE BELIEVE YOU SO EASILY?
I'M NOT THAT SURE WE CAN TRUST HIM TO REALLY BE ON OUR SIDE, ACTUALLY...
THIS WAY, PLEASE.
DOWN HERE IS MY BASEMENT STUDIO.

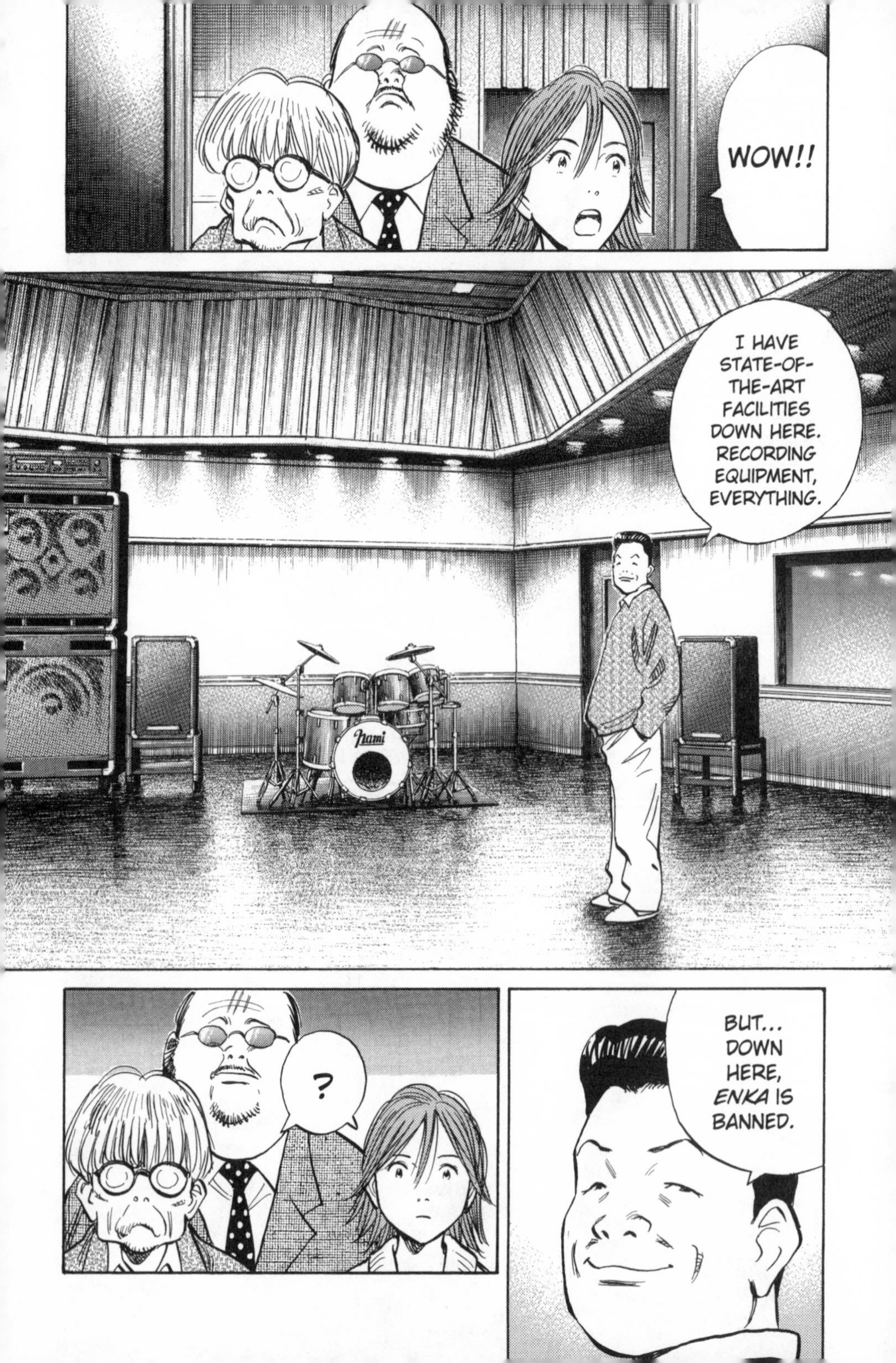
WOW!!
I HAVE STATE-OF-THE-ART FACILITIES DOWN HERE. RECORDING EQUIPMENT, EVERYTHING.
BUT... DOWN HERE, *ENKA* IS BANNED.
?

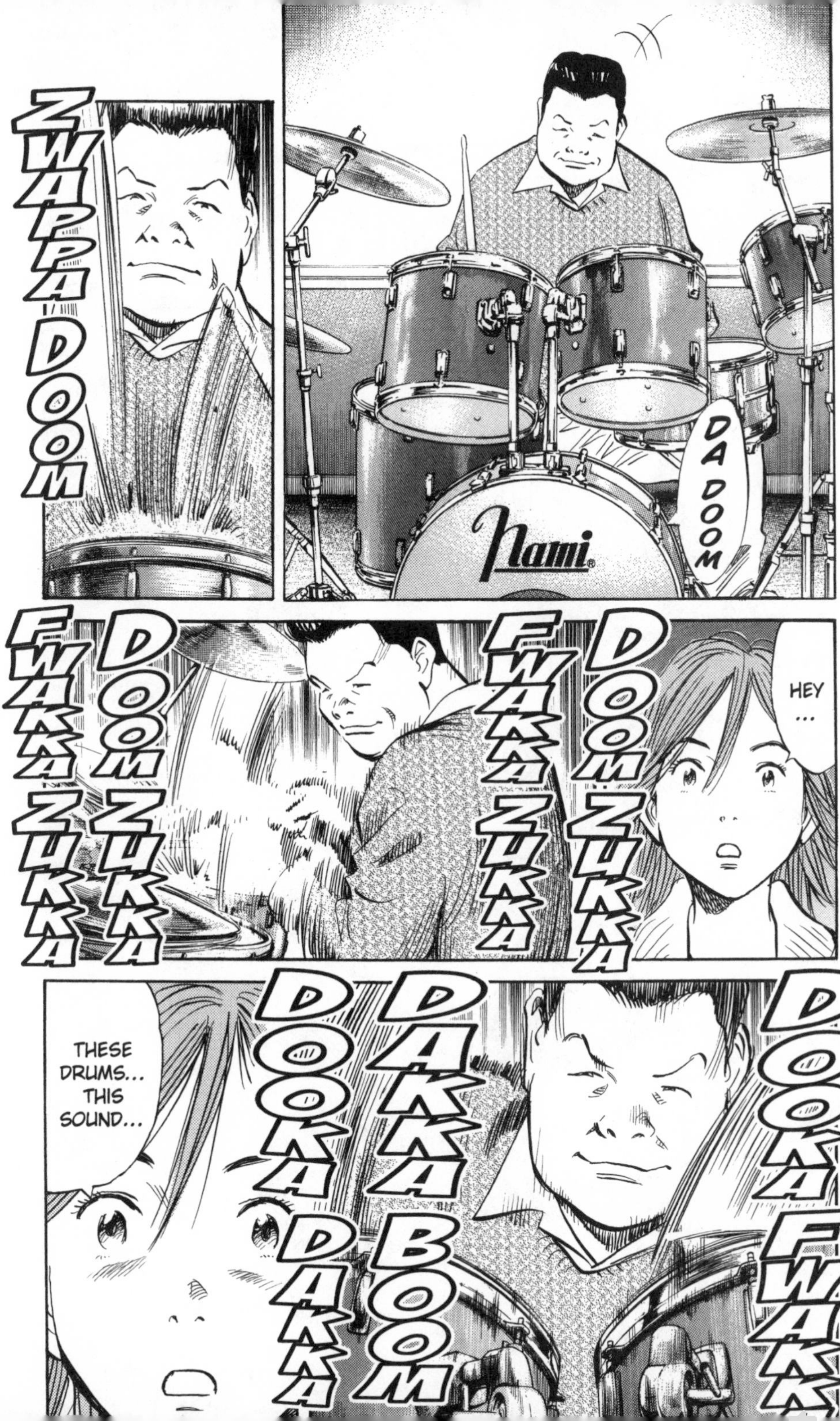
DA DOOOM
ZWAPPA DOOM
HEY ...
DOOM ZUKKA
FWAKKA ZUKKA
DOOM ZUKKA
FWAKKA ZUKKA
DOOOKA FWAKK
DAKKA BOOM
DOOKA DAKKA
THESE DRUMS... THIS SOUND...

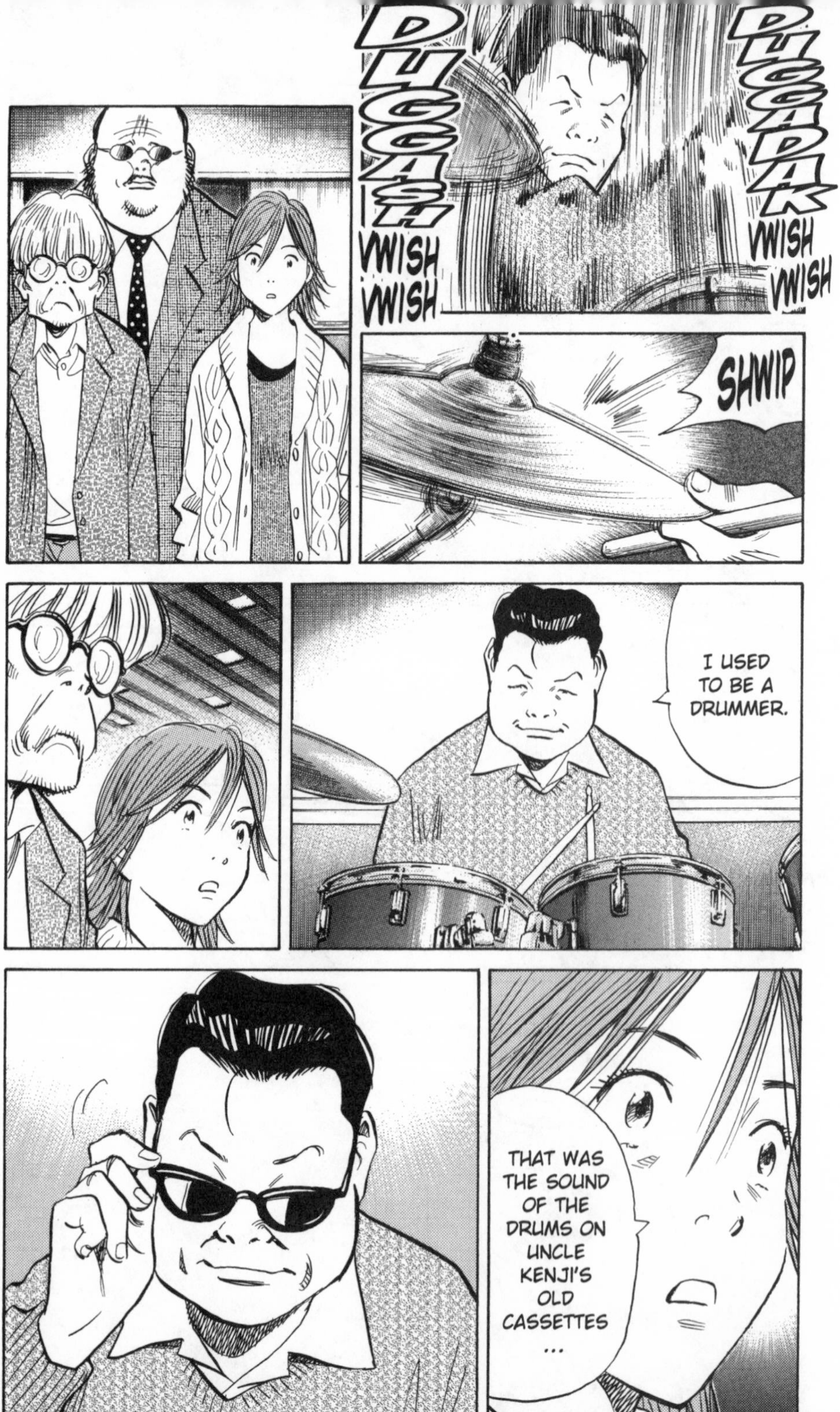
DUGGADAK
VWISH VWISH
DUGGASH
VWISH VWISH
SHWIP
I USED TO BE A DRUMMER.
THAT WAS THE SOUND OF THE DRUMS ON UNCLE KENJI'S OLD CASSETTES ...

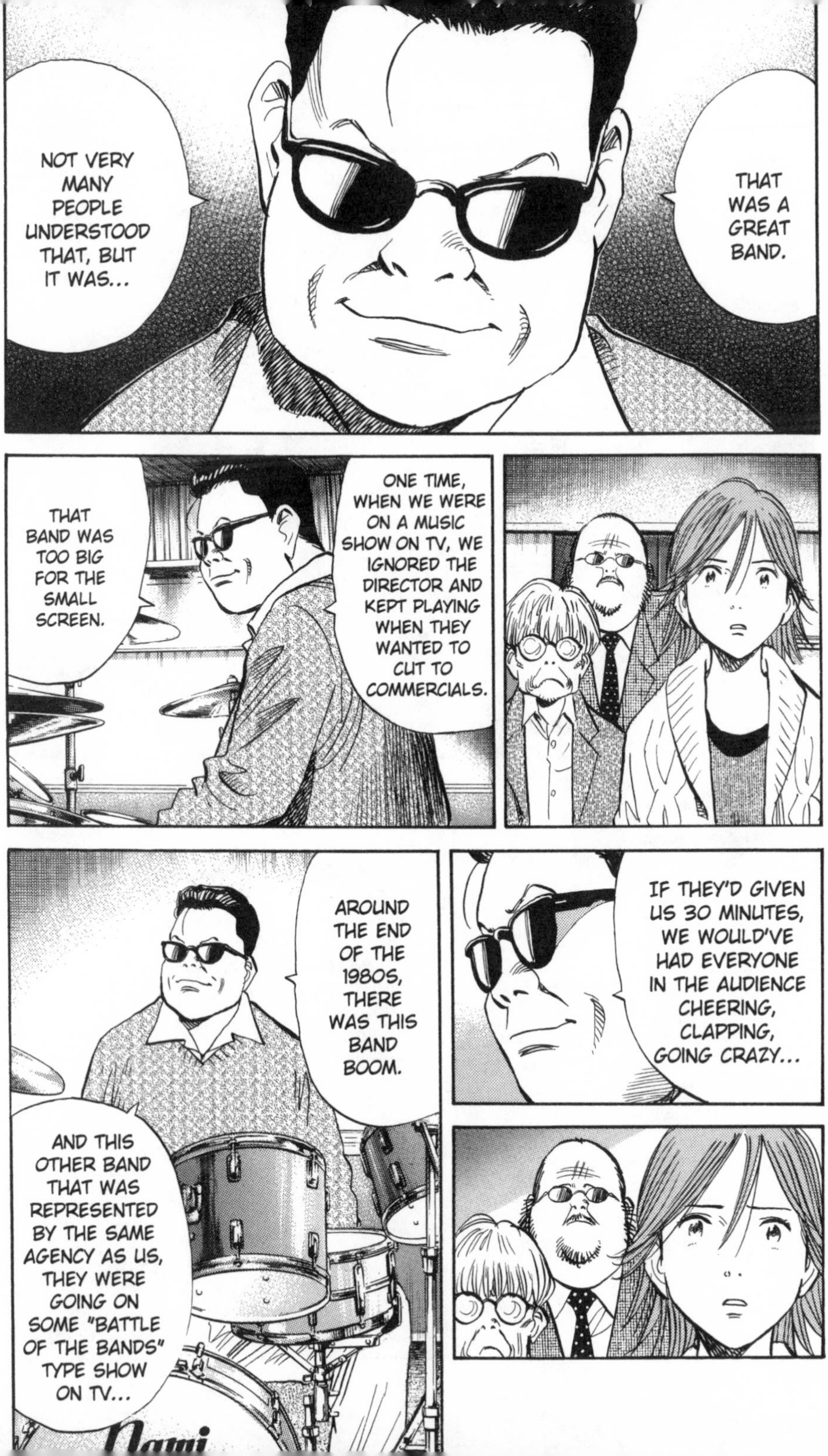
THAT WAS A GREAT BAND.
NOT VERY MANY PEOPLE UNDERSTOOD THAT, BUT IT WAS...
ONE TIME, WHEN WE WERE ON A MUSIC SHOW ON TV, WE IGNORED THE DIRECTOR AND KEPT PLAYING WHEN THEY WANTED TO CUT TO COMMERCIALS.
THAT BAND WAS TOO BIG FOR THE SMALL SCREEN.
IF THEY'D GIVEN US 30 MINUTES, WE WOULD'VE HAD EVERYONE IN THE AUDIENCE CHEERING, CLAPPING, GOING CRAZY...
AROUND THE END OF THE 1980S, THERE WAS THIS BAND BOOM.
AND THIS OTHER BAND THAT WAS REPRESENTED BY THE SAME AGENCY AS US, THEY WERE GOING ON SOME "BATTLE OF THE BANDS" TYPE SHOW ON TV...

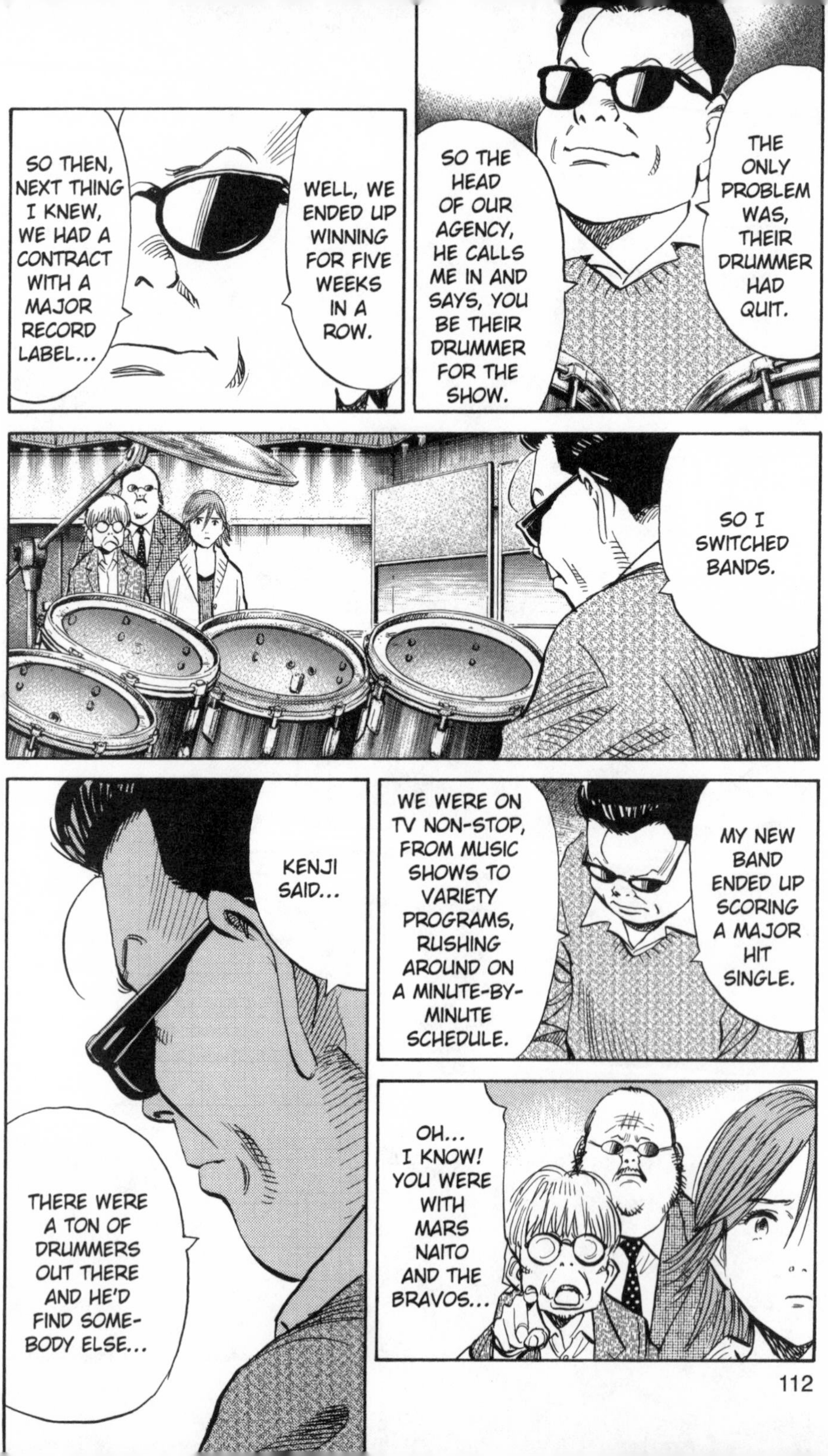
THE ONLY PROBLEM WAS, THEIR DRUMMER HAD QUIT.
SO THE HEAD OF OUR AGENCY, HE CALLS ME IN AND SAYS, YOU BE THEIR DRUMMER FOR THE SHOW.
WELL, WE ENDED UP WINNING FOR FIVE WEEKS IN A ROW.
SO THEN, NEXT THING I KNEW, WE HAD A CONTRACT WITH A MAJOR RECORD LABEL...
SO I SWITCHED BANDS.
MY NEW BAND ENDED UP SCORING A MAJOR HIT SINGLE.
WE WERE ON TV NON-STOP, FROM MUSIC SHOWS TO VARIETY PROGRAMS, RUSHING AROUND ON A MINUTE-BY-MINUTE SCHEDULE.
OH... I KNOW! YOU WERE WITH MARS NAITO AND THE BRAVOS...
KENJI SAID...
THERE WERE A TON OF DRUMMERS OUT THERE AND HE'D FIND SOME-BODY ELSE...

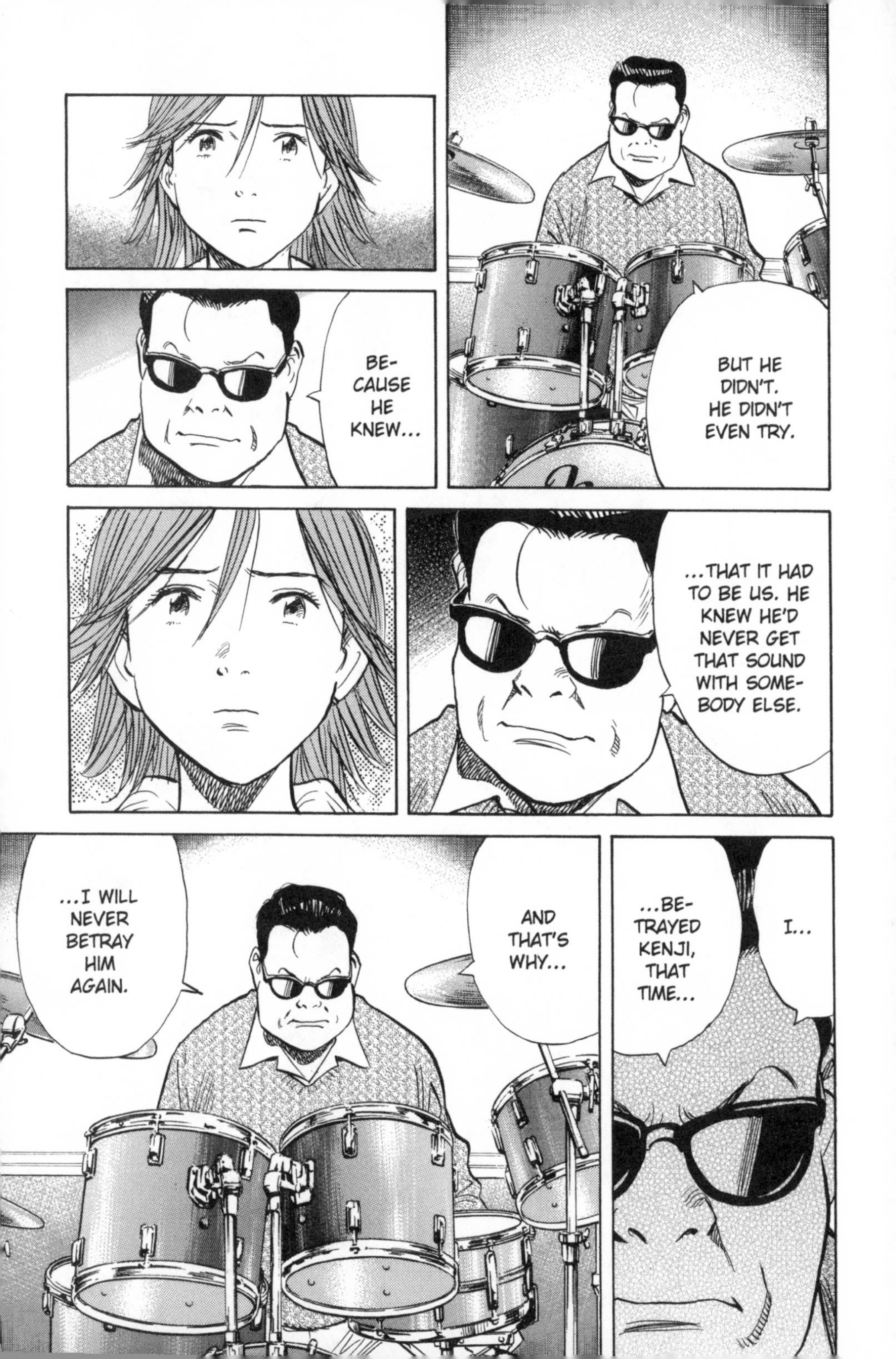
BUT HE DIDN'T. HE DIDN'T EVEN TRY.
BE-CAUSE HE KNEW...
...THAT IT HAD TO BE US. HE KNEW HE'D NEVER GET THAT SOUND WITH SOME-BODY ELSE.
I...
...BE-TRAYED KENJI, THAT TIME...
AND THAT'S WHY...
...I WILL NEVER BETRAY HIM AGAIN.

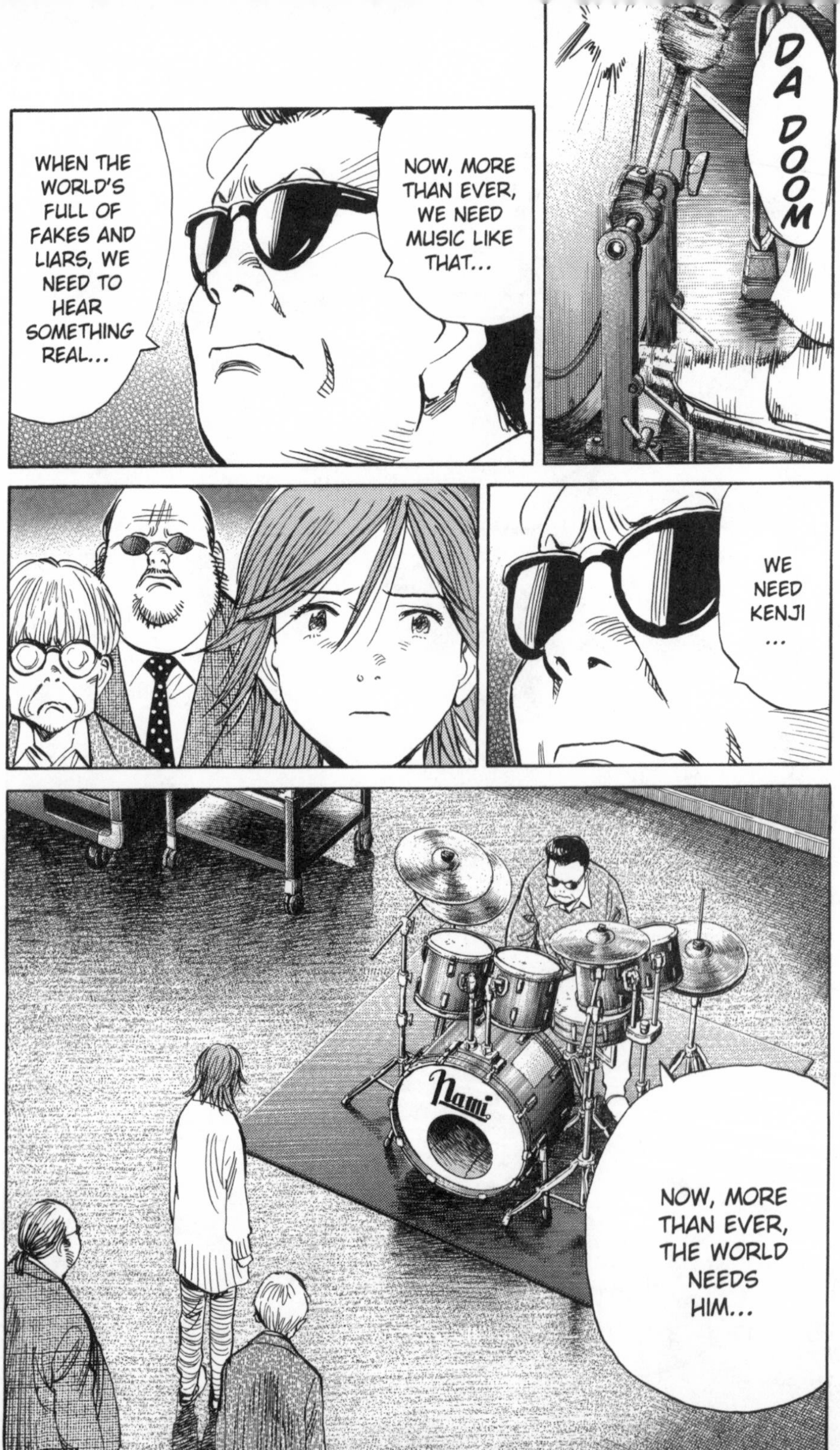
DA DOOM
NOW, MORE THAN EVER, WE NEED MUSIC LIKE THAT...
WHEN THE WORLD'S FULL OF FAKES AND LIARS, WE NEED TO HEAR SOMETHING REAL...
WE NEED KENJI ...
NOW, MORE THAN EVER, THE WORLD NEEDS HIM...

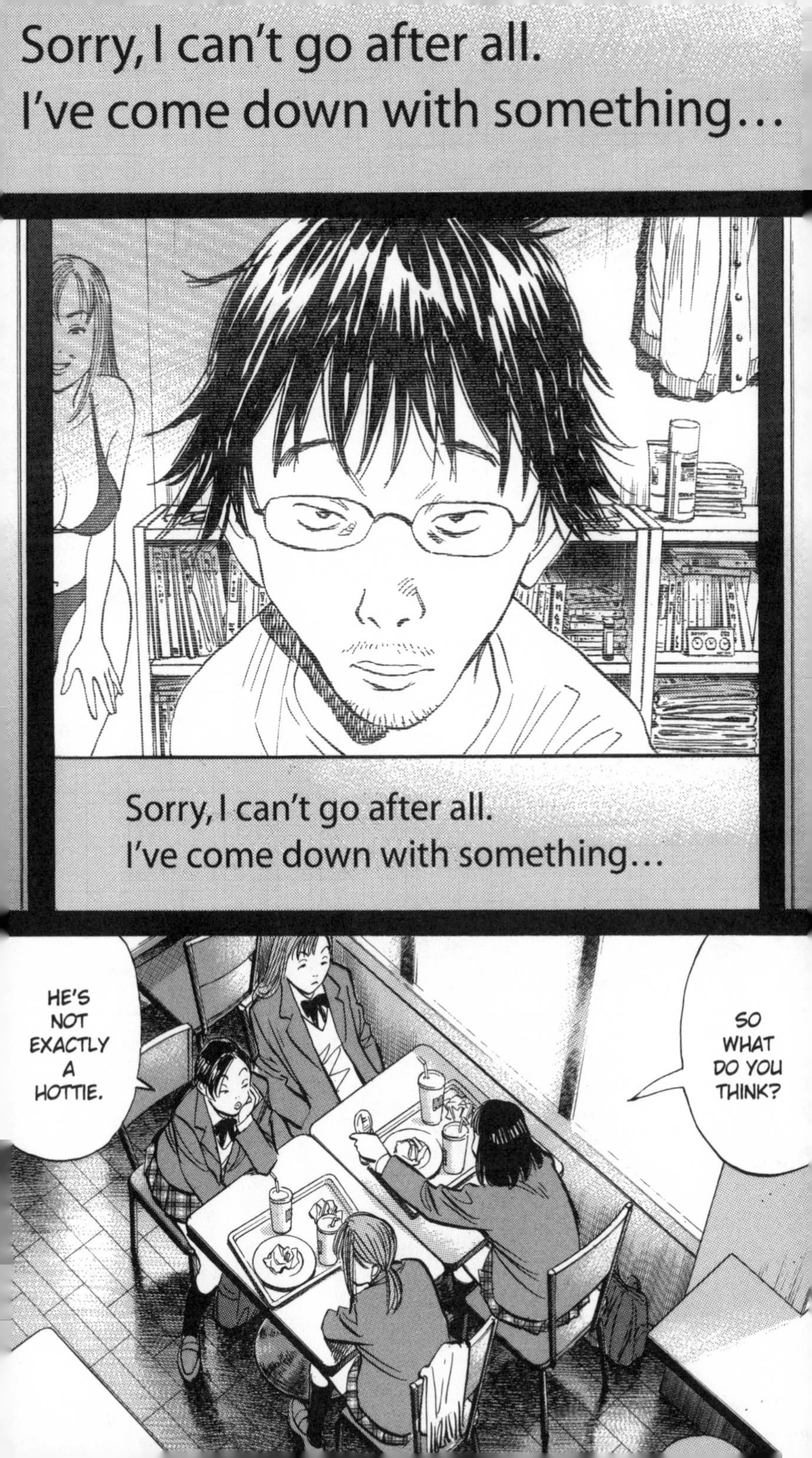
Sorry, I can't go after all. I've come down with something…
Sorry, I can't go after all. I've come down with something…
SO WHAT DO YOU THINK?
HE'S NOT EXACTLY A HOTTIE.

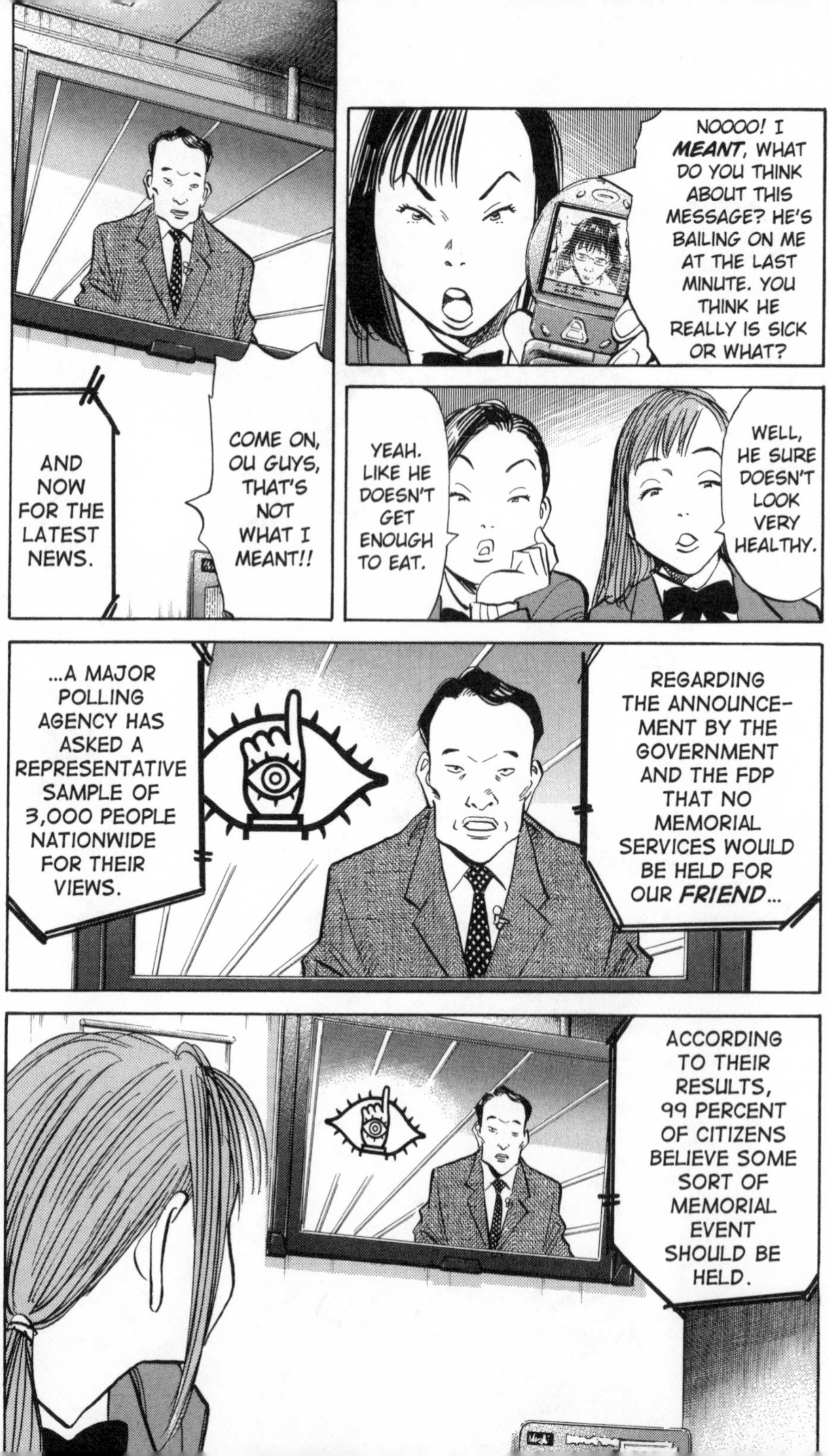
NOOOO! I **MEANT**, WHAT DO YOU THINK ABOUT THIS MESSAGE? HE'S BAILING ON ME AT THE LAST MINUTE. YOU THINK HE REALLY IS SICK OR WHAT?
WELL, HE SURE DOESN'T LOOK VERY HEALTHY.
YEAH. LIKE HE DOESN'T GET ENOUGH TO EAT.
COME ON, OU GUYS, THAT'S NOT WHAT I MEANT!!
AND NOW FOR THE LATEST NEWS.
REGARDING THE ANNOUNCE-MENT BY THE GOVERNMENT AND THE FDP THAT NO MEMORIAL SERVICES WOULD BE HELD FOR OUR **FRIEND**...
...A MAJOR POLLING AGENCY HAS ASKED A REPRESENTATIVE SAMPLE OF 3,000 PEOPLE NATIONWIDE FOR THEIR VIEWS.
ACCORDING TO THEIR RESULTS, 99 PERCENT OF CITIZENS BELIEVE SOME SORT OF MEMORIAL EVENT SHOULD BE HELD.

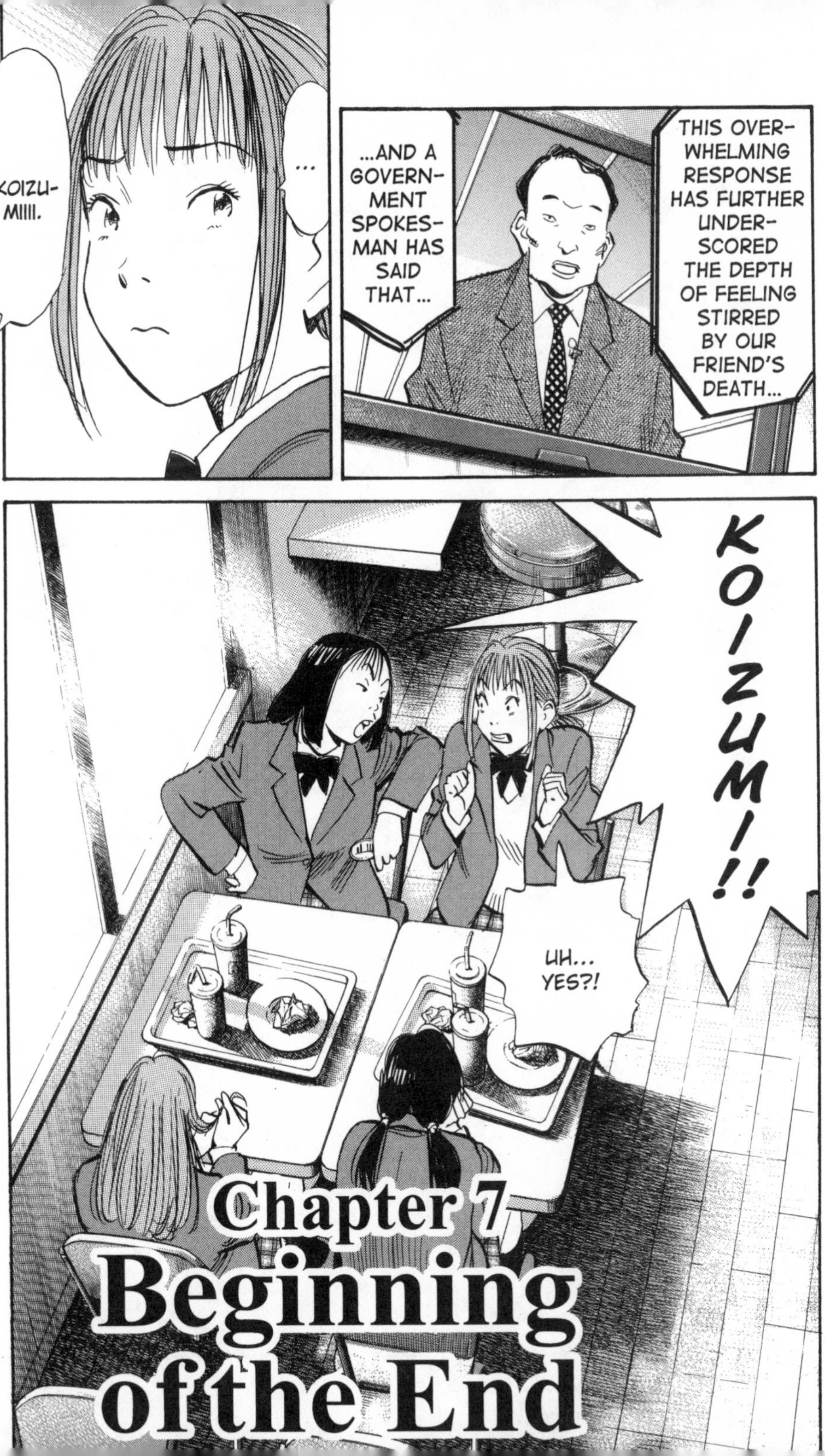
THIS OVER-WHELMING RESPONSE HAS FURTHER UNDER-SCORED THE DEPTH OF FEELING STIRRED BY OUR FRIEND'S DEATH...
...AND A GOVERN-MENT SPOKES-MAN HAS SAID THAT...
...
KOIZU-MIIII.
KOIZUMI!!
UH... YES?!

Chapter 7
Beginning of the End

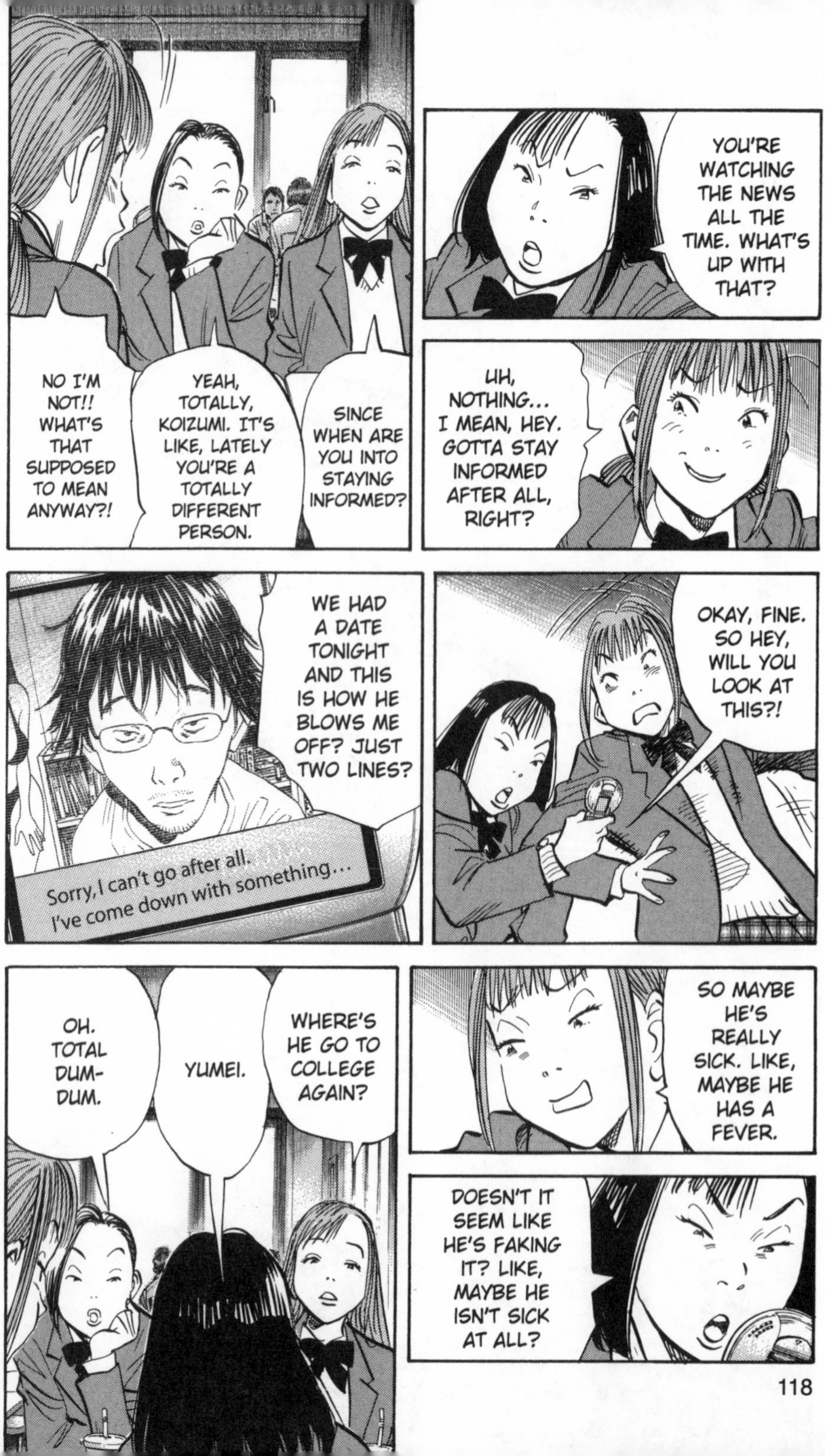
YOU'RE WATCHING THE NEWS ALL THE TIME. WHAT'S UP WITH THAT?
UH, NOTHING... I MEAN, HEY. GOTTA STAY INFORMED AFTER ALL, RIGHT?
SINCE WHEN ARE YOU INTO STAYING INFORMED?
YEAH, TOTALLY, KOIZUMI. IT'S LIKE, LATELY YOU'RE A TOTALLY DIFFERENT PERSON.
NO I'M NOT!! WHAT'S THAT SUPPOSED TO MEAN ANYWAY?!
OKAY, FINE. SO HEY, WILL YOU LOOK AT THIS?!
WE HAD A DATE TONIGHT AND THIS IS HOW HE BLOWS ME OFF? JUST TWO LINES?
Sorry, I can't go after all.
I've come down with something...
SO MAYBE HE'S REALLY SICK. LIKE, MAYBE HE HAS A FEVER.
DOESN'T IT SEEM LIKE HE'S FAKING IT? LIKE, MAYBE HE ISN'T SICK AT ALL?
WHERE'S HE GO TO COLLEGE AGAIN?
YUMEI.
OH. TOTAL DUM-DUM.

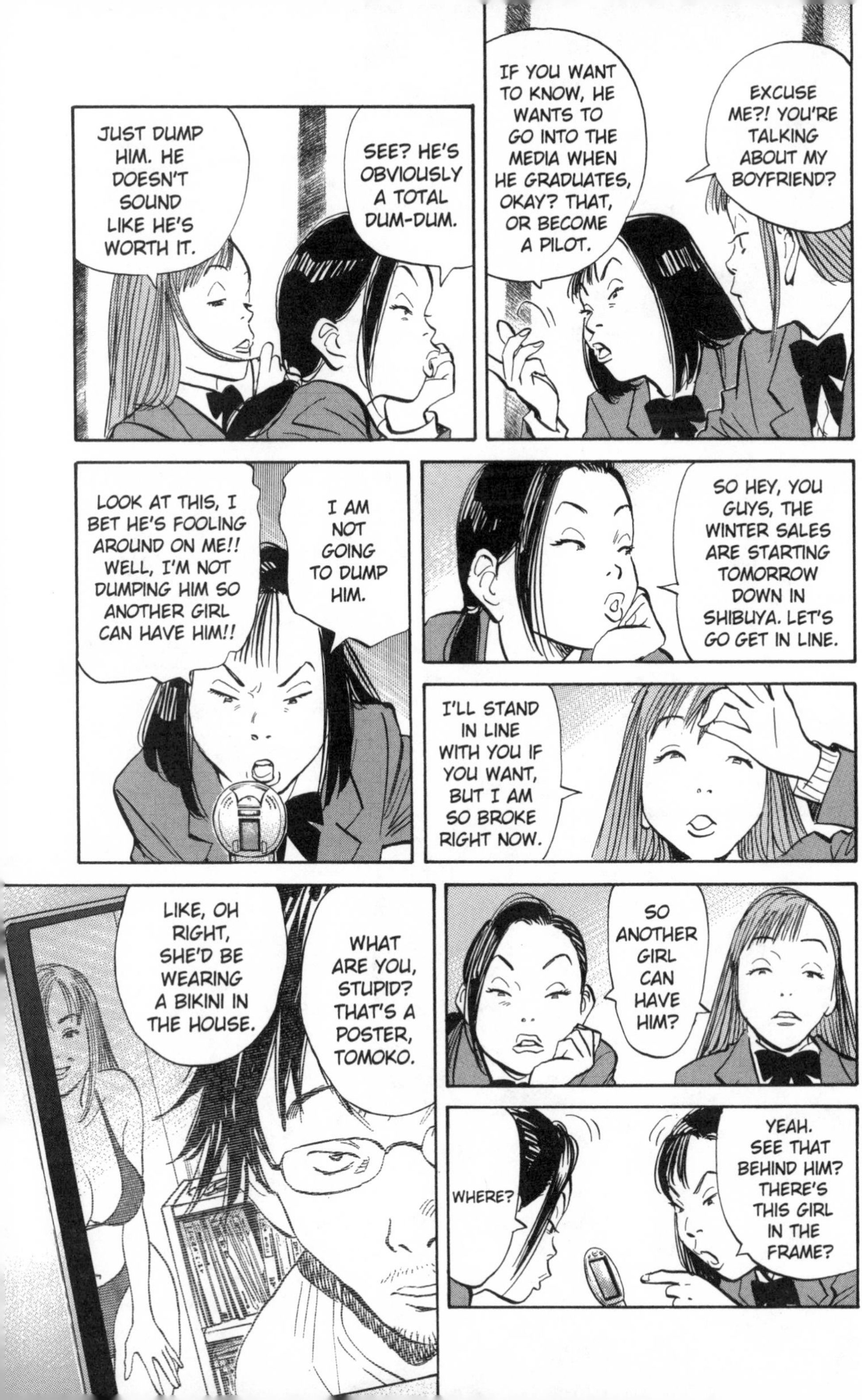
EXCUSE ME?! YOU'RE TALKING ABOUT MY BOYFRIEND?
IF YOU WANT TO KNOW, HE WANTS TO GO INTO THE MEDIA WHEN HE GRADUATES, OKAY? THAT, OR BECOME A PILOT.
SEE? HE'S OBVIOUSLY A TOTAL DUM-DUM.
JUST DUMP HIM. HE DOESN'T SOUND LIKE HE'S WORTH IT.
SO HEY, YOU GUYS, THE WINTER SALES ARE STARTING TOMORROW DOWN IN SHIBUYA. LET'S GO GET IN LINE.
I'LL STAND IN LINE WITH YOU IF YOU WANT, BUT I AM SO BROKE RIGHT NOW.
I AM NOT GOING TO DUMP HIM.
LOOK AT THIS, I BET HE'S FOOLING AROUND ON ME!! WELL, I'M NOT DUMPING HIM SO ANOTHER GIRL CAN HAVE HIM!!
SO ANOTHER GIRL CAN HAVE HIM?
YEAH. SEE THAT BEHIND HIM? THERE'S THIS GIRL IN THE FRAME?
WHERE?
WHAT ARE YOU, STUPID? THAT'S A POSTER, TOMOKO.
LIKE, OH RIGHT, SHE'D BE WEARING A BIKINI IN THE HOUSE.

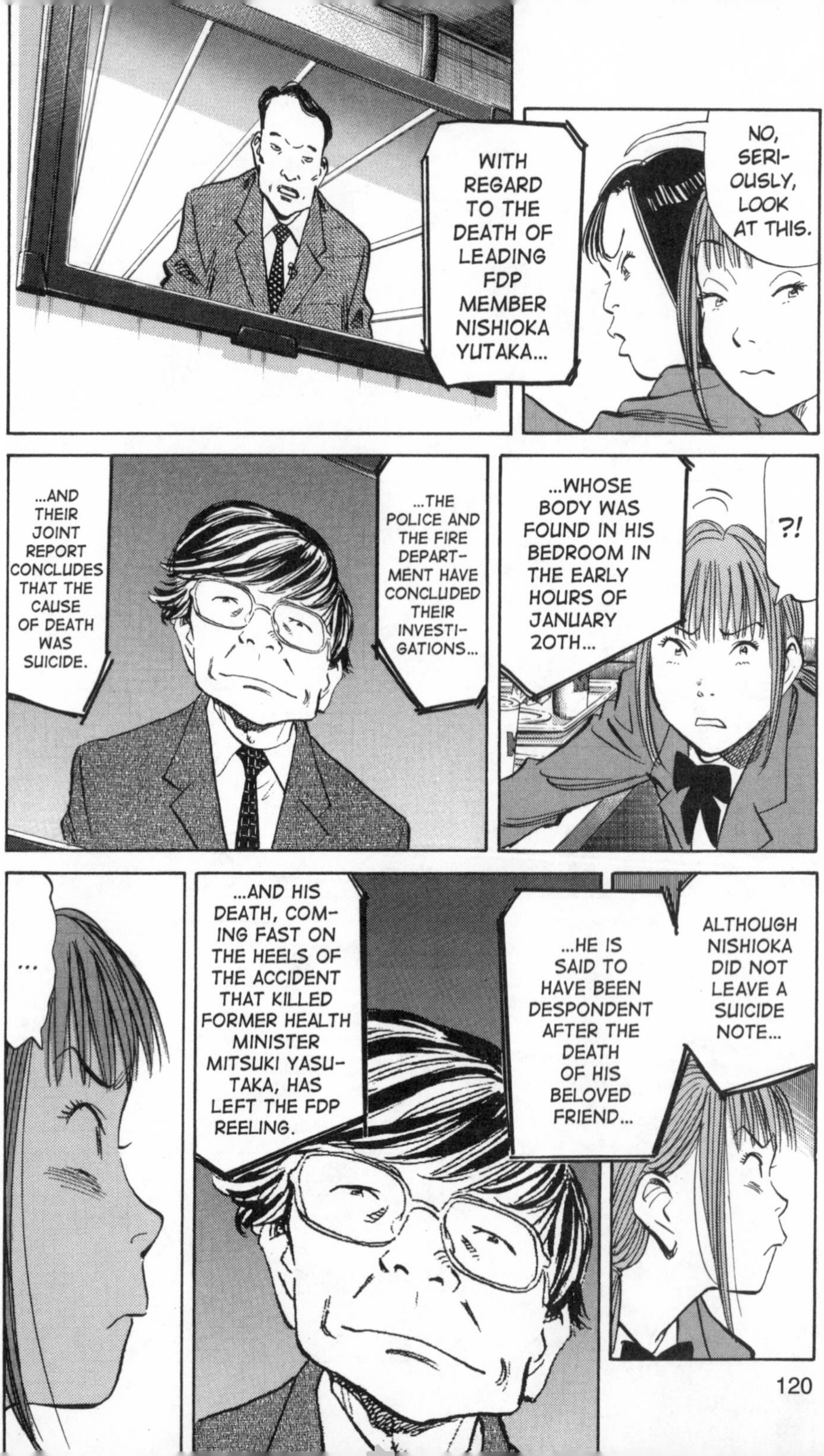
NO, SERIOUSLY, LOOK AT THIS.
WITH REGARD TO THE DEATH OF LEADING FDP MEMBER NISHIOKA YUTAKA...
...WHOSE BODY WAS FOUND IN HIS BEDROOM IN THE EARLY HOURS OF JANUARY 20TH...
?!
...THE POLICE AND THE FIRE DEPARTMENT HAVE CONCLUDED THEIR INVESTIGATIONS...
...AND THEIR JOINT REPORT CONCLUDES THAT THE CAUSE OF DEATH WAS SUICIDE.
ALTHOUGH NISHIOKA DID NOT LEAVE A SUICIDE NOTE...
...HE IS SAID TO HAVE BEEN DESPONDENT AFTER THE DEATH OF HIS BELOVED FRIEND...
...AND HIS DEATH, COMING FAST ON THE HEELS OF THE ACCIDENT THAT KILLED FORMER HEALTH MINISTER MITSUKI YASUTAKA, HAS LEFT THE FDP REELING.
...

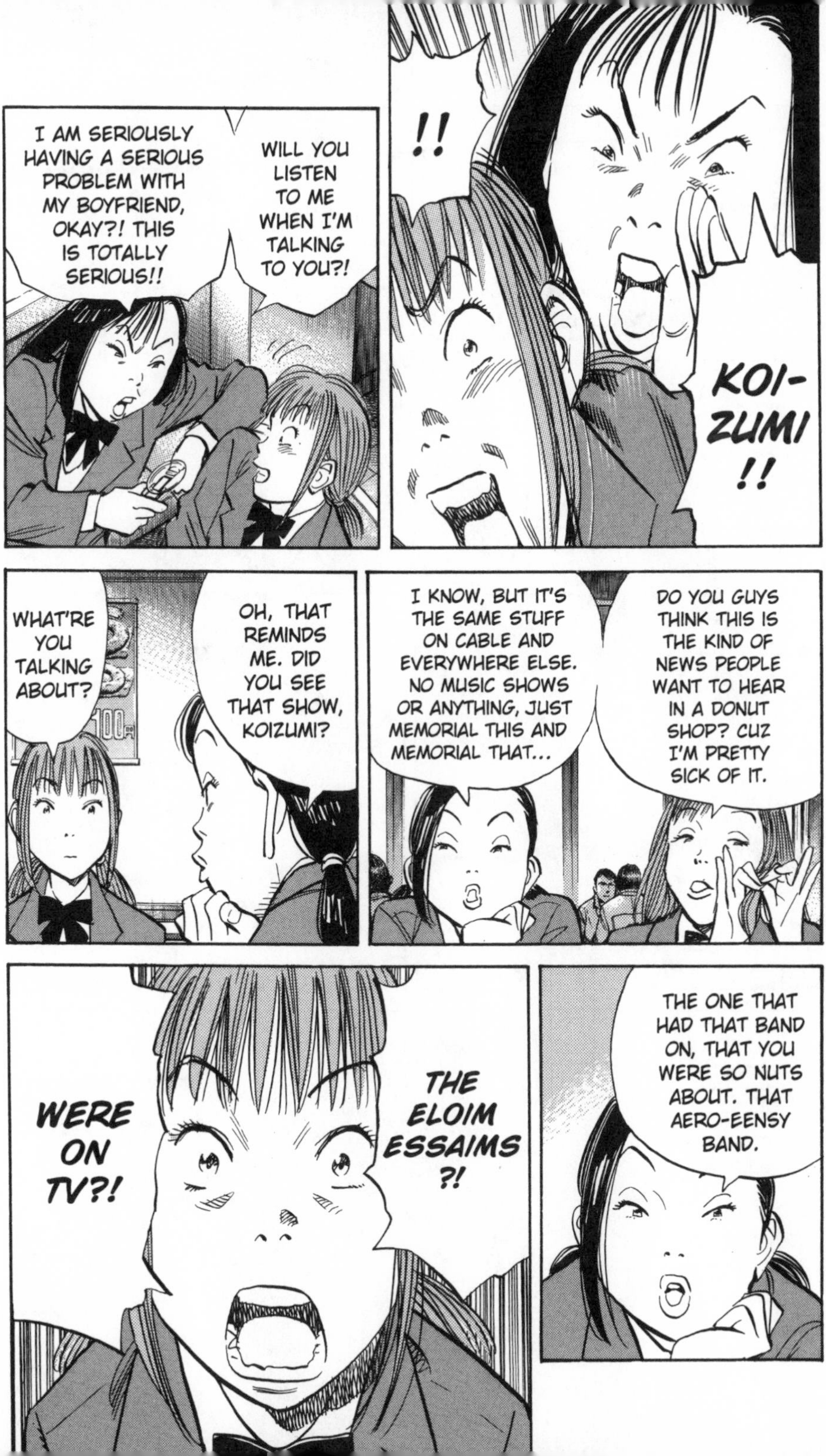
!!
KOI-ZUMI!!
WILL YOU LISTEN TO ME WHEN I'M TALKING TO YOU?!
I AM SERIOUSLY HAVING A SERIOUS PROBLEM WITH MY BOYFRIEND, OKAY?! THIS IS TOTALLY SERIOUS!!
DO YOU GUYS THINK THIS IS THE KIND OF NEWS PEOPLE WANT TO HEAR IN A DONUT SHOP? CUZ I'M PRETTY SICK OF IT.
I KNOW, BUT IT'S THE SAME STUFF ON CABLE AND EVERYWHERE ELSE. NO MUSIC SHOWS OR ANYTHING, JUST MEMORIAL THIS AND MEMORIAL THAT...
OH, THAT REMINDS ME. DID YOU SEE THAT SHOW, KOIZUMI?
WHAT'RE YOU TALKING ABOUT?
100円
THE ONE THAT HAD THAT BAND ON, THAT YOU WERE SO NUTS ABOUT. THAT AERO-EENSY BAND.
THE ELOIM ESSAIMS?!
WERE ON TV?!

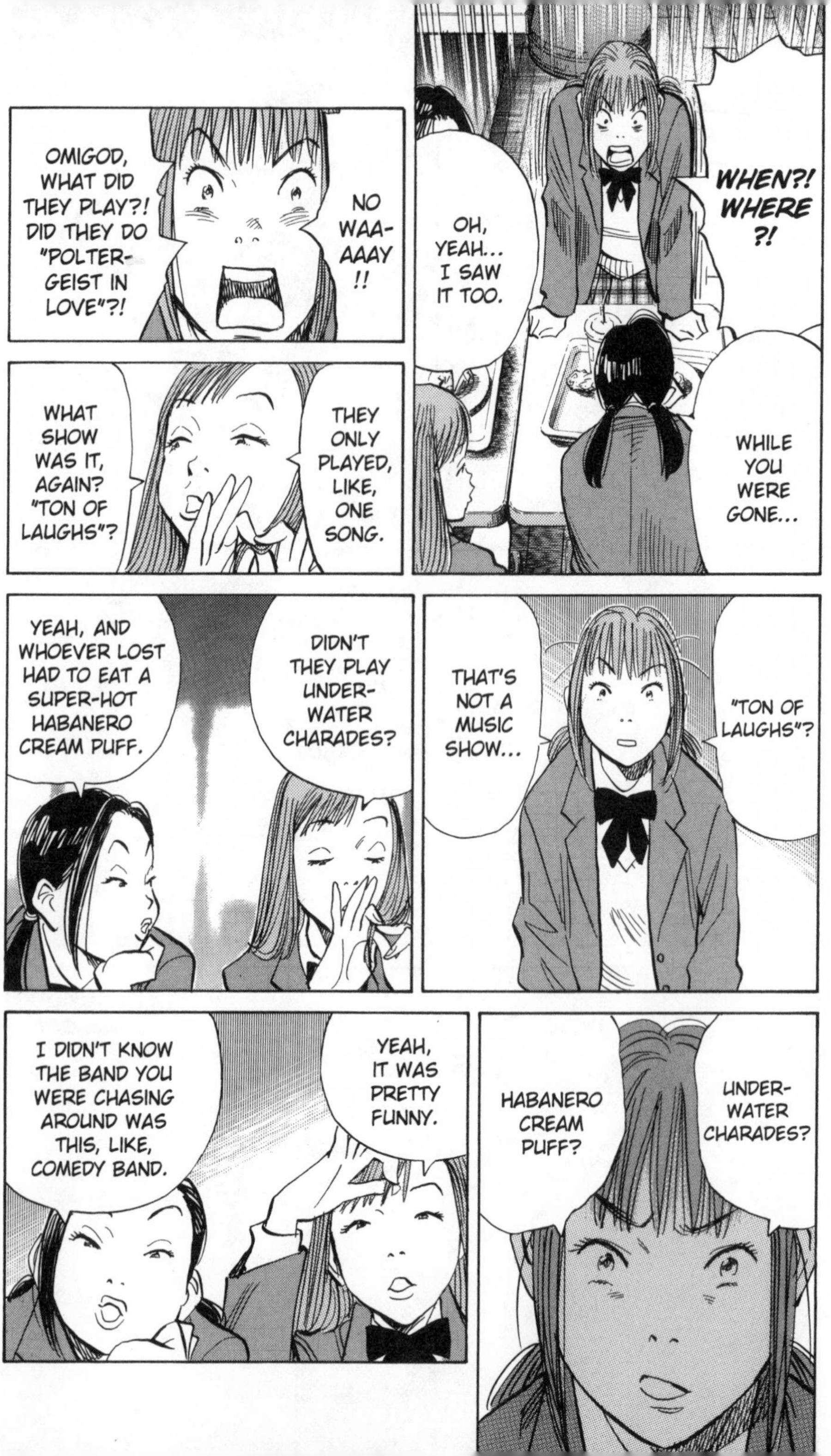
WHEN?! WHERE ?!
OH, YEAH... I SAW IT TOO.
WHILE YOU WERE GONE...
NO WAA-AAAY !!
OMIGOD, WHAT DID THEY PLAY?! DID THEY DO "POLTER-GEIST IN LOVE"?!
THEY ONLY PLAYED, LIKE, ONE SONG.
WHAT SHOW WAS IT, AGAIN? "TON OF LAUGHS"?
"TON OF LAUGHS"?
THAT'S NOT A MUSIC SHOW...
DIDN'T THEY PLAY UNDER-WATER CHARADES?
YEAH, AND WHOEVER LOST HAD TO EAT A SUPER-HOT HABANERO CREAM PUFF.
UNDER-WATER CHARADES?
HABANERO CREAM PUFF?
YEAH, IT WAS PRETTY FUNNY.
I DIDN'T KNOW THE BAND YOU WERE CHASING AROUND WAS THIS, LIKE, COMEDY BAND.

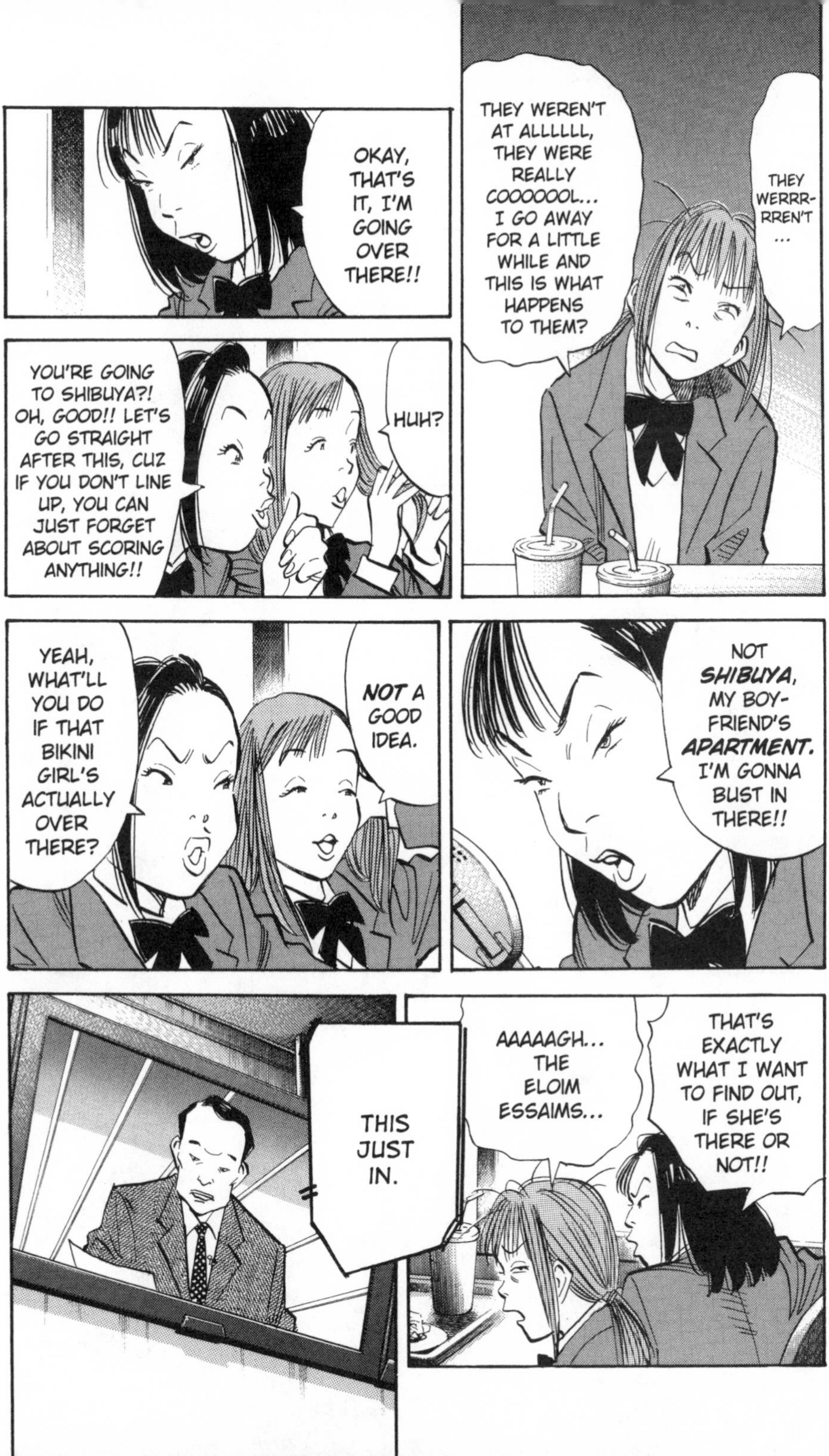
THEY WERRRRREN'T ...
THEY WEREN'T AT ALLLLLL, THEY WERE REALLY COOOOOOL... I GO AWAY FOR A LITTLE WHILE AND THIS IS WHAT HAPPENS TO THEM?
OKAY, THAT'S IT, I'M GOING OVER THERE!!
HUH?
YOU'RE GOING TO SHIBUYA?! OH, GOOD!! LET'S GO STRAIGHT AFTER THIS, CUZ IF YOU DON'T LINE UP, YOU CAN JUST FORGET ABOUT SCORING ANYTHING!!
NOT SHIBUYA, MY BOY-FRIEND'S APARTMENT. I'M GONNA BUST IN THERE!!
NOT A GOOD IDEA.
YEAH, WHAT'LL YOU DO IF THAT BIKINI GIRL'S ACTUALLY OVER THERE?
THAT'S EXACTLY WHAT I WANT TO FIND OUT, IF SHE'S THERE OR NOT!!
AAAAAGH... THE ELOIM ESSAIMS...
THIS JUST IN.

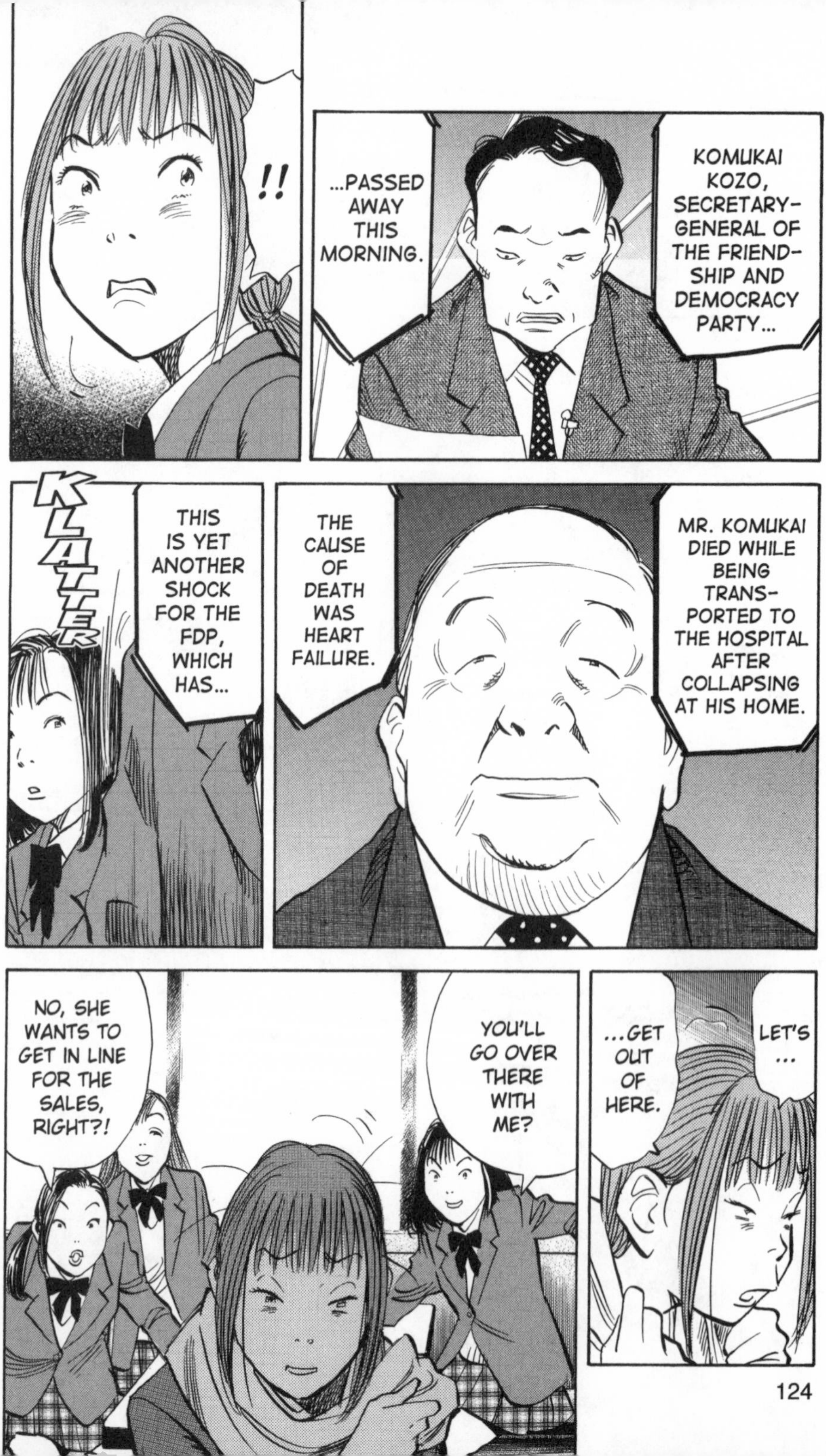
KOMUKAI KOZO, SECRETARY-GENERAL OF THE FRIENDSHIP AND DEMOCRACY PARTY...
...PASSED AWAY THIS MORNING.
!!
MR. KOMUKAI DIED WHILE BEING TRANS-PORTED TO THE HOSPITAL AFTER COLLAPSING AT HIS HOME.
THE CAUSE OF DEATH WAS HEART FAILURE.
THIS IS YET ANOTHER SHOCK FOR THE FDP, WHICH HAS...
KLATTER
LET'S...
...GET OUT OF HERE.
YOU'LL GO OVER THERE WITH ME?
NO, SHE WANTS TO GET IN LINE FOR THE SALES, RIGHT?!

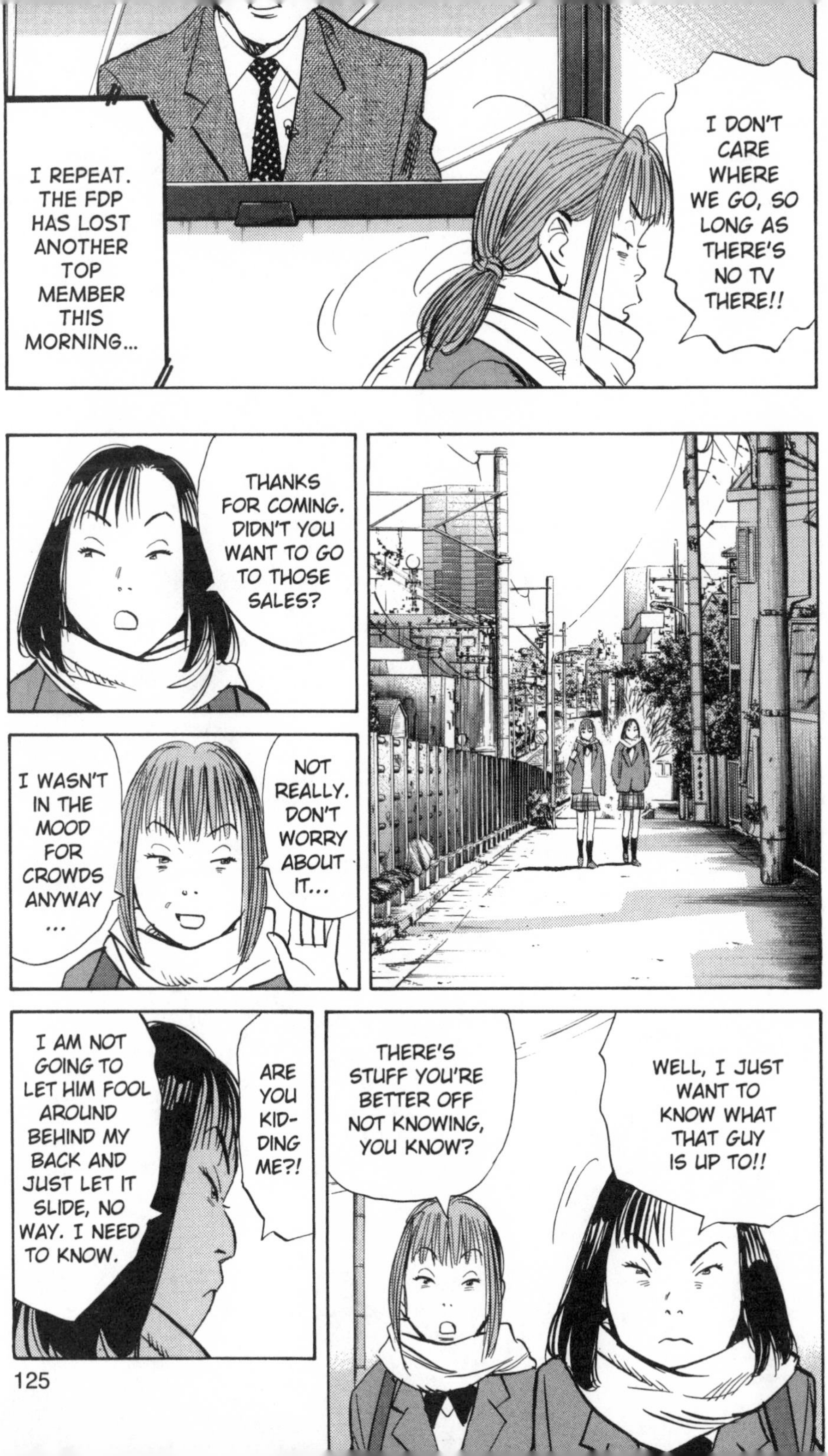
I DON'T CARE WHERE WE GO, SO LONG AS THERE'S NO TV THERE!!
I REPEAT. THE FDP HAS LOST ANOTHER TOP MEMBER THIS MORNING...
THANKS FOR COMING. DIDN'T YOU WANT TO GO TO THOSE SALES?
NOT REALLY. DON'T WORRY ABOUT IT...
I WASN'T IN THE MOOD FOR CROWDS ANYWAY...
WELL, I JUST WANT TO KNOW WHAT THAT GUY IS UP TO!!
THERE'S STUFF YOU'RE BETTER OFF NOT KNOWING, YOU KNOW?
ARE YOU KID-DING ME?!
I AM NOT GOING TO LET HIM FOOL AROUND BEHIND MY BACK AND JUST LET IT SLIDE, NO WAY. I NEED TO KNOW.

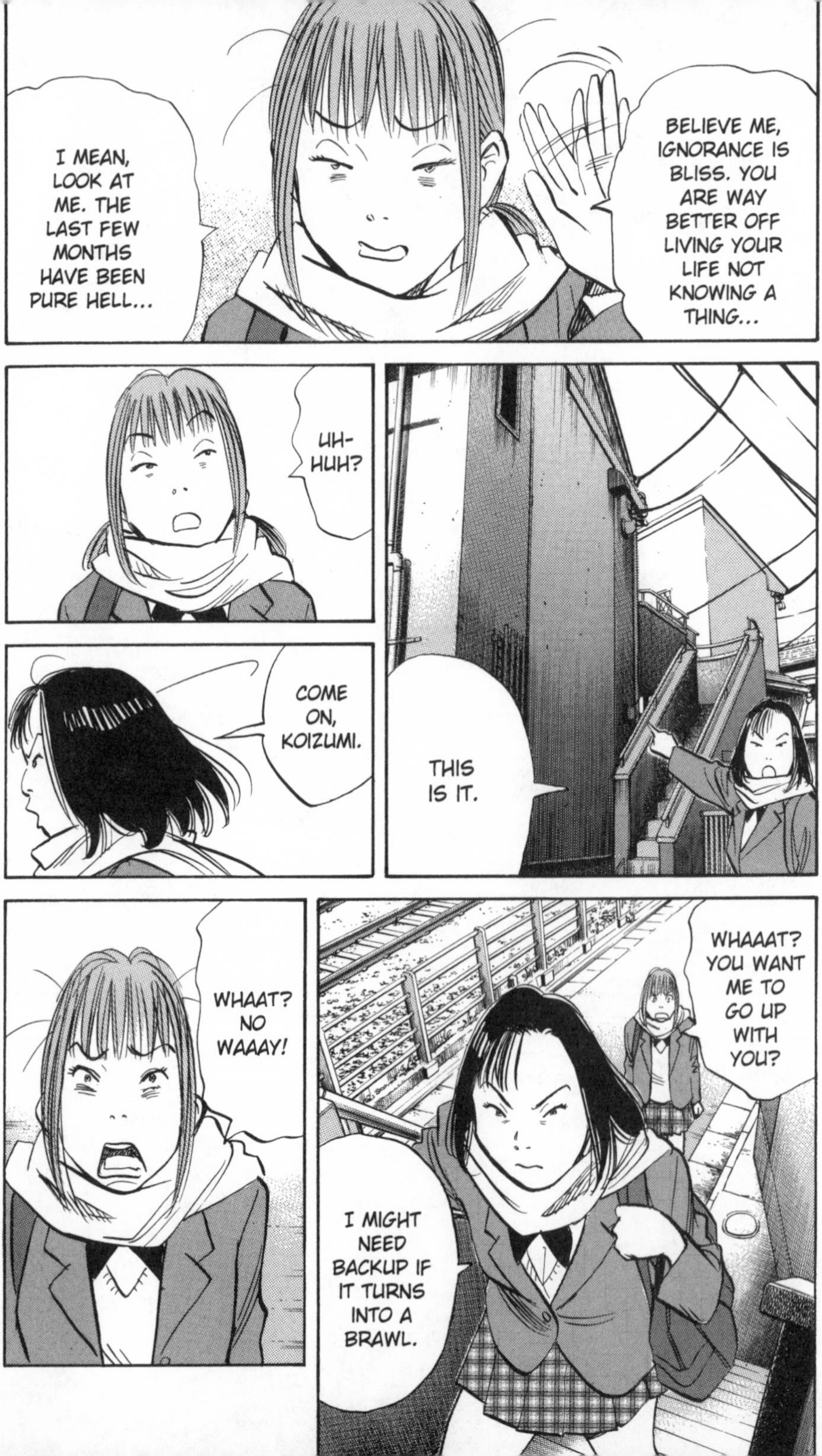
BELIEVE ME, IGNORANCE IS BLISS. YOU ARE WAY BETTER OFF LIVING YOUR LIFE NOT KNOWING A THING...
I MEAN, LOOK AT ME. THE LAST FEW MONTHS HAVE BEEN PURE HELL...
THIS IS IT.
UH-HUH?
COME ON, KOIZUMI.
WHAAAT? YOU WANT ME TO GO UP WITH YOU?
I MIGHT NEED BACKUP IF IT TURNS INTO A BRAWL.
WHAAT? NO WAAAY!

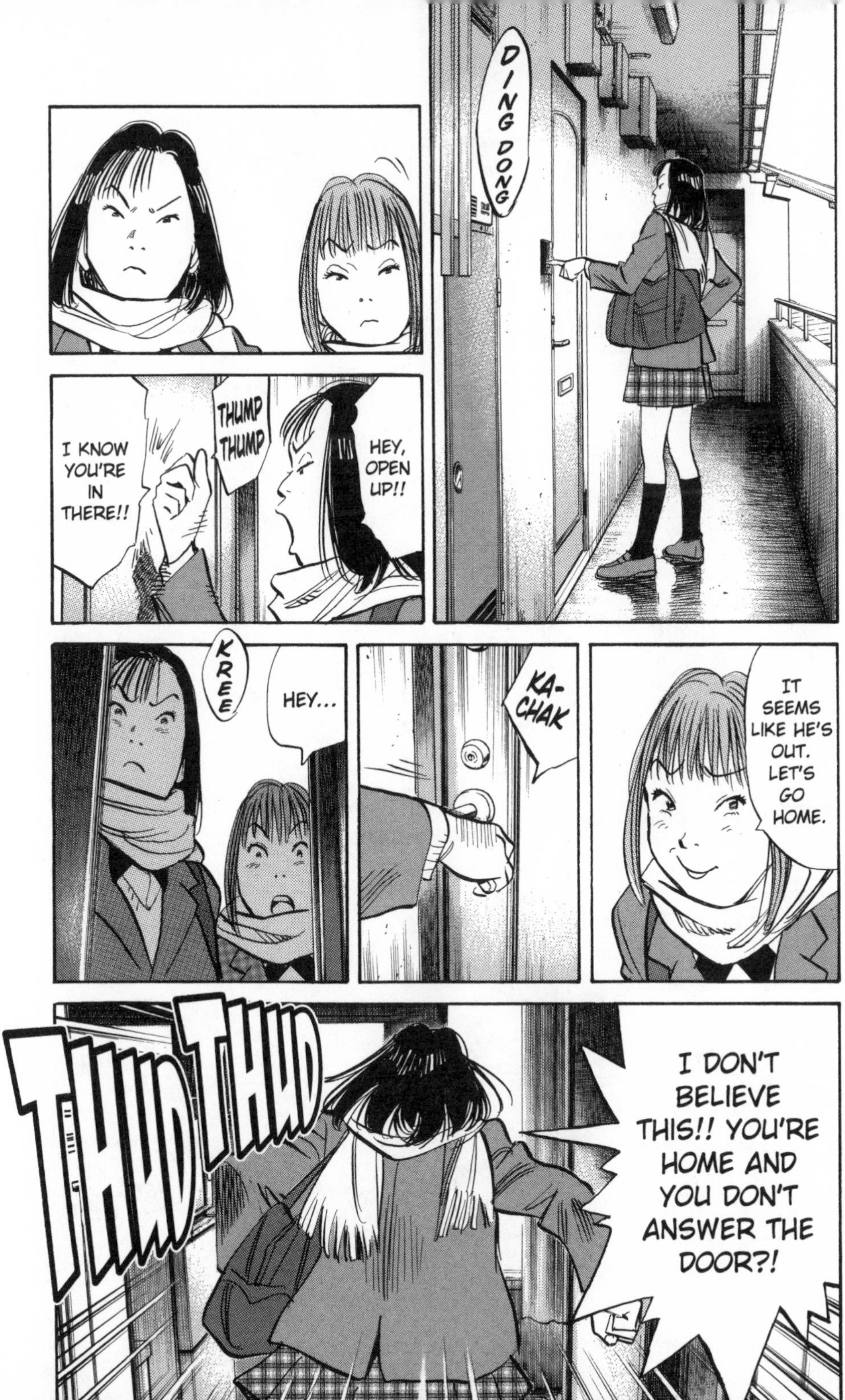
DING DONG
HEY, OPEN UP!!
THUMP THUMP
I KNOW YOU'RE IN THERE!!
IT SEEMS LIKE HE'S OUT. LET'S GO HOME.
KA-CHAK
HEY...
KREE
I DON'T BELIEVE THIS!! YOU'RE HOME AND YOU DON'T ANSWER THE DOOR?!
THUD THUD

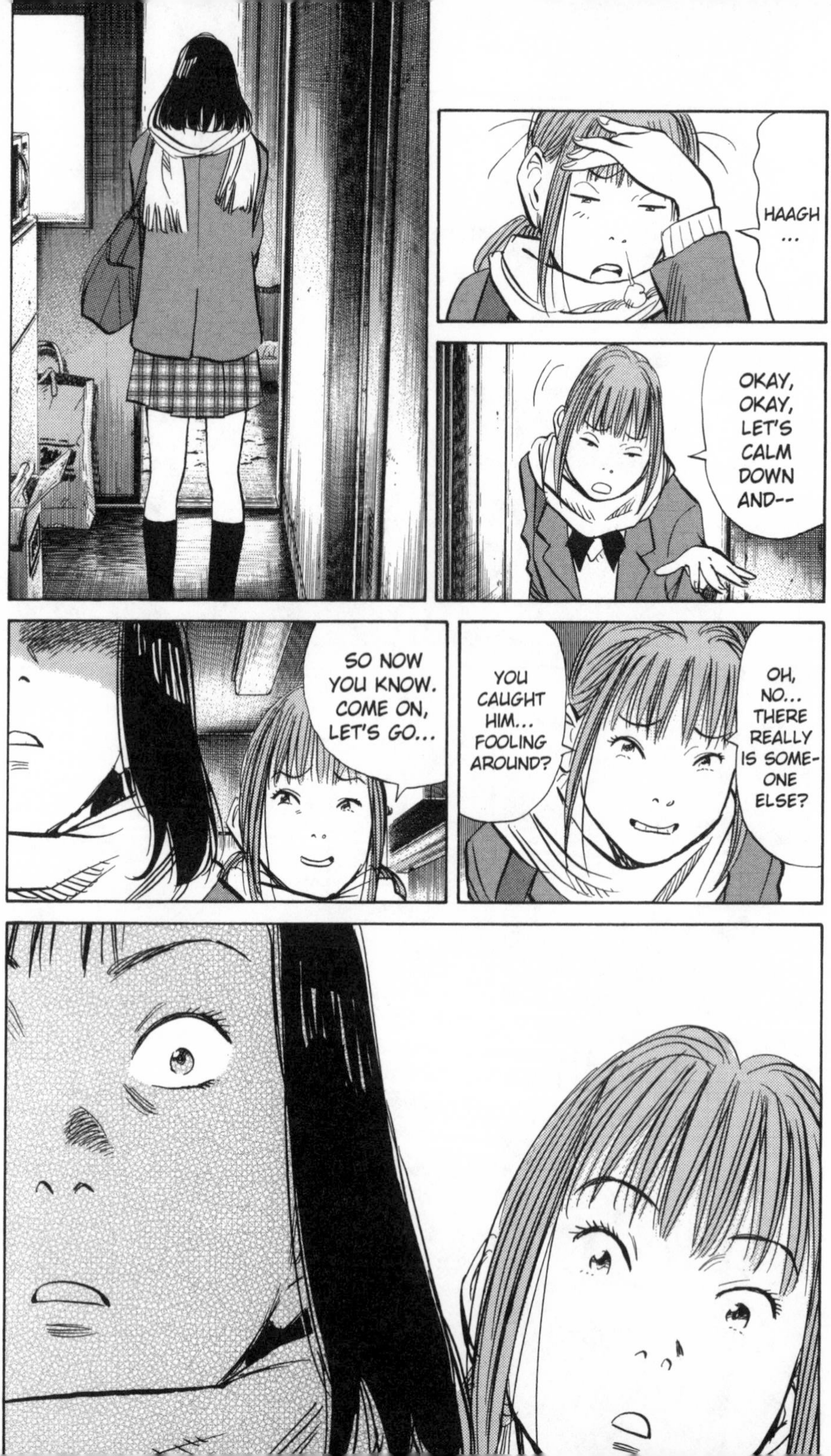
HAAGH...
OKAY, OKAY, LET'S CALM DOWN AND--
OH, NO... THERE REALLY IS SOME-ONE ELSE?
YOU CAUGHT HIM... FOOLING AROUND?
SO NOW YOU KNOW. COME ON, LET'S GO...

MY...
GOD...

URGH
!!

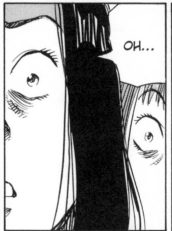

OH...

OMI-
GOD...

...AN
AMBU-
LANCE!

CALL
...

WAAGH
...

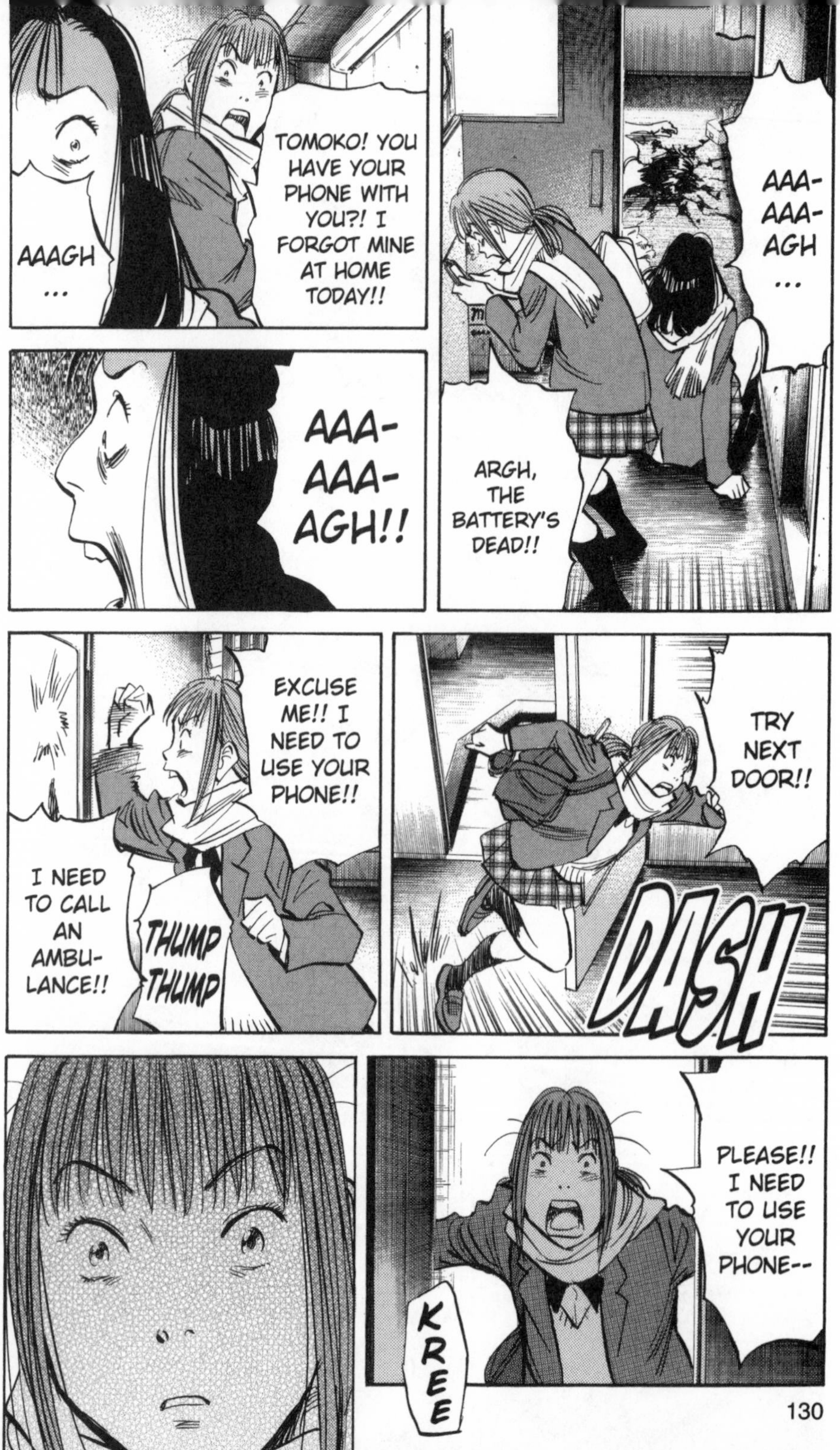
AAA-AAA-AGH ...
ARGH, THE BATTERY'S DEAD!!
TOMOKO! YOU HAVE YOUR PHONE WITH YOU?! I FORGOT MINE AT HOME TODAY!!
AAAGH ...
AAA-AAA-AGH!!
TRY NEXT DOOR!!
DASH
EXCUSE ME!! I NEED TO USE YOUR PHONE!!
I NEED TO CALL AN AMBU-LANCE!!
THUMP THUMP
PLEASE!! I NEED TO USE YOUR PHONE--
KREE

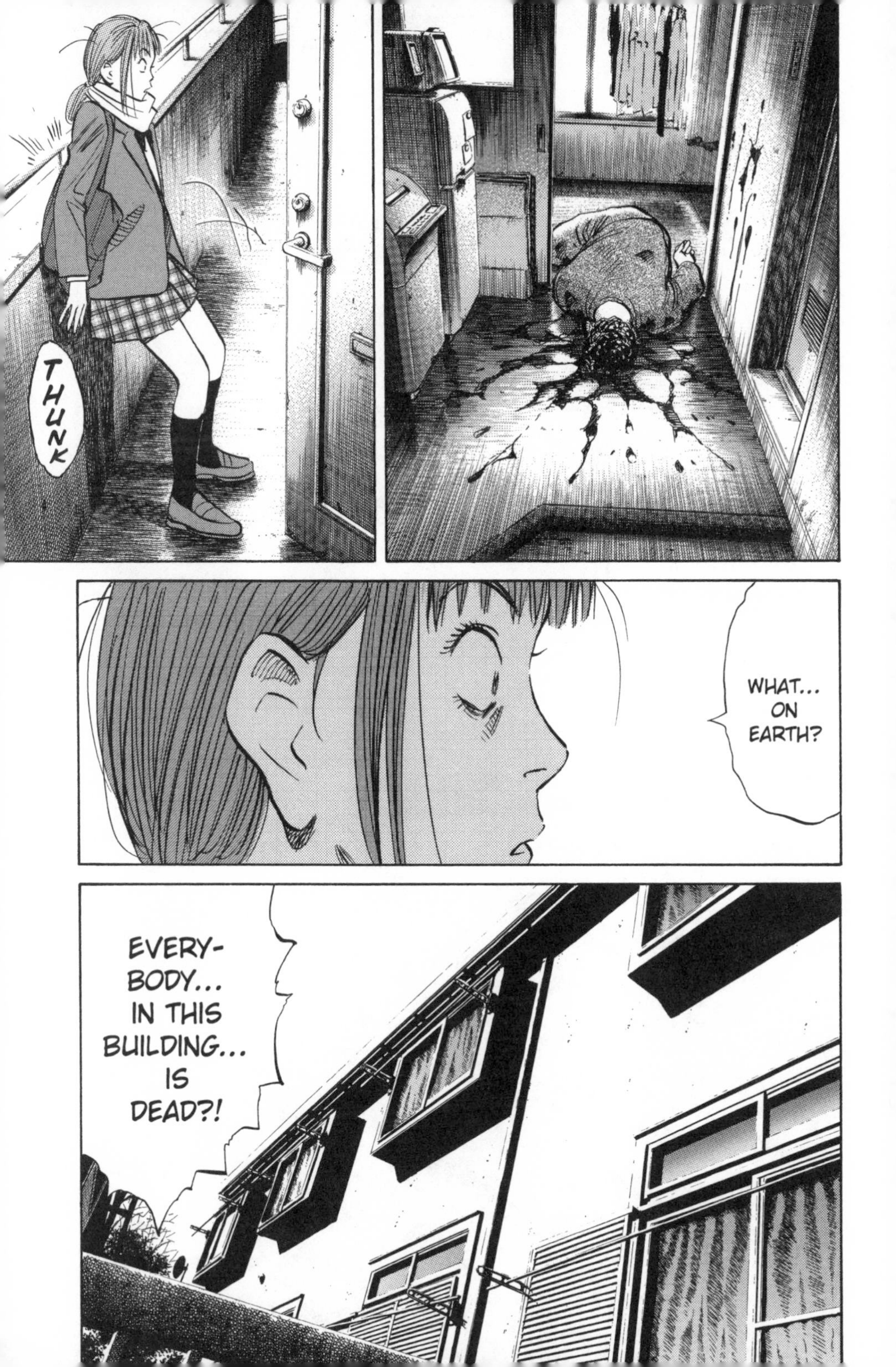
THUNK
WHAT... ON EARTH?
EVERY-BODY... IN THIS BUILDING... IS DEAD?!

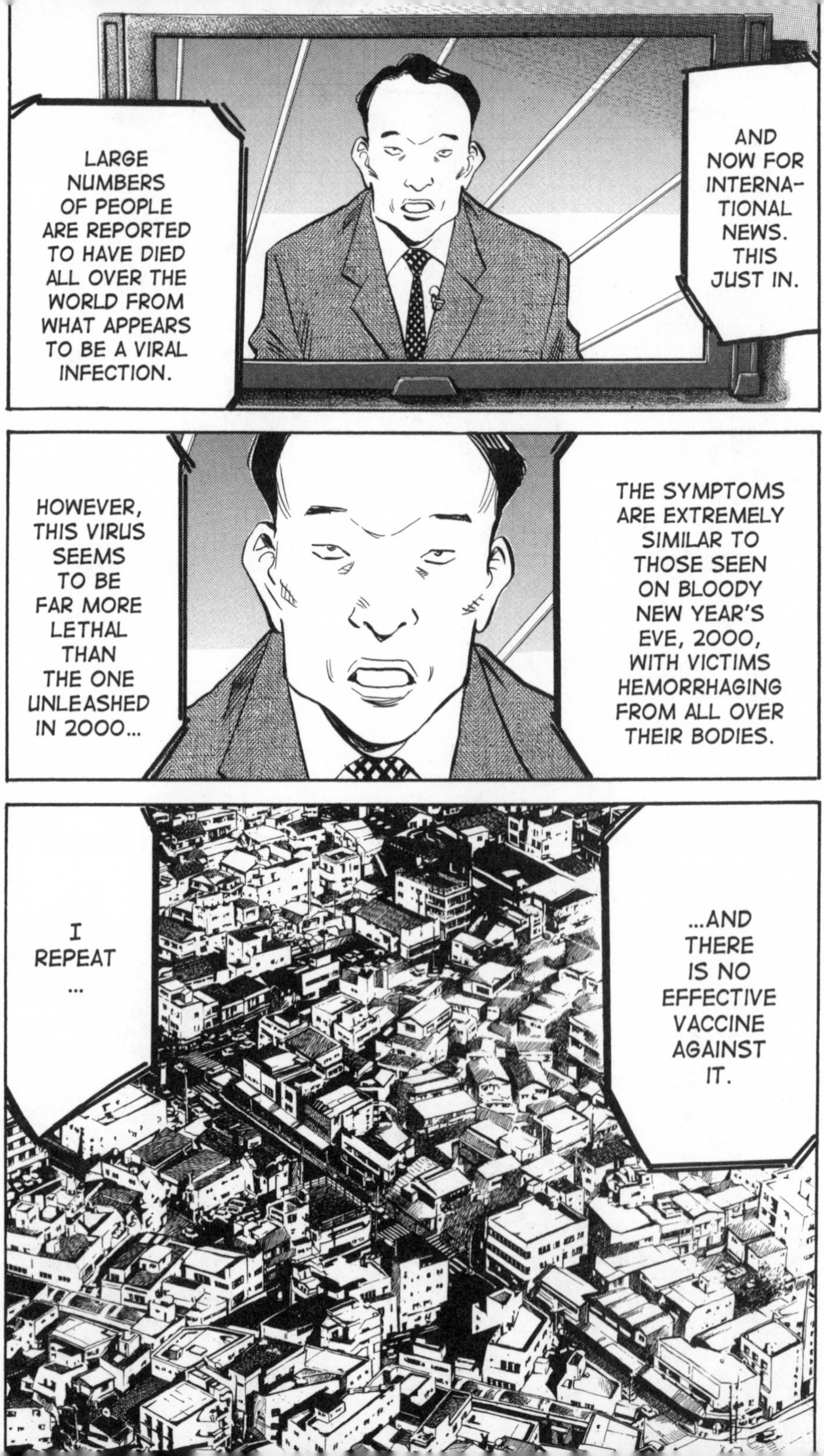
AND NOW FOR INTERNATIONAL NEWS. THIS JUST IN.
LARGE NUMBERS OF PEOPLE ARE REPORTED TO HAVE DIED ALL OVER THE WORLD FROM WHAT APPEARS TO BE A VIRAL INFECTION.
THE SYMPTOMS ARE EXTREMELY SIMILAR TO THOSE SEEN ON BLOODY NEW YEAR'S EVE, 2000, WITH VICTIMS HEMORRHAGING FROM ALL OVER THEIR BODIES.
HOWEVER, THIS VIRUS SEEMS TO BE FAR MORE LETHAL THAN THE ONE UNLEASHED IN 2000...
...AND THERE IS NO EFFECTIVE VACCINE AGAINST IT.
I REPEAT ...

Chapter 8 Revenge of Frogdoom ①

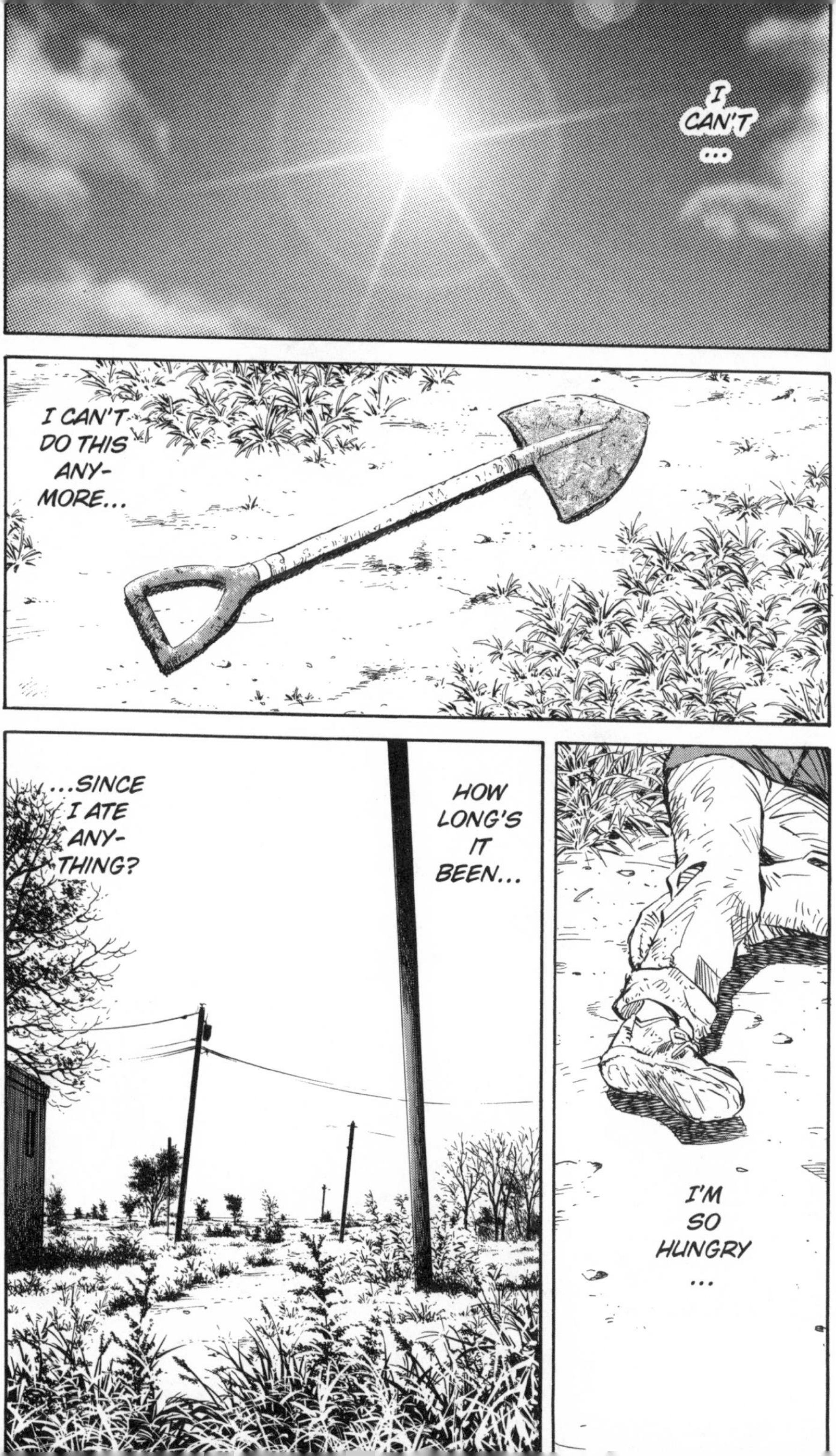
I CAN'T ...
I CAN'T DO THIS ANY-MORE...
I'M SO HUNGRY ...
HOW LONG'S IT BEEN...
...SINCE I ATE ANY-THING?

AM I...

...GOING TO DIE RIGHT HERE?

Chapter 8
Revenge of Frogdoom ①

NEW MEXICO, U.S.A

VRUM VRUM VRUM

VRUM VRUM VRUM

2015

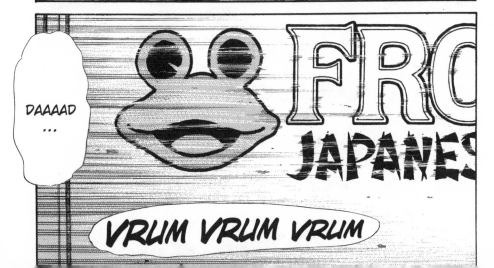

DAAAAD
...

VRUM VRUM VRUM

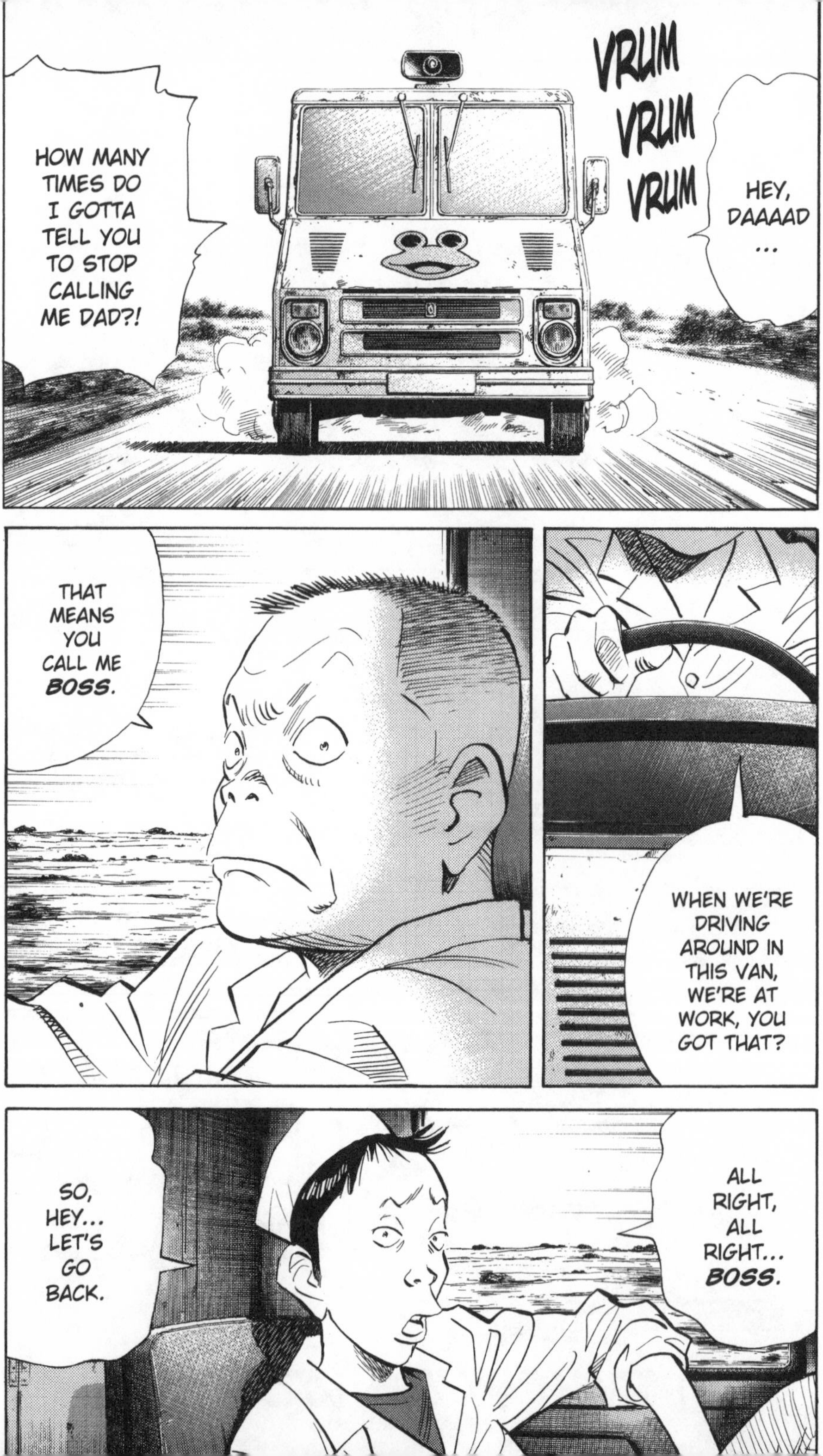
HEY, DAAAAD ...
VRUM VRUM VRUM
HOW MANY TIMES DO I GOTTA TELL YOU TO STOP CALLING ME DAD?!
WHEN WE'RE DRIVING AROUND IN THIS VAN, WE'RE AT WORK, YOU GOT THAT?
THAT MEANS YOU CALL ME BOSS.
ALL RIGHT, ALL RIGHT... BOSS.
SO, HEY... LET'S GO BACK.

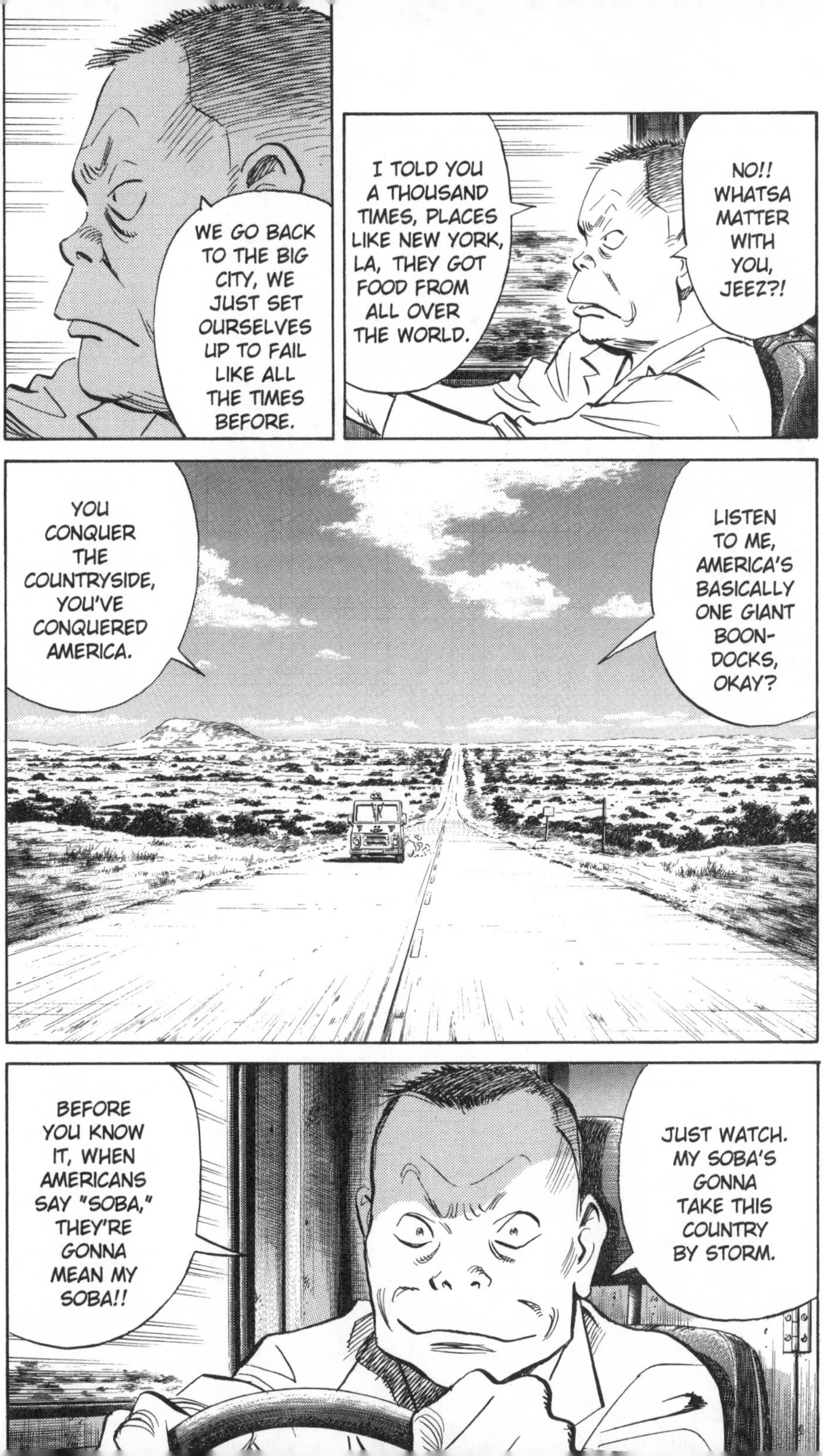
NO!! WHATSA MATTER WITH YOU, JEEZ?!
I TOLD YOU A THOUSAND TIMES, PLACES LIKE NEW YORK, LA, THEY GOT FOOD FROM ALL OVER THE WORLD.
WE GO BACK TO THE BIG CITY, WE JUST SET OURSELVES UP TO FAIL LIKE ALL THE TIMES BEFORE.
LISTEN TO ME, AMERICA'S BASICALLY ONE GIANT BOON-DOCKS, OKAY?
YOU CONQUER THE COUNTRYSIDE, YOU'VE CONQUERED AMERICA.
JUST WATCH. MY SOBA'S GONNA TAKE THIS COUNTRY BY STORM.
BEFORE YOU KNOW IT, WHEN AMERICANS SAY "SOBA," THEY'RE GONNA MEAN MY SOBA!!

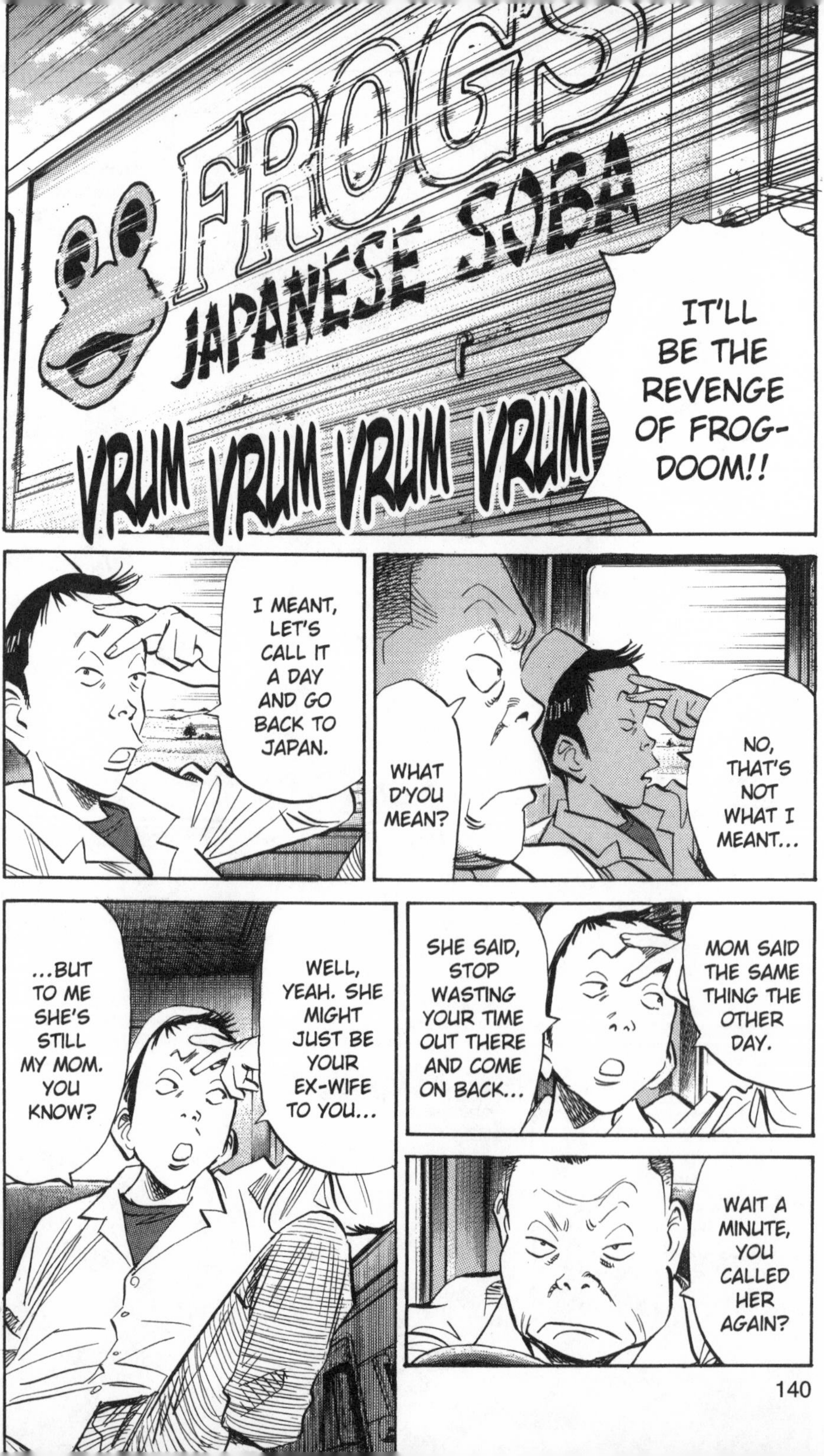
IT'LL BE THE REVENGE OF FROG-DOOM!!
FROG'S
JAPANESE SOBA
VRUM VRUM VRUM VRUM
NO, THAT'S NOT WHAT I MEANT...
WHAT D'YOU MEAN?
I MEANT, LET'S CALL IT A DAY AND GO BACK TO JAPAN.
MOM SAID THE SAME THING THE OTHER DAY.
SHE SAID, STOP WASTING YOUR TIME OUT THERE AND COME ON BACK...
WAIT A MINUTE, YOU CALLED HER AGAIN?
WELL, YEAH. SHE MIGHT JUST BE YOUR EX-WIFE TO YOU...
...BUT TO ME SHE'S STILL MY MOM. YOU KNOW?

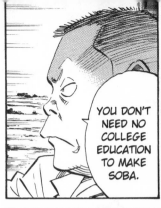

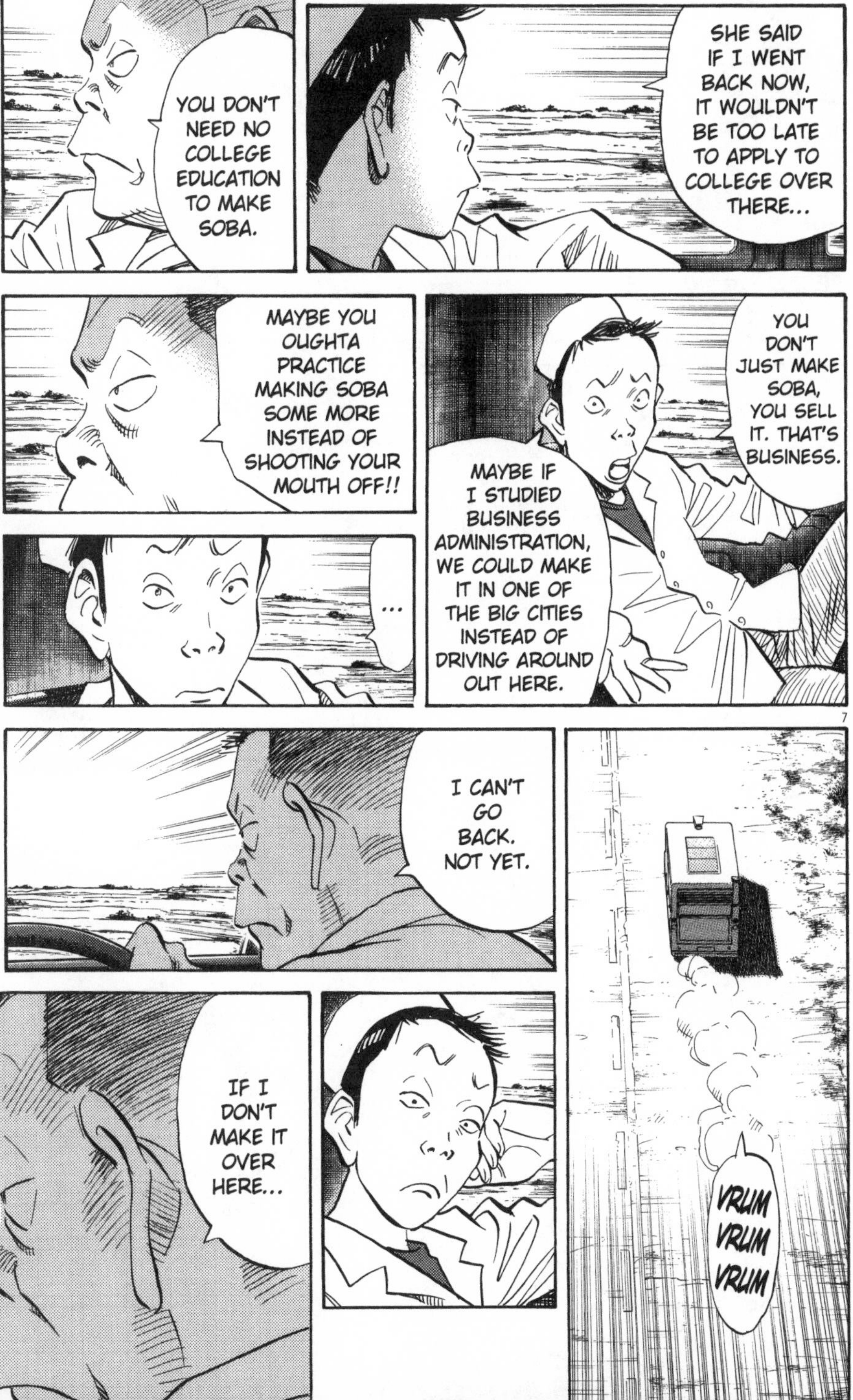
SHE SAID IF I WENT BACK NOW, IT WOULDN'T BE TOO LATE TO APPLY TO COLLEGE OVER THERE...
YOU DON'T NEED NO COLLEGE EDUCATION TO MAKE SOBA.
YOU DON'T JUST MAKE SOBA, YOU SELL IT. THAT'S BUSINESS.
MAYBE IF I STUDIED BUSINESS ADMINISTRATION, WE COULD MAKE IT IN ONE OF THE BIG CITIES INSTEAD OF DRIVING AROUND OUT HERE.
MAYBE YOU OUGHTA PRACTICE MAKING SOBA SOME MORE INSTEAD OF SHOOTING YOUR MOUTH OFF!!
...
VRUM VRUM VRUM
I CAN'T GO BACK. NOT YET.
IF I DON'T MAKE IT OVER HERE...

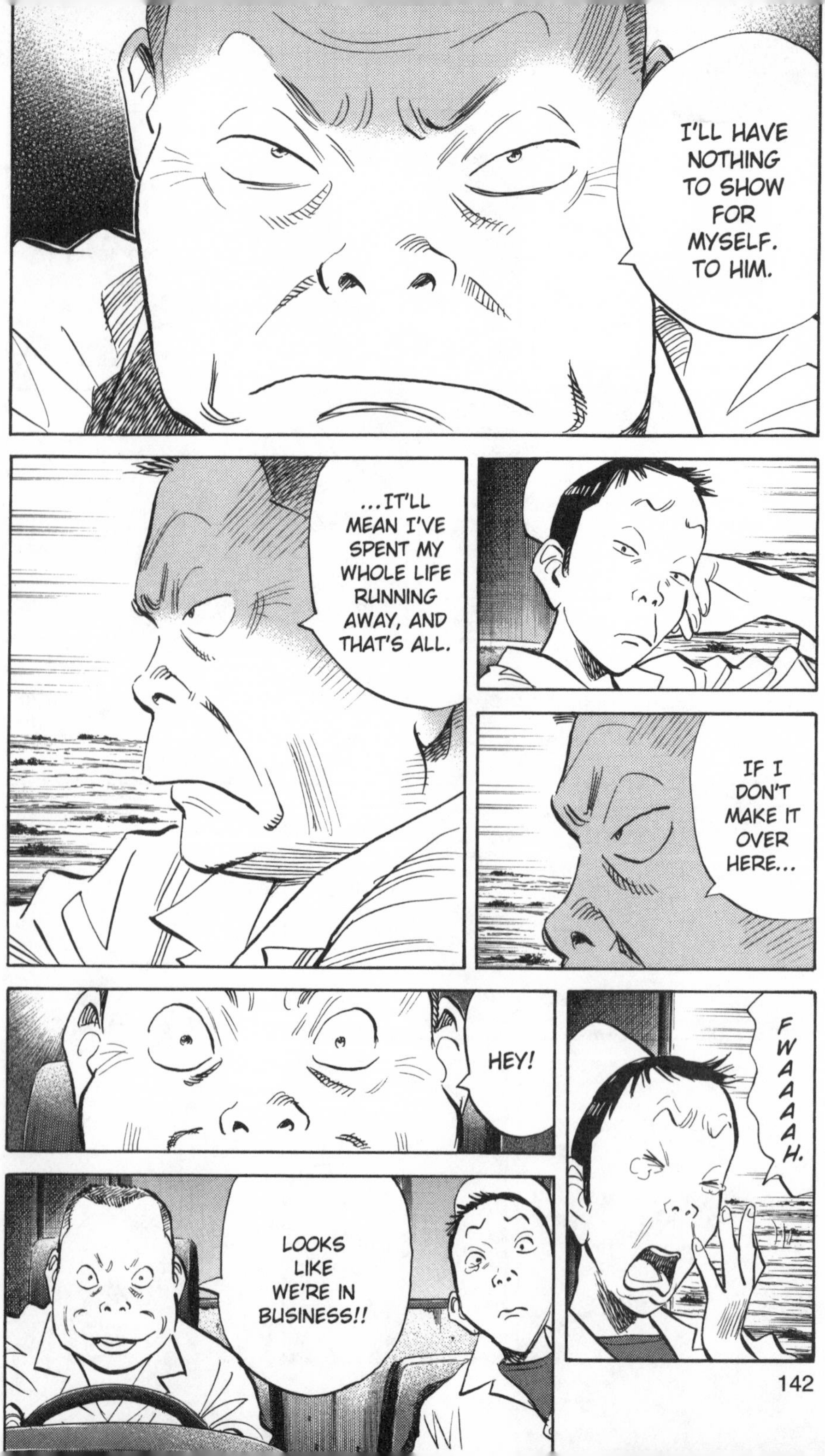

I'LL HAVE NOTHING TO SHOW FOR MYSELF. TO HIM.
IF I DON'T MAKE IT OVER HERE...
...IT'LL MEAN I'VE SPENT MY WHOLE LIFE RUNNING AWAY, AND THAT'S ALL.
FWAAAAAH.
HEY!
LOOKS LIKE WE'RE IN BUSINESS!!

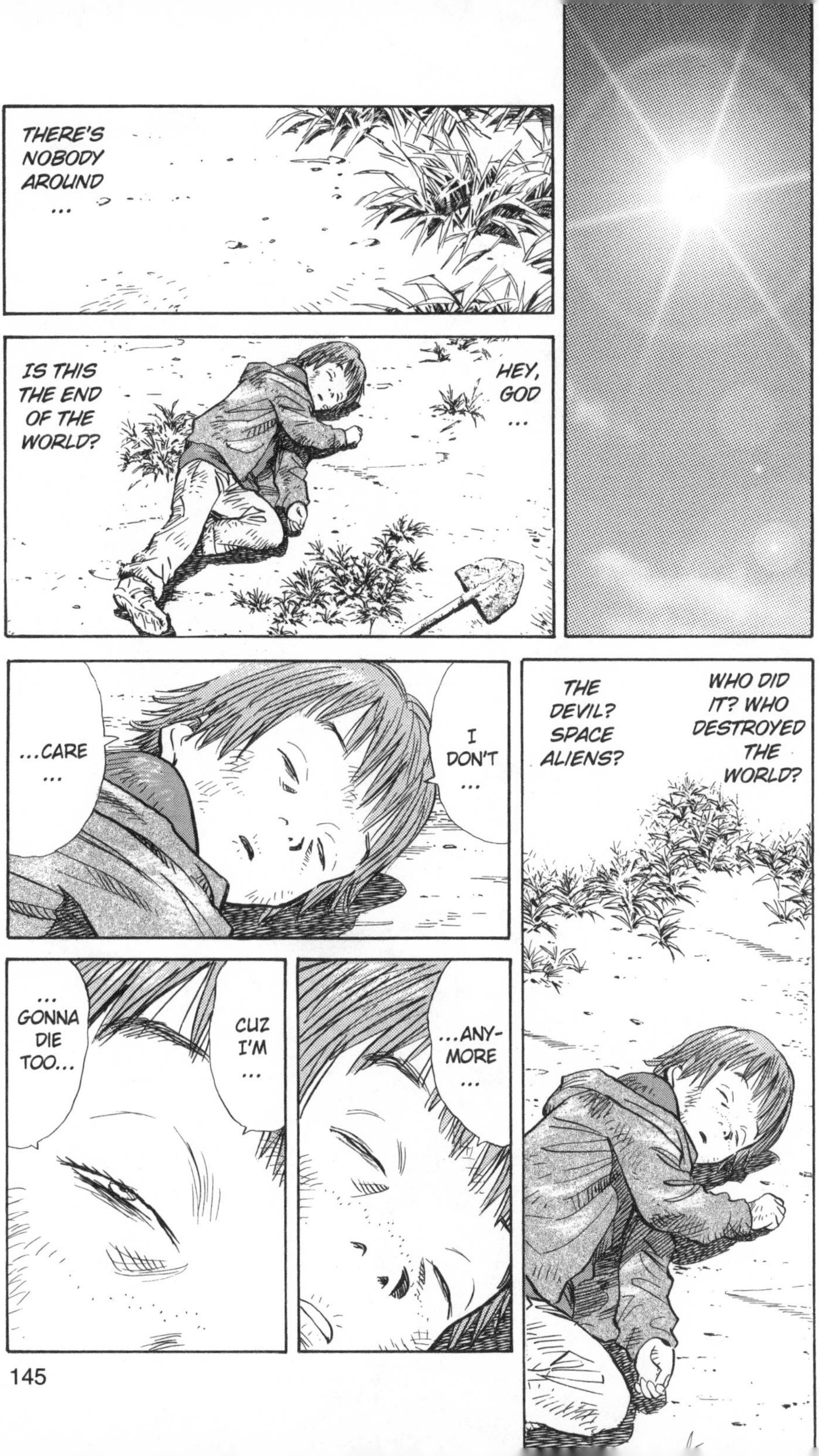
THERE'S NOBODY AROUND ...
HEY, GOD ...
IS THIS THE END OF THE WORLD?
WHO DID IT? WHO DESTROYED THE WORLD?
THE DEVIL? SPACE ALIENS?
I DON'T ...
...CARE ...
...ANY-MORE ...
CUZ I'M ...
... GONNA DIE TOO...

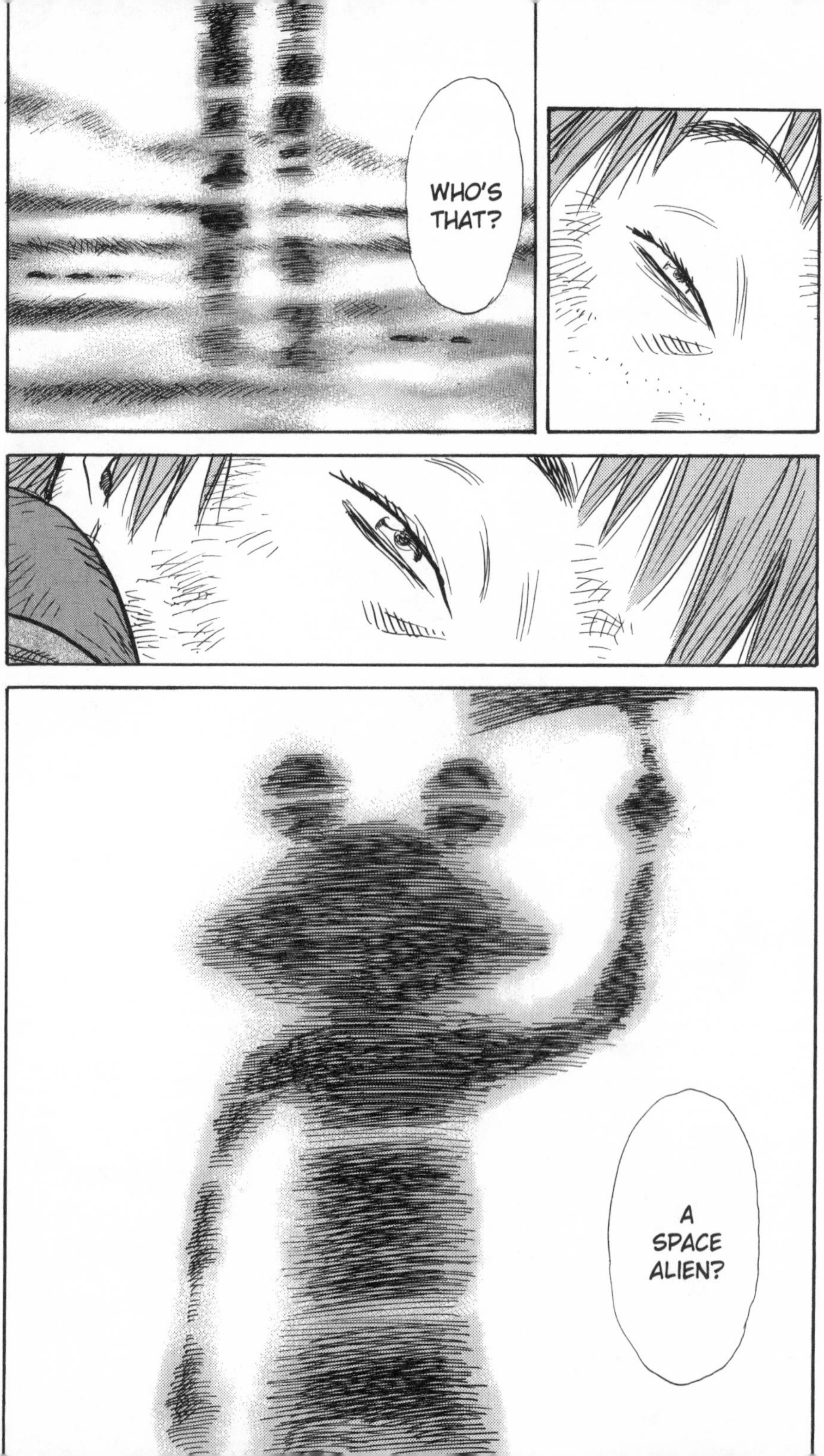
WHO'S THAT?
A SPACE ALIEN?

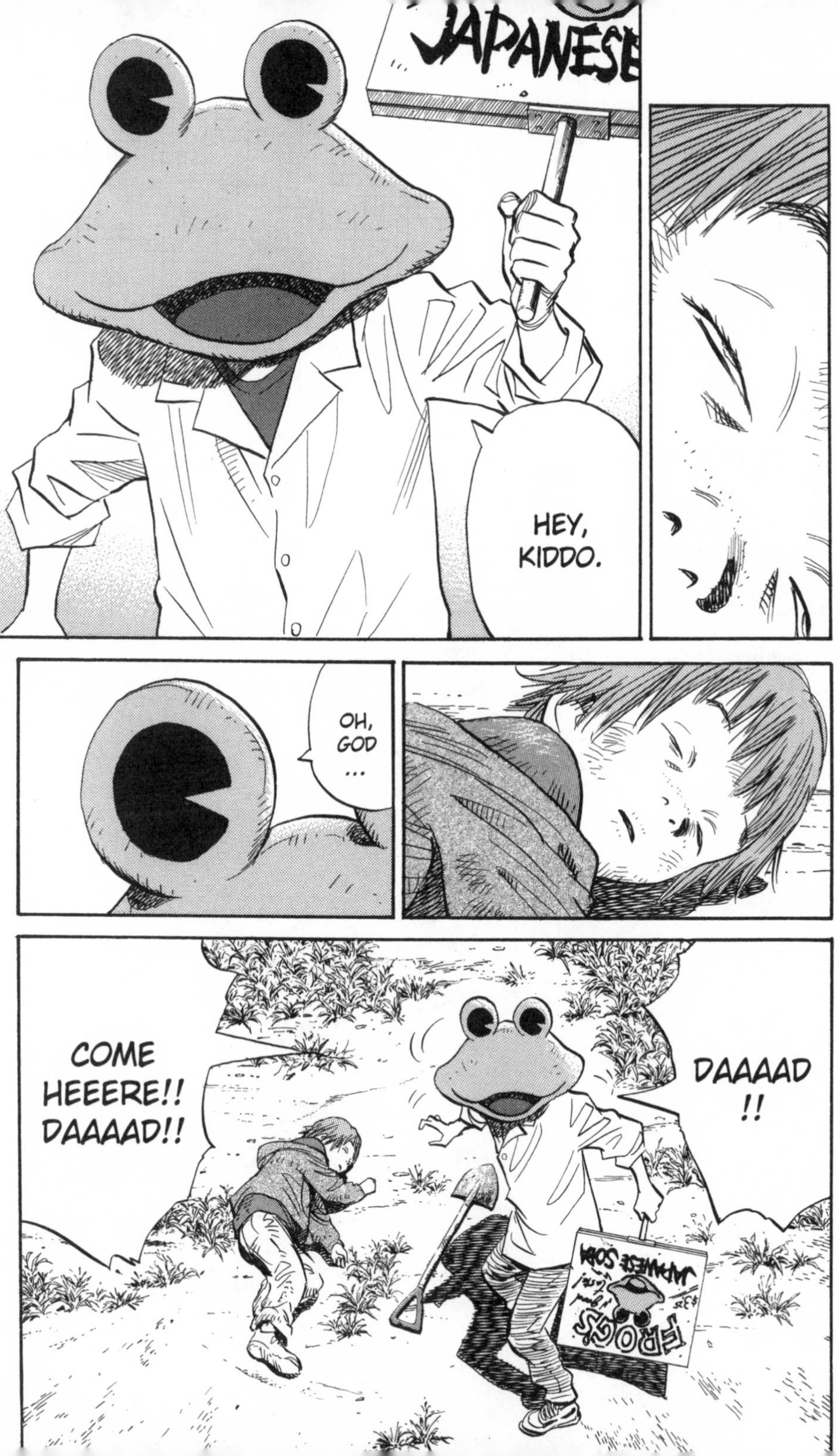
JAPANESE
HEY, KIDDO.
OH, GOD ...
DAAAAD !!
COME HEEERE!! DAAAAD!!

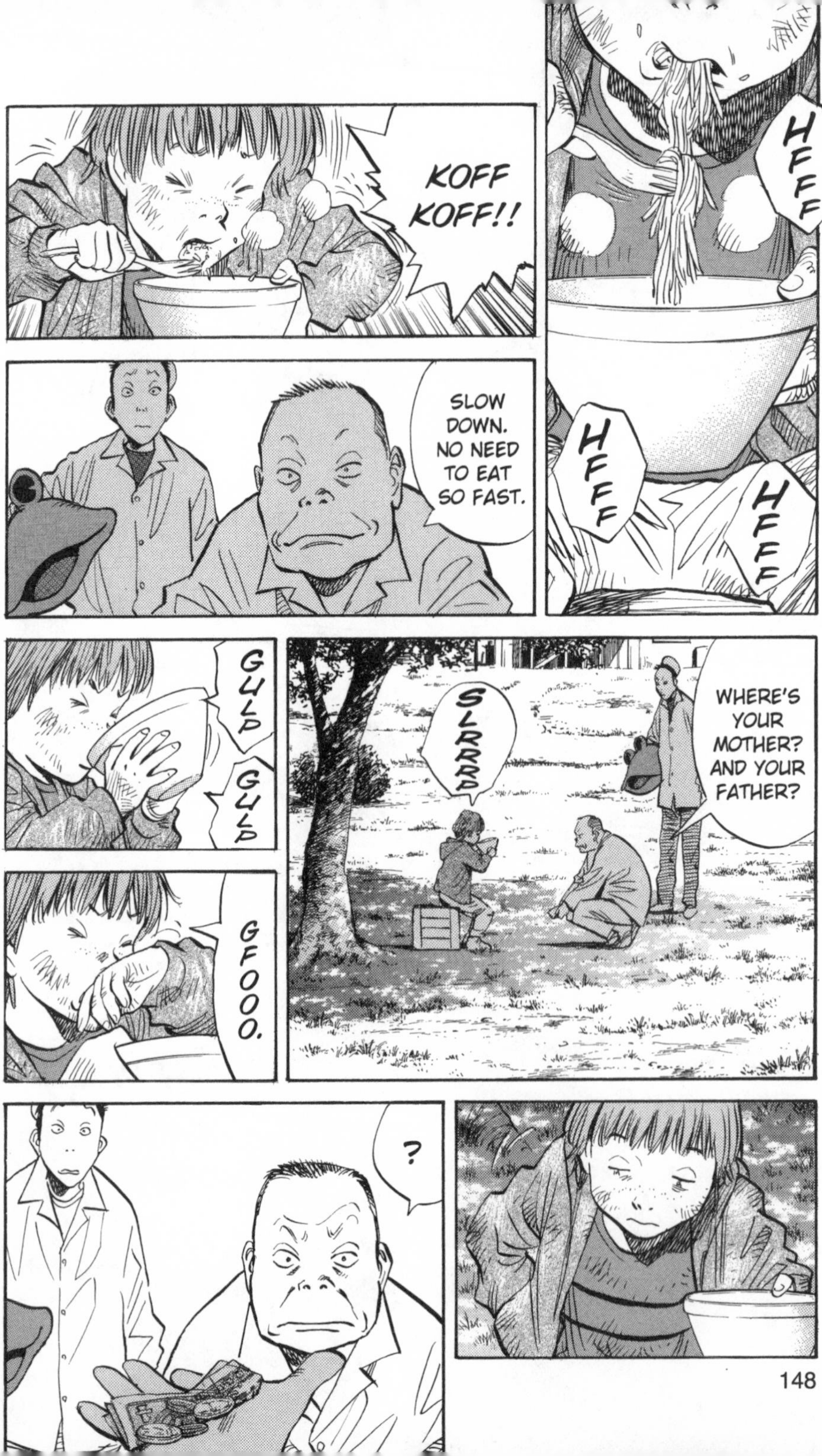
HFFF
HFFF
HFFF
KOFF KOFF!!
SLOW DOWN. NO NEED TO EAT SO FAST.
WHERE'S YOUR MOTHER? AND YOUR FATHER?
SLRRRP
GULP
GULP
GFOOO.
?

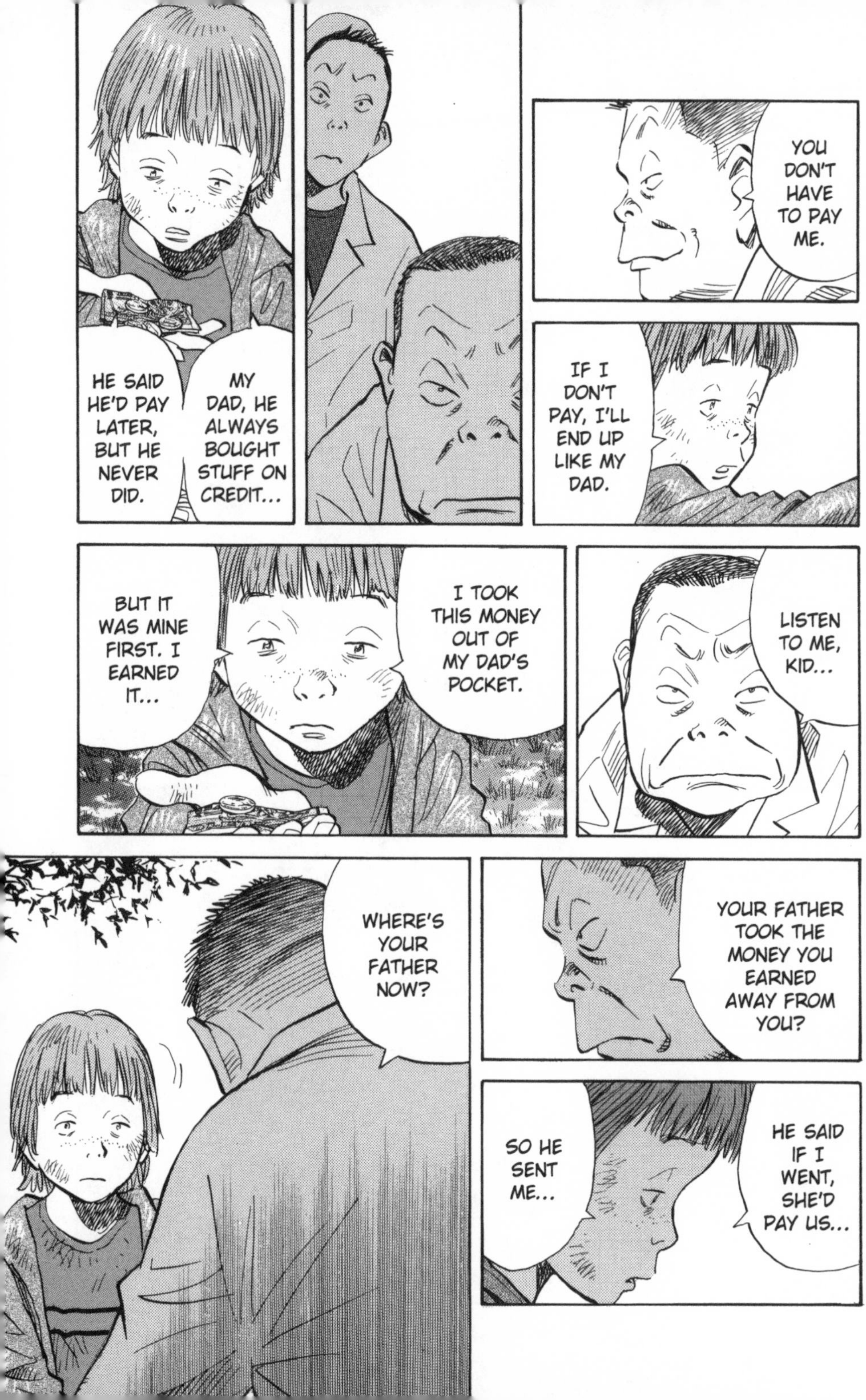
YOU DON'T HAVE TO PAY ME.
IF I DON'T PAY, I'LL END UP LIKE MY DAD.
MY DAD, HE ALWAYS BOUGHT STUFF ON CREDIT...
HE SAID HE'D PAY LATER, BUT HE NEVER DID.
LISTEN TO ME, KID...
I TOOK THIS MONEY OUT OF MY DAD'S POCKET.
BUT IT WAS MINE FIRST. I EARNED IT...
YOUR FATHER TOOK THE MONEY YOU EARNED AWAY FROM YOU?
HE SAID IF I WENT, SHE'D PAY US...
SO HE SENT ME...
WHERE'S YOUR FATHER NOW?

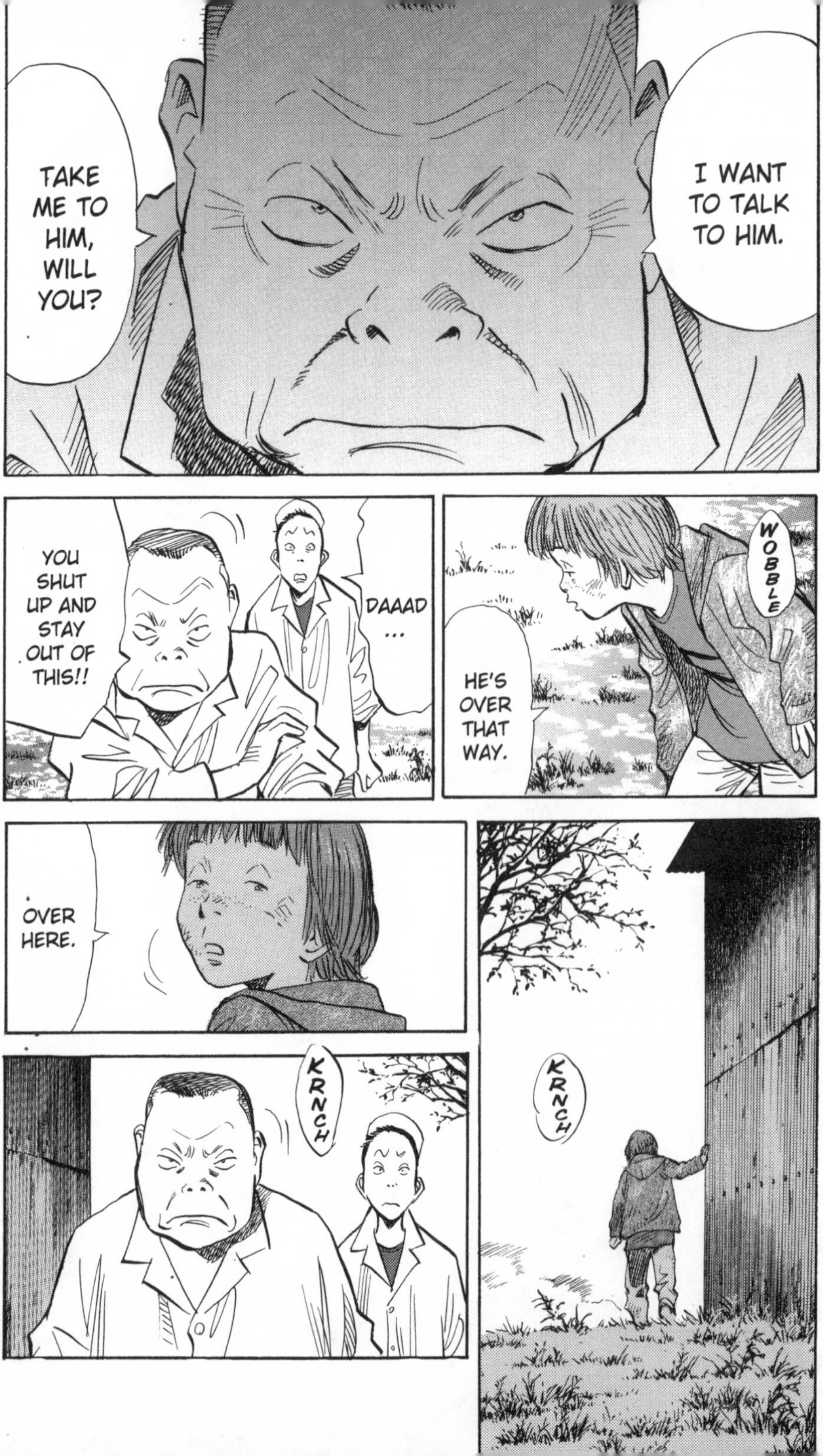
I WANT TO TALK TO HIM.
TAKE ME TO HIM, WILL YOU?
WOBBLE
HE'S OVER THAT WAY.
DAAAD...
YOU SHUT UP AND STAY OUT OF THIS!!
KRNCH
OVER HERE.
KRNCH

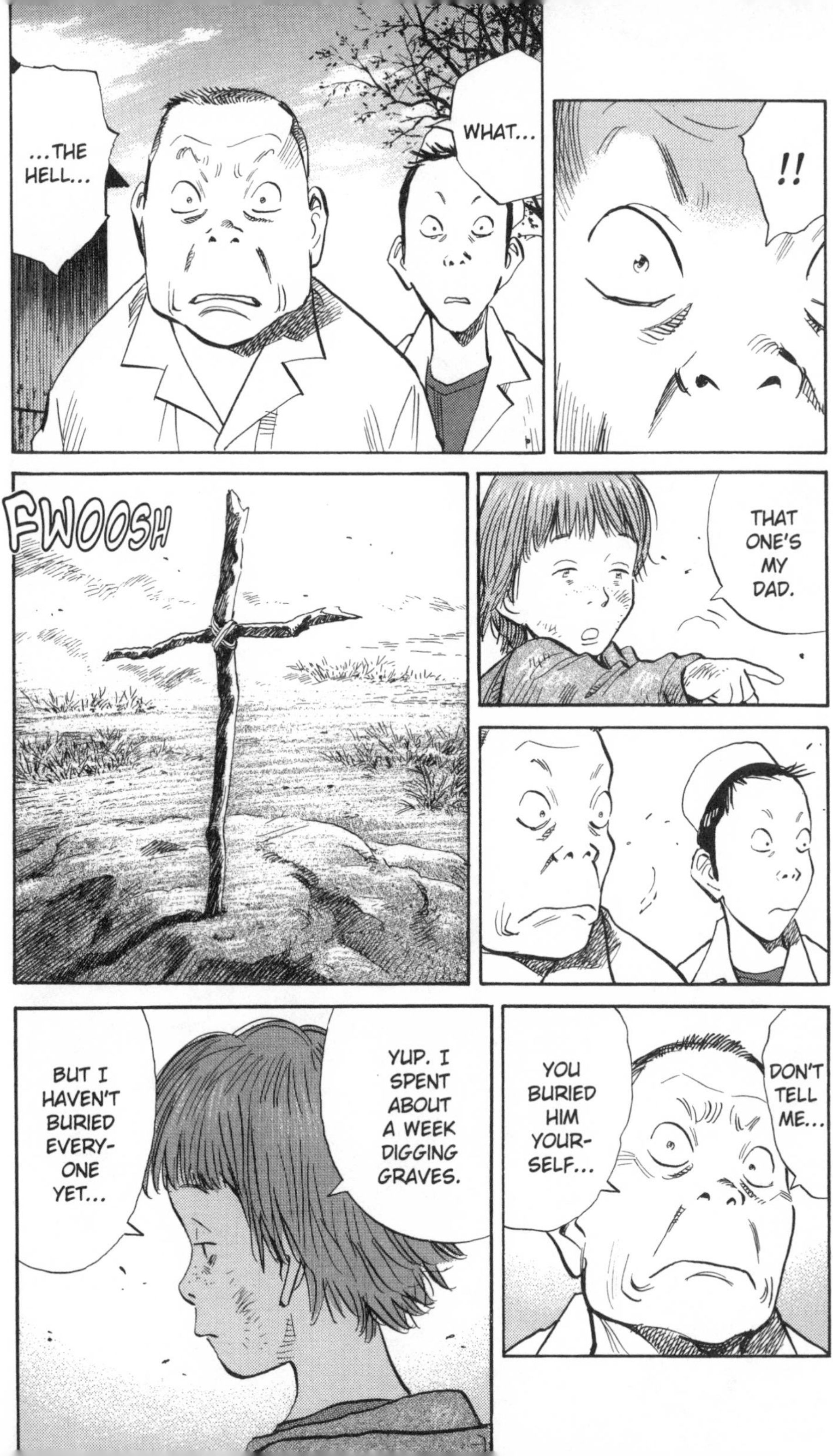
!!
WHAT...
...THE HELL...
THAT ONE'S MY DAD.
FWOOSH
DON'T TELL ME...
YOU BURIED HIM YOURSELF...
YUP. I SPENT ABOUT A WEEK DIGGING GRAVES.
BUT I HAVEN'T BURIED EVERYONE YET...

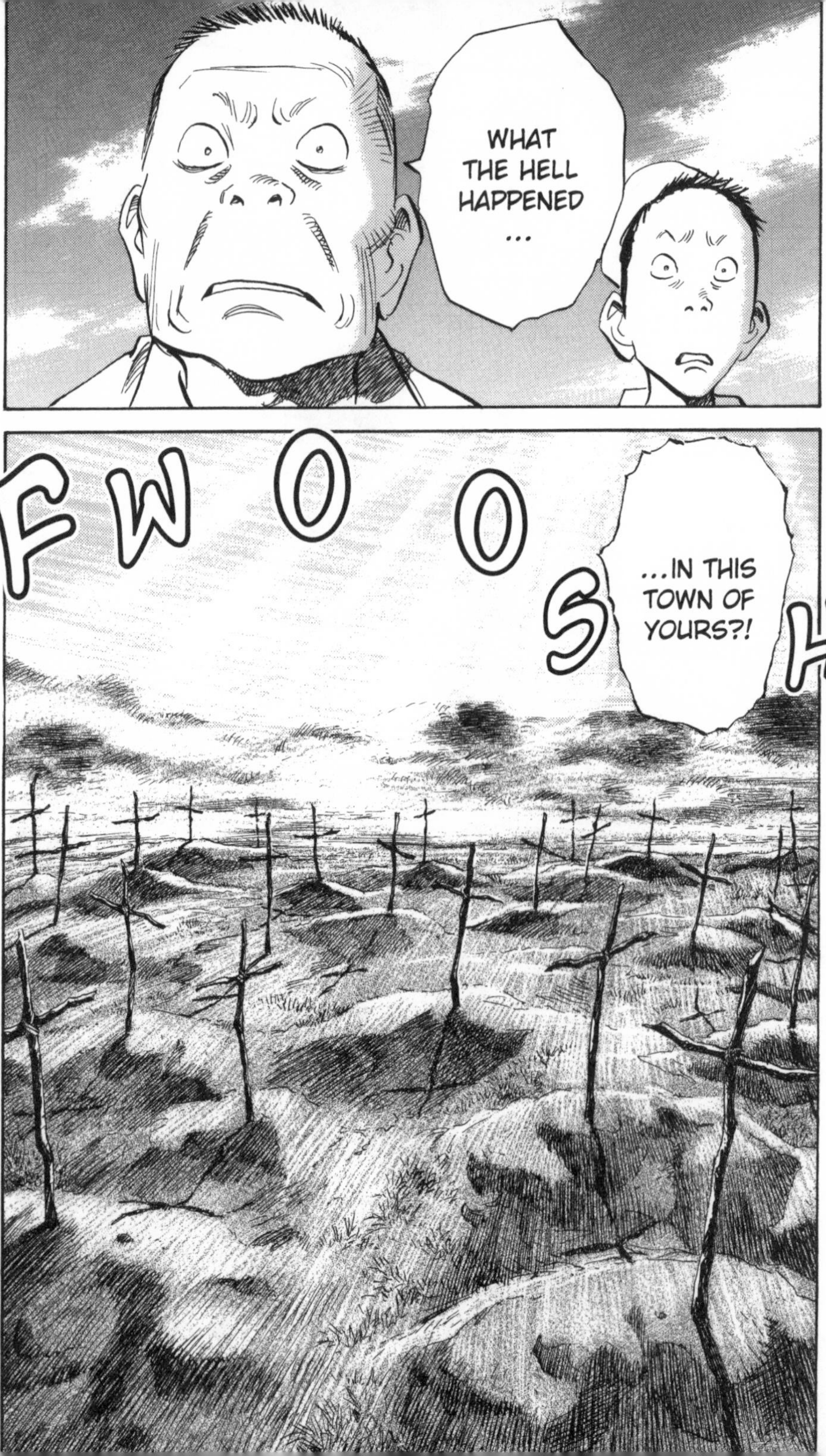
WHAT THE HELL HAPPENED ...
...IN THIS TOWN OF YOURS?!
FWOOSH

Chapter 9 Revenge of Frogdoom②

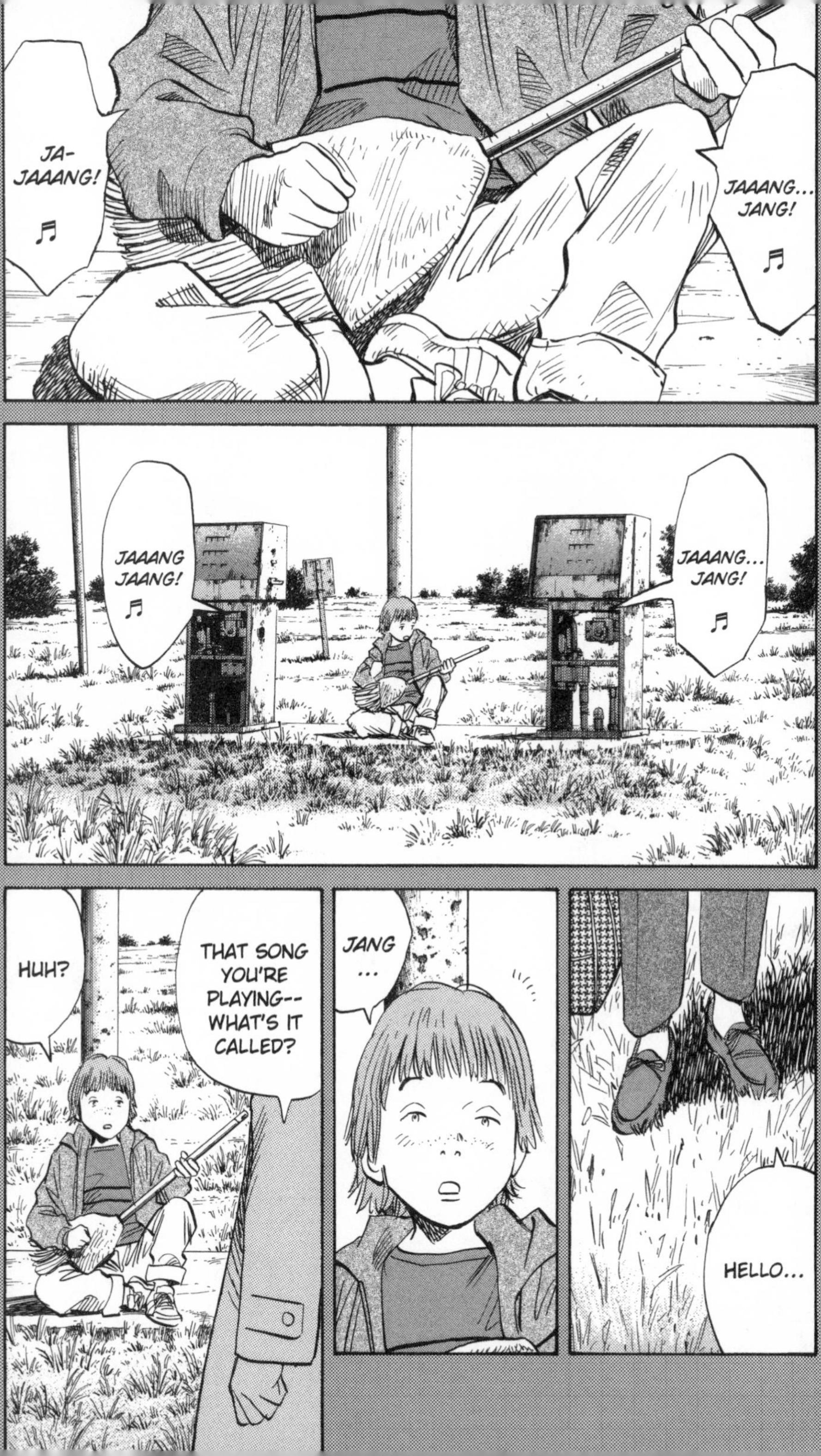
JAAANG... JANG! ♬
JA-JAAANG! ♬
JAAANG... JANG! ♬
JAAANG JAANG! ♬
HELLO...
JANG ...
THAT SONG YOU'RE PLAYING-- WHAT'S IT CALLED?
HUH?

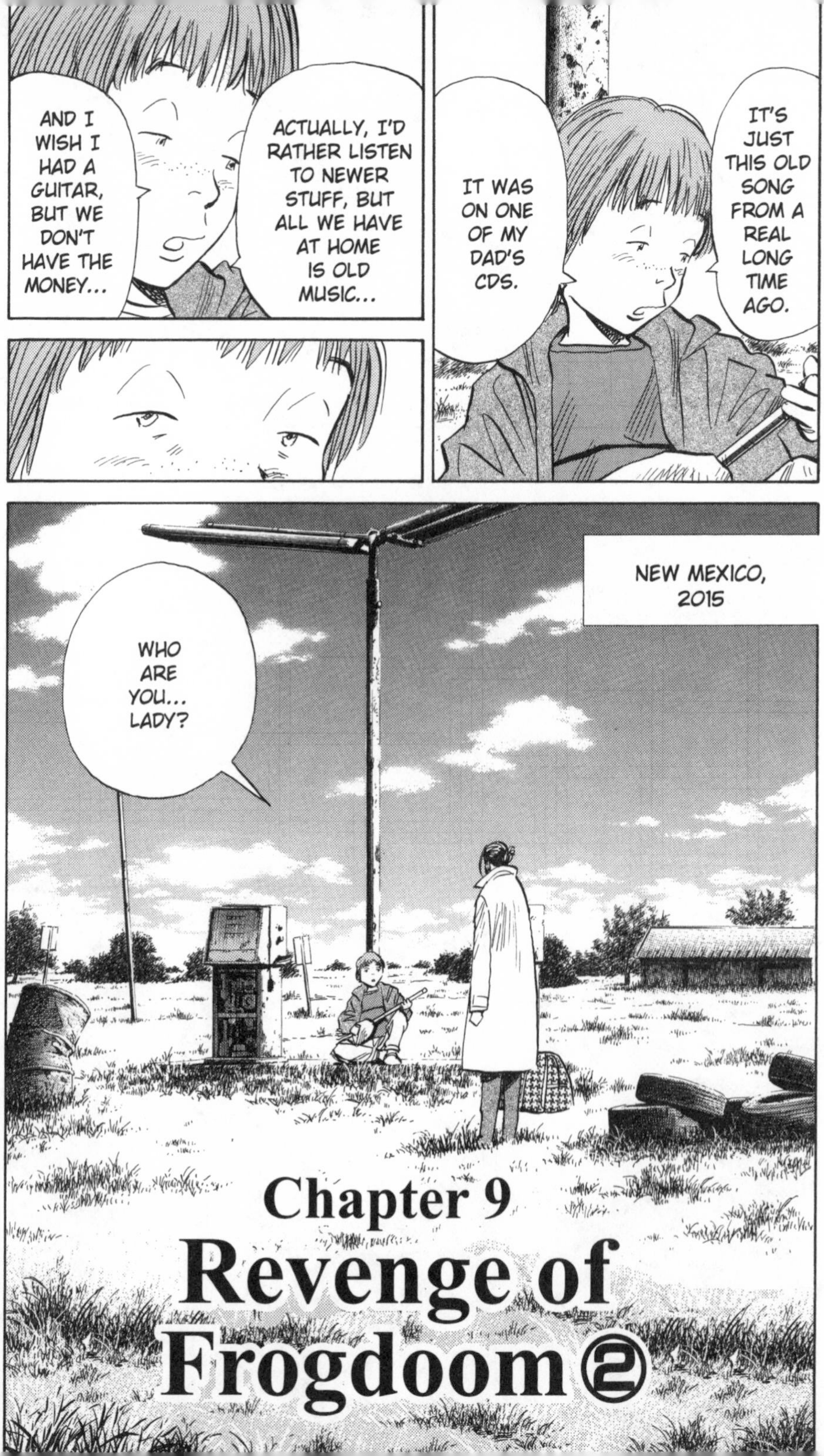
IT'S JUST THIS OLD SONG FROM A REAL LONG TIME AGO.
IT WAS ON ONE OF MY DAD'S CDS.
ACTUALLY, I'D RATHER LISTEN TO NEWER STUFF, BUT ALL WE HAVE AT HOME IS OLD MUSIC...
AND I WISH I HAD A GUITAR, BUT WE DON'T HAVE THE MONEY...
NEW MEXICO, 2015
WHO ARE YOU... LADY?
Chapter 9
Revenge of Frogdoom ②

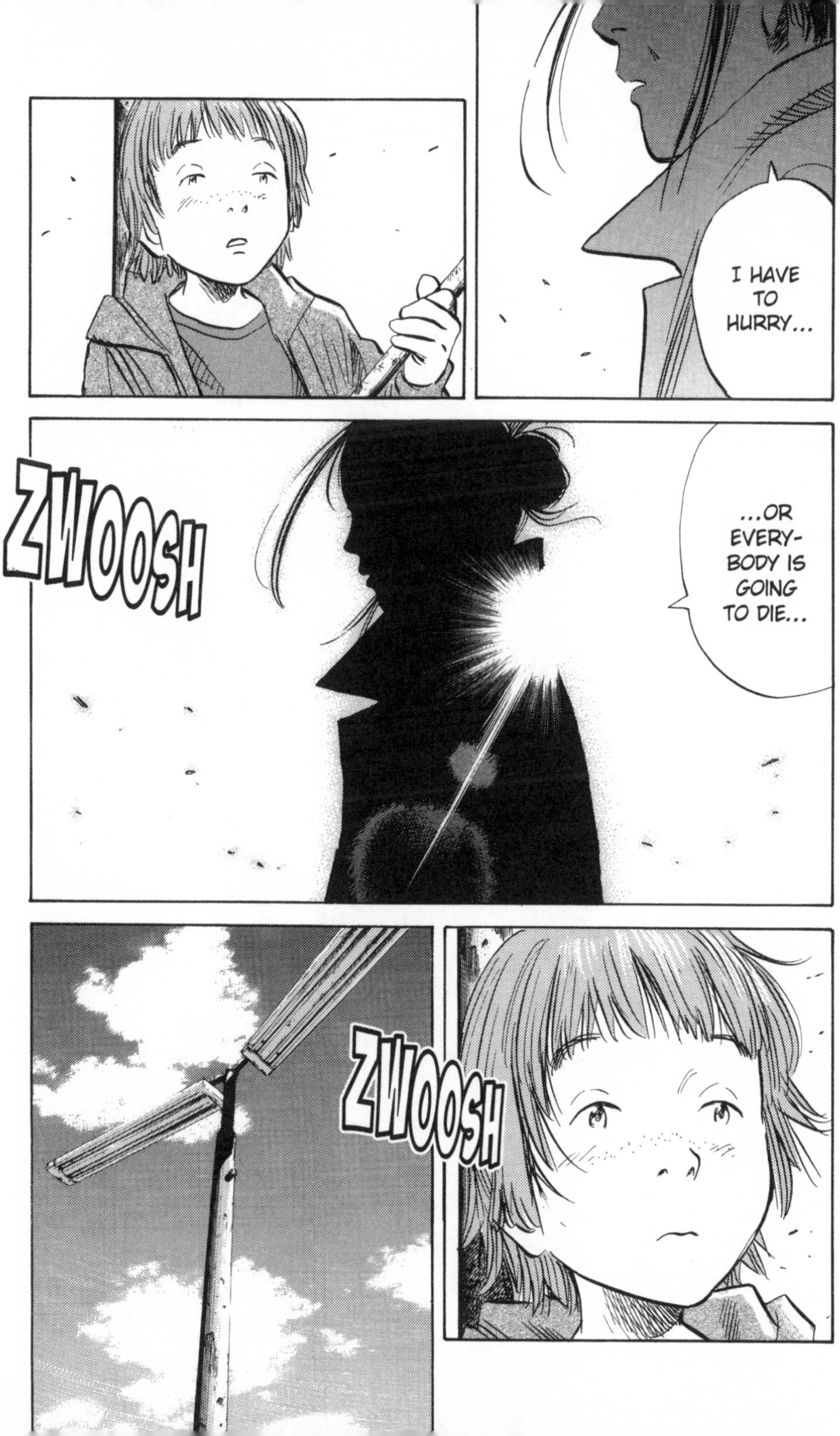
I HAVE TO HURRY...
...OR EVERY-BODY IS GOING TO DIE...
ZWOOSH
ZWOOSH

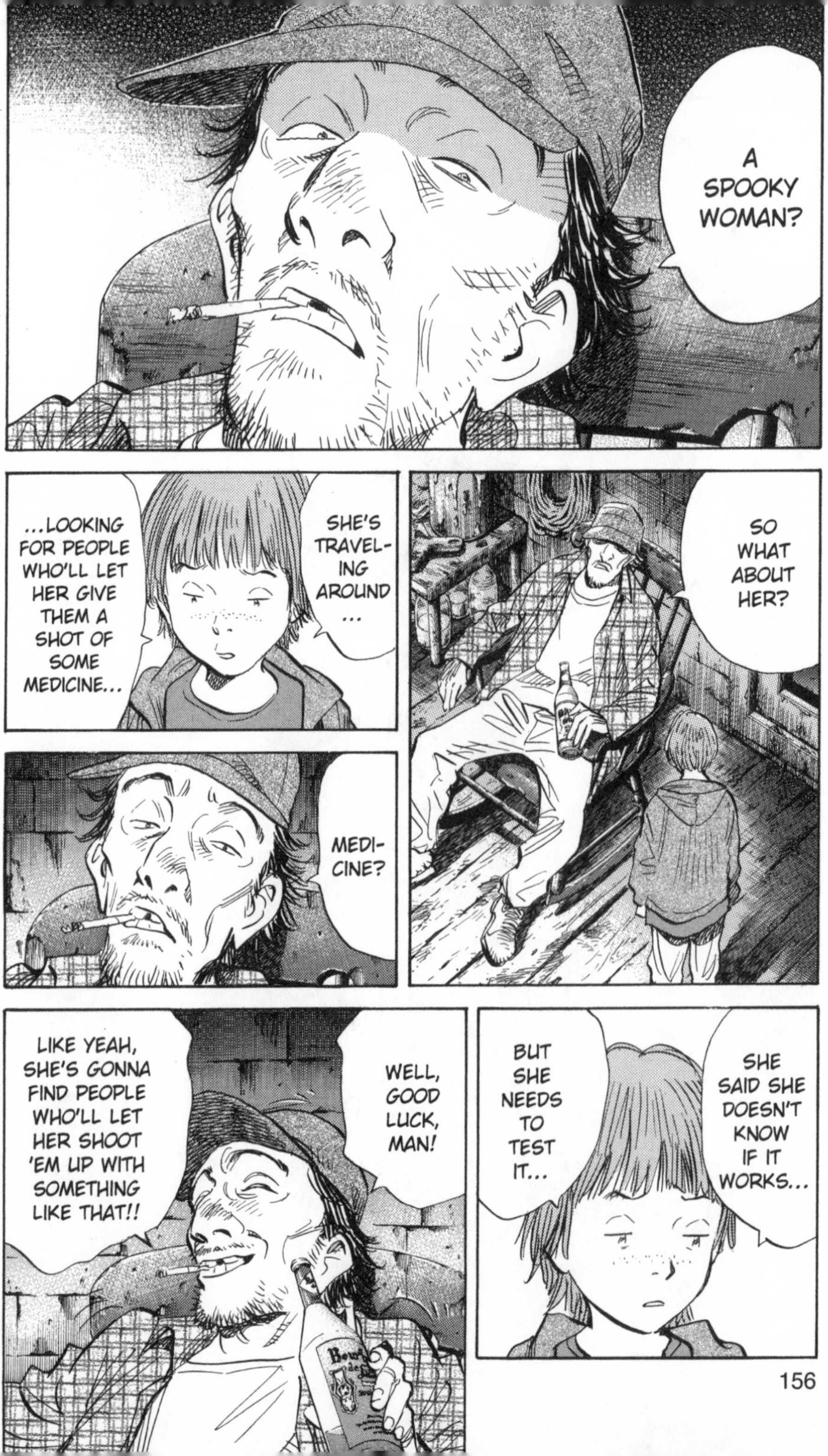
A SPOOKY WOMAN?
SO WHAT ABOUT HER?
SHE'S TRAVELING AROUND...
...LOOKING FOR PEOPLE WHO'LL LET HER GIVE THEM A SHOT OF SOME MEDICINE...
MEDICINE?
SHE SAID SHE DOESN'T KNOW IF IT WORKS...
BUT SHE NEEDS TO TEST IT...
WELL, GOOD LUCK, MAN!
LIKE YEAH, SHE'S GONNA FIND PEOPLE WHO'LL LET HER SHOOT 'EM UP WITH SOMETHING LIKE THAT!!

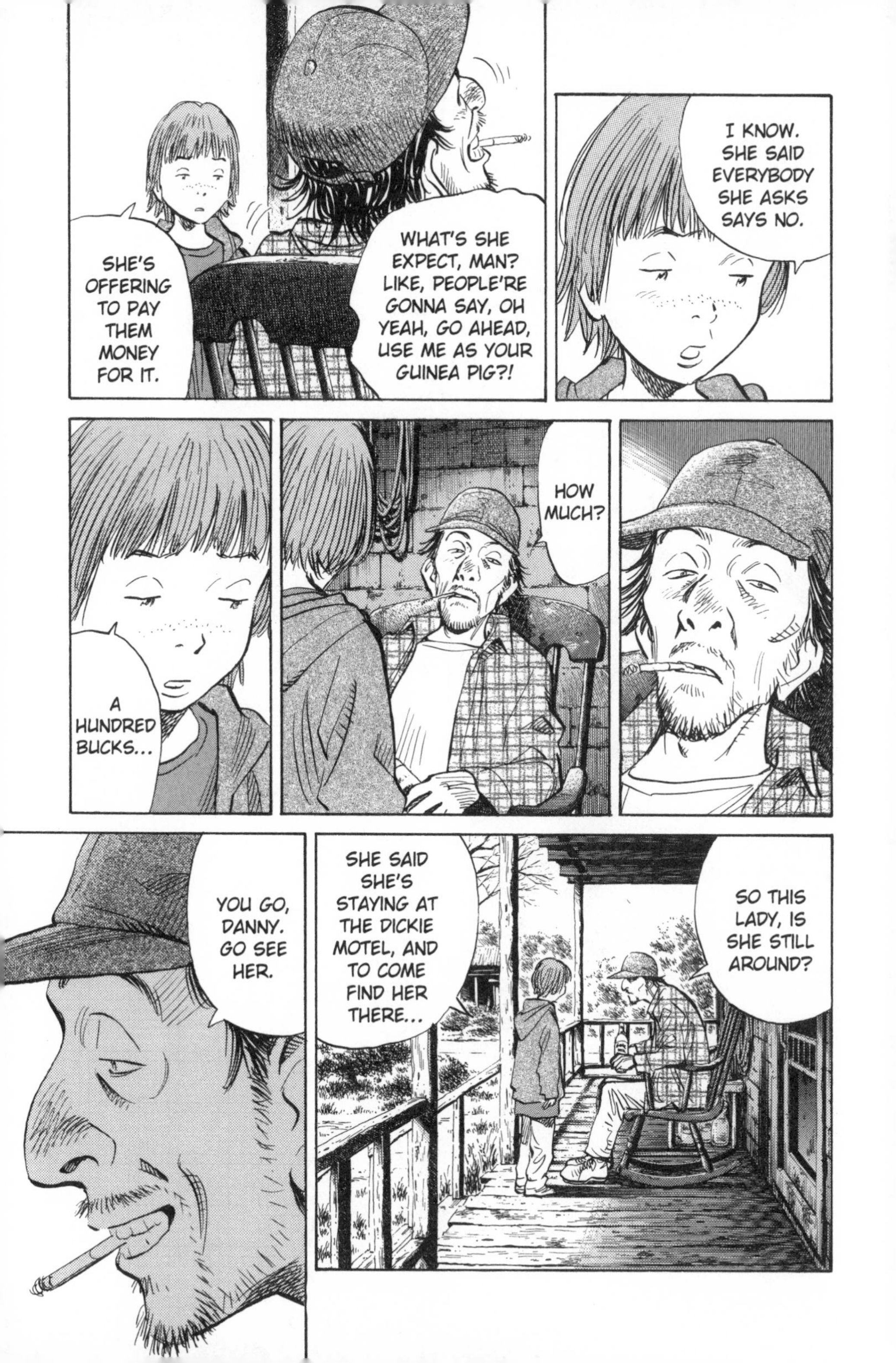
I KNOW. SHE SAID EVERYBODY SHE ASKS SAYS NO.
WHAT'S SHE EXPECT, MAN? LIKE, PEOPLE'RE GONNA SAY, OH YEAH, GO AHEAD, USE ME AS YOUR GUINEA PIG?!
SHE'S OFFERING TO PAY THEM MONEY FOR IT.
HOW MUCH?
A HUNDRED BUCKS...
SO THIS LADY, IS SHE STILL AROUND?
SHE SAID SHE'S STAYING AT THE DICKIE MOTEL, AND TO COME FIND HER THERE...
YOU GO, DANNY. GO SEE HER.

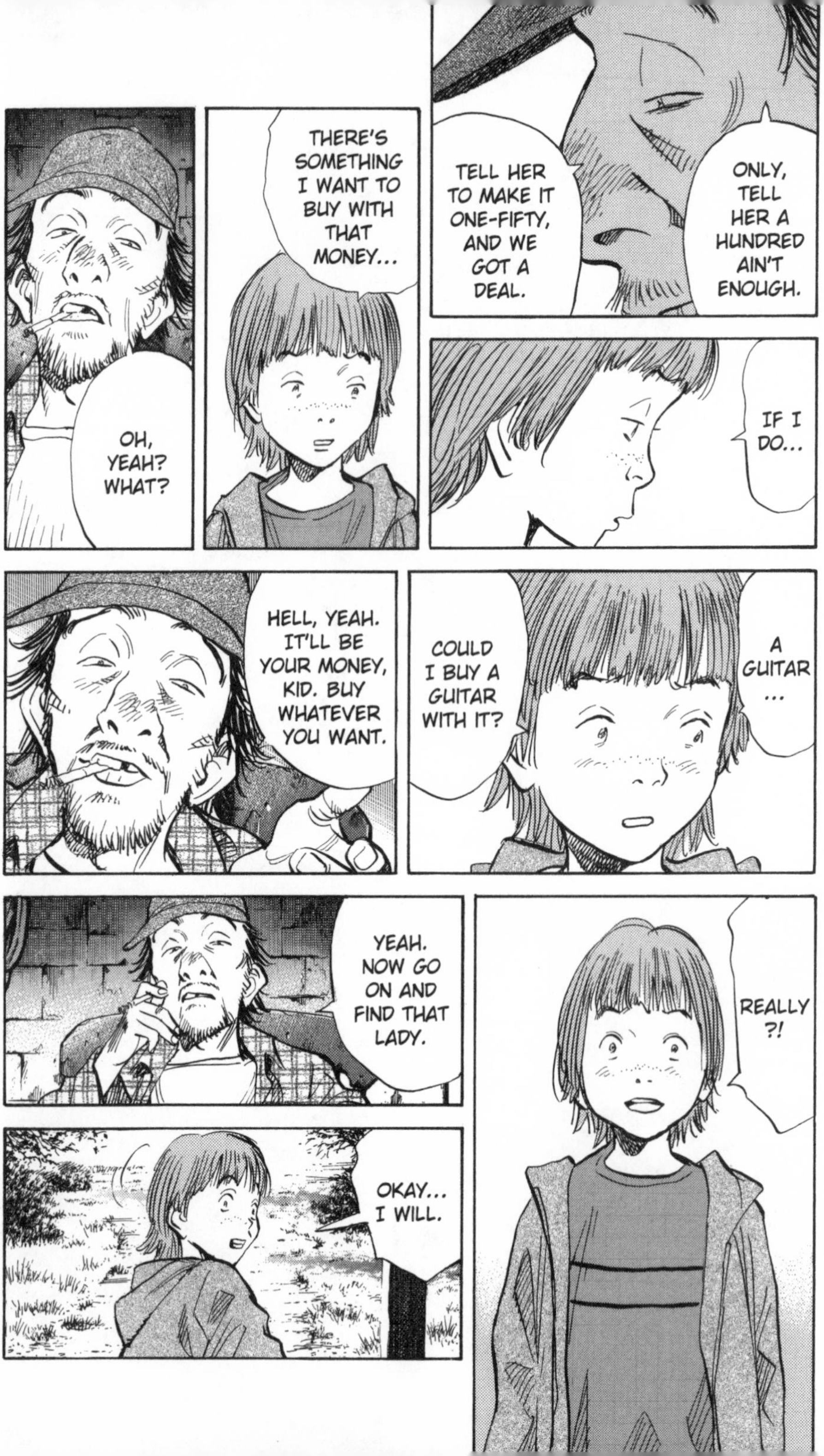
ONLY, TELL HER A HUNDRED AIN'T ENOUGH.
TELL HER TO MAKE IT ONE-FIFTY, AND WE GOT A DEAL.
IF I DO...
THERE'S SOMETHING I WANT TO BUY WITH THAT MONEY...
OH, YEAH? WHAT?
A GUITAR ...
COULD I BUY A GUITAR WITH IT?
HELL, YEAH. IT'LL BE YOUR MONEY, KID. BUY WHATEVER YOU WANT.
REALLY ?!
YEAH. NOW GO ON AND FIND THAT LADY.
OKAY... I WILL.

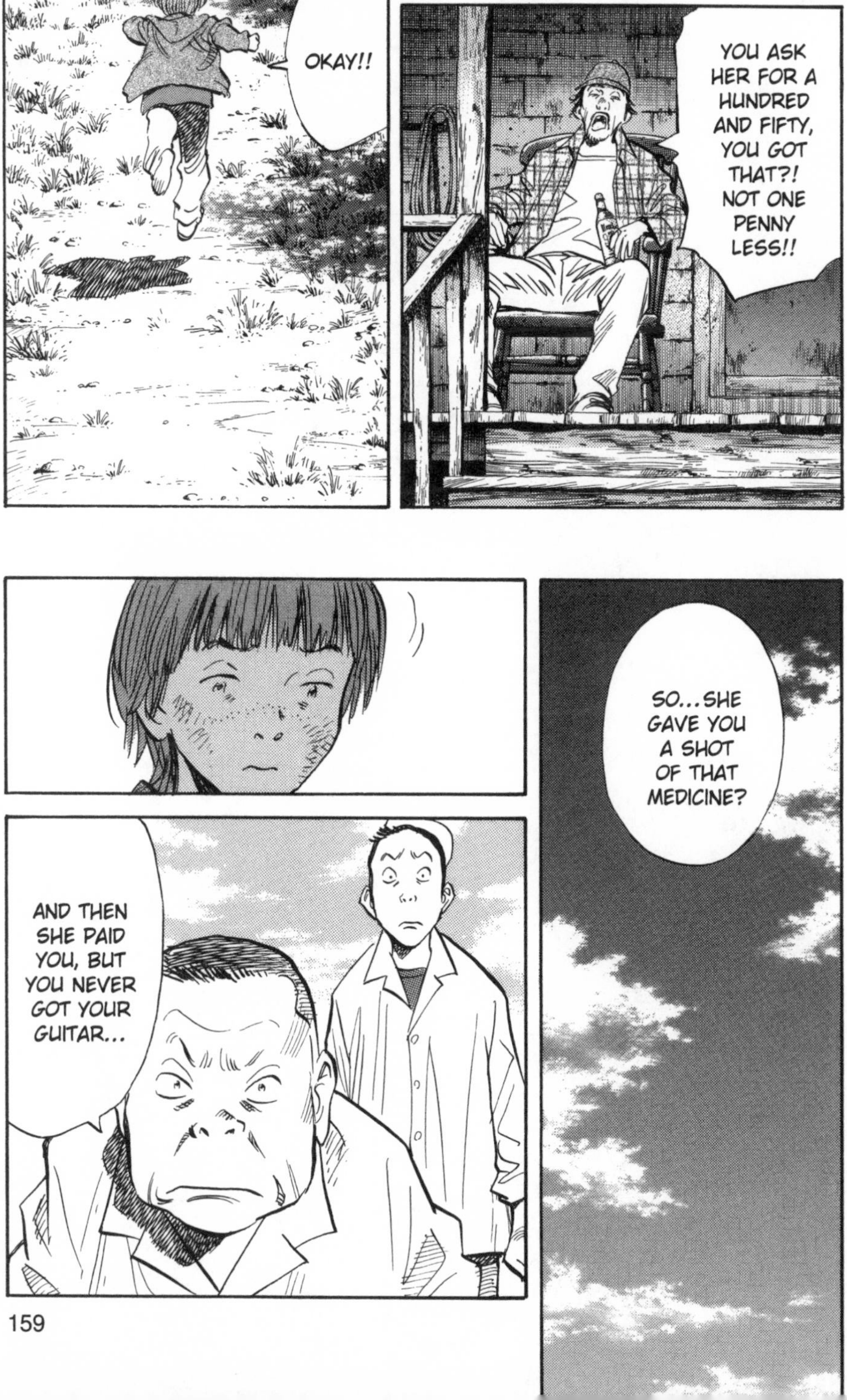
YOU ASK HER FOR A HUNDRED AND FIFTY, YOU GOT THAT?! NOT ONE PENNY LESS!!
OKAY!!
SO...SHE GAVE YOU A SHOT OF THAT MEDICINE?
AND THEN SHE PAID YOU, BUT YOU NEVER GOT YOUR GUITAR...

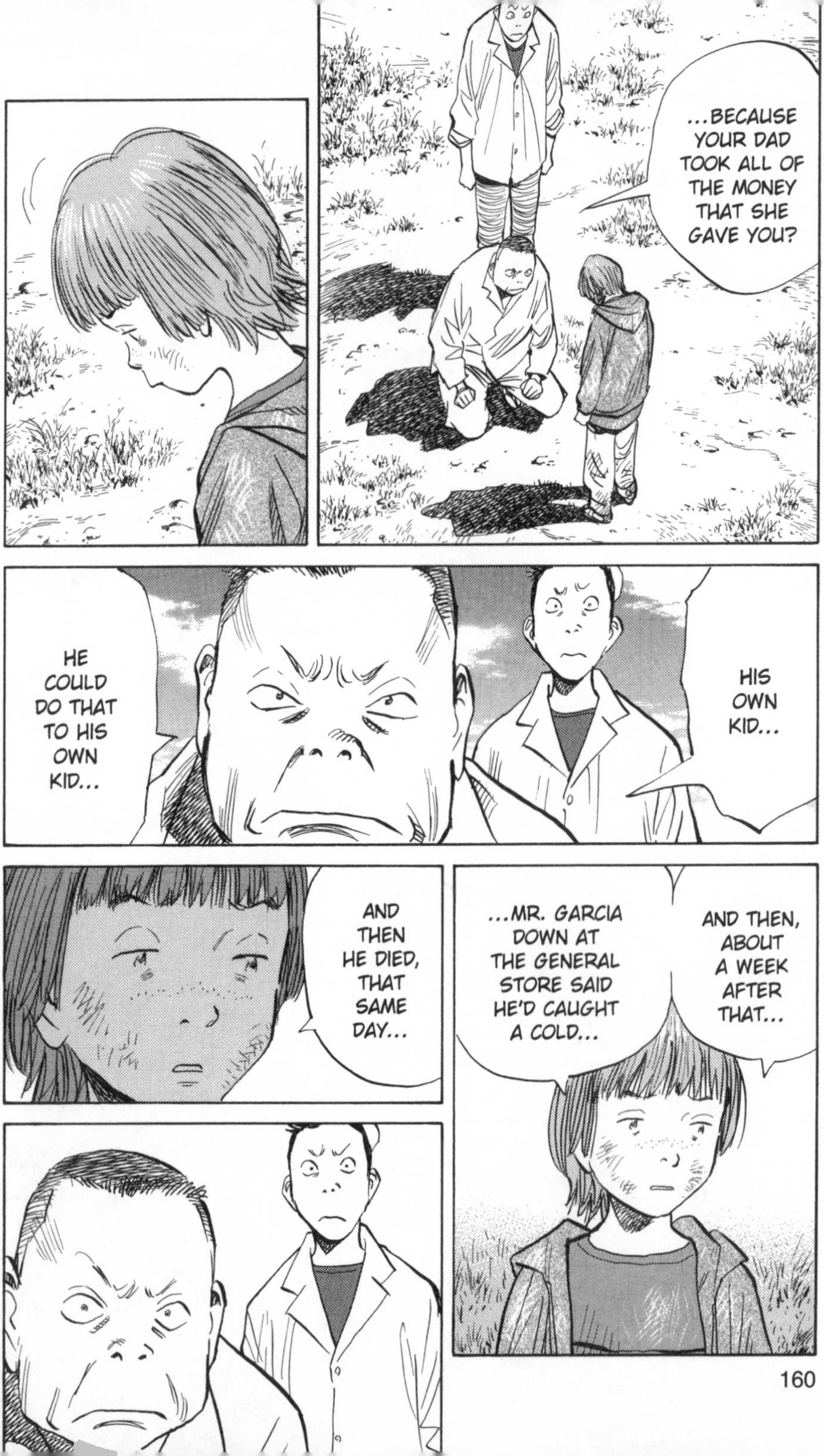

...BECAUSE YOUR DAD TOOK ALL OF THE MONEY THAT SHE GAVE YOU?
HIS OWN KID...
HE COULD DO THAT TO HIS OWN KID...
AND THEN, ABOUT A WEEK AFTER THAT...
...MR. GARCIA DOWN AT THE GENERAL STORE SAID HE'D CAUGHT A COLD...
AND THEN HE DIED, THAT SAME DAY...

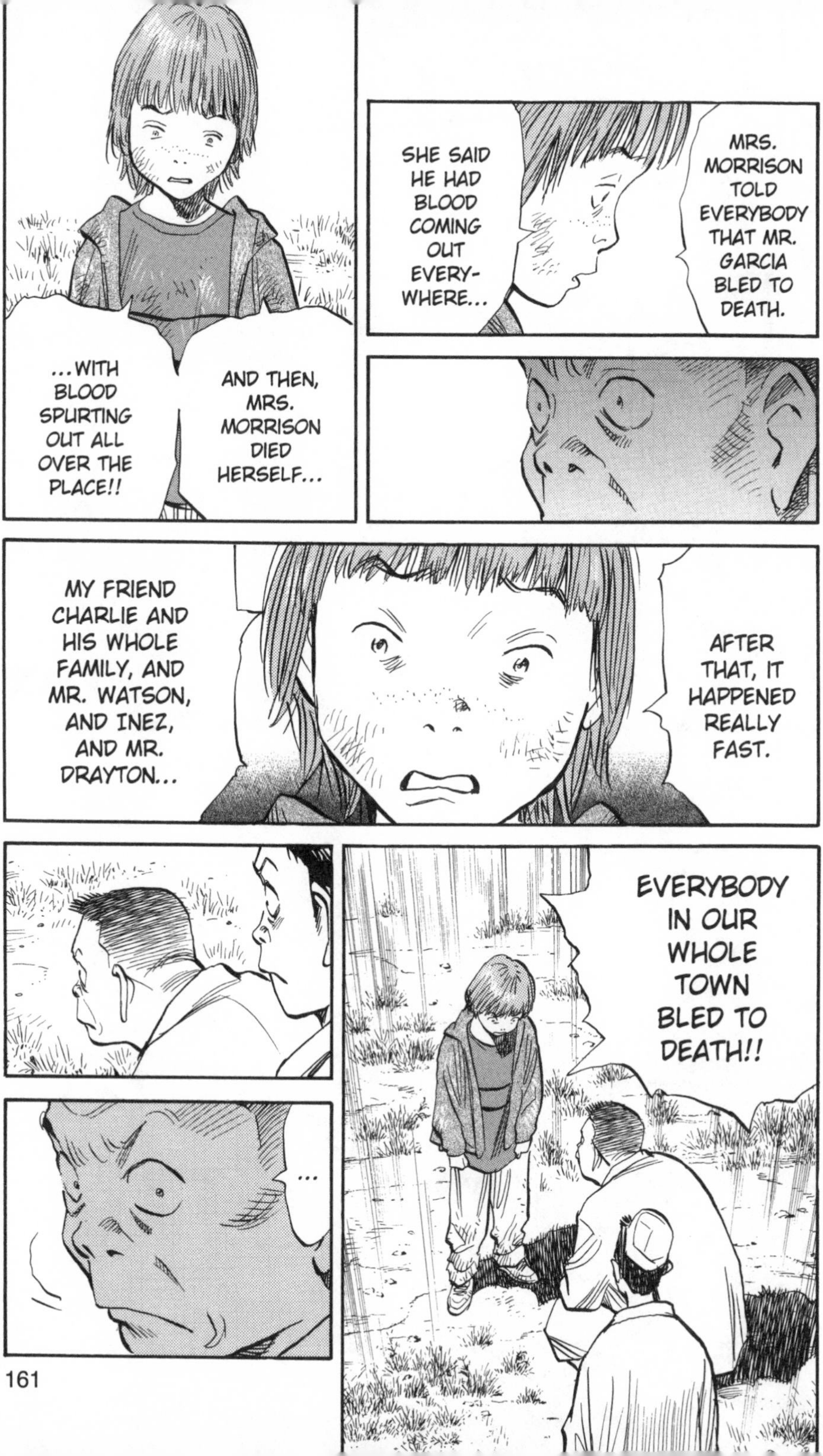

MRS. MORRISON TOLD EVERYBODY THAT MR. GARCIA BLED TO DEATH.
SHE SAID HE HAD BLOOD COMING OUT EVERY-WHERE...
AND THEN, MRS. MORRISON DIED HERSELF...
...WITH BLOOD SPURTING OUT ALL OVER THE PLACE!!
AFTER THAT, IT HAPPENED REALLY FAST.
MY FRIEND CHARLIE AND HIS WHOLE FAMILY, AND MR. WATSON, AND INEZ, AND MR. DRAYTON...
EVERYBODY IN OUR WHOLE TOWN BLED TO DEATH!!
...

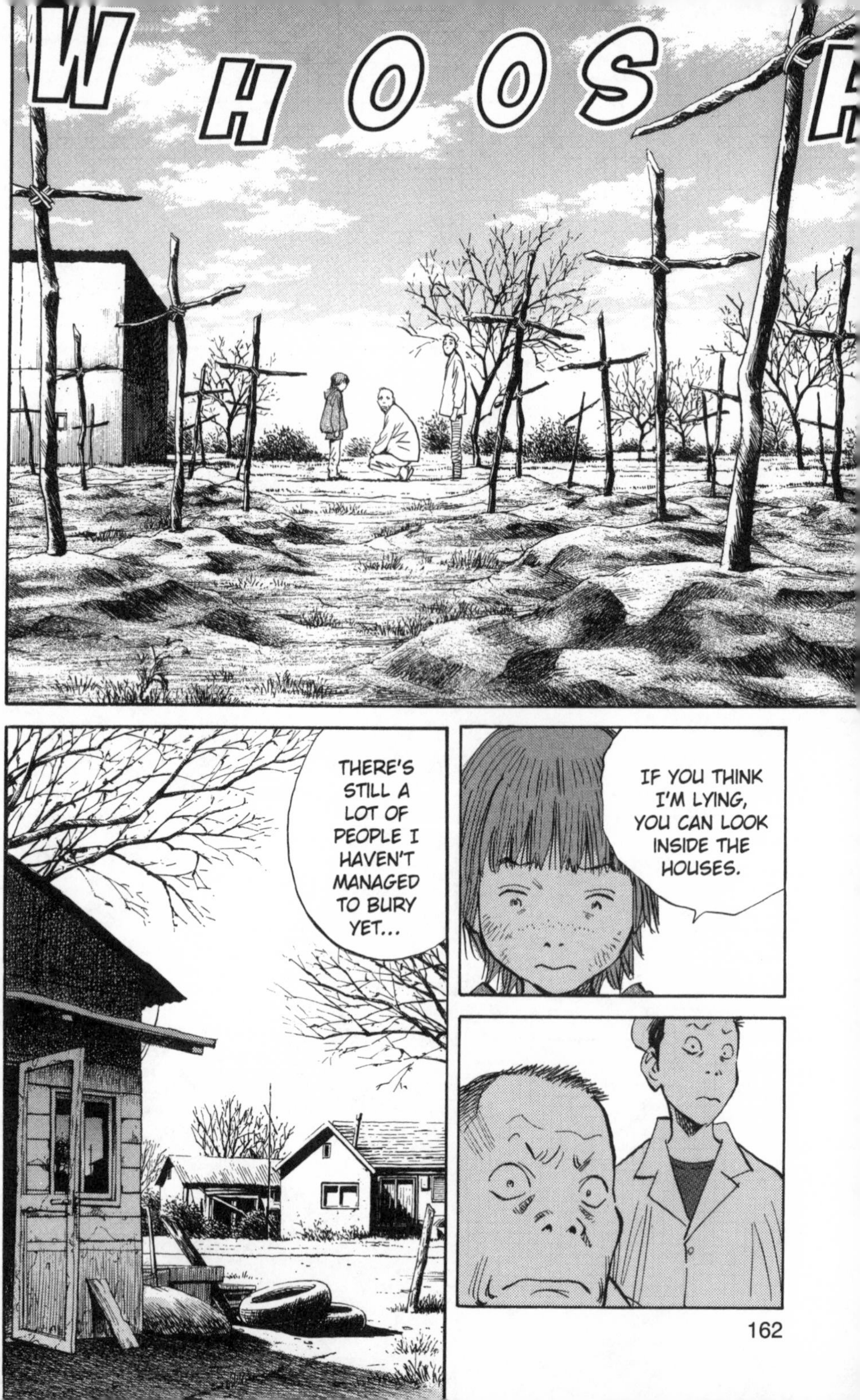
WHOOSH
IF YOU THINK I'M LYING, YOU CAN LOOK INSIDE THE HOUSES.
THERE'S STILL A LOT OF PEOPLE I HAVEN'T MANAGED TO BURY YET...

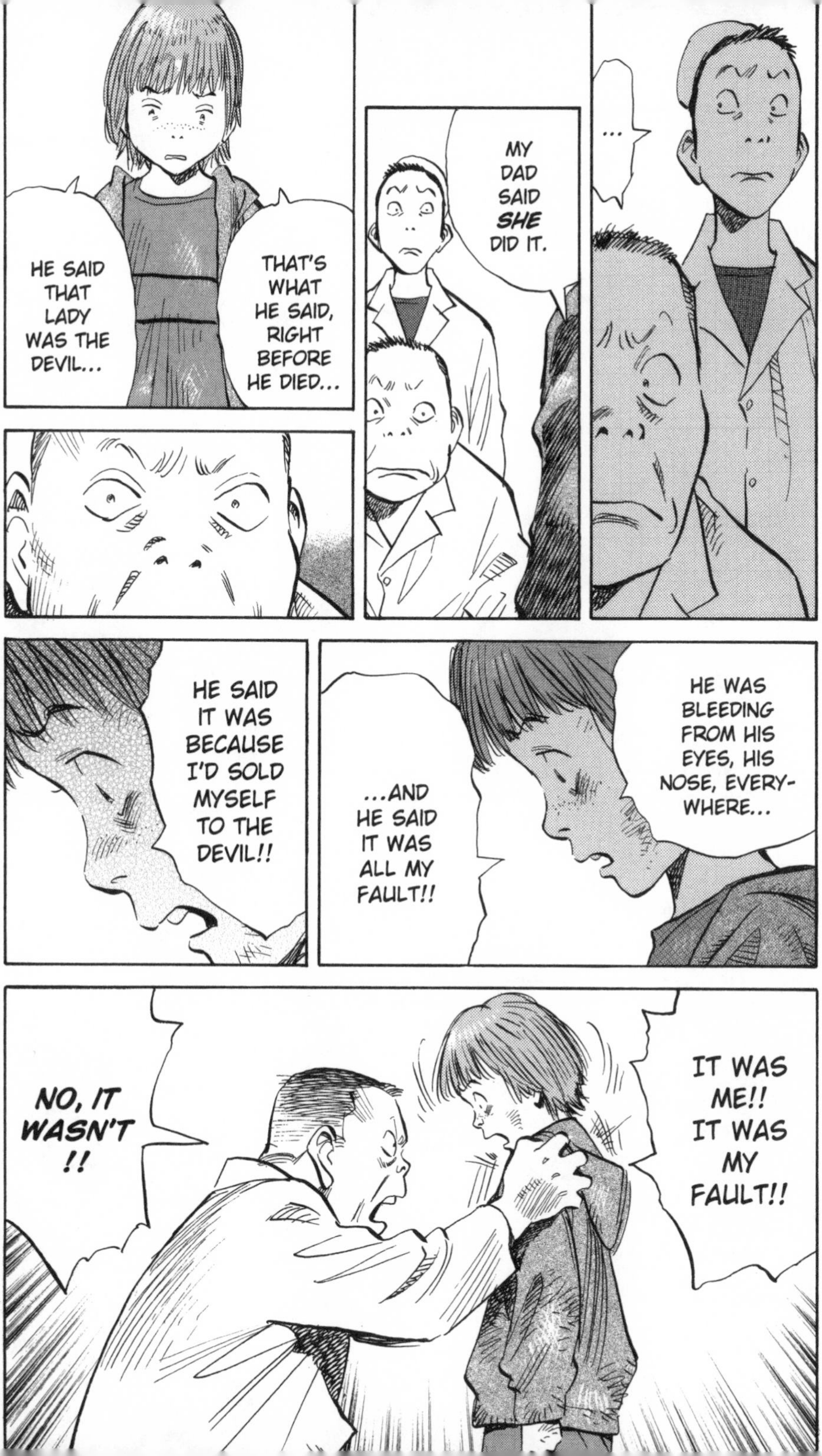

...
MY DAD SAID SHE DID IT.
HE SAID THAT LADY WAS THE DEVIL...
THAT'S WHAT HE SAID, RIGHT BEFORE HE DIED...
HE WAS BLEEDING FROM HIS EYES, HIS NOSE, EVERY-WHERE...
...AND HE SAID IT WAS ALL MY FAULT!!
HE SAID IT WAS BECAUSE I'D SOLD MYSELF TO THE DEVIL!!
IT WAS ME!! IT WAS MY FAULT!!
NO, IT WASN'T !!

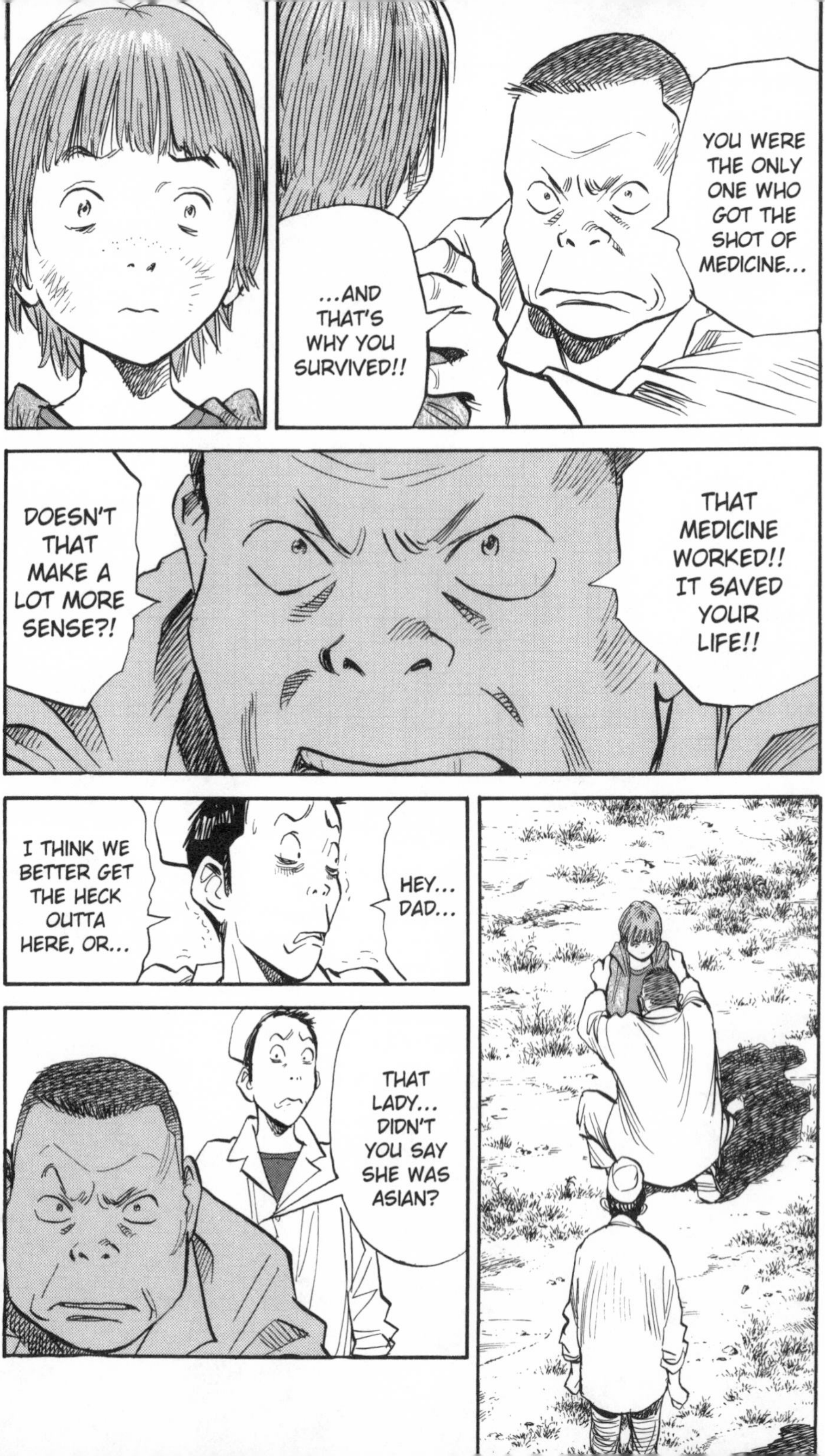
YOU WERE THE ONLY ONE WHO GOT THE SHOT OF MEDICINE...
...AND THAT'S WHY YOU SURVIVED!!
THAT MEDICINE WORKED!! IT SAVED YOUR LIFE!!
DOESN'T THAT MAKE A LOT MORE SENSE?!
HEY... DAD...
I THINK WE BETTER GET THE HECK OUTTA HERE, OR...
THAT LADY... DIDN'T YOU SAY SHE WAS ASIAN?

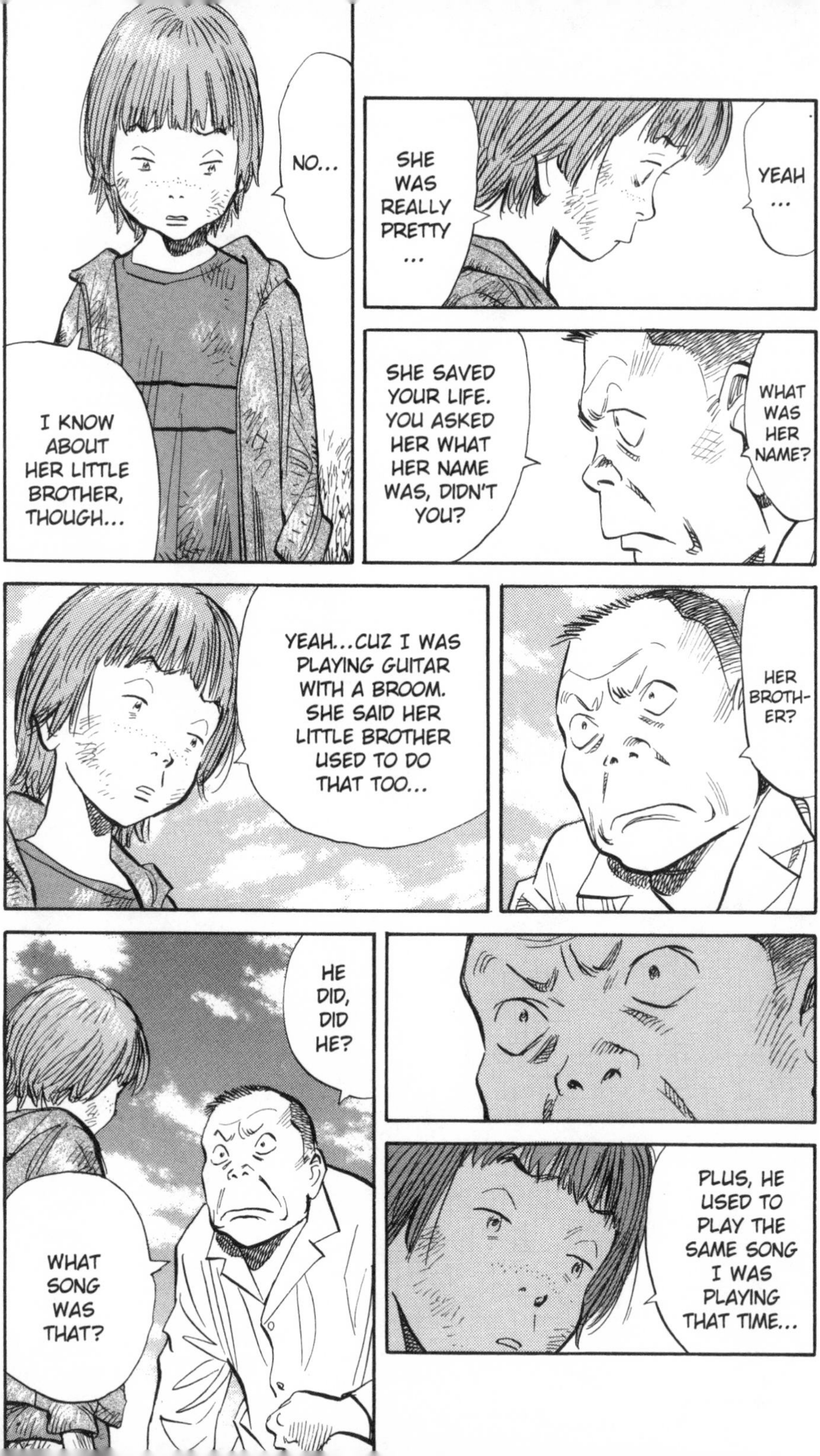
YEAH ...
SHE WAS REALLY PRETTY ...
WHAT WAS HER NAME?
SHE SAVED YOUR LIFE. YOU ASKED HER WHAT HER NAME WAS, DIDN'T YOU?
NO...
I KNOW ABOUT HER LITTLE BROTHER, THOUGH...
HER BROTH-ER?
YEAH...CUZ I WAS PLAYING GUITAR WITH A BROOM. SHE SAID HER LITTLE BROTHER USED TO DO THAT TOO...
PLUS, HE USED TO PLAY THE SAME SONG I WAS PLAYING THAT TIME...
HE DID, DID HE?
WHAT SONG WAS THAT?

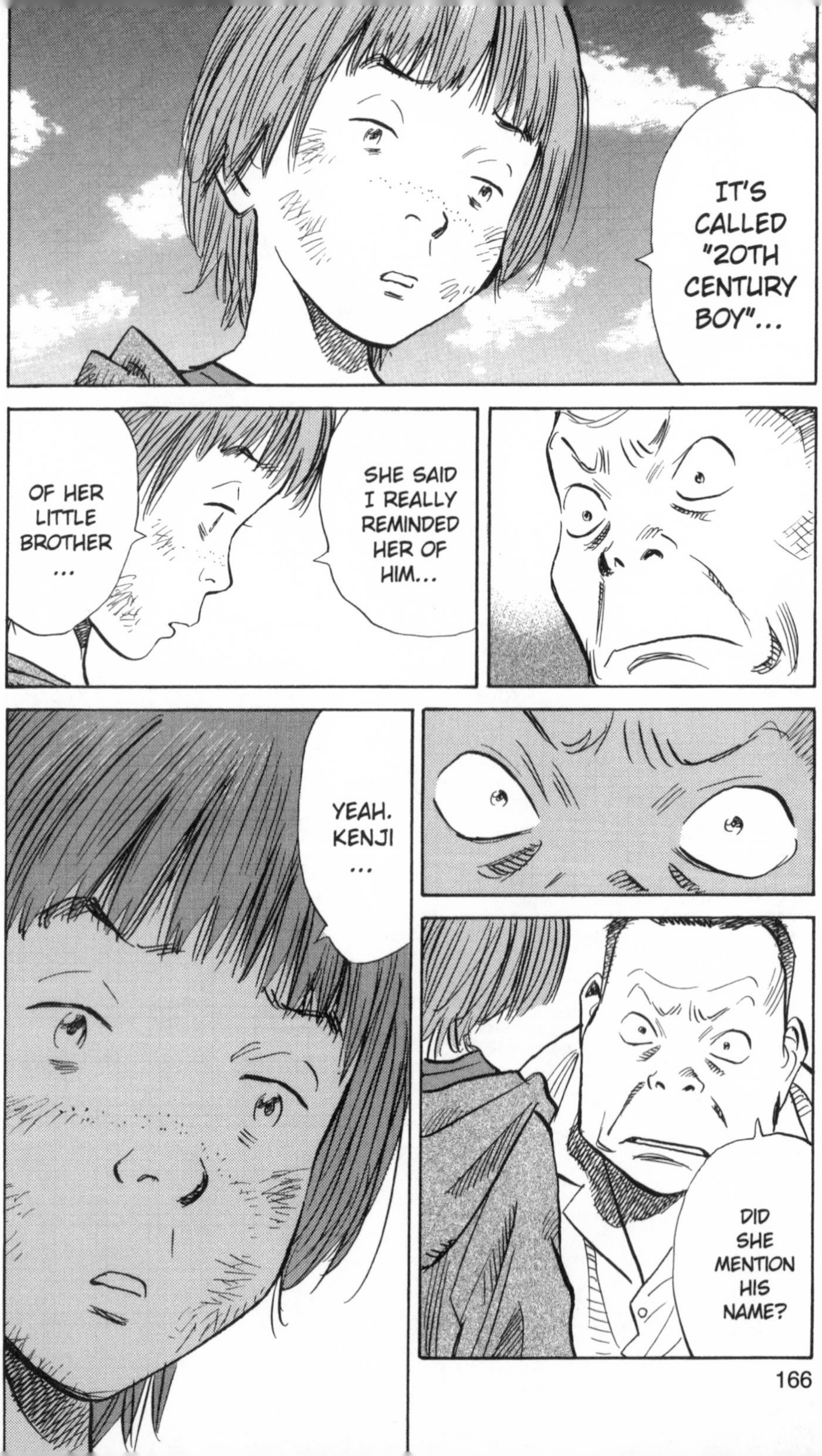
IT'S CALLED "20TH CENTURY BOY"...
SHE SAID I REALLY REMINDED HER OF HIM...
OF HER LITTLE BROTHER ...
DID SHE MENTION HIS NAME?
YEAH. KENJI ...

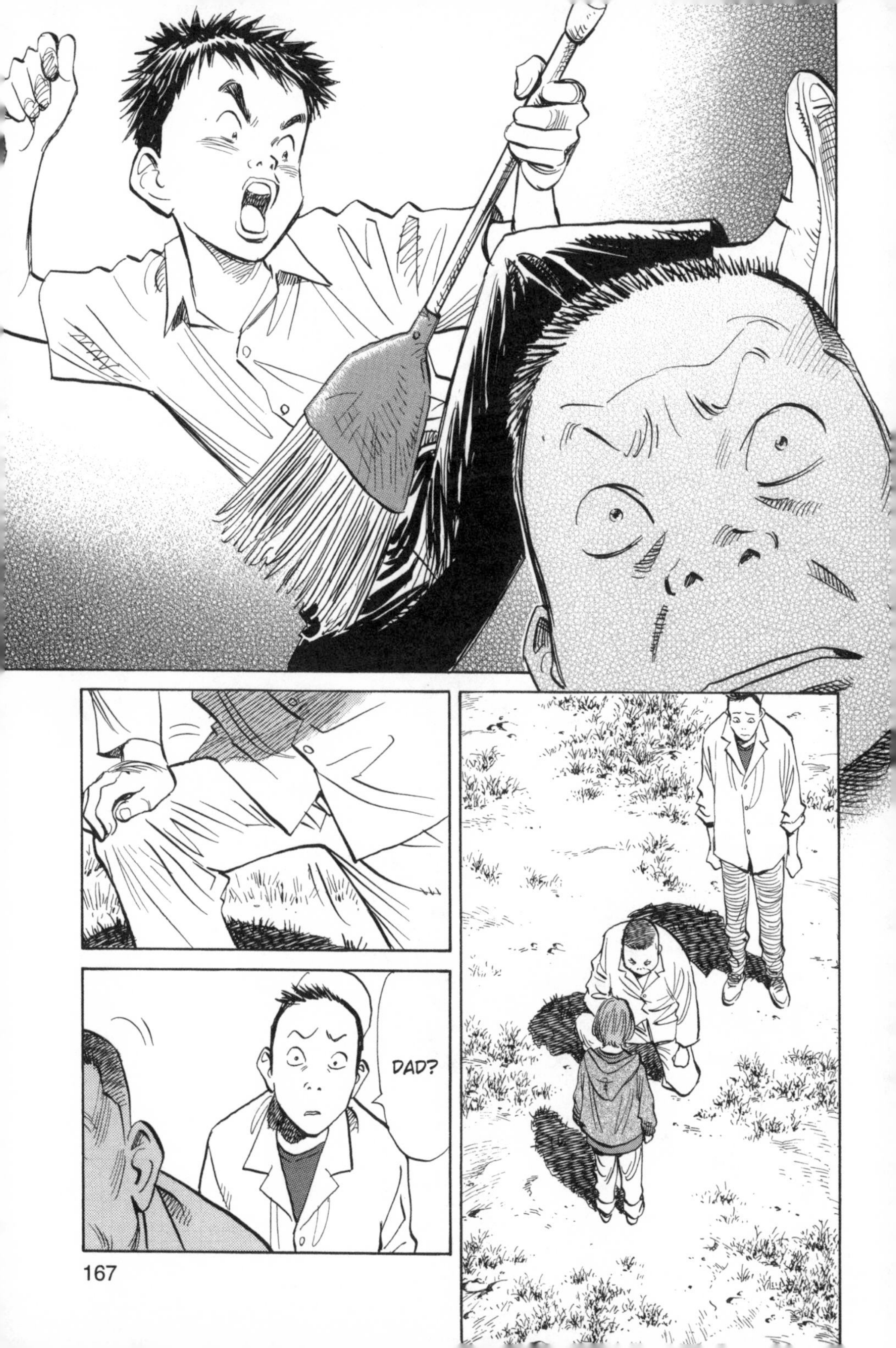
DAD?

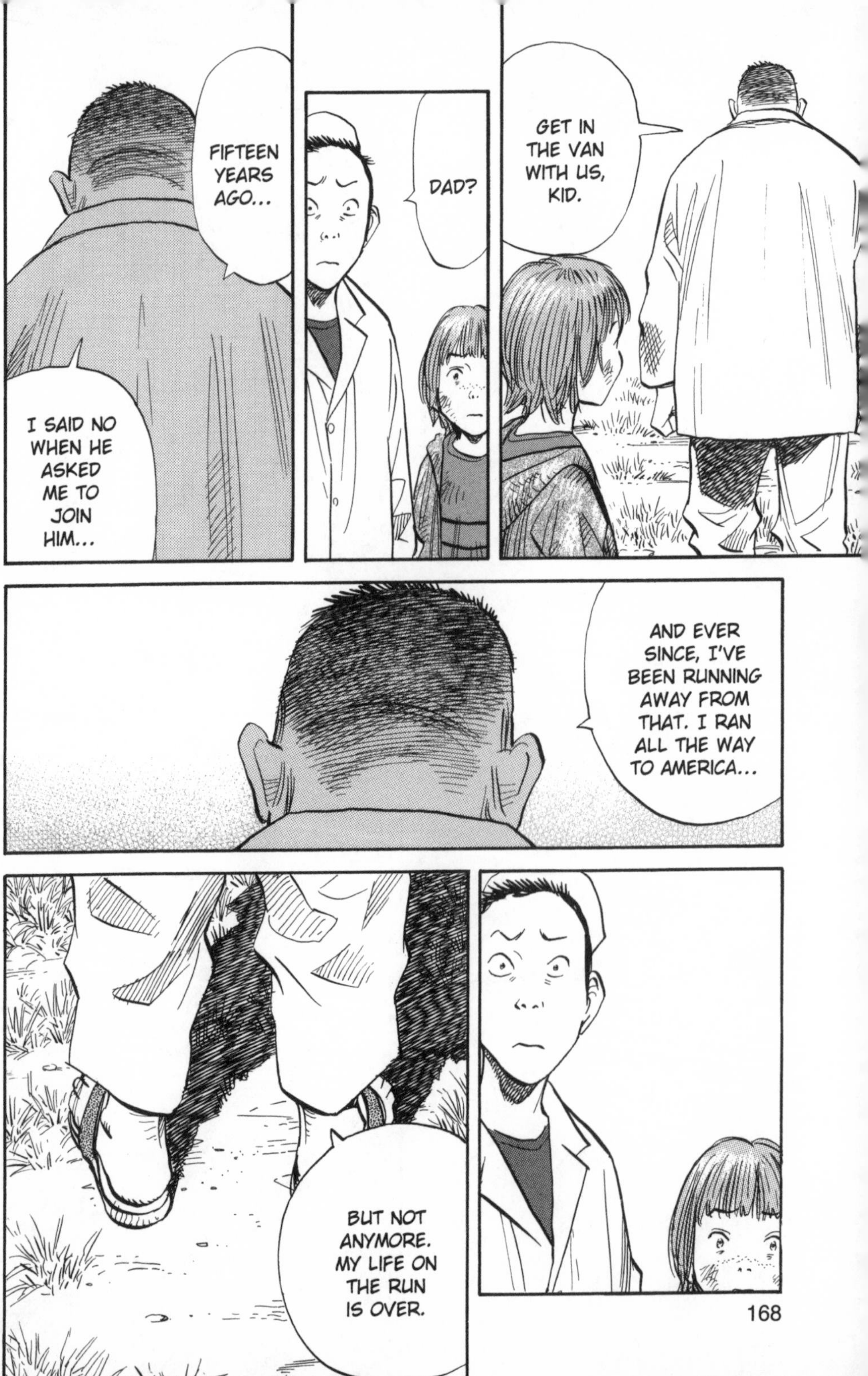
GET IN THE VAN WITH US, KID.
DAD?
FIFTEEN YEARS AGO...
I SAID NO WHEN HE ASKED ME TO JOIN HIM...
AND EVER SINCE, I'VE BEEN RUNNING AWAY FROM THAT. I RAN ALL THE WAY TO AMERICA...
BUT NOT ANYMORE. MY LIFE ON THE RUN IS OVER.

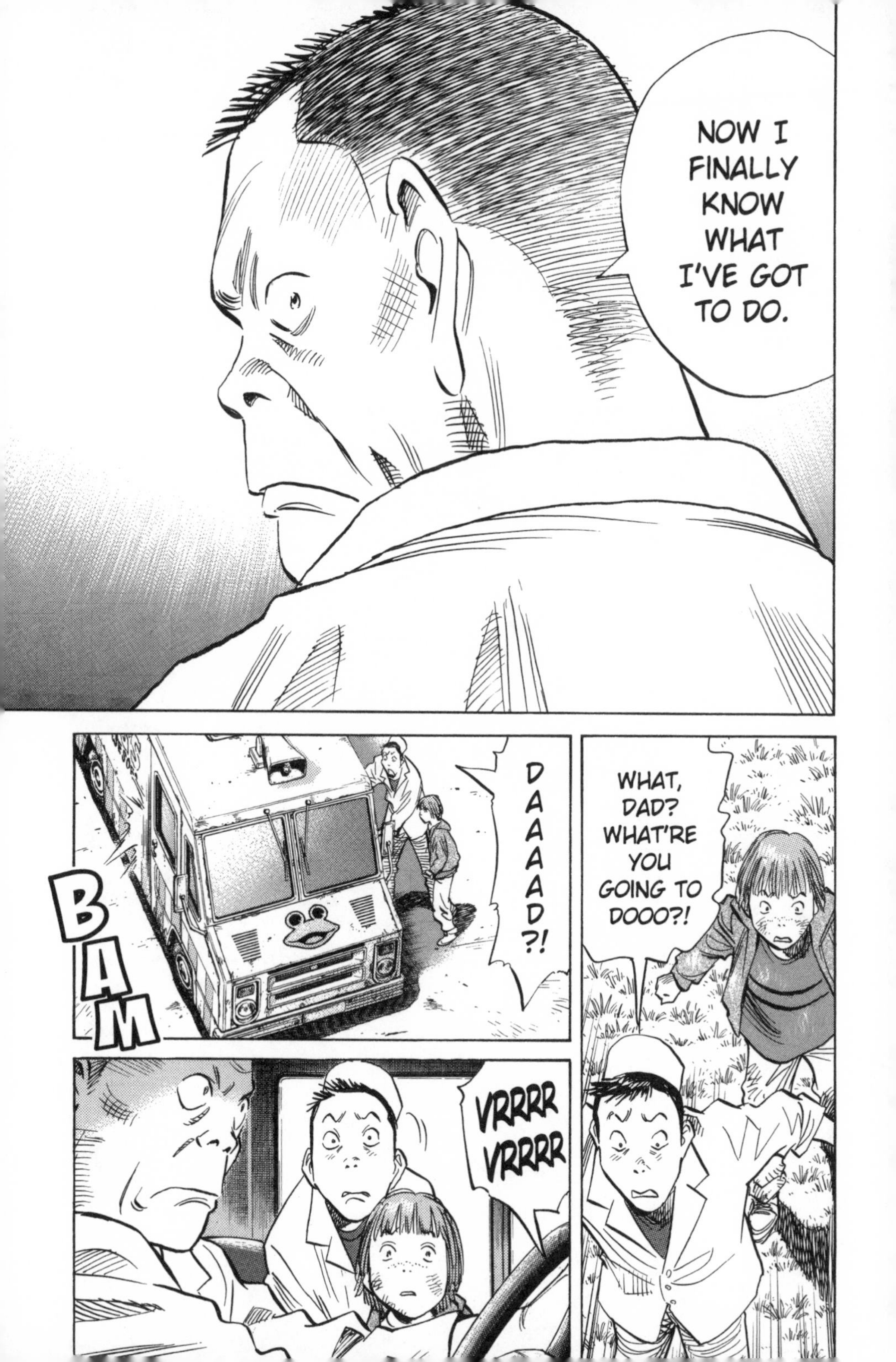
NOW I FINALLY KNOW WHAT I'VE GOT TO DO.
WHAT, DAD? WHAT'RE YOU GOING TO DOOO?!
DAAAAAAD?!
BAM
VRRRR VRRRR

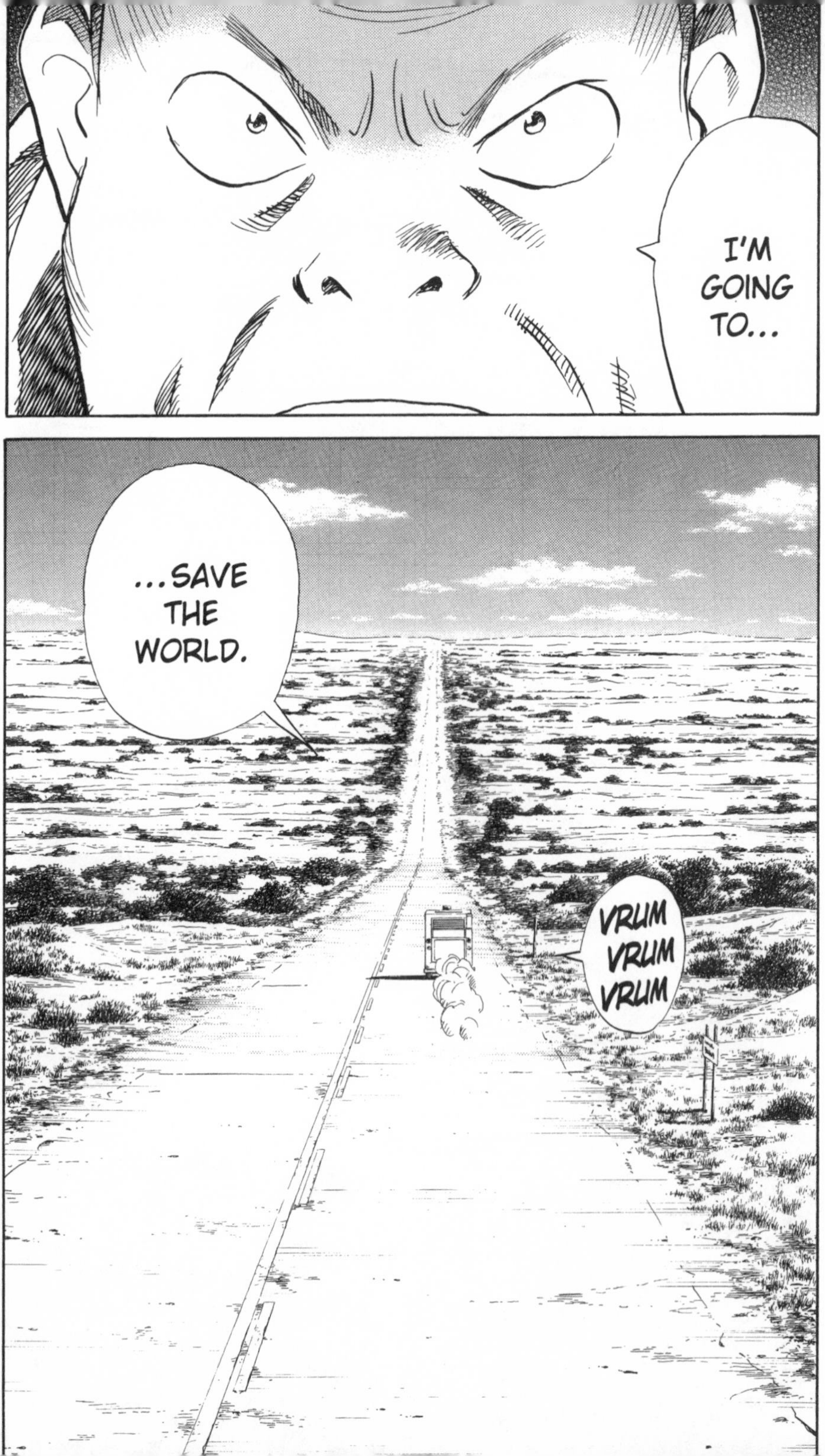
I'M GOING TO...
...SAVE THE WORLD.
VRUM VRUM VRUM

Chapter 10 A Quiet Town in Germany

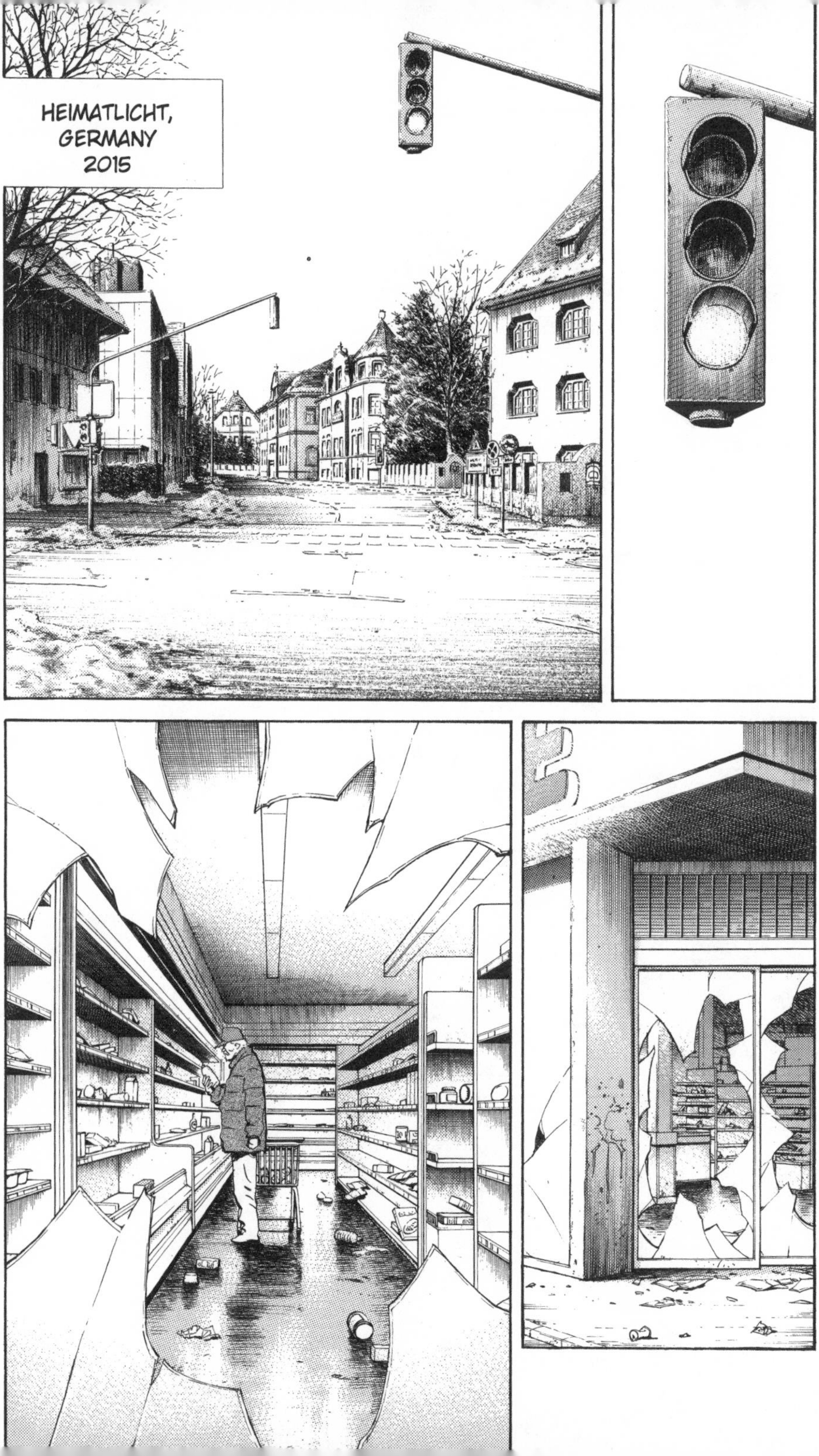
HEIMATLICHT,
GERMANY
2015

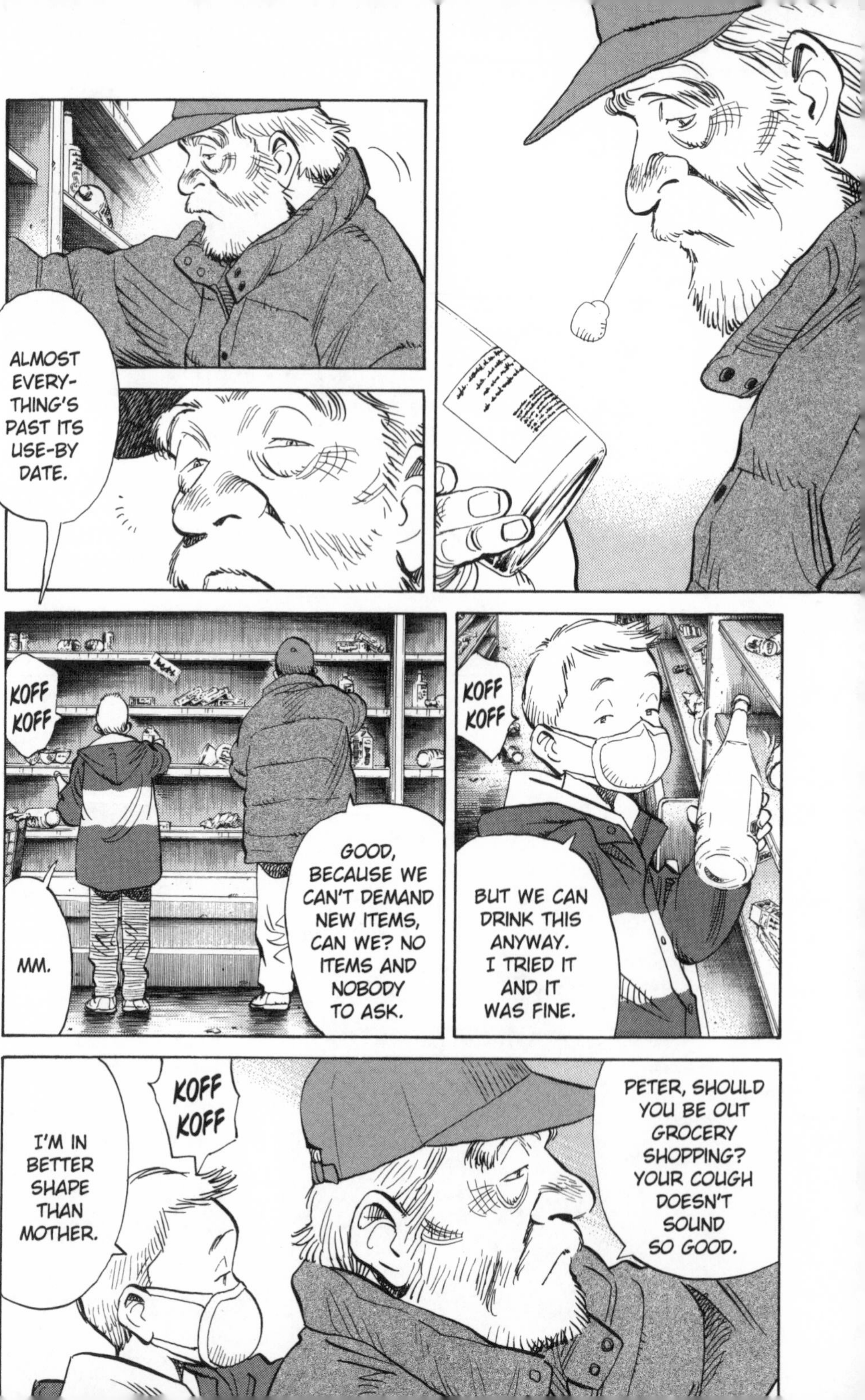
ALMOST EVERY-THING'S PAST ITS USE-BY DATE.
KOFF KOFF
BUT WE CAN DRINK THIS ANYWAY. I TRIED IT AND IT WAS FINE.
KOFF KOFF
GOOD, BECAUSE WE CAN'T DEMAND NEW ITEMS, CAN WE? NO ITEMS AND NOBODY TO ASK.
MM.
PETER, SHOULD YOU BE OUT GROCERY SHOPPING? YOUR COUGH DOESN'T SOUND SO GOOD.
KOFF KOFF
I'M IN BETTER SHAPE THAN MOTHER.

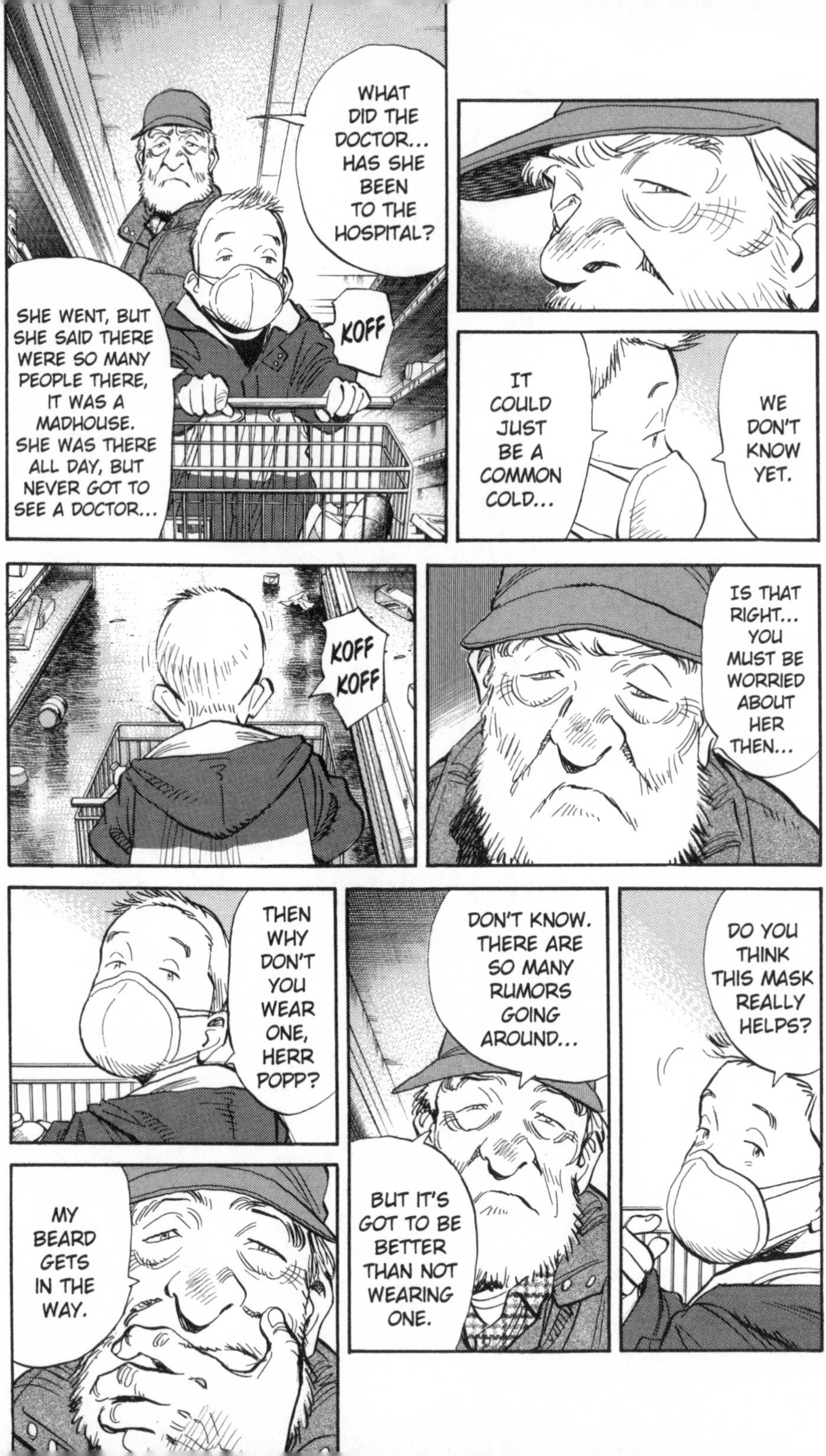
WE DON'T KNOW YET.
IT COULD JUST BE A COMMON COLD...
WHAT DID THE DOCTOR... HAS SHE BEEN TO THE HOSPITAL?
KOFF
SHE WENT, BUT SHE SAID THERE WERE SO MANY PEOPLE THERE, IT WAS A MADHOUSE. SHE WAS THERE ALL DAY, BUT NEVER GOT TO SEE A DOCTOR...
IS THAT RIGHT... YOU MUST BE WORRIED ABOUT HER THEN...
KOFF KOFF
DO YOU THINK THIS MASK REALLY HELPS?
DON'T KNOW. THERE ARE SO MANY RUMORS GOING AROUND...
BUT IT'S GOT TO BE BETTER THAN NOT WEARING ONE.
THEN WHY DON'T YOU WEAR ONE, HERR POPP?
MY BEARD GETS IN THE WAY.

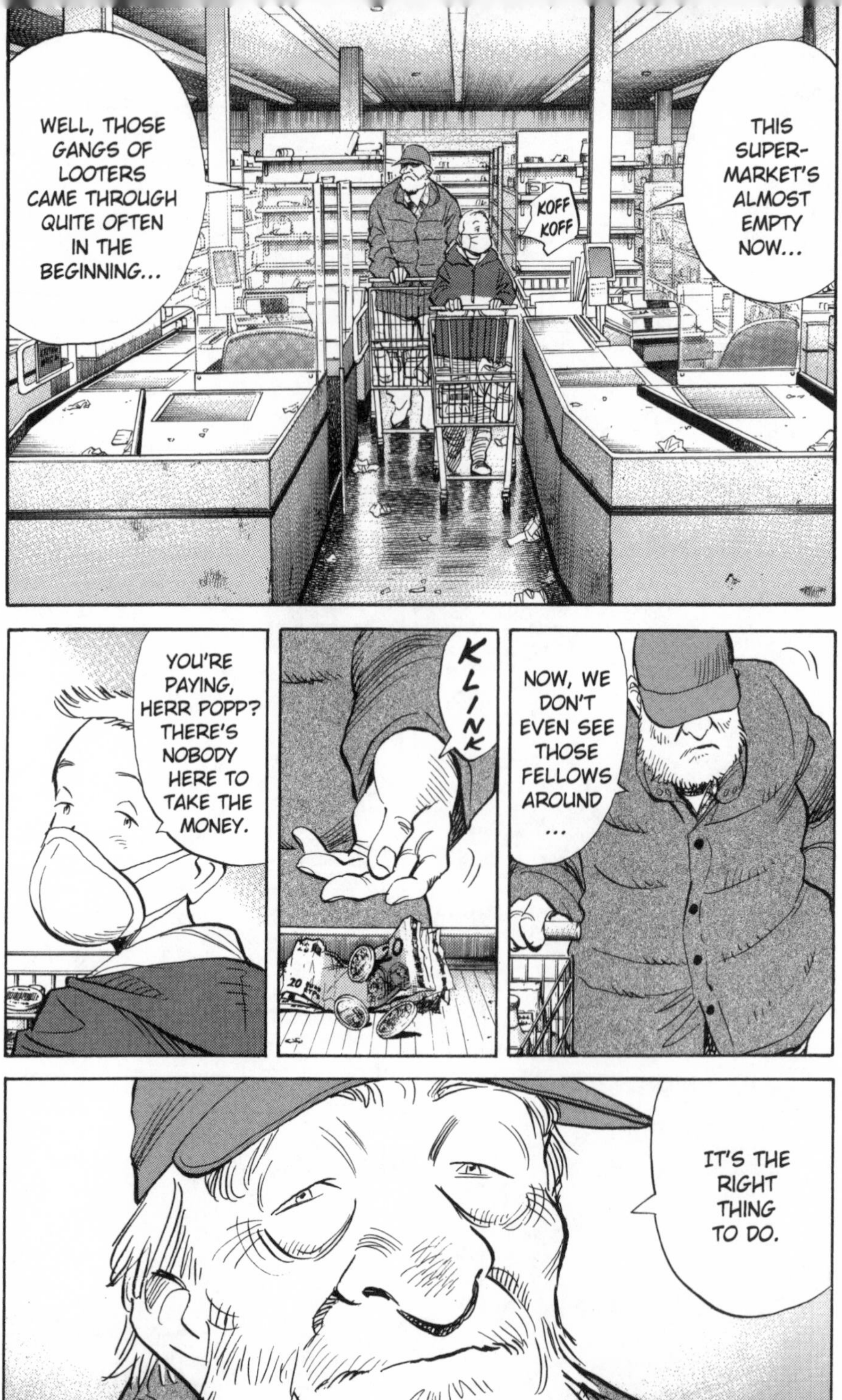

THIS SUPER-MARKET'S ALMOST EMPTY NOW...
KOFF KOFF
WELL, THOSE GANGS OF LOOTERS CAME THROUGH QUITE OFTEN IN THE BEGINNING...
NOW, WE DON'T EVEN SEE THOSE FELLOWS AROUND ...
KLINK
YOU'RE PAYING, HERR POPP? THERE'S NOBODY HERE TO TAKE THE MONEY.
IT'S THE RIGHT THING TO DO.

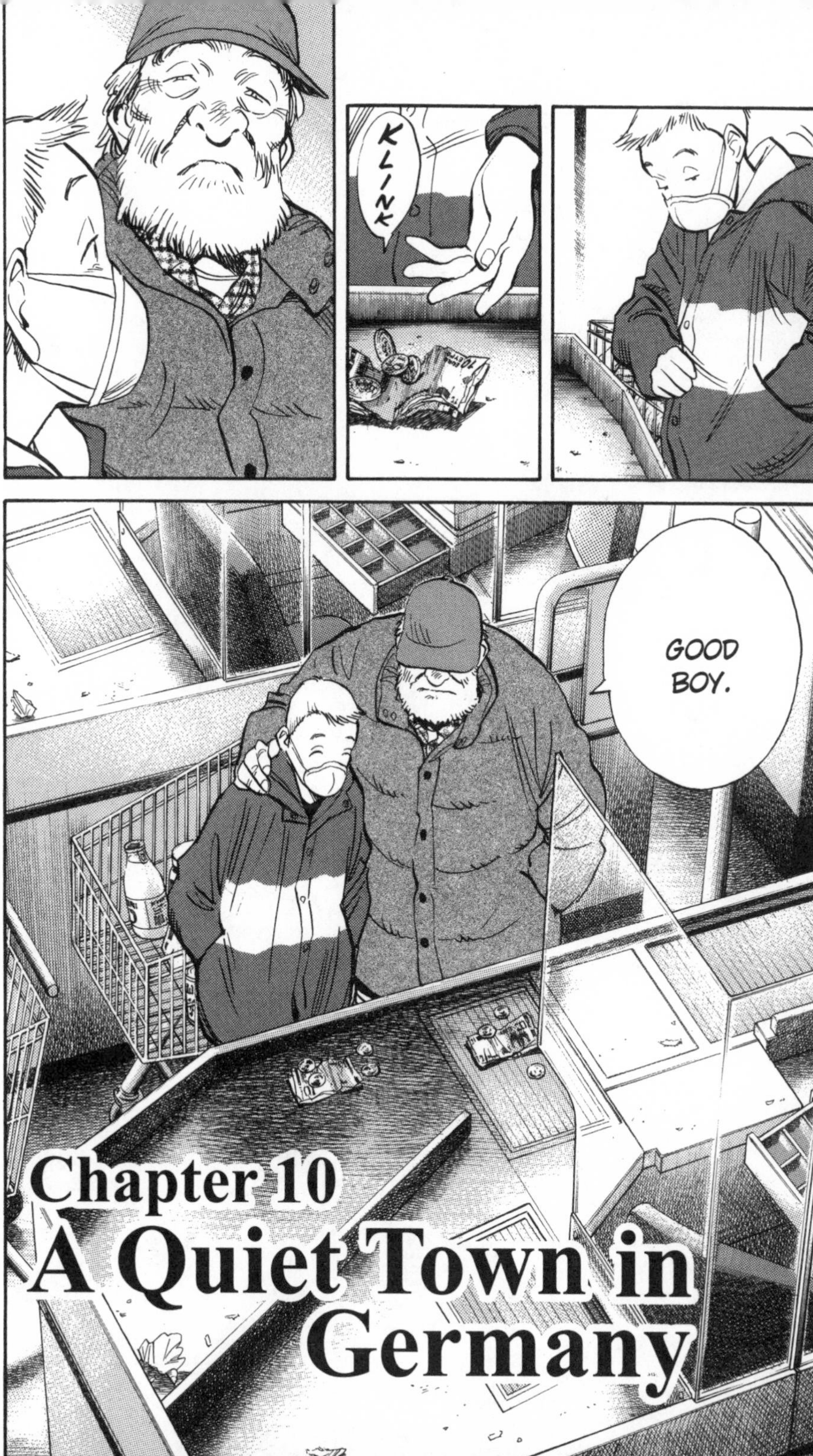
KLINK
GOOD BOY.
Chapter 10
A Quiet Town in Germany

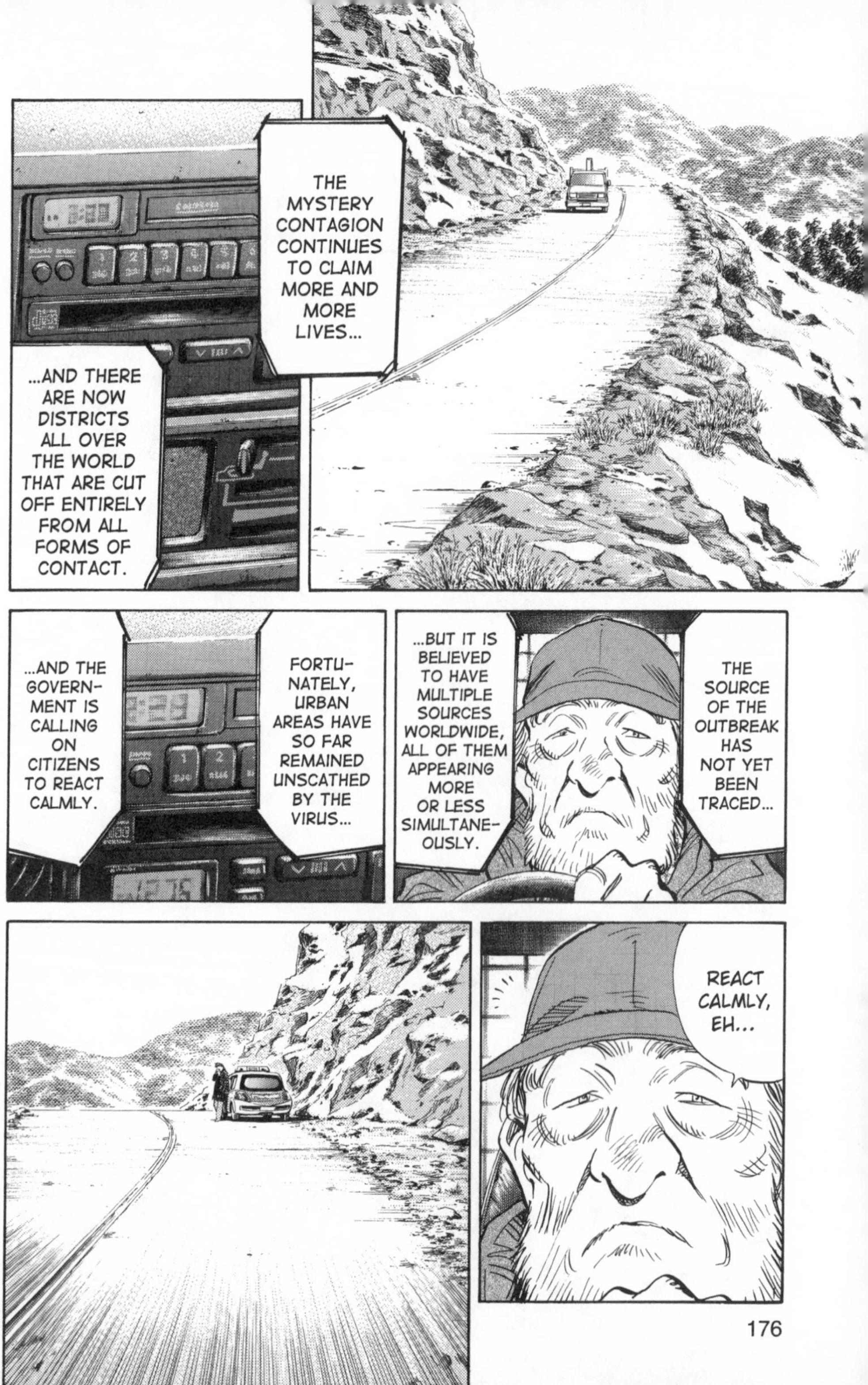
THE MYSTERY CONTAGION CONTINUES TO CLAIM MORE AND MORE LIVES...
...AND THERE ARE NOW DISTRICTS ALL OVER THE WORLD THAT ARE CUT OFF ENTIRELY FROM ALL FORMS OF CONTACT.
THE SOURCE OF THE OUTBREAK HAS NOT YET BEEN TRACED...
...BUT IT IS BELIEVED TO HAVE MULTIPLE SOURCES WORLDWIDE, ALL OF THEM APPEARING MORE OR LESS SIMULTANE-OUSLY.
FORTU-NATELY, URBAN AREAS HAVE SO FAR REMAINED UNSCATHED BY THE VIRUS...
...AND THE GOVERN-MENT IS CALLING ON CITIZENS TO REACT CALMLY.
REACT CALMLY, EH...

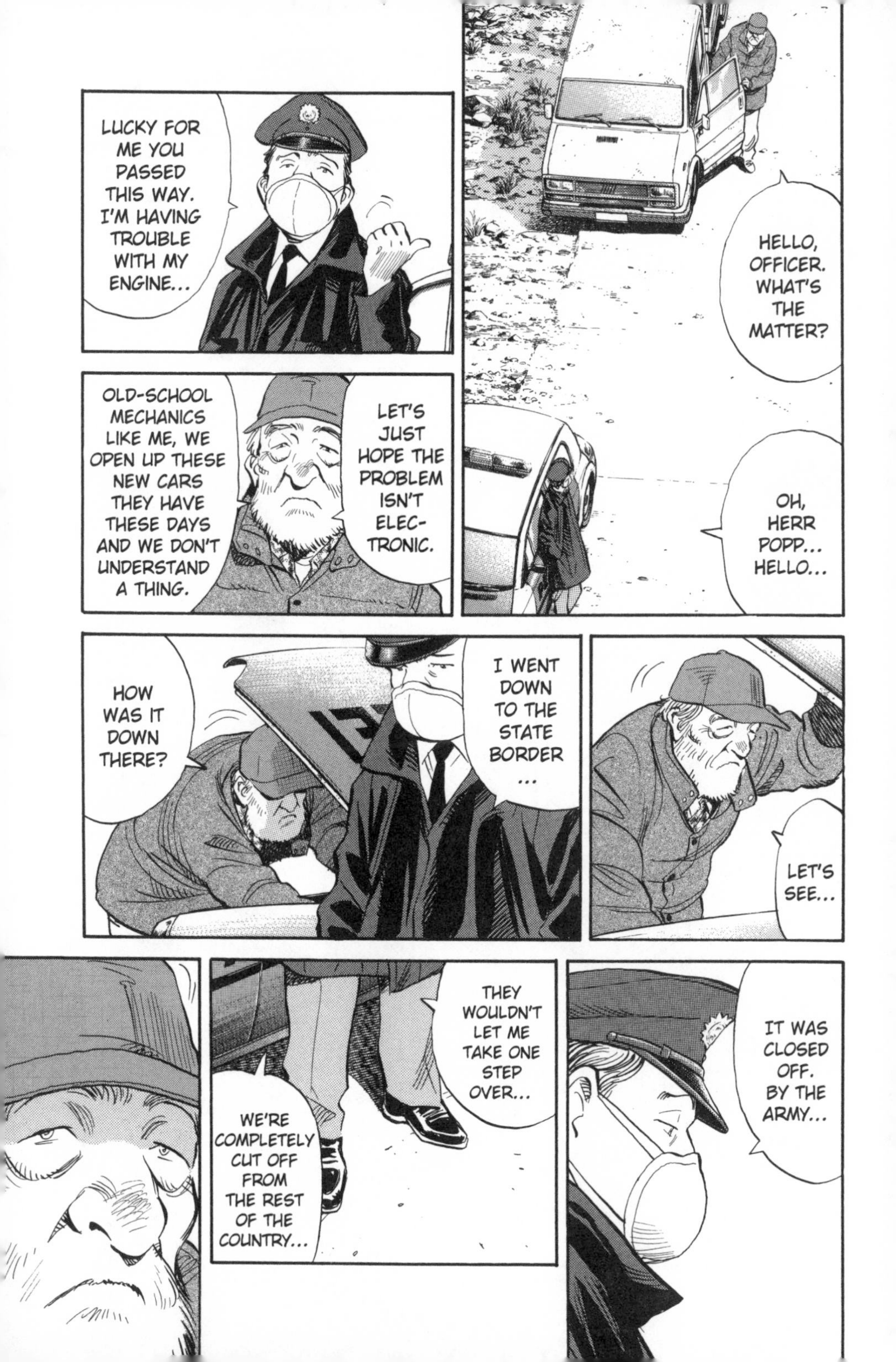
HELLO, OFFICER. WHAT'S THE MATTER?
OH, HERR POPP... HELLO...
LUCKY FOR ME YOU PASSED THIS WAY. I'M HAVING TROUBLE WITH MY ENGINE...
LET'S JUST HOPE THE PROBLEM ISN'T ELEC-TRONIC.
OLD-SCHOOL MECHANICS LIKE ME, WE OPEN UP THESE NEW CARS THEY HAVE THESE DAYS AND WE DON'T UNDERSTAND A THING.
LET'S SEE...
I WENT DOWN TO THE STATE BORDER ...
HOW WAS IT DOWN THERE?
IT WAS CLOSED OFF. BY THE ARMY...
THEY WOULDN'T LET ME TAKE ONE STEP OVER...
WE'RE COMPLETELY CUT OFF FROM THE REST OF THE COUNTRY...

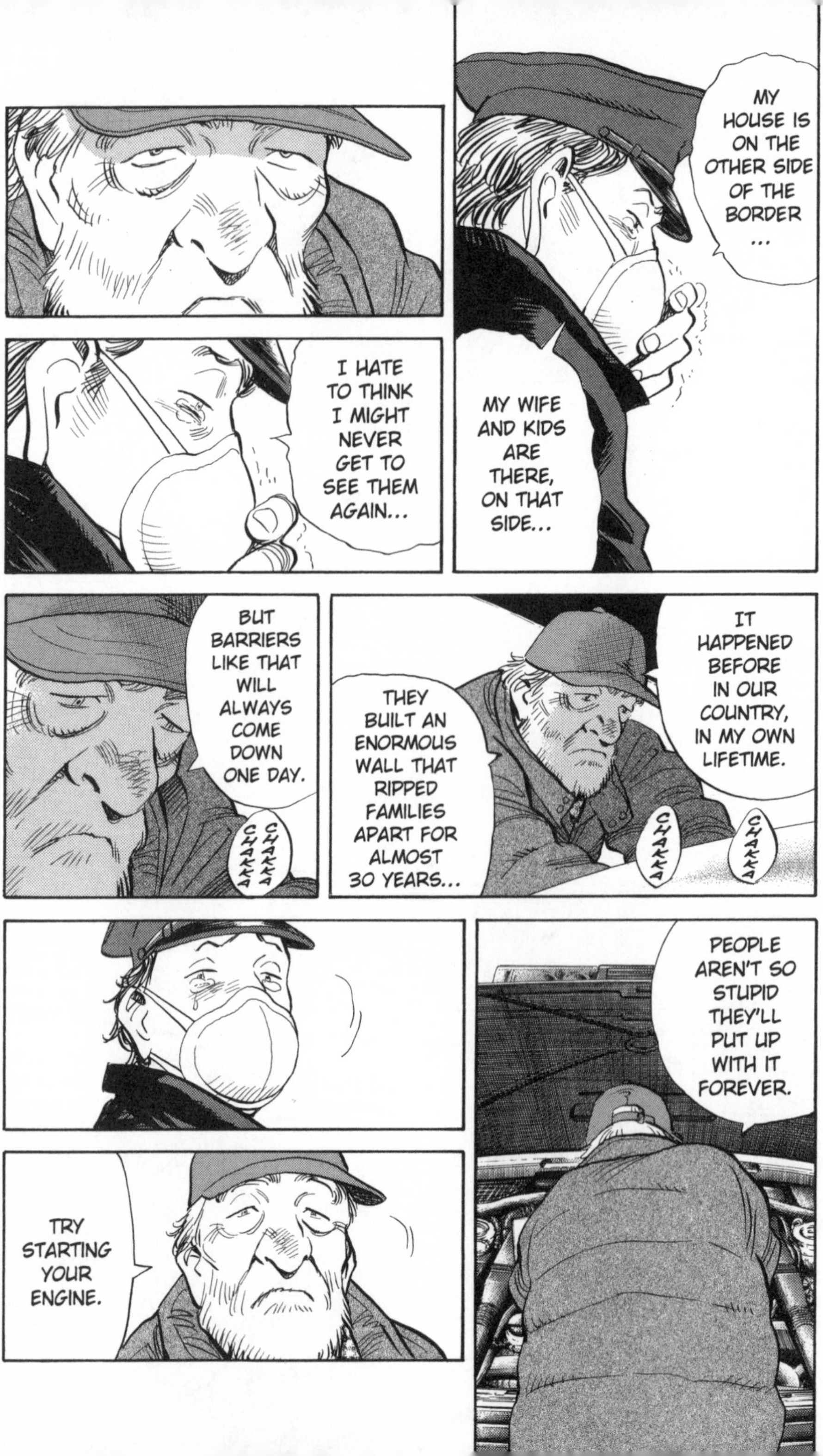
MY HOUSE IS ON THE OTHER SIDE OF THE BORDER...
MY WIFE AND KIDS ARE THERE, ON THAT SIDE...
I HATE TO THINK I MIGHT NEVER GET TO SEE THEM AGAIN...
IT HAPPENED BEFORE IN OUR COUNTRY, IN MY OWN LIFETIME.
THEY BUILT AN ENORMOUS WALL THAT RIPPED FAMILIES APART FOR ALMOST 30 YEARS...
CHAKKA
CHAKKA
BUT BARRIERS LIKE THAT WILL ALWAYS COME DOWN ONE DAY.
CHAKKA CHAKKA
PEOPLE AREN'T SO STUPID THEY'LL PUT UP WITH IT FOREVER.
TRY STARTING YOUR ENGINE.

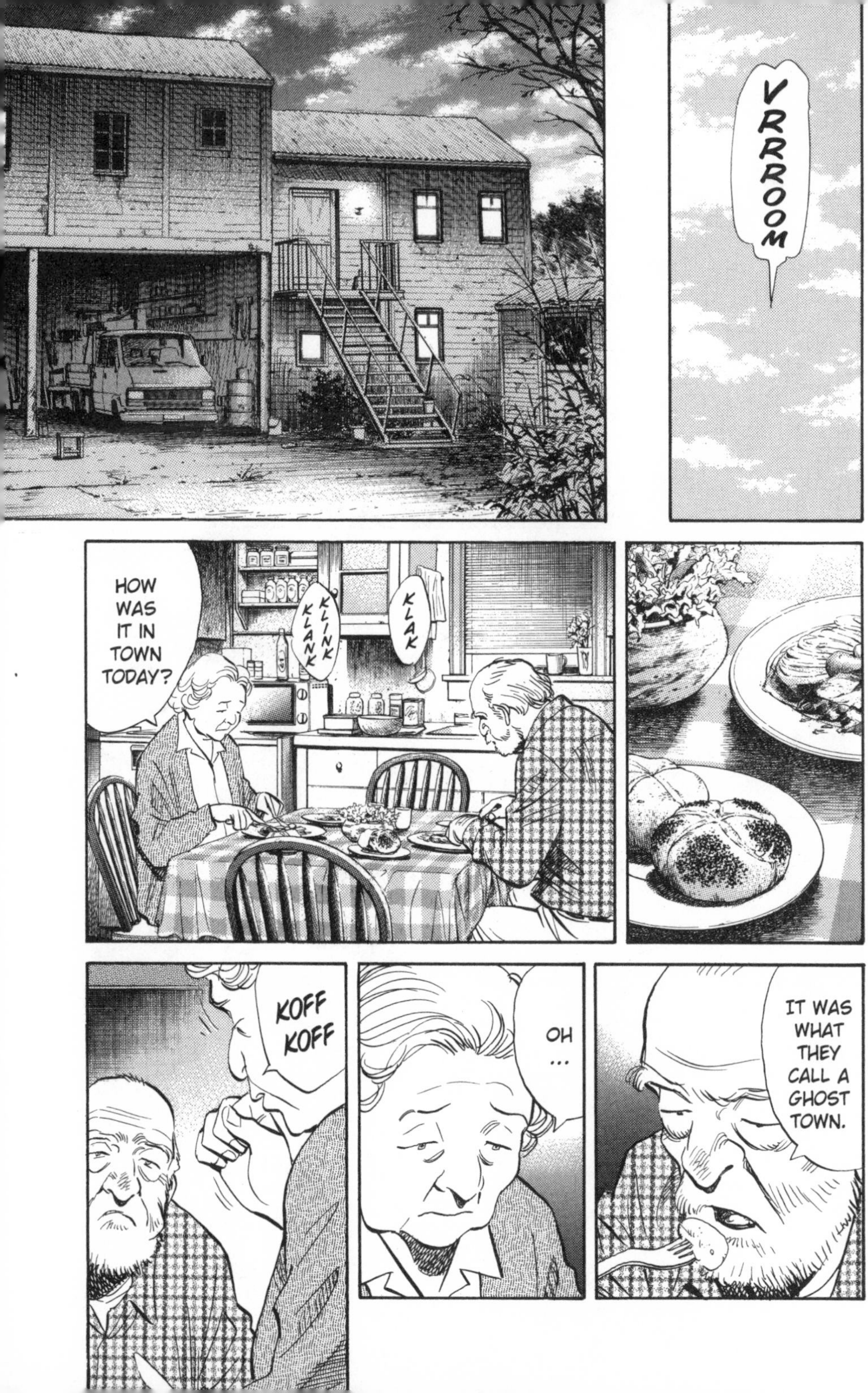
VRRROOM
HOW WAS IT IN TOWN TODAY?
KLINK KLANK
KLAK
IT WAS WHAT THEY CALL A GHOST TOWN.
OH ...
KOFF KOFF

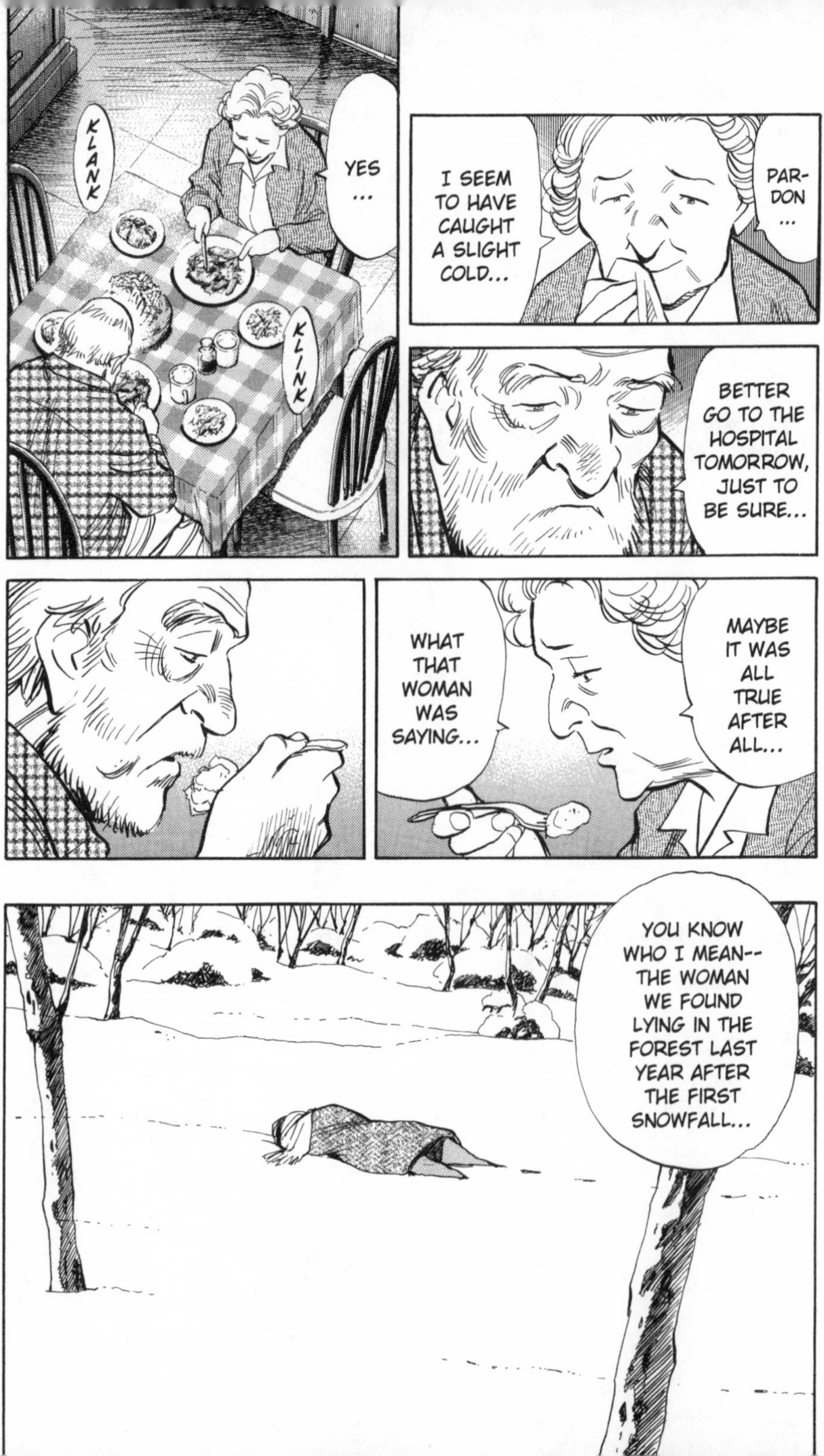
PAR-DON...
I SEEM TO HAVE CAUGHT A SLIGHT COLD...
BETTER GO TO THE HOSPITAL TOMORROW, JUST TO BE SURE...
YES...
KLINK
KLANK
MAYBE IT WAS ALL TRUE AFTER ALL...
WHAT THAT WOMAN WAS SAYING...
YOU KNOW WHO I MEAN-- THE WOMAN WE FOUND LYING IN THE FOREST LAST YEAR AFTER THE FIRST SNOWFALL...

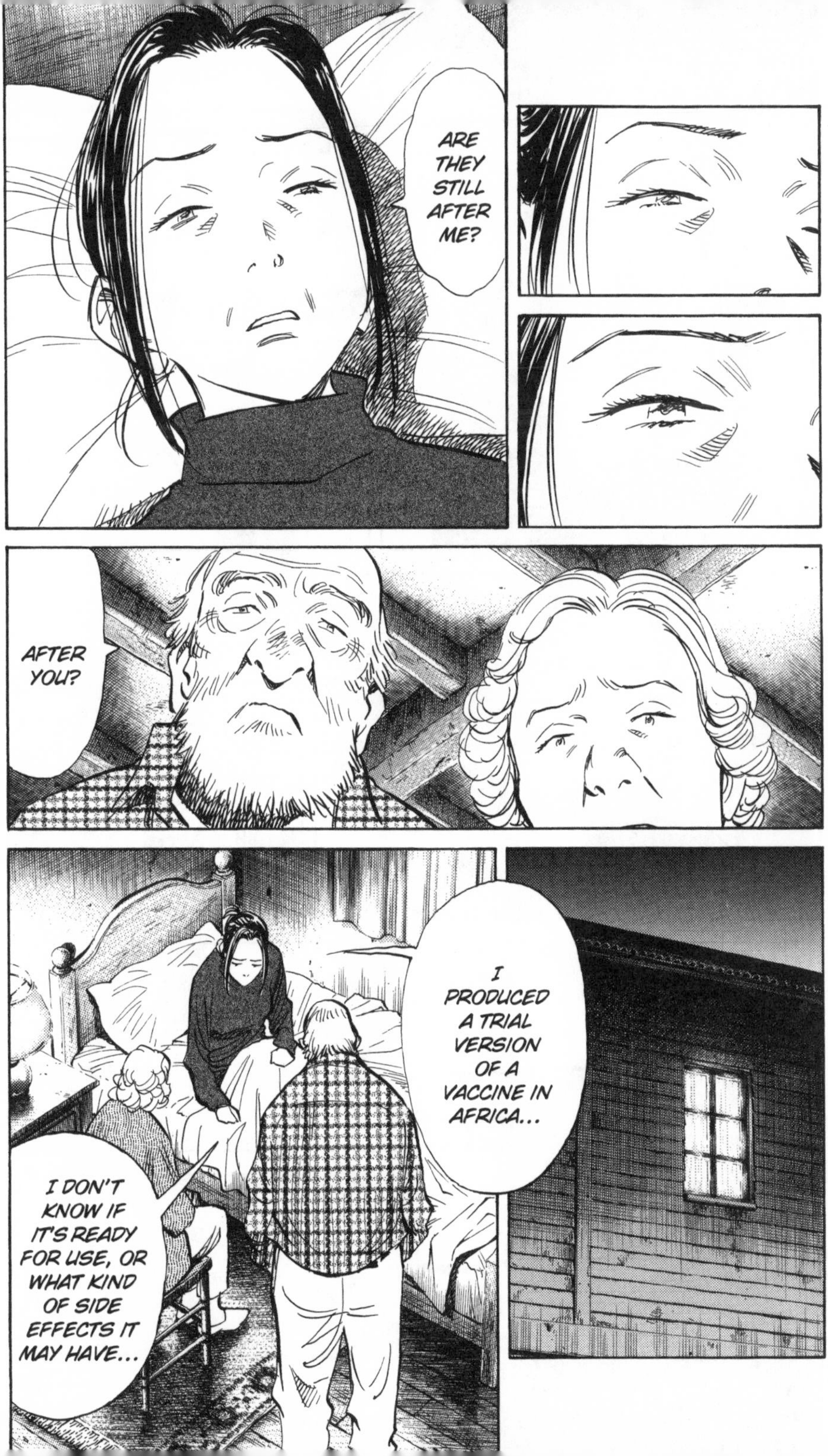
ARE THEY STILL AFTER ME?
AFTER YOU?
I PRODUCED A TRIAL VERSION OF A VACCINE IN AFRICA...
I DON'T KNOW IF IT'S READY FOR USE, OR WHAT KIND OF SIDE EFFECTS IT MAY HAVE...

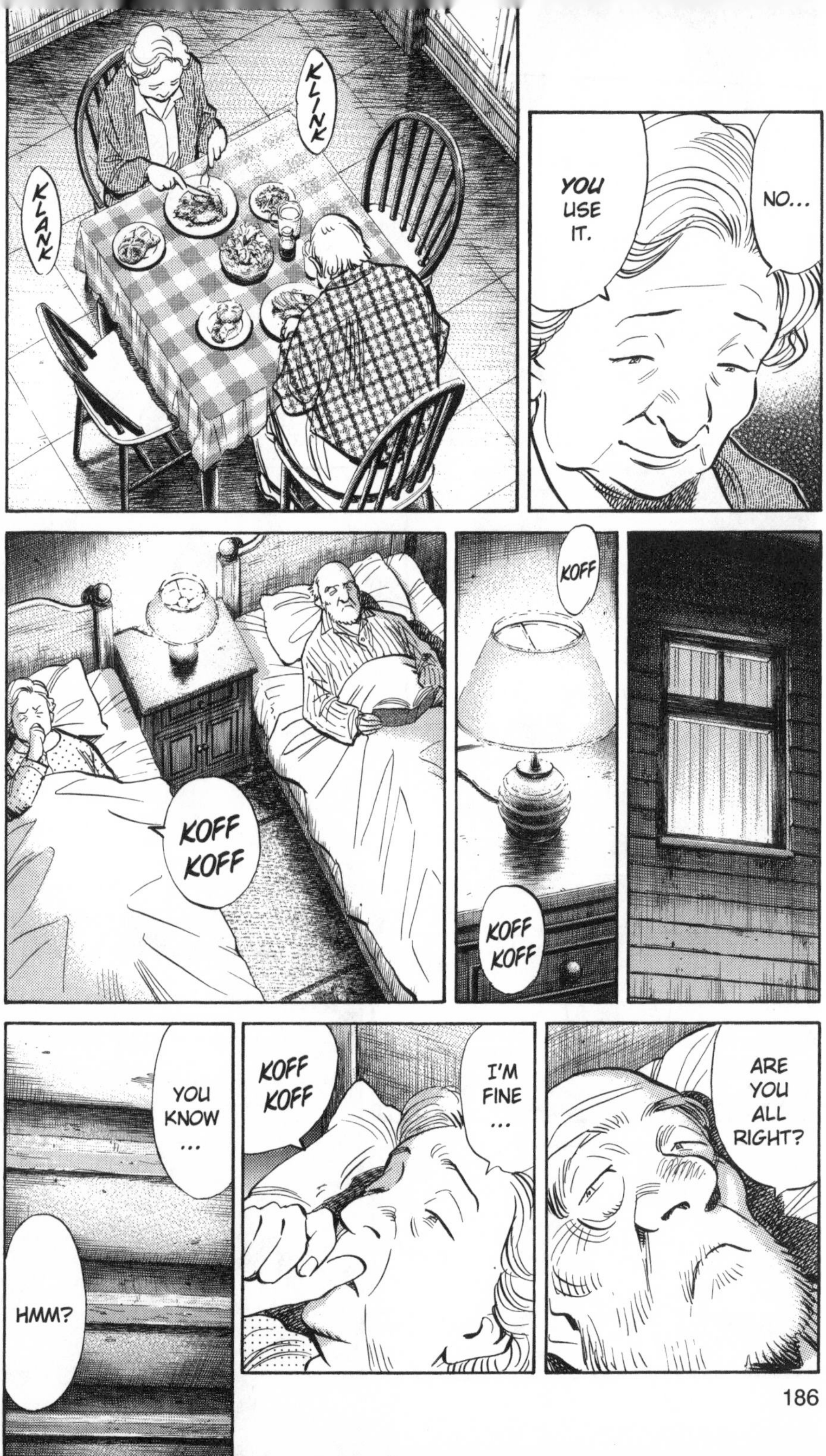
NO...
YOU USE IT.
KLINK
KLANK
KOFF
KOFF KOFF
KOFF KOFF
ARE YOU ALL RIGHT?
I'M FINE ...
KOFF KOFF
YOU KNOW ...
HMM?

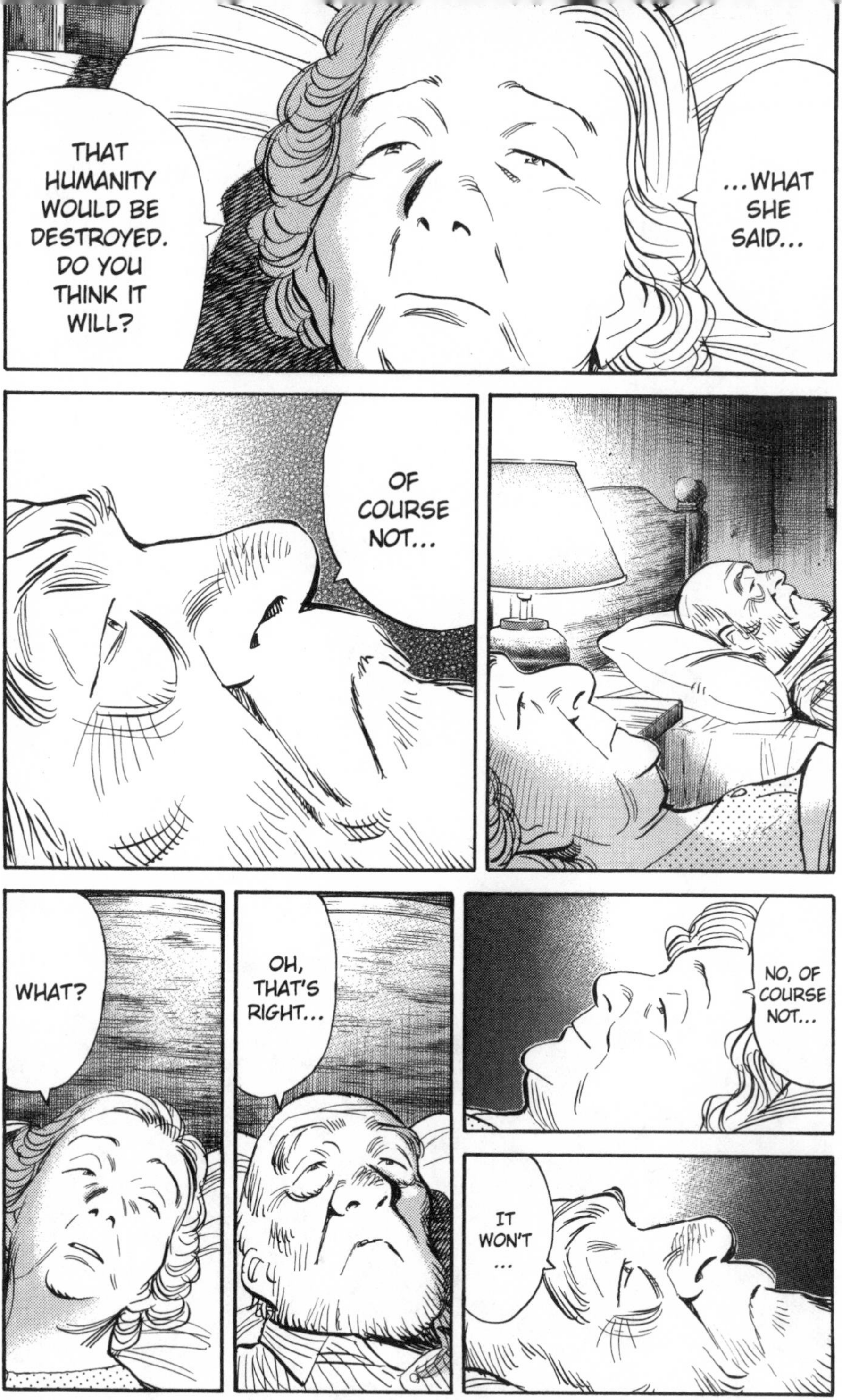
...WHAT SHE SAID...
THAT HUMANITY WOULD BE DESTROYED. DO YOU THINK IT WILL?
OF COURSE NOT...
NO, OF COURSE NOT...
IT WON'T ...
OH, THAT'S RIGHT...
WHAT?

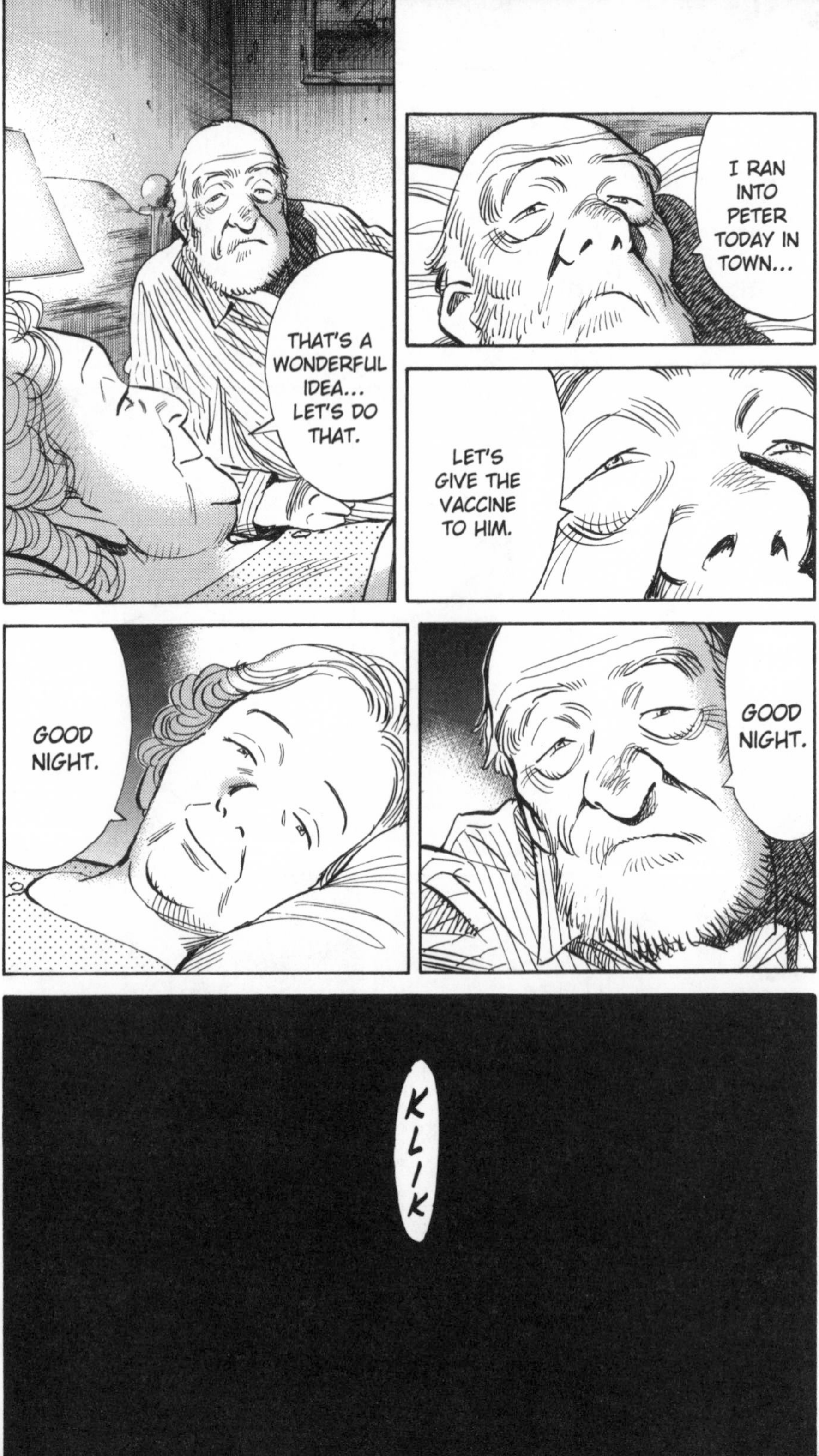
I RAN INTO PETER TODAY IN TOWN...
LET'S GIVE THE VACCINE TO HIM.
THAT'S A WONDERFUL IDEA... LET'S DO THAT.
GOOD NIGHT.
GOOD NIGHT.
KLIK

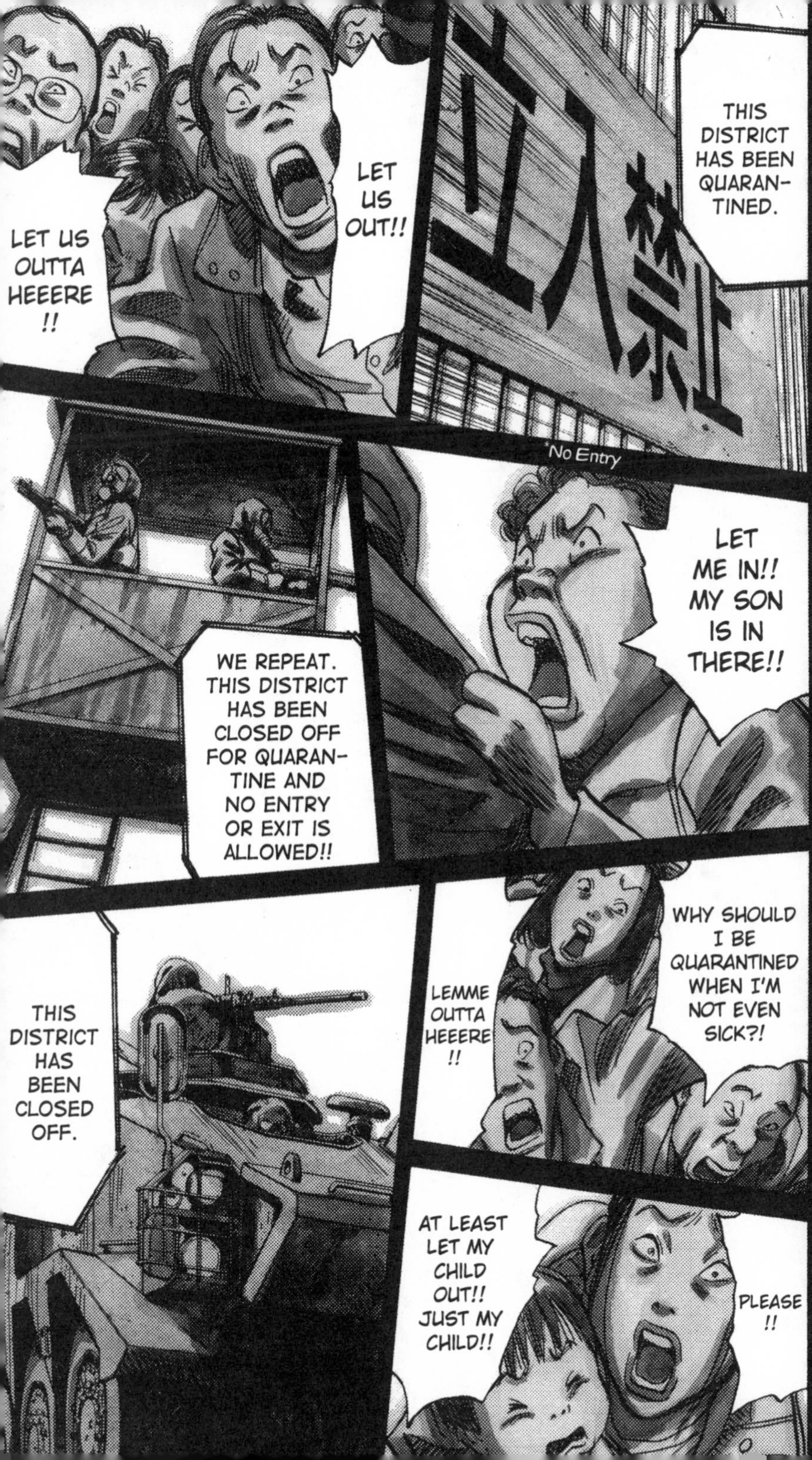
THIS DISTRICT HAS BEEN QUARANTINED.
*No Entry
LET US OUT!!
LET US OUTTA HEEERE !!
LET ME IN!! MY SON IS IN THERE!!
WE REPEAT. THIS DISTRICT HAS BEEN CLOSED OFF FOR QUARANTINE AND NO ENTRY OR EXIT IS ALLOWED!!
WHY SHOULD I BE QUARANTINED WHEN I'M NOT EVEN SICK?!
LEMME OUTTA HEEERE !!
PLEASE !!
AT LEAST LET MY CHILD OUT!! JUST MY CHILD!!
THIS DISTRICT HAS BEEN CLOSED OFF.

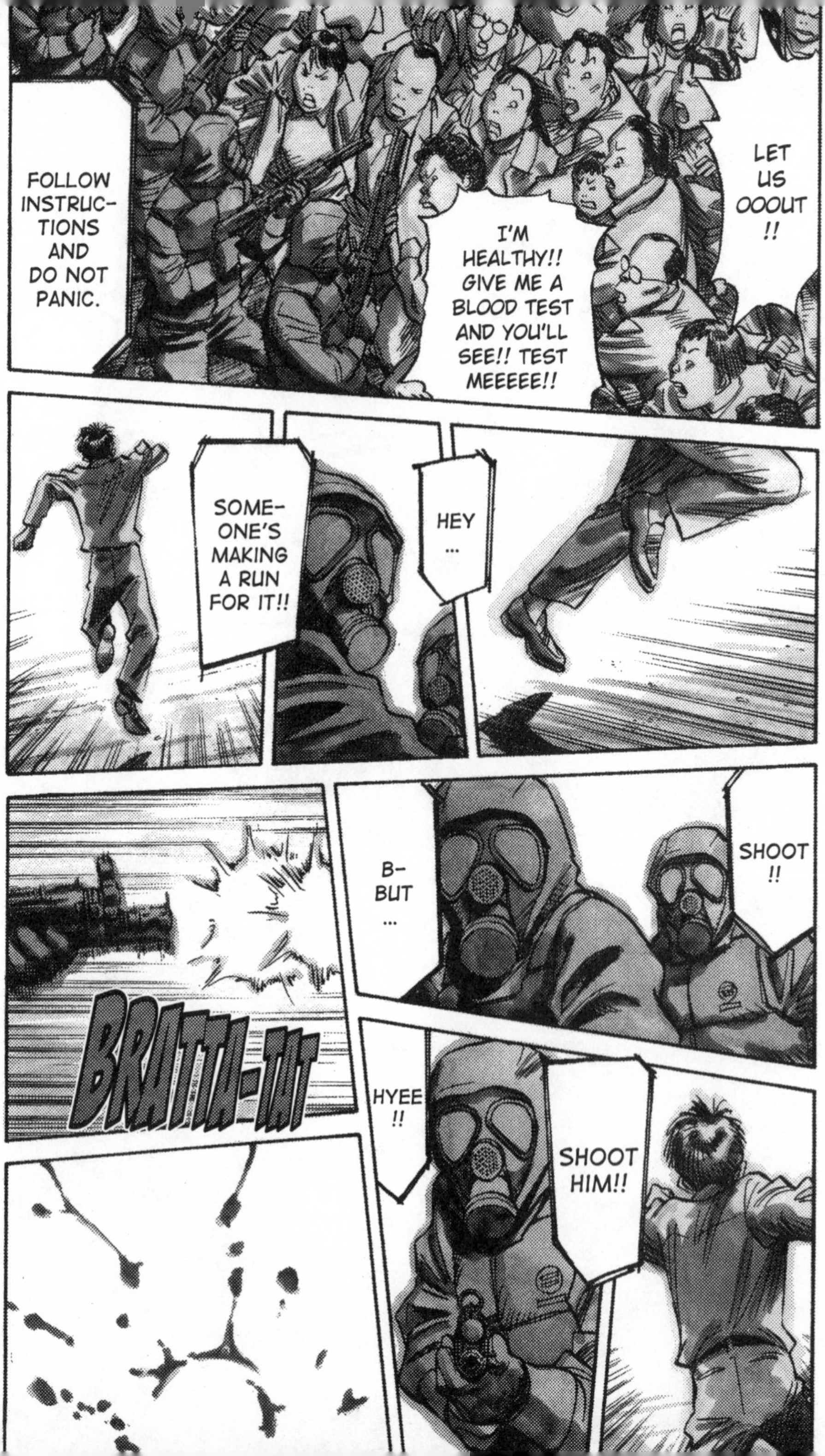
LET US OOOUT!!
I'M HEALTHY!! GIVE ME A BLOOD TEST AND YOU'LL SEE!! TEST MEEEEE!!
FOLLOW INSTRUC-TIONS AND DO NOT PANIC.
HEY ...
SOME-ONE'S MAKING A RUN FOR IT!!
SHOOT!!
B-BUT ...
SHOOT HIM!!
HYEE!!
BRATTA-TAT

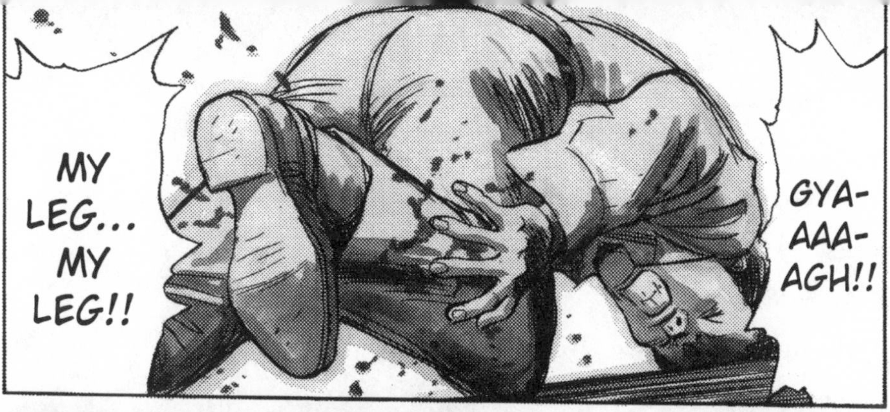
GYA-AAAA-AGH!!
MY LEG... MY LEG!!

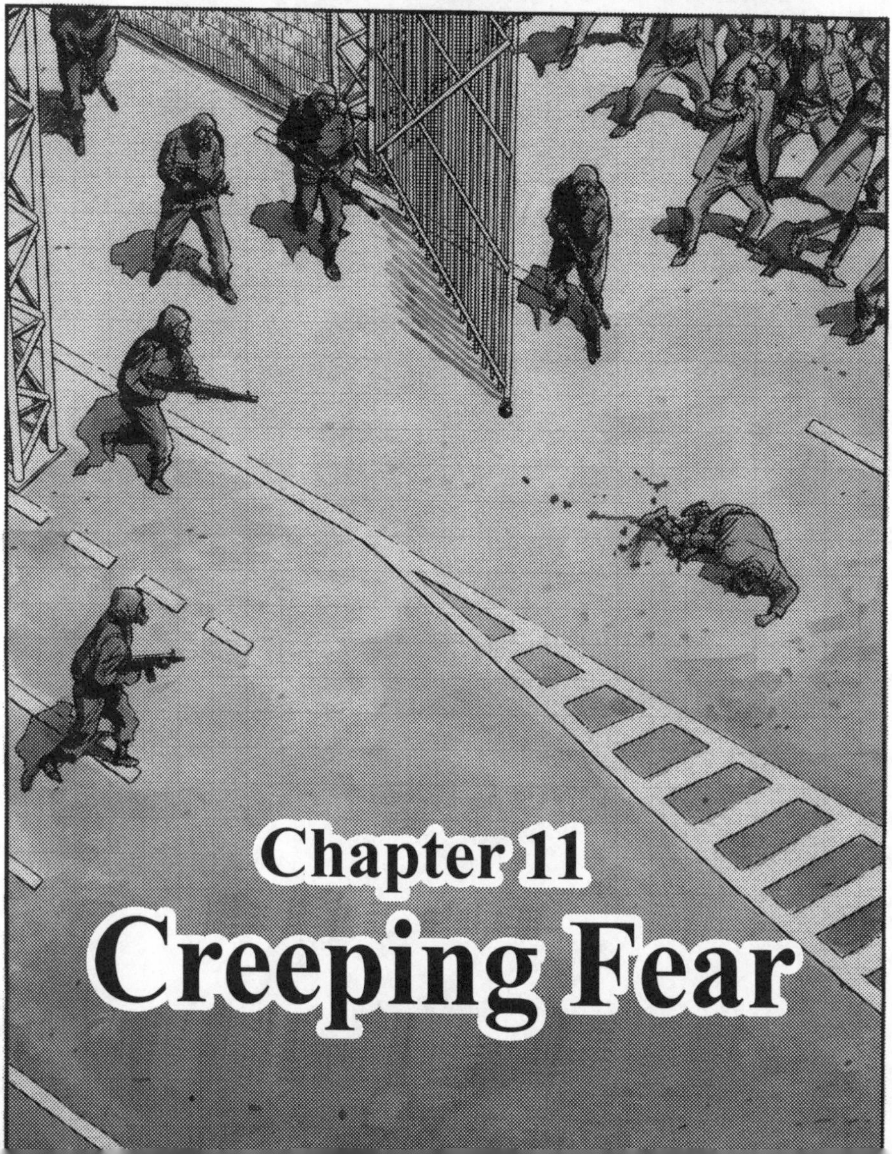
Chapter 11
Creeping Fear

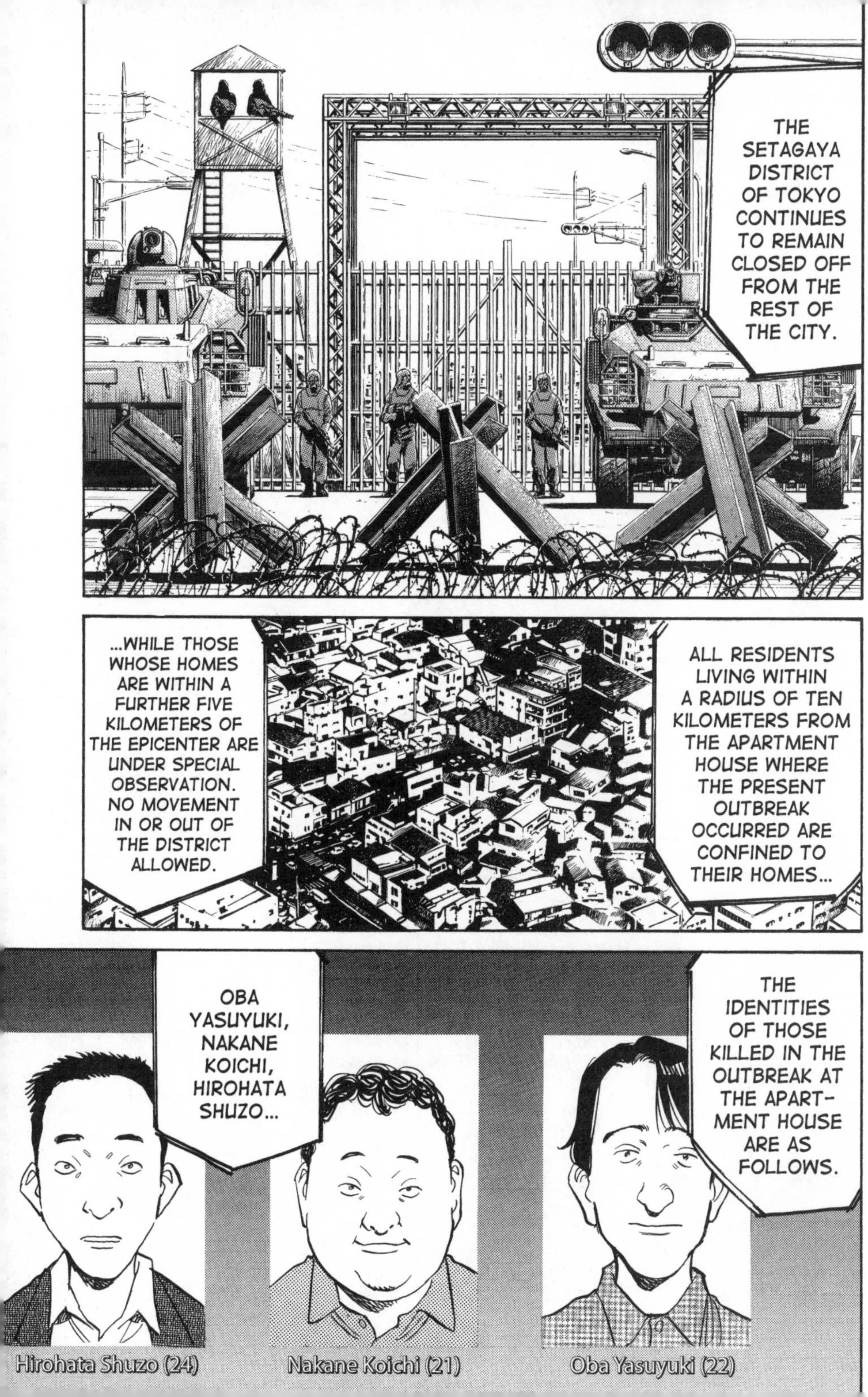
THE SETAGAYA DISTRICT OF TOKYO CONTINUES TO REMAIN CLOSED OFF FROM THE REST OF THE CITY.
ALL RESIDENTS LIVING WITHIN A RADIUS OF TEN KILOMETERS FROM THE APARTMENT HOUSE WHERE THE PRESENT OUTBREAK OCCURRED ARE CONFINED TO THEIR HOMES...
...WHILE THOSE WHOSE HOMES ARE WITHIN A FURTHER FIVE KILOMETERS OF THE EPICENTER ARE UNDER SPECIAL OBSERVATION. NO MOVEMENT IN OR OUT OF THE DISTRICT ALLOWED.
THE IDENTITIES OF THOSE KILLED IN THE OUTBREAK AT THE APART-MENT HOUSE ARE AS FOLLOWS.
OBA YASUYUKI, NAKANE KOICHI, HIROHATA SHUZO...
Oba Yasuyuki (22)
Nakane Koichi (21)
Hirohata Shuzo (24)

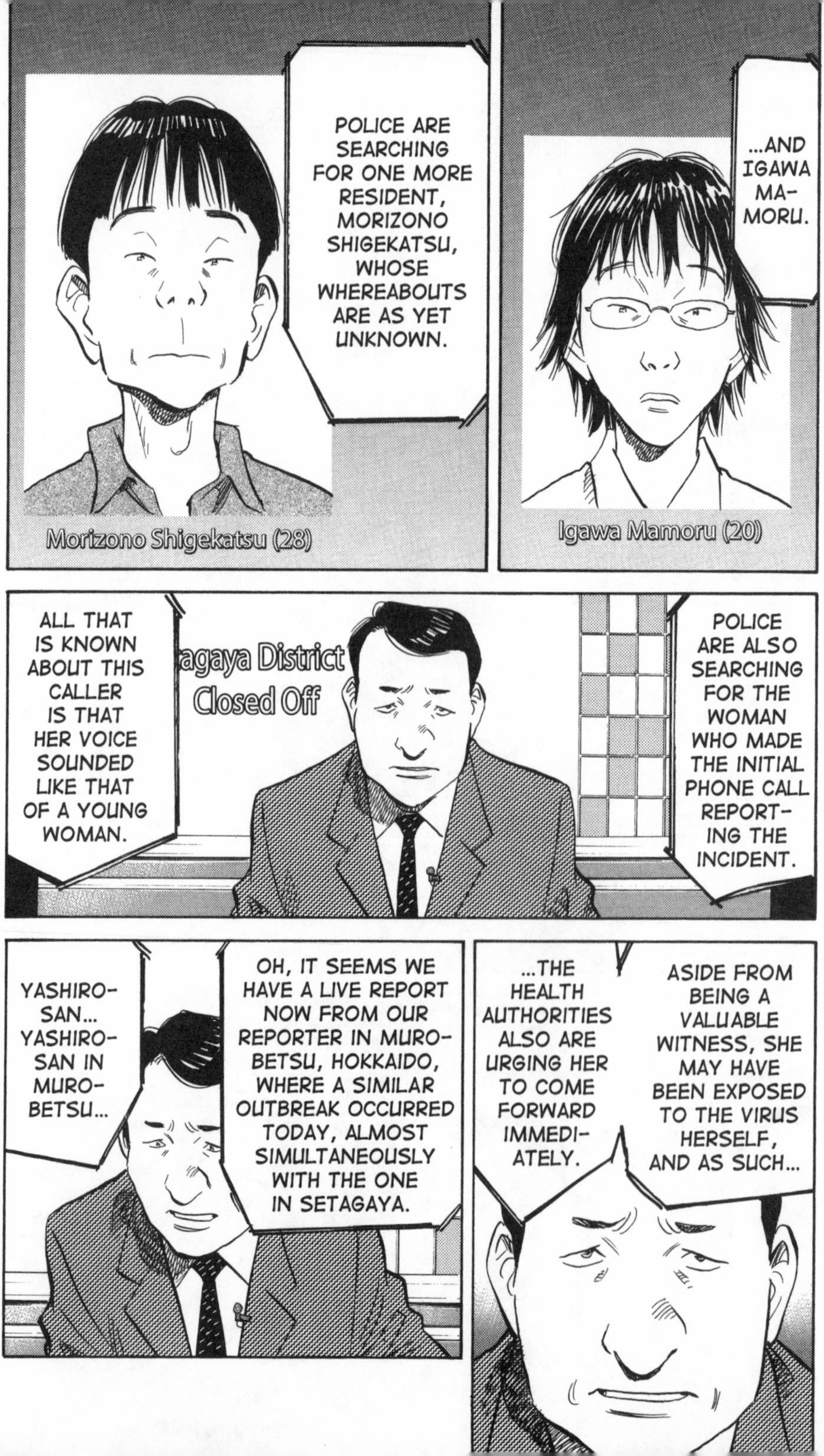
POLICE ARE SEARCHING FOR ONE MORE RESIDENT, MORIZONO SHIGEKATSU, WHOSE WHEREABOUTS ARE AS YET UNKNOWN.
Morizono Shigekatsu (28)
...AND IGAWA MA-MORU.
Igawa Mamoru (20)
POLICE ARE ALSO SEARCHING FOR THE WOMAN WHO MADE THE INITIAL PHONE CALL REPORT-ING THE INCIDENT.
agaya District
Closed Off
ALL THAT IS KNOWN ABOUT THIS CALLER IS THAT HER VOICE SOUNDED LIKE THAT OF A YOUNG WOMAN.
ASIDE FROM BEING A VALUABLE WITNESS, SHE MAY HAVE BEEN EXPOSED TO THE VIRUS HERSELF, AND AS SUCH...
...THE HEALTH AUTHORITIES ALSO ARE URGING HER TO COME FORWARD IMMEDI-ATELY.
OH, IT SEEMS WE HAVE A LIVE REPORT NOW FROM OUR REPORTER IN MURO-BETSU, HOKKAIDO, WHERE A SIMILAR OUTBREAK OCCURRED TODAY, ALMOST SIMULTANEOUSLY WITH THE ONE IN SETAGAYA.
YASHIRO-SAN... YASHIRO-SAN IN MURO-BETSU...

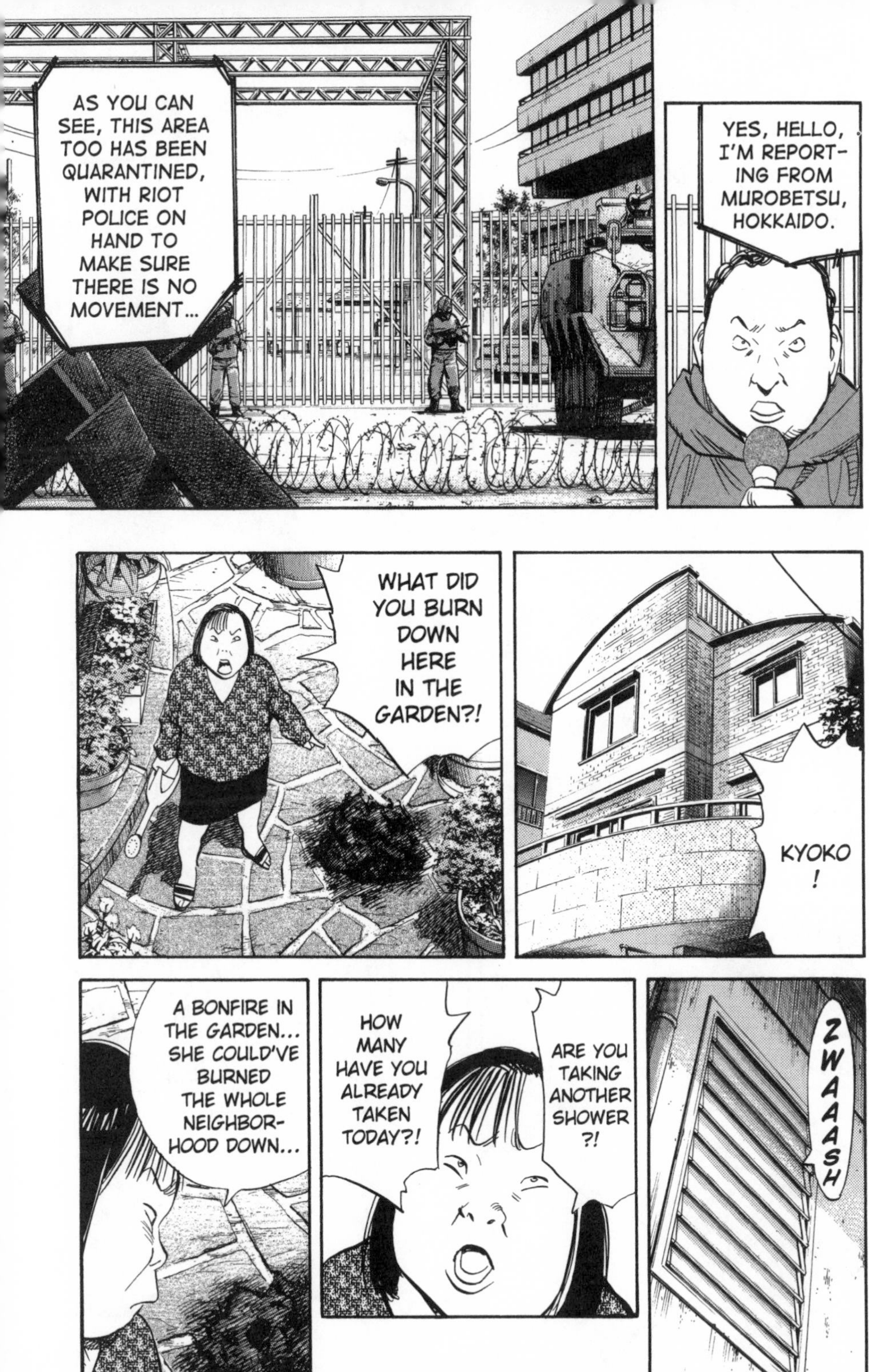
YES, HELLO, I'M REPORTING FROM MUROBETSU, HOKKAIDO.
AS YOU CAN SEE, THIS AREA TOO HAS BEEN QUARANTINED, WITH RIOT POLICE ON HAND TO MAKE SURE THERE IS NO MOVEMENT...
KYOKO!
WHAT DID YOU BURN DOWN HERE IN THE GARDEN?!
ZWAAAASH
ARE YOU TAKING ANOTHER SHOWER?!
HOW MANY HAVE YOU ALREADY TAKEN TODAY?!
A BONFIRE IN THE GARDEN... SHE COULD'VE BURNED THE WHOLE NEIGHBORHOOD DOWN...

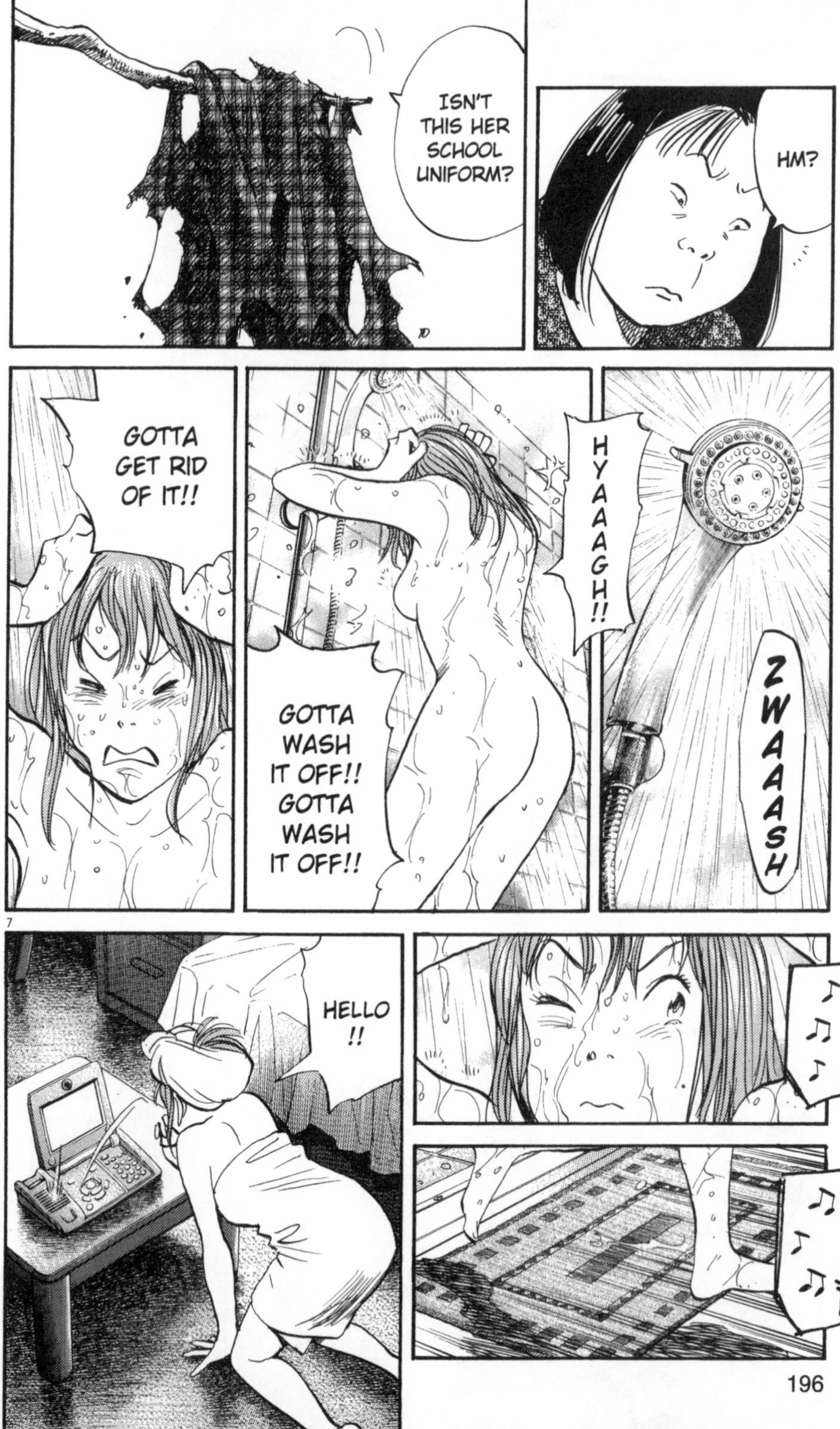
HM?
ISN'T THIS HER SCHOOL UNIFORM?
HYAAAAGH!!
ZWAAAASH
GOTTA WASH IT OFF!! GOTTA WASH IT OFF!!
GOTTA GET RID OF IT!!
HELLO !!

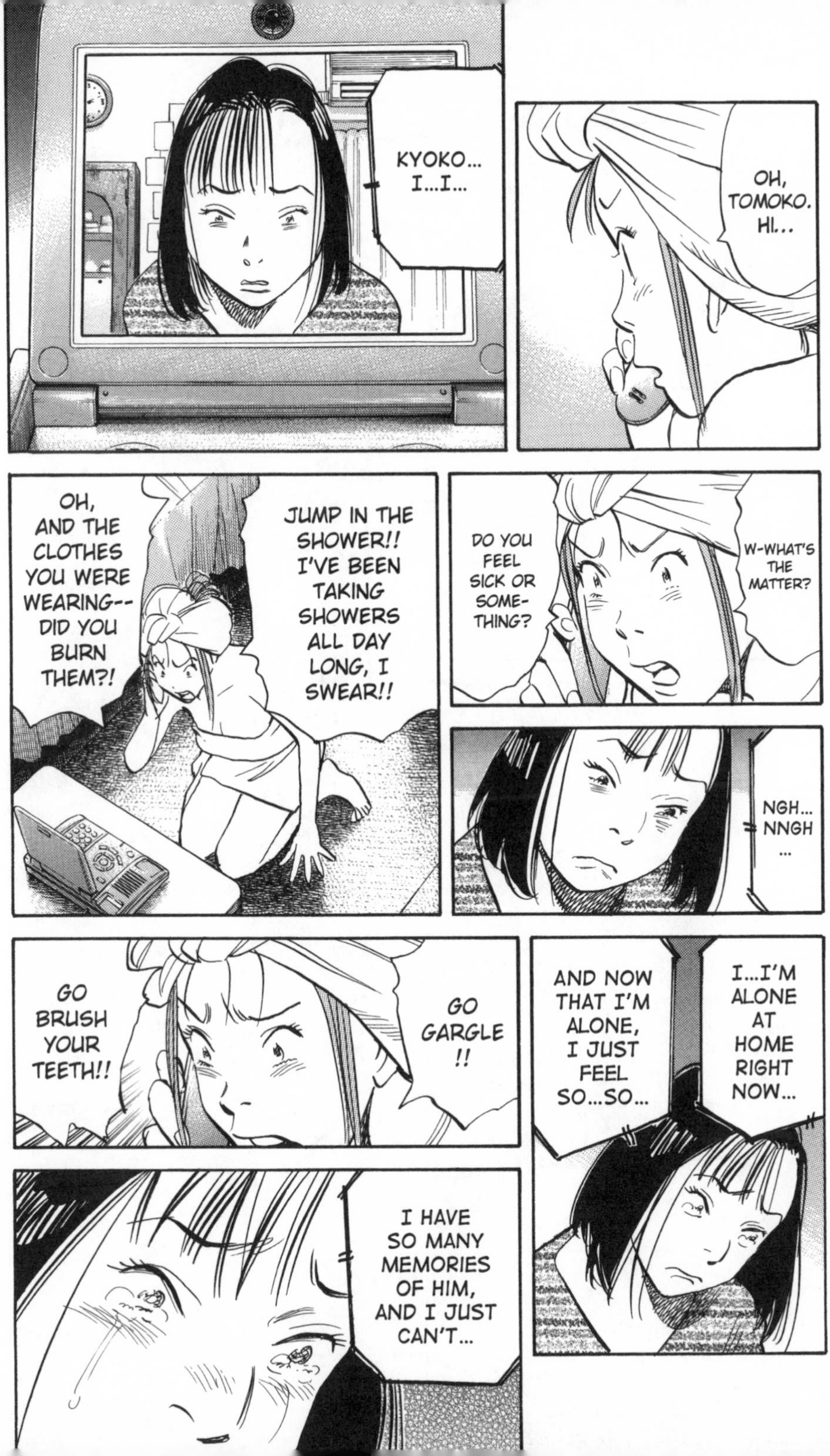

OH, TOMOKO. HI...
KYOKO... I...I...
W-WHAT'S THE MATTER?
DO YOU FEEL SICK OR SOME-THING?
NGH... NNGH ...
JUMP IN THE SHOWER!! I'VE BEEN TAKING SHOWERS ALL DAY LONG, I SWEAR!!
OH, AND THE CLOTHES YOU WERE WEARING-- DID YOU BURN THEM?!
I...I'M ALONE AT HOME RIGHT NOW...
AND NOW THAT I'M ALONE, I JUST FEEL SO...SO...
GO GARGLE !!
GO BRUSH YOUR TEETH!!
I HAVE SO MANY MEMORIES OF HIM, AND I JUST CAN'T...

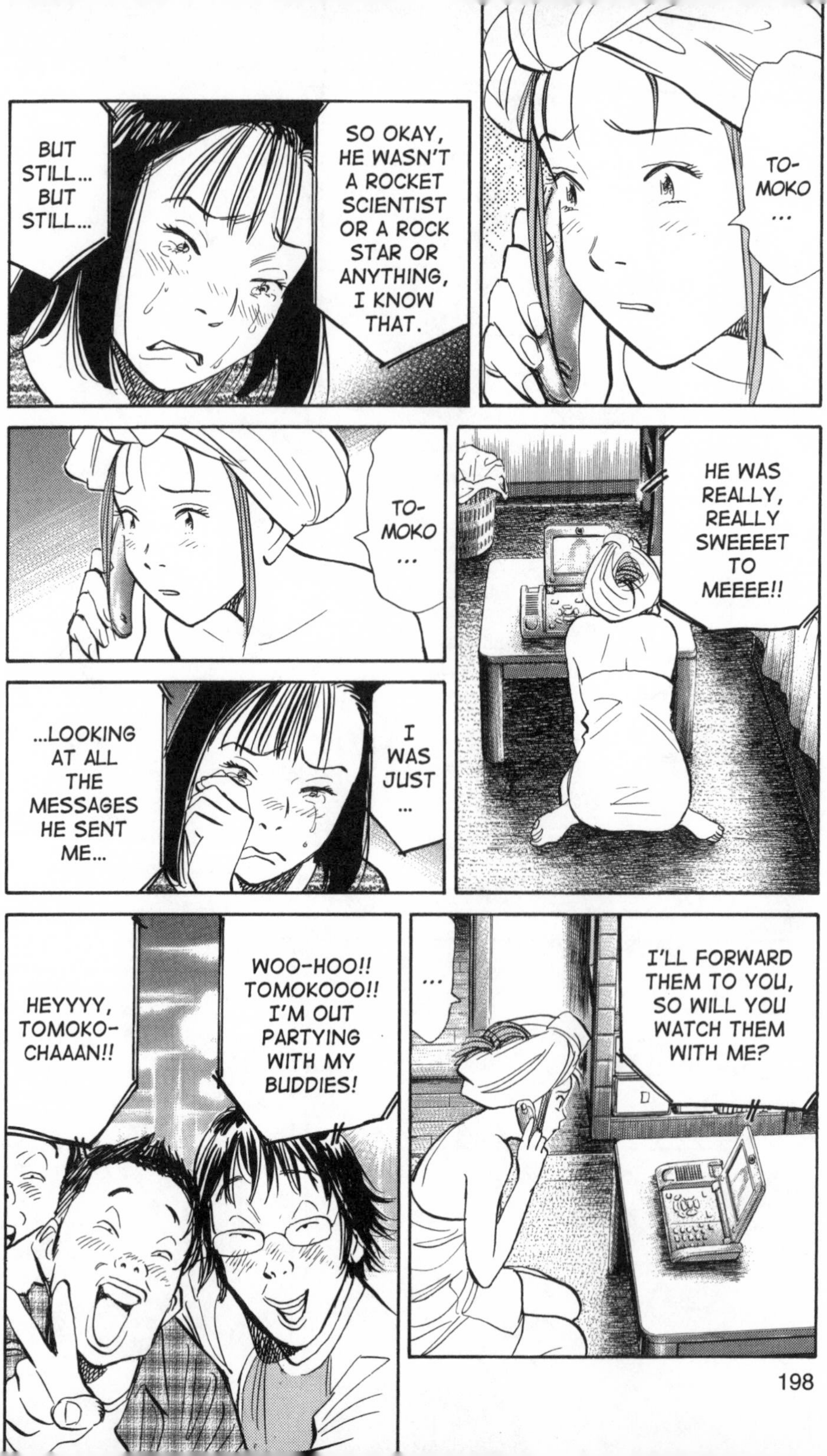

TO-MOKO ...
SO OKAY, HE WASN'T A ROCKET SCIENTIST OR A ROCK STAR OR ANYTHING, I KNOW THAT.
BUT STILL... BUT STILL...
HE WAS REALLY, REALLY SWEEEET TO MEEEE!!
TO-MOKO ...
I WAS JUST ...
...LOOKING AT ALL THE MESSAGES HE SENT ME...
I'LL FORWARD THEM TO YOU, SO WILL YOU WATCH THEM WITH ME?
...
WOO-HOO!! TOMOKOOO!! I'M OUT PARTYING WITH MY BUDDIES!
HEYYYY, TOMOKO-CHAAAN!!

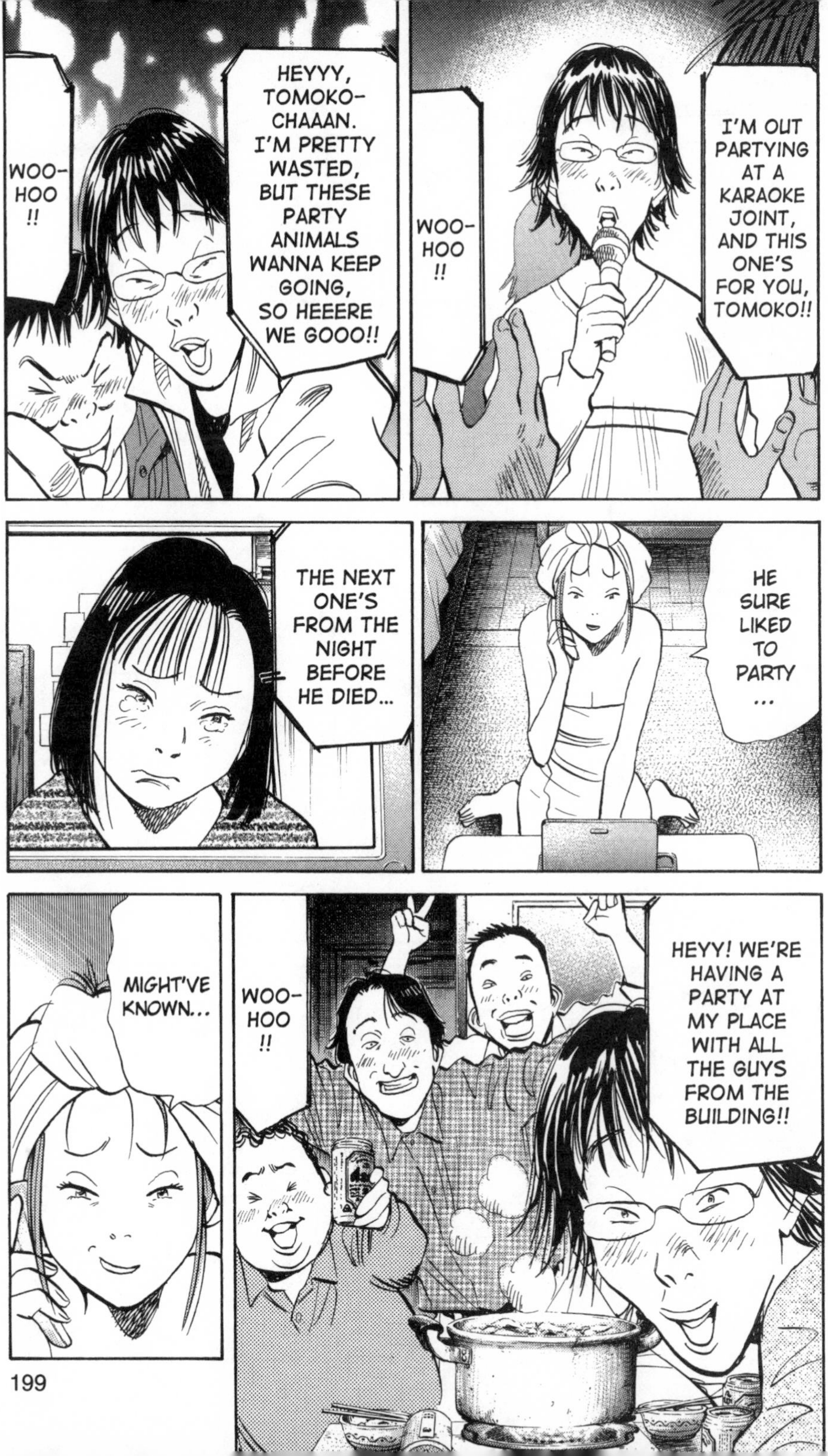
I'M OUT PARTYING AT A KARAOKE JOINT, AND THIS ONE'S FOR YOU, TOMOKO!!
WOO-HOO !!
HEYYY, TOMOKO-CHAAAN. I'M PRETTY WASTED, BUT THESE PARTY ANIMALS WANNA KEEP GOING, SO HEEERE WE GOOO!!
WOO-HOO !!
HE SURE LIKED TO PARTY ...
THE NEXT ONE'S FROM THE NIGHT BEFORE HE DIED...
HEYY! WE'RE HAVING A PARTY AT MY PLACE WITH ALL THE GUYS FROM THE BUILDING!!
WOO-HOO !!
MIGHT'VE KNOWN...

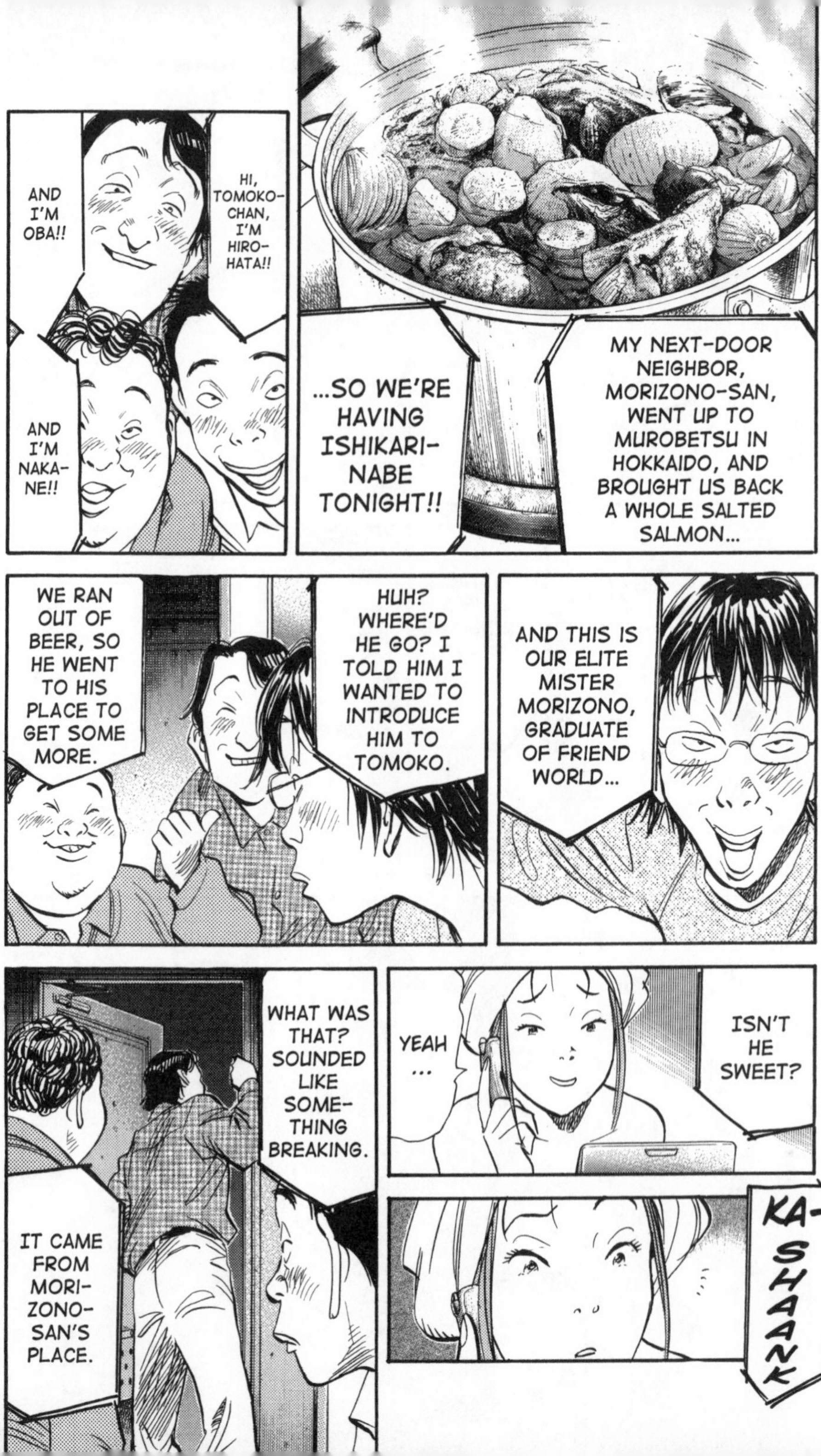
MY NEXT-DOOR NEIGHBOR, MORIZONO-SAN, WENT UP TO MUROBETSU IN HOKKAIDO, AND BROUGHT US BACK A WHOLE SALTED SALMON...
...SO WE'RE HAVING ISHIKARI-NABE TONIGHT!!
HI, TOMOKO-CHAN, I'M HIRO-HATA!!
AND I'M OBA!!
AND I'M NAKA-NE!!
AND THIS IS OUR ELITE MISTER MORIZONO, GRADUATE OF FRIEND WORLD...
HUH? WHERE'D HE GO? I TOLD HIM I WANTED TO INTRODUCE HIM TO TOMOKO.
WE RAN OUT OF BEER, SO HE WENT TO HIS PLACE TO GET SOME MORE.
ISN'T HE SWEET?
YEAH ...
KA-SHAANK
WHAT WAS THAT? SOUNDED LIKE SOME-THING BREAKING.
IT CAME FROM MORI-ZONO-SAN'S PLACE.

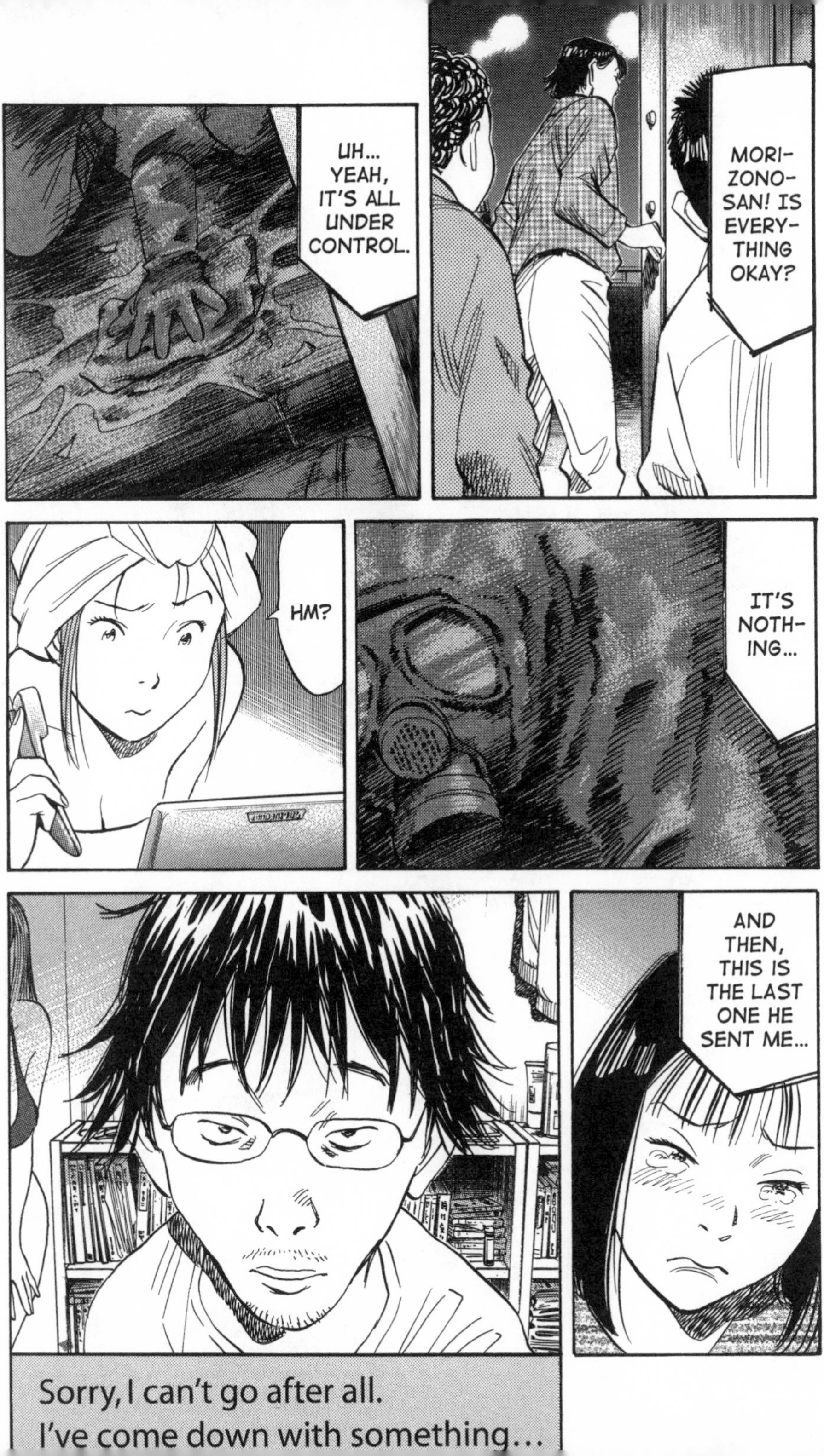
MORI-ZONO-SAN! IS EVERY-THING OKAY?
UH... YEAH, IT'S ALL UNDER CONTROL.
IT'S NOTH-ING...
HM?
AND THEN, THIS IS THE LAST ONE HE SENT ME...
Sorry, I can't go after all.
I've come down with something...

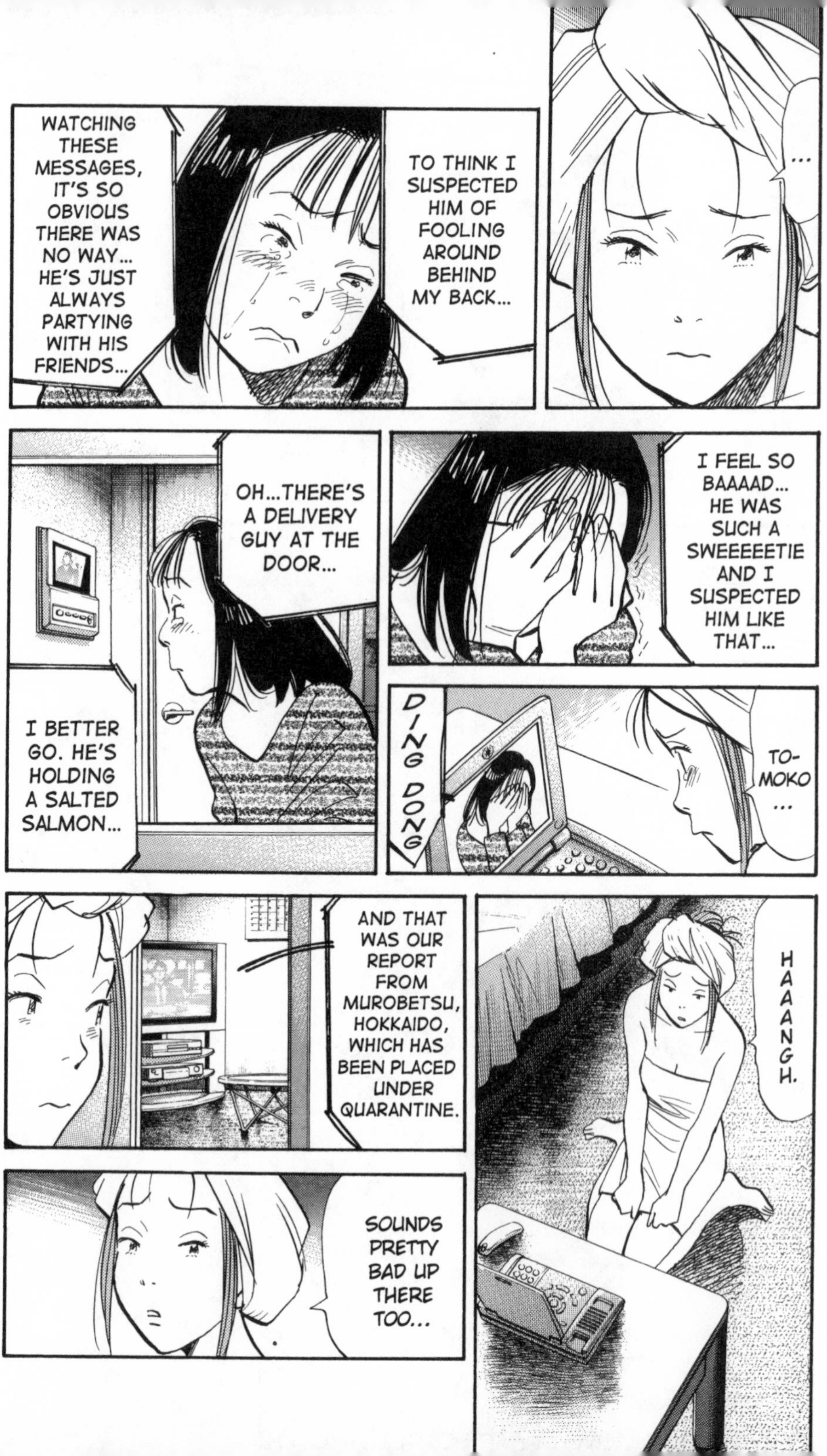
...
TO THINK I SUSPECTED HIM OF FOOLING AROUND BEHIND MY BACK...
WATCHING THESE MESSAGES, IT'S SO OBVIOUS THERE WAS NO WAY... HE'S JUST ALWAYS PARTYING WITH HIS FRIENDS...
I FEEL SO BAAAAD... HE WAS SUCH A SWEEEEETIE AND I SUSPECTED HIM LIKE THAT...
TO-MOKO...
DING DONG
OH...THERE'S A DELIVERY GUY AT THE DOOR...
I BETTER GO. HE'S HOLDING A SALTED SALMON...
HAAAANGH.
AND THAT WAS OUR REPORT FROM MUROBETSU, HOKKAIDO, WHICH HAS BEEN PLACED UNDER QUARANTINE.
SOUNDS PRETTY BAD UP THERE TOO...

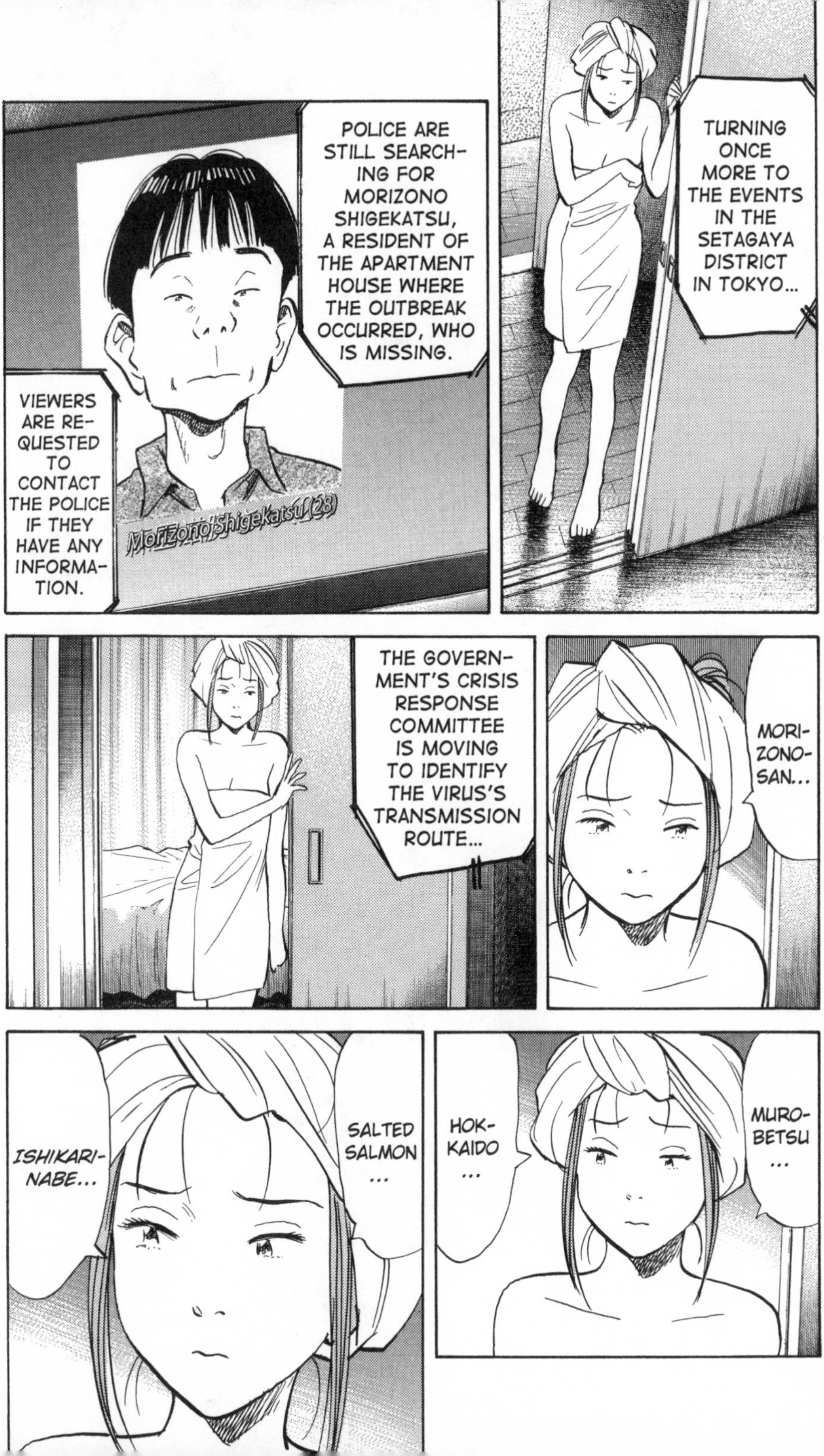
TURNING ONCE MORE TO THE EVENTS IN THE SETAGAYA DISTRICT IN TOKYO...
POLICE ARE STILL SEARCHING FOR MORIZONO SHIGEKATSU, A RESIDENT OF THE APARTMENT HOUSE WHERE THE OUTBREAK OCCURRED, WHO IS MISSING.
VIEWERS ARE REQUESTED TO CONTACT THE POLICE IF THEY HAVE ANY INFORMATION.
Morizono Shigekatsu (28)
MORIZONO-SAN...
THE GOVERNMENT'S CRISIS RESPONSE COMMITTEE IS MOVING TO IDENTIFY THE VIRUS'S TRANSMISSION ROUTE...
MUROBETSU...
HOKKAIDO...
SALTED SALMON...
ISHIKARI-NABE...

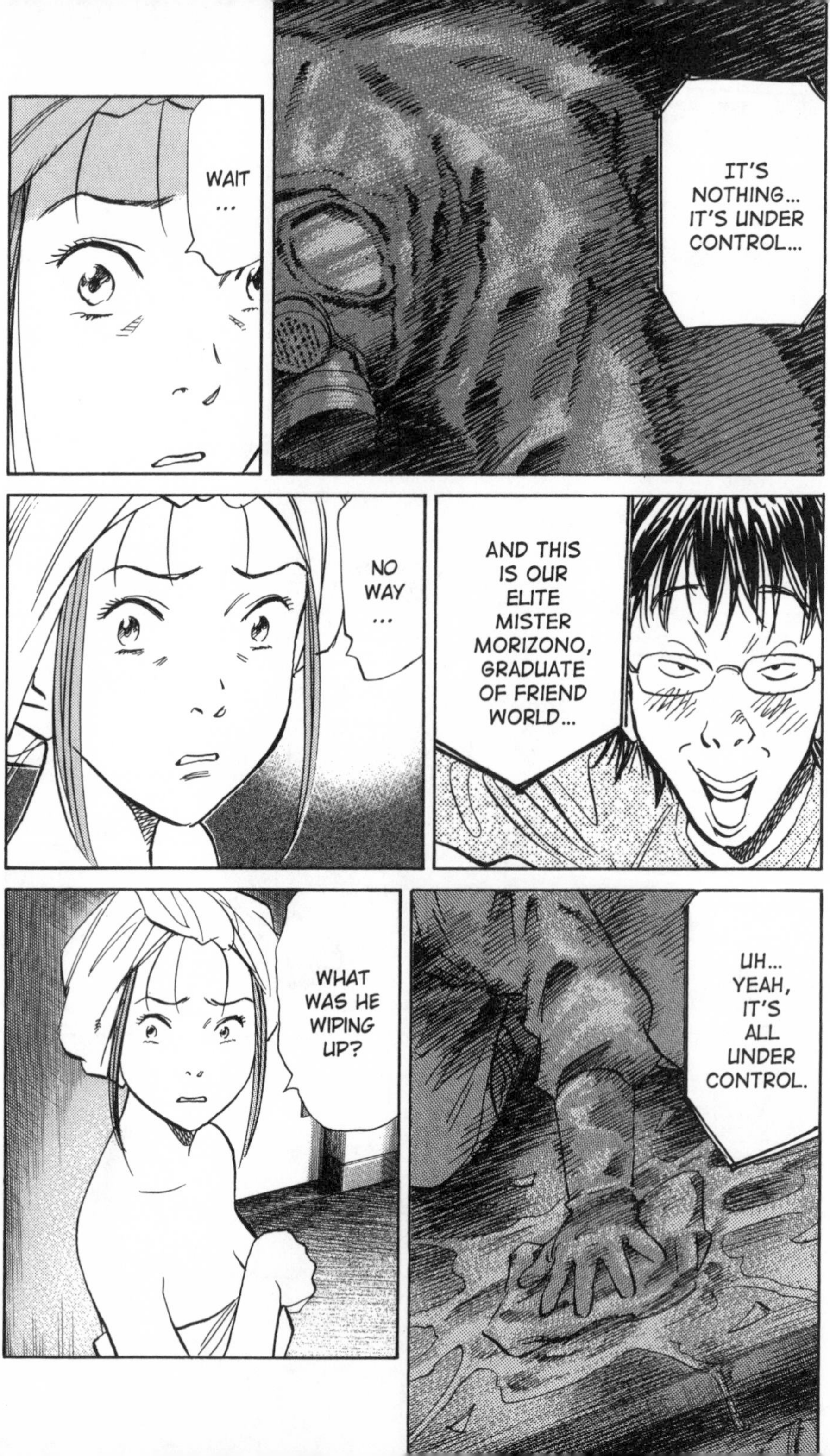
IT'S NOTHING... IT'S UNDER CONTROL...
WAIT ...
AND THIS IS OUR ELITE MISTER MORIZONO, GRADUATE OF FRIEND WORLD...
NO WAY ...
UH... YEAH, IT'S ALL UNDER CONTROL.
WHAT WAS HE WIPING UP?

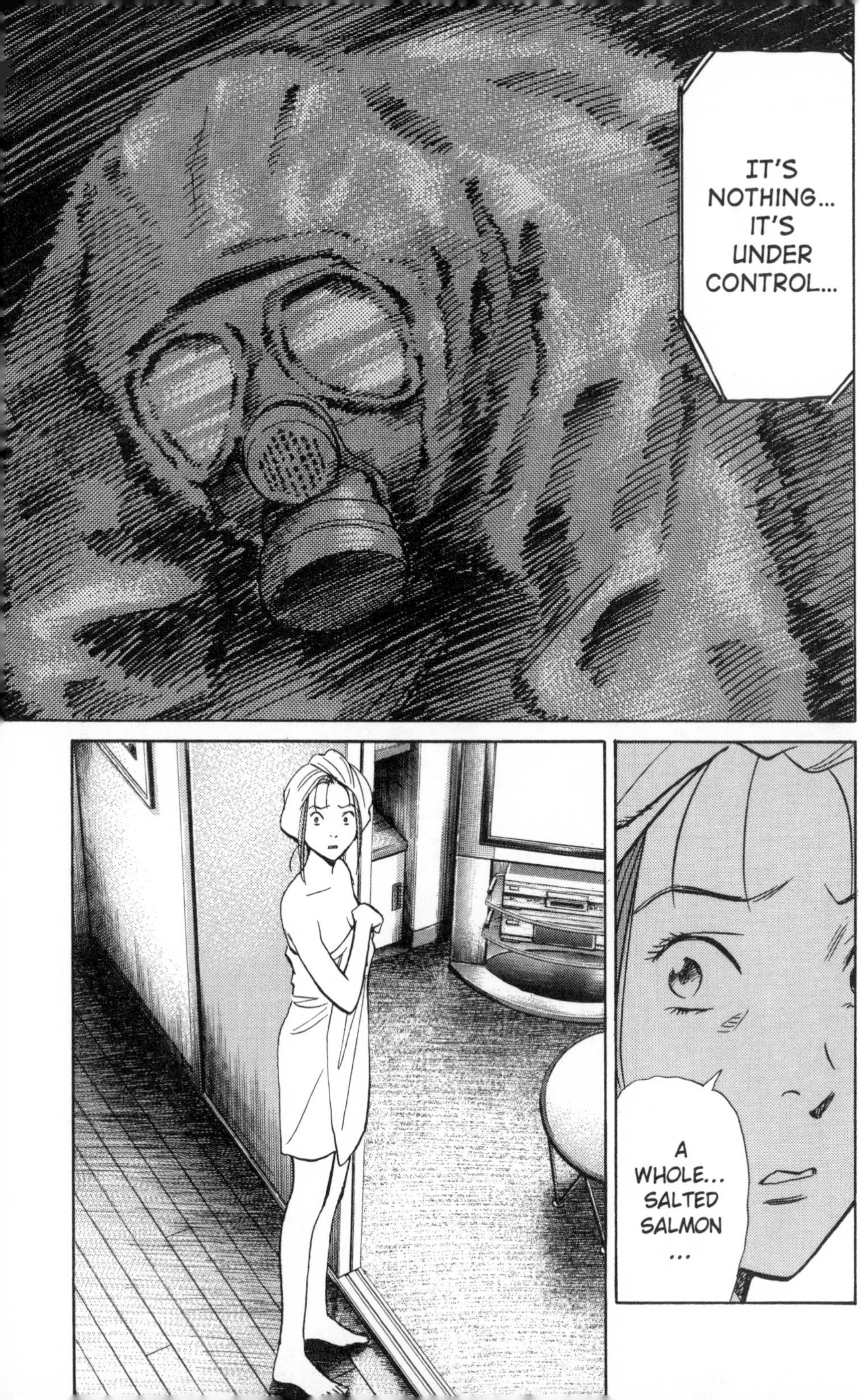
IT'S NOTHING... IT'S UNDER CONTROL...
A WHOLE... SALTED SALMON ...

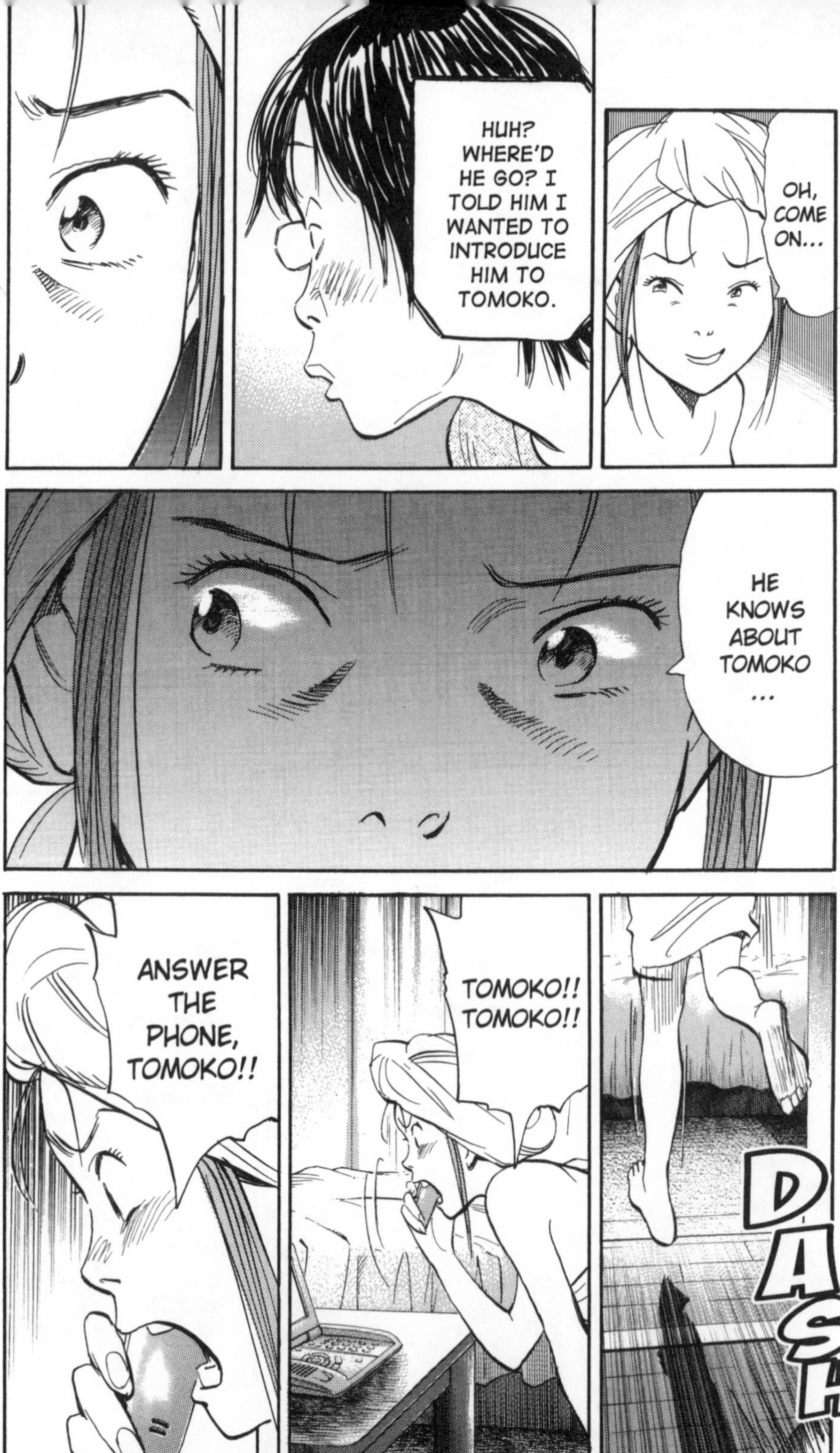
OH, COME ON...
HUH? WHERE'D HE GO? I TOLD HIM I WANTED TO INTRODUCE HIM TO TOMOKO.
HE KNOWS ABOUT TOMOKO ...
DASH
TOMOKO!! TOMOKO!!
ANSWER THE PHONE, TOMOKO!!

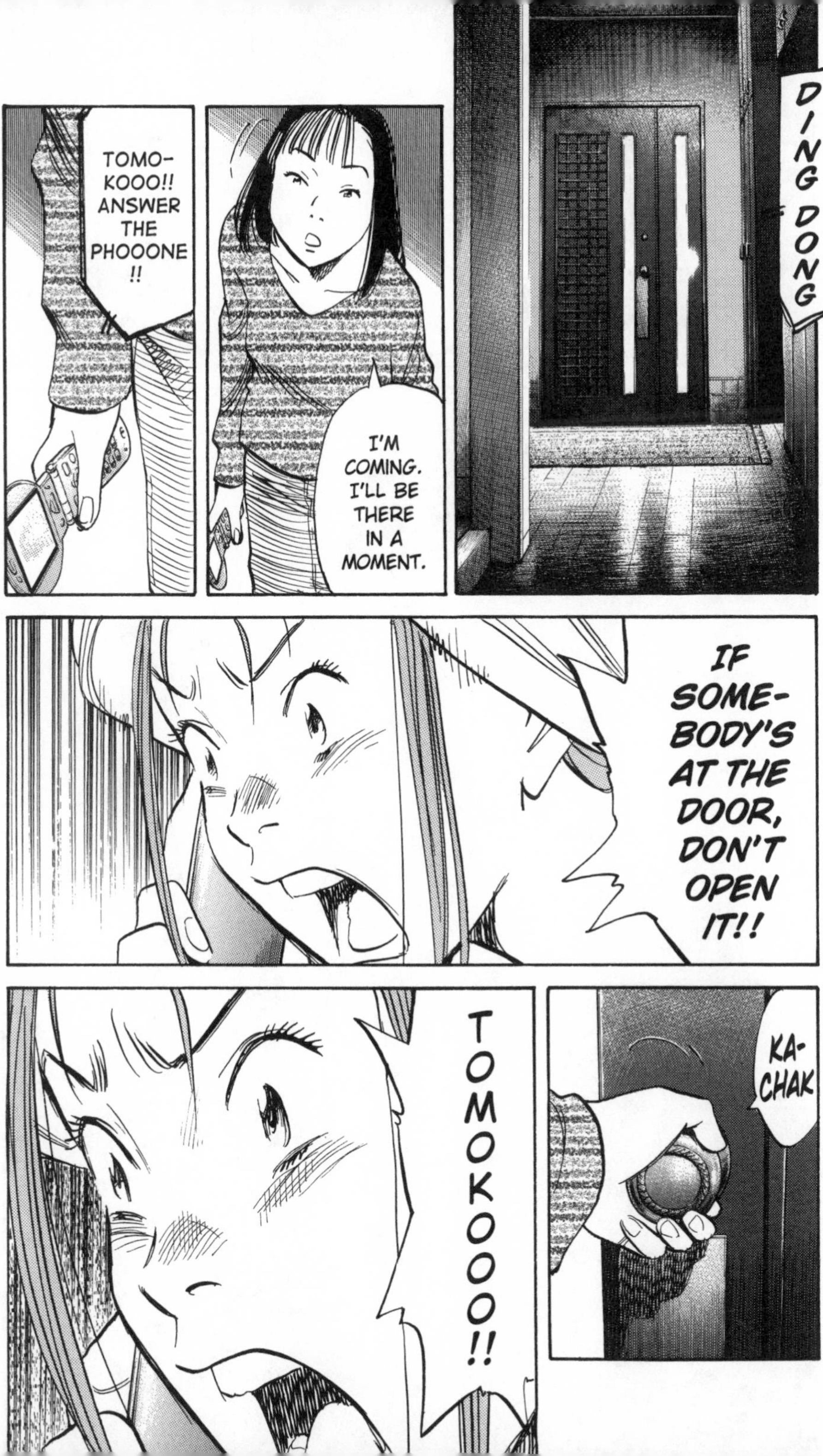
DING DONG
I'M COMING. I'LL BE THERE IN A MOMENT.
TOMO-KOOO!! ANSWER THE PHOOONE!!
IF SOME-BODY'S AT THE DOOR, DON'T OPEN IT!!
KA-CHAK
TOMOKOOOO!!

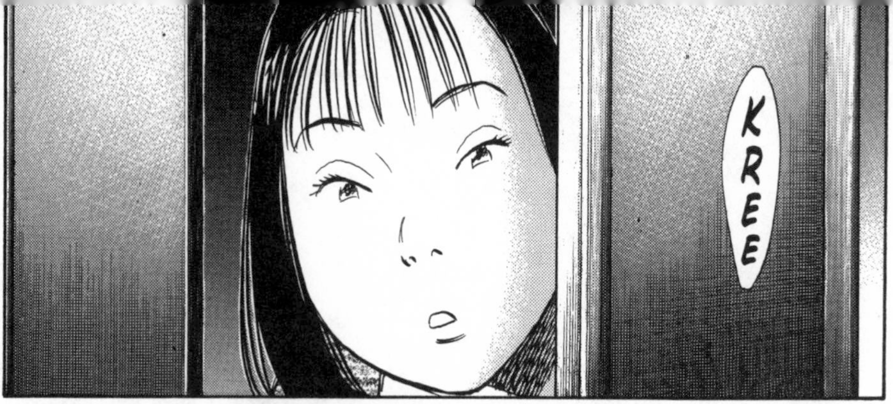
KREE

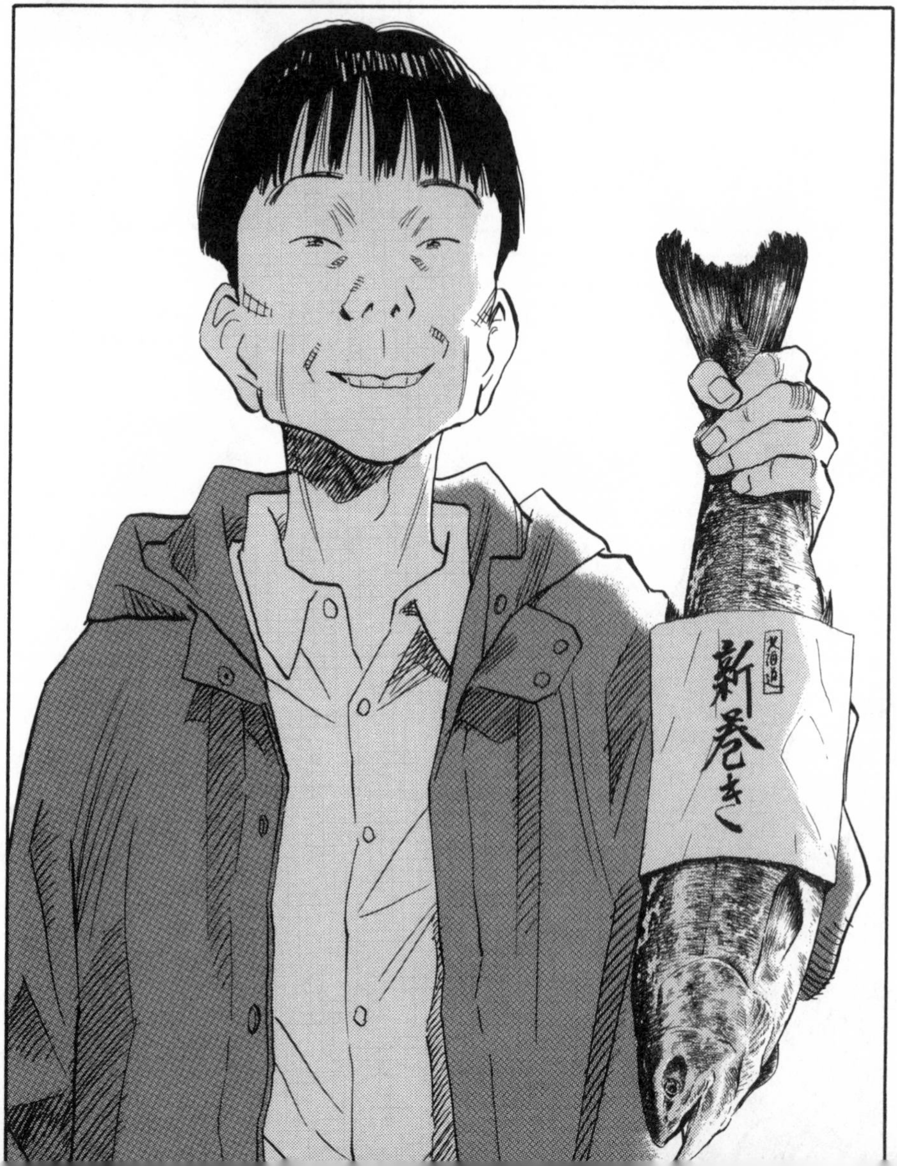
新巻き

Chapter 12 New Command

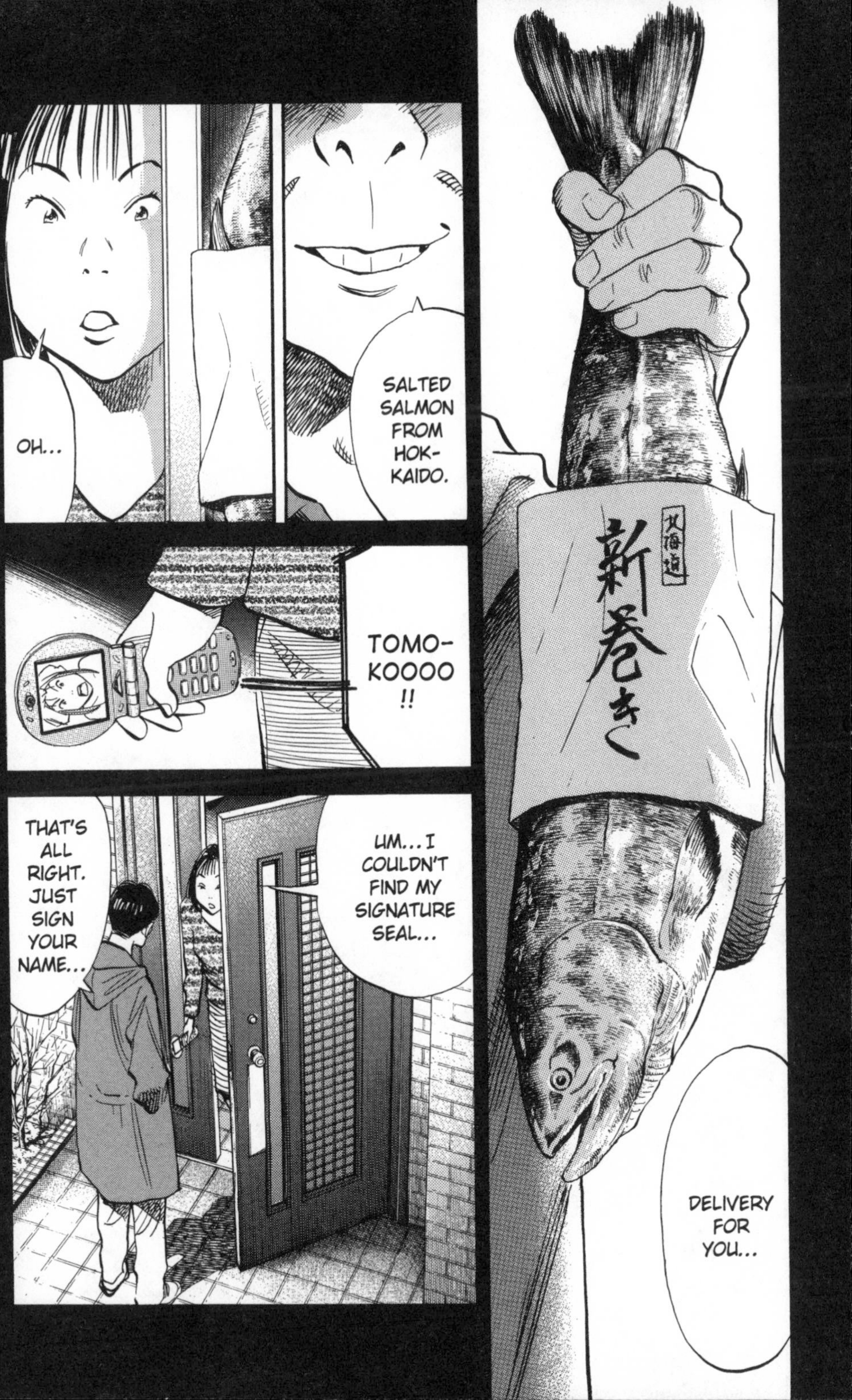

DELIVERY FOR YOU...
北海道
新巻き
SALTED SALMON FROM HOK-KAIDO.
OH...
TOMO-KOOOO!!
UM... I COULDN'T FIND MY SIGNATURE SEAL...
THAT'S ALL RIGHT. JUST SIGN YOUR NAME...

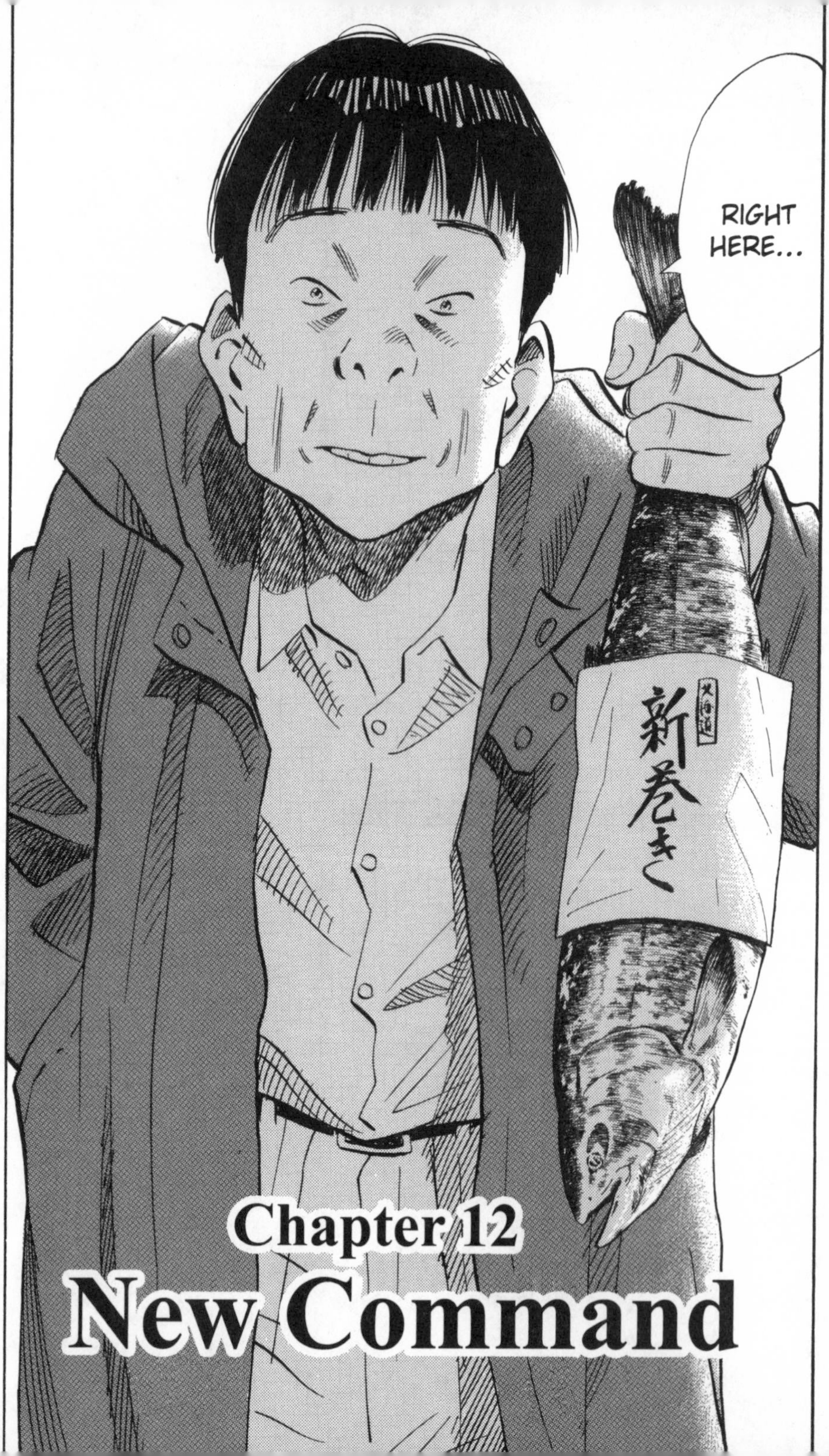
RIGHT HERE...
新巻き

Chapter 12
New Command

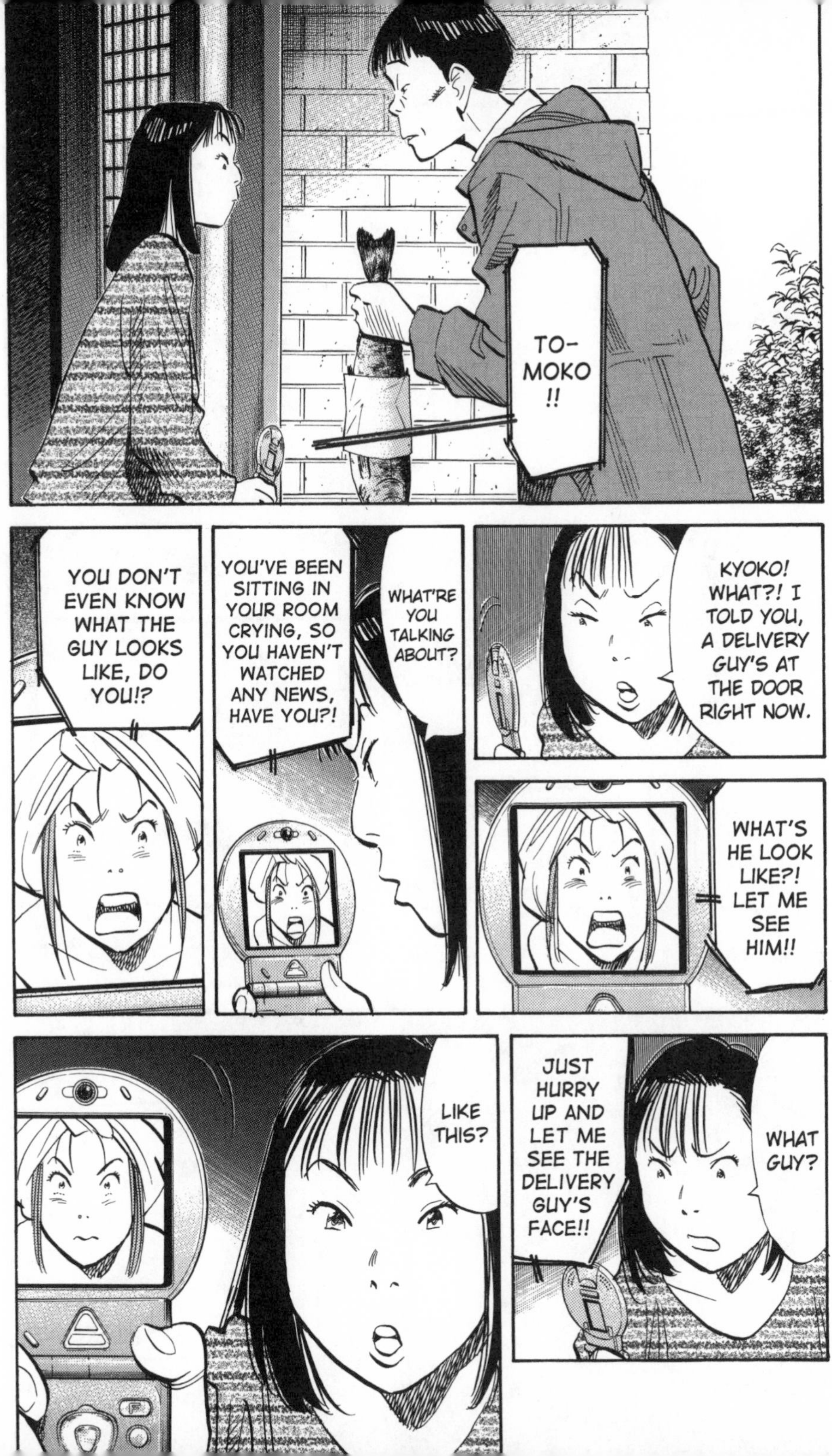
TO-MOKO !!
KYOKO! WHAT?! I TOLD YOU, A DELIVERY GUY'S AT THE DOOR RIGHT NOW.
WHAT'S HE LOOK LIKE?! LET ME SEE HIM!!
WHAT'RE YOU TALKING ABOUT?
YOU'VE BEEN SITTING IN YOUR ROOM CRYING, SO YOU HAVEN'T WATCHED ANY NEWS, HAVE YOU?!
YOU DON'T EVEN KNOW WHAT THE GUY LOOKS LIKE, DO YOU!?
WHAT GUY?
JUST HURRY UP AND LET ME SEE THE DELIVERY GUY'S FACE!!
LIKE THIS?

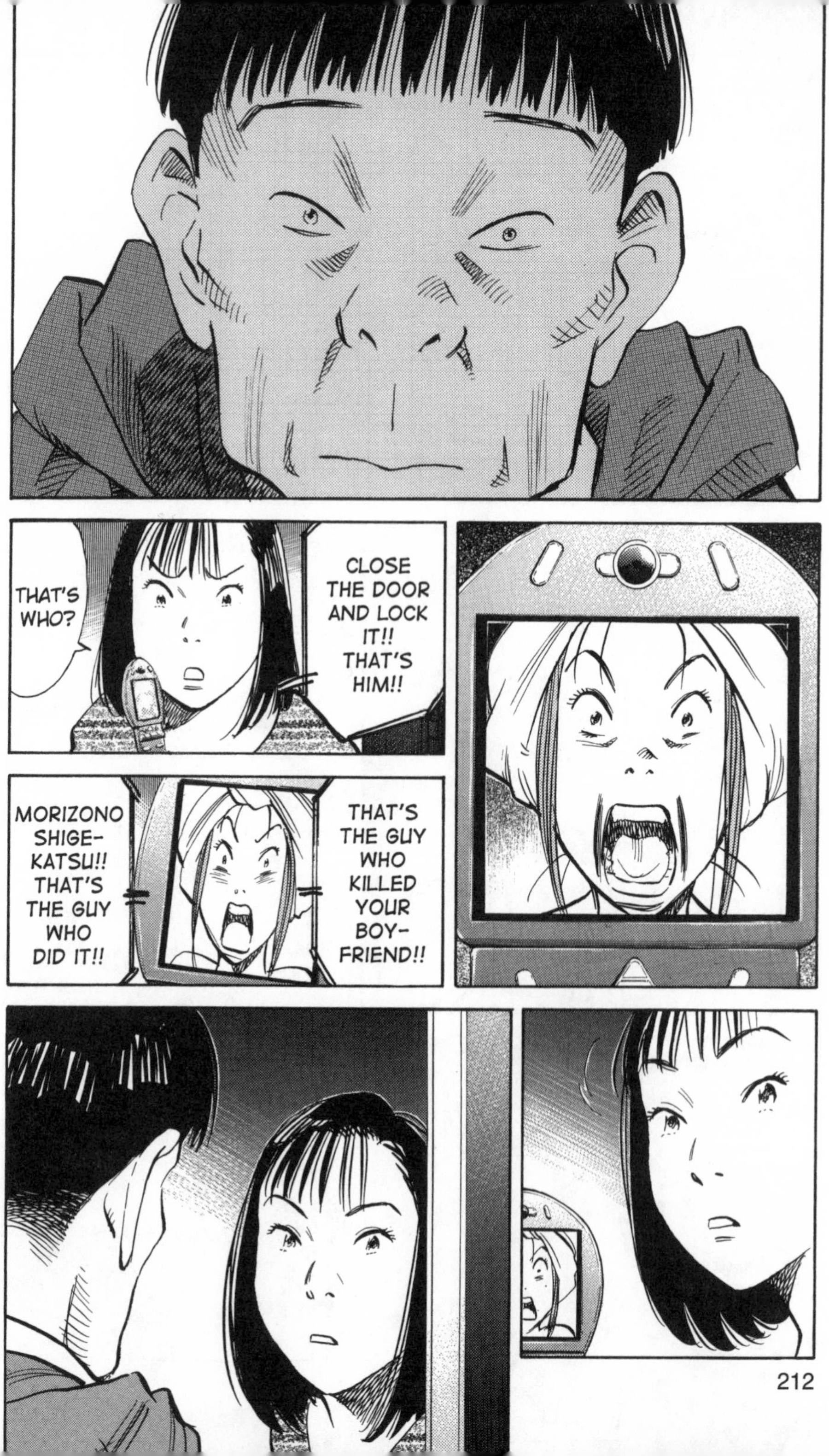
CLOSE THE DOOR AND LOCK IT!! THAT'S HIM!!
THAT'S WHO?
THAT'S THE GUY WHO KILLED YOUR BOY-FRIEND!!
MORIZONO SHIGE-KATSU!! THAT'S THE GUY WHO DID IT!!

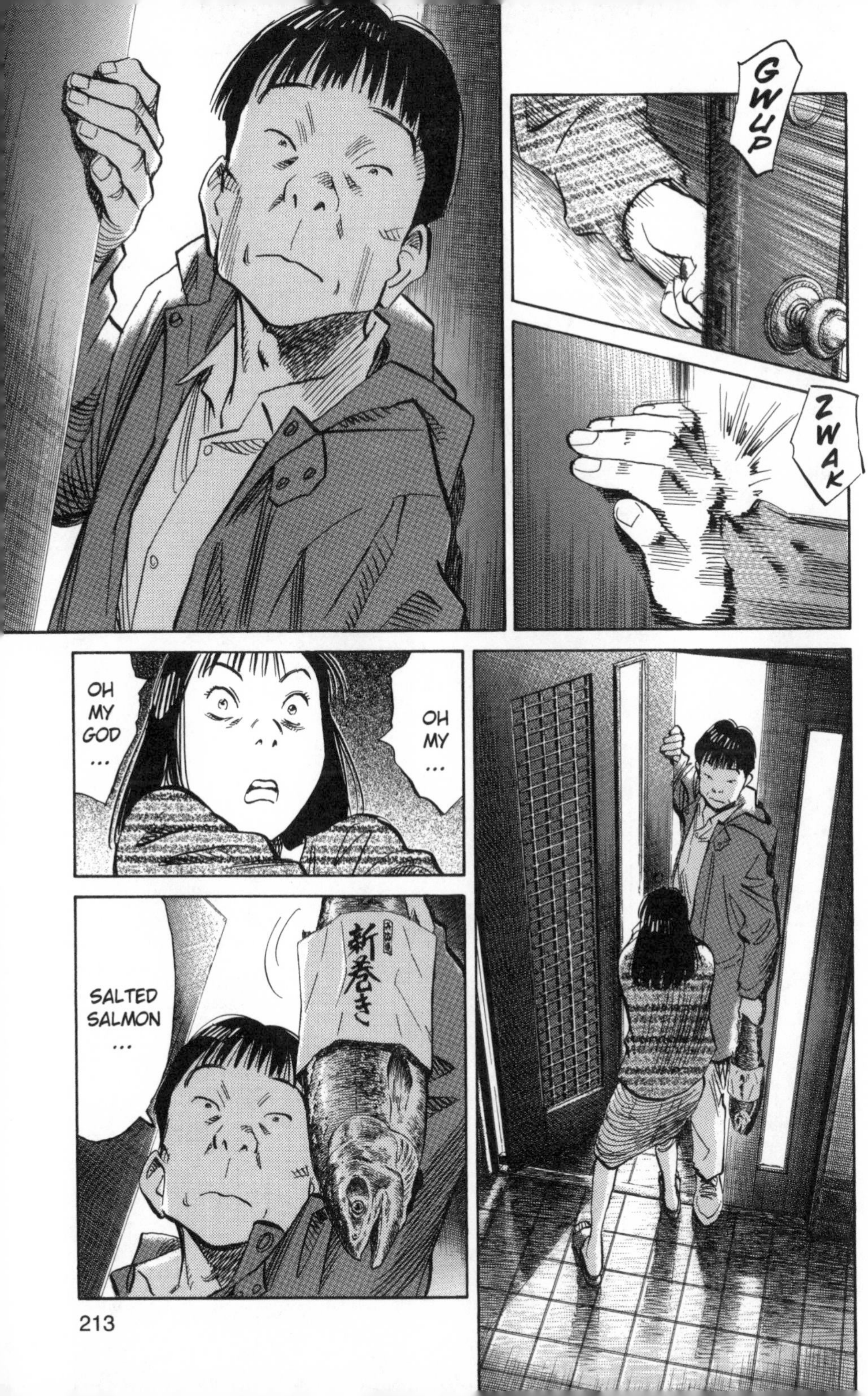
GWUP
ZWAK
OH MY ...
OH MY GOD ...
新巻き
SALTED SALMON ...

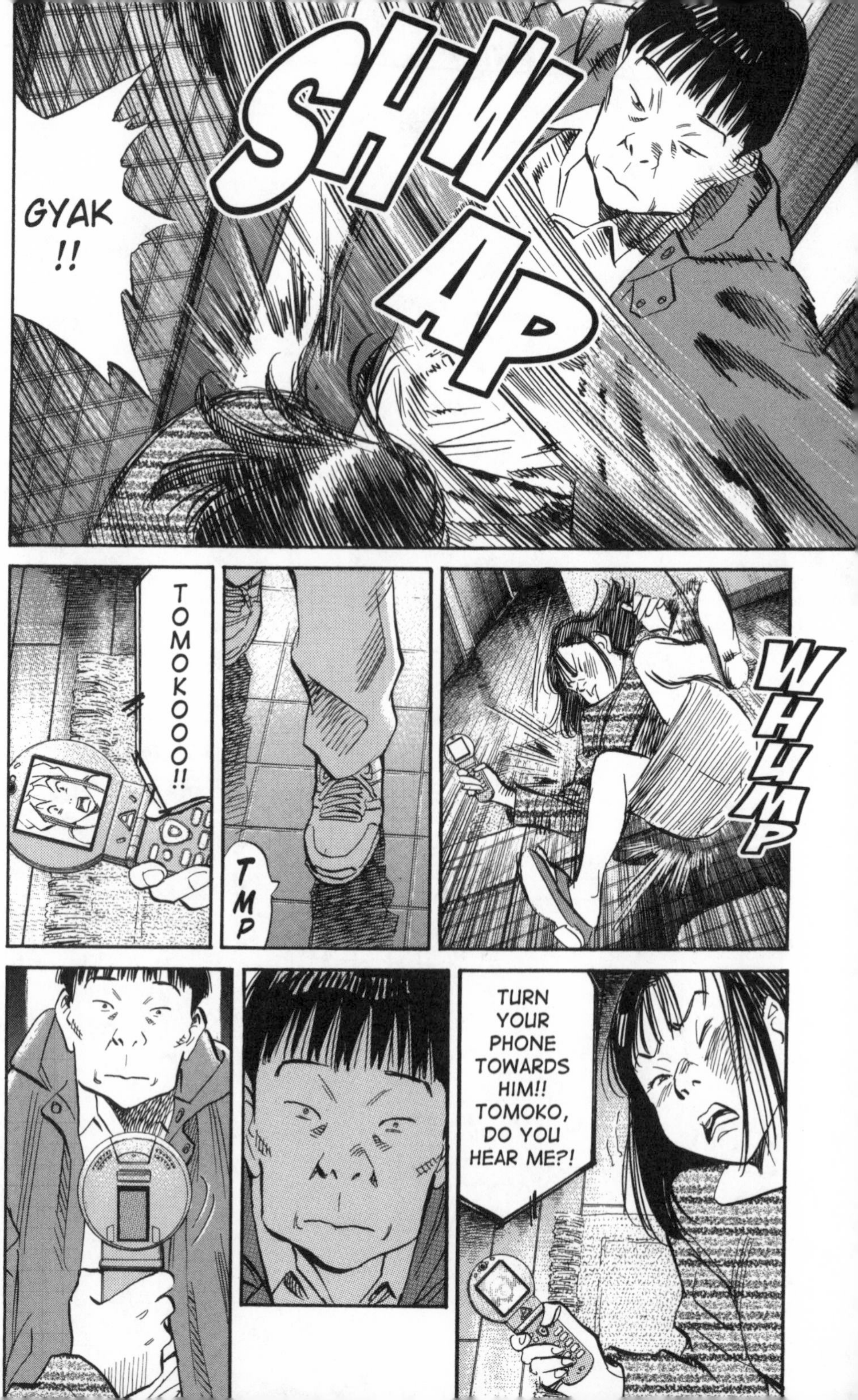
SHWAP
GYAK!!
WHUMP
TMP
TOMOKOOO!!
TURN YOUR PHONE TOWARDS HIM!! TOMOKO, DO YOU HEAR ME?!

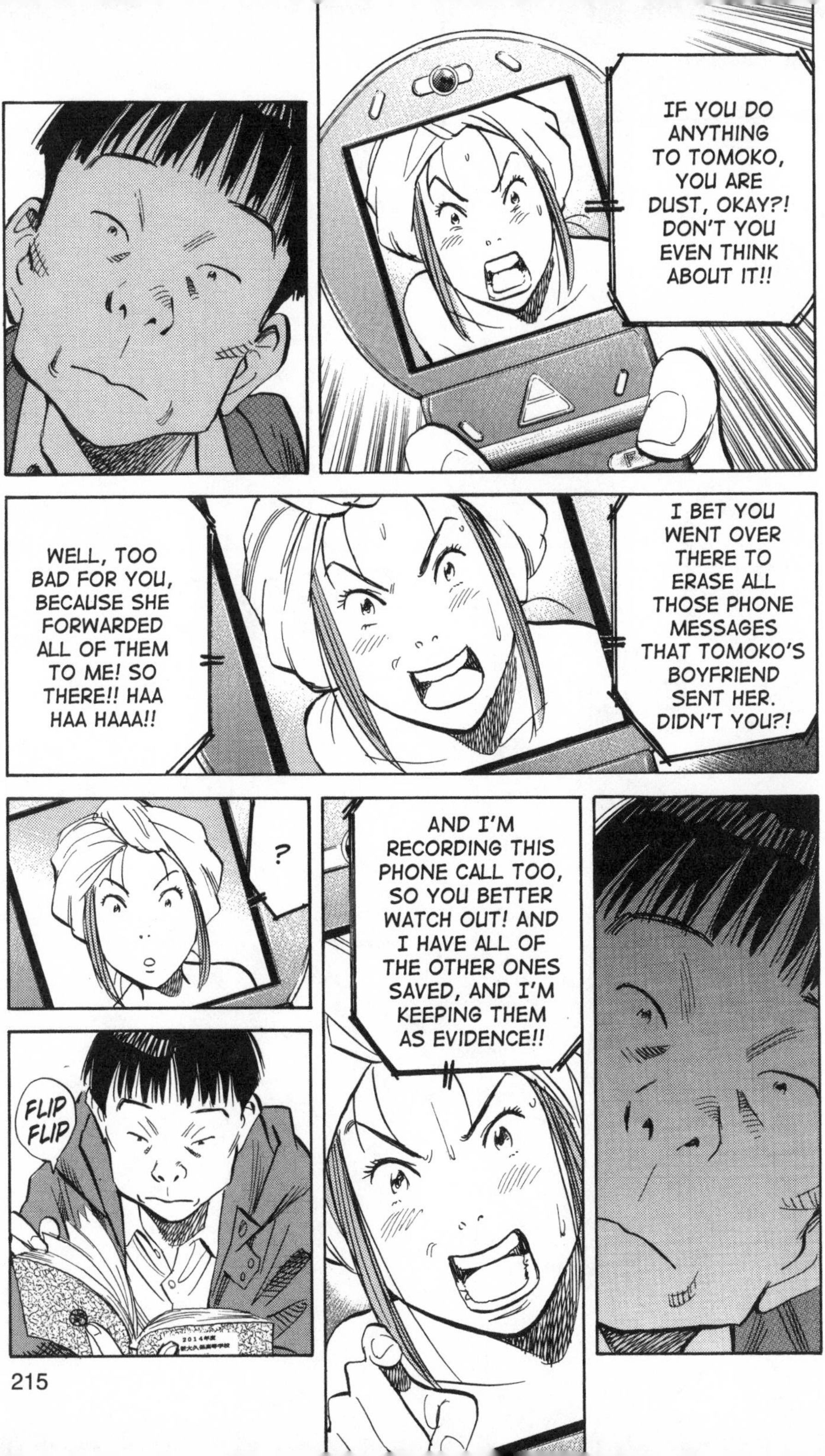
IF YOU DO ANYTHING TO TOMOKO, YOU ARE DUST, OKAY?! DON'T YOU EVEN THINK ABOUT IT!!
I BET YOU WENT OVER THERE TO ERASE ALL THOSE PHONE MESSAGES THAT TOMOKO'S BOYFRIEND SENT HER. DIDN'T YOU?!
WELL, TOO BAD FOR YOU, BECAUSE SHE FORWARDED ALL OF THEM TO ME! SO THERE!! HAA HAA HAAA!!
AND I'M RECORDING THIS PHONE CALL TOO, SO YOU BETTER WATCH OUT! AND I HAVE ALL OF THE OTHER ONES SAVED, AND I'M KEEPING THEM AS EVIDENCE!!
?
FLIP FLIP

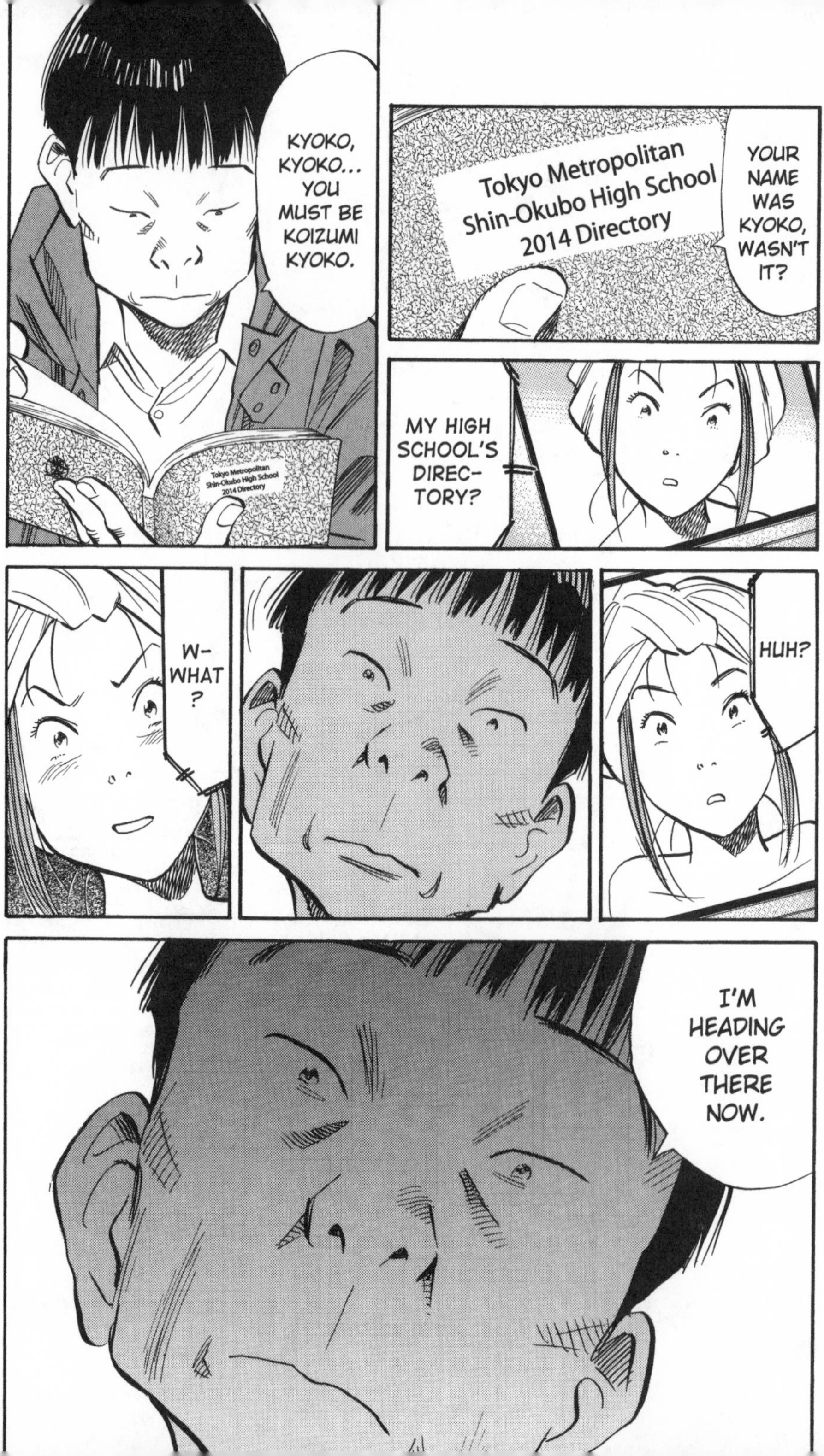
YOUR NAME WAS KYOKO, WASN'T IT?
Tokyo Metropolitan Shin-Okubo High School 2014 Directory
MY HIGH SCHOOL'S DIRECTORY?
KYOKO, KYOKO... YOU MUST BE KOIZUMI KYOKO.
Tokyo Metropolitan Shin-Okubo High School 2014 Directory
HUH?
W-WHAT?
I'M HEADING OVER THERE NOW.

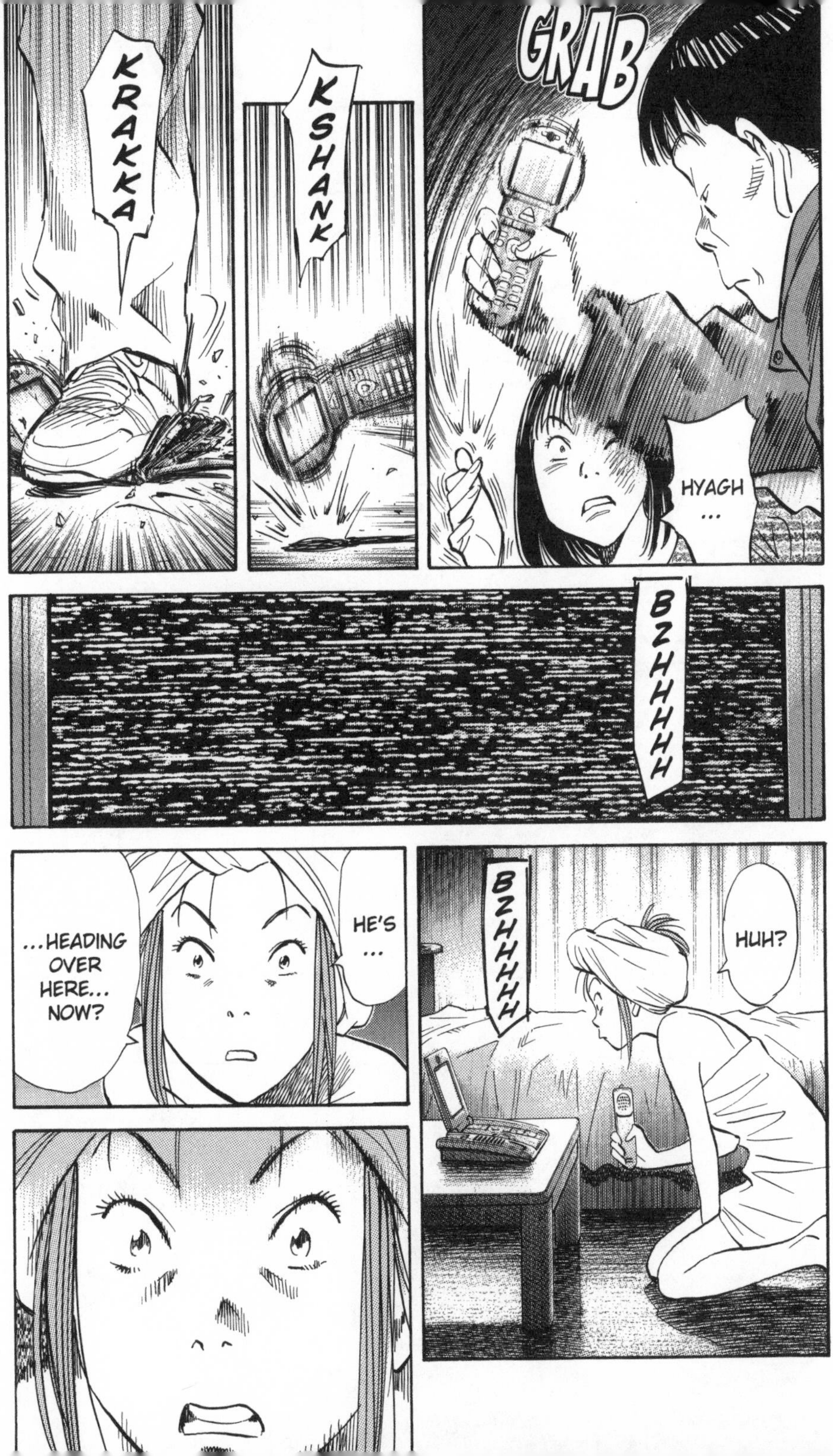
GRAB
HYAGH ...
KSHANK
KRAKKA
BZHHHHHH
BZHHHHHH
HUH?
HE'S ...
...HEADING OVER HERE... NOW?

OMI-GOD!! WHAT DO I DO?!

OMI-GOD!! WHAT DO I DO?!

DA

GYAAARGH!!

HE'S COMING OVER HERE!!

HE'S COM-ING!!

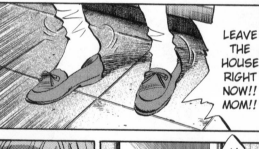

LEAVE THE HOUSE RIGHT NOW!! MOM!!

KRIK

THUDDA DUDDA

MOOOOOMM!!

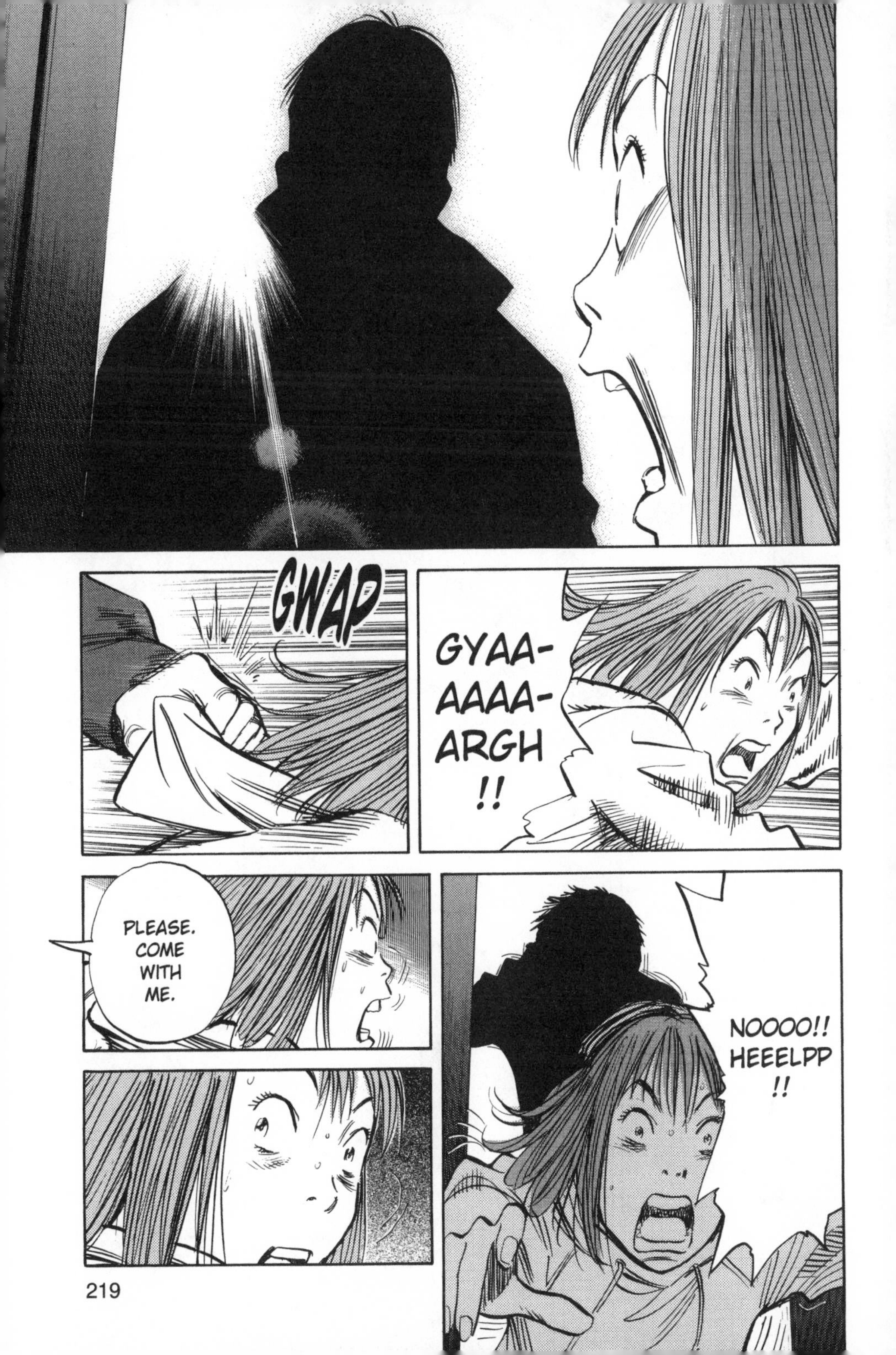
GYAA-AAAA-ARGH!!
GWAP
NOOOO!! HEEELPP!!
PLEASE. COME WITH ME.

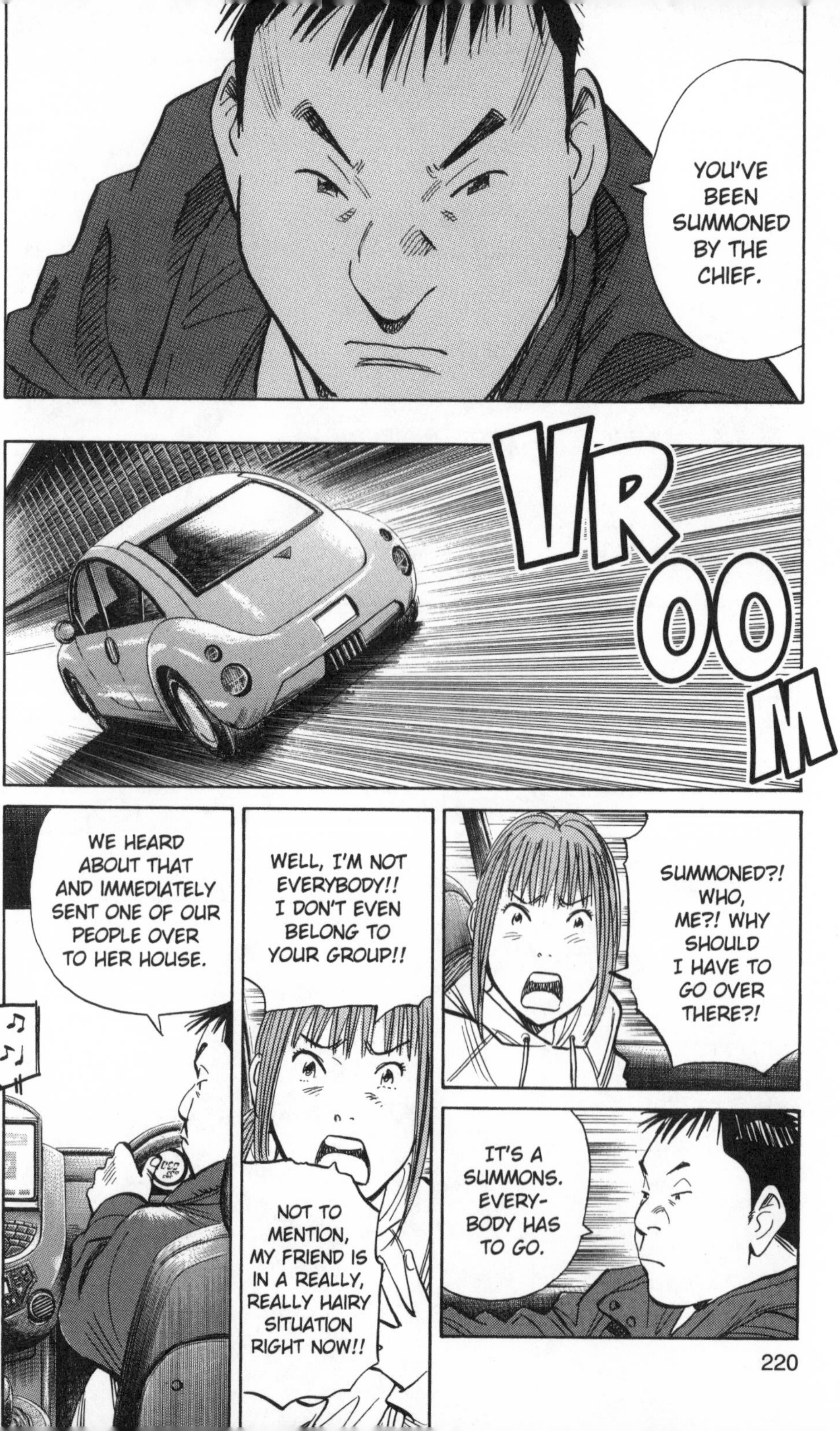
YOU'VE BEEN SUMMONED BY THE CHIEF.
VROOOM
SUMMONED?! WHO, ME?! WHY SHOULD I HAVE TO GO OVER THERE?!
IT'S A SUMMONS. EVERYBODY HAS TO GO.
WELL, I'M NOT EVERYBODY!! I DON'T EVEN BELONG TO YOUR GROUP!!
NOT TO MENTION, MY FRIEND IS IN A REALLY, REALLY HAIRY SITUATION RIGHT NOW!!
WE HEARD ABOUT THAT AND IMMEDIATELY SENT ONE OF OUR PEOPLE OVER TO HER HOUSE.
♪ ♪

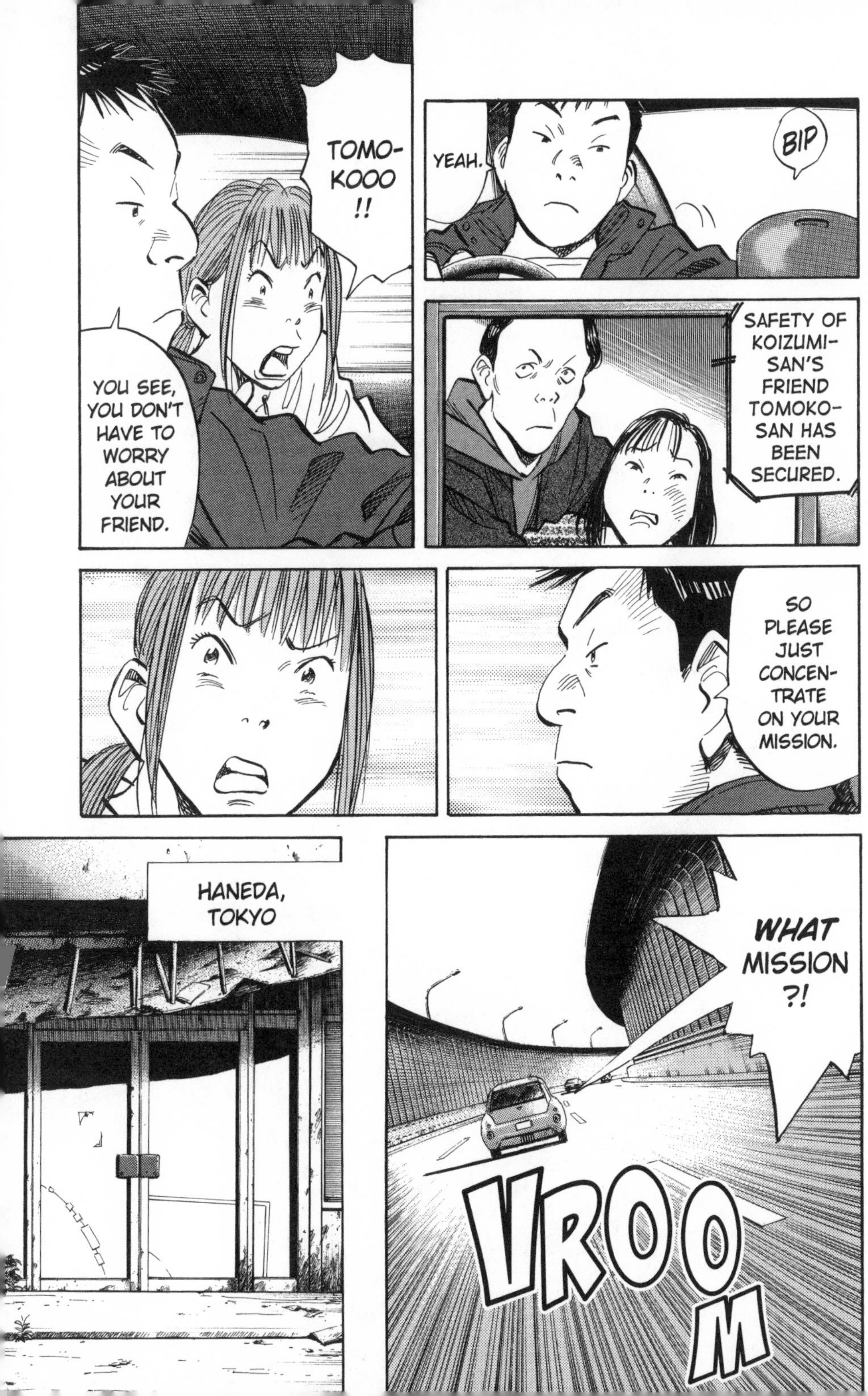
BIP
YEAH.
SAFETY OF KOIZUMI-SAN'S FRIEND TOMOKO-SAN HAS BEEN SECURED.
TOMO-KOOO !!
YOU SEE, YOU DON'T HAVE TO WORRY ABOUT YOUR FRIEND.
SO PLEASE JUST CONCEN-TRATE ON YOUR MISSION.
WHAT MISSION ?!
VROOM
HANEDA, TOKYO

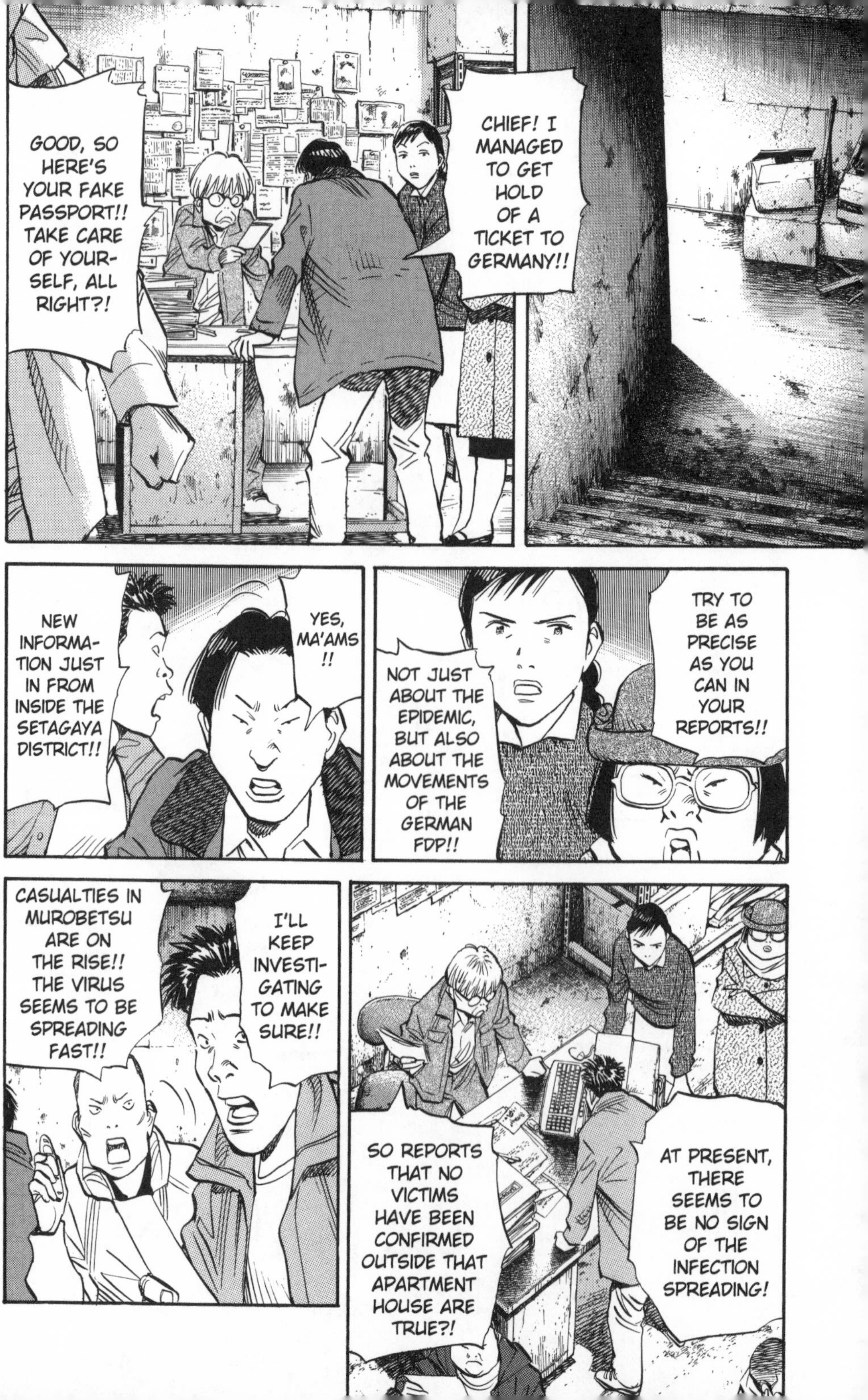
CHIEF! I MANAGED TO GET HOLD OF A TICKET TO GERMANY!!
GOOD, SO HERE'S YOUR FAKE PASSPORT!! TAKE CARE OF YOUR-SELF, ALL RIGHT?!
TRY TO BE AS PRECISE AS YOU CAN IN YOUR REPORTS!!
NOT JUST ABOUT THE EPIDEMIC, BUT ALSO ABOUT THE MOVEMENTS OF THE GERMAN FDP!!
YES, MA'AMS!!
NEW INFORMA-TION JUST IN FROM INSIDE THE SETAGAYA DISTRICT!!
AT PRESENT, THERE SEEMS TO BE NO SIGN OF THE INFECTION SPREADING!
SO REPORTS THAT NO VICTIMS HAVE BEEN CONFIRMED OUTSIDE THAT APARTMENT HOUSE ARE TRUE?!
I'LL KEEP INVESTI-GATING TO MAKE SURE!!
CASUALTIES IN MUROBETSU ARE ON THE RISE!! THE VIRUS SEEMS TO BE SPREADING FAST!!

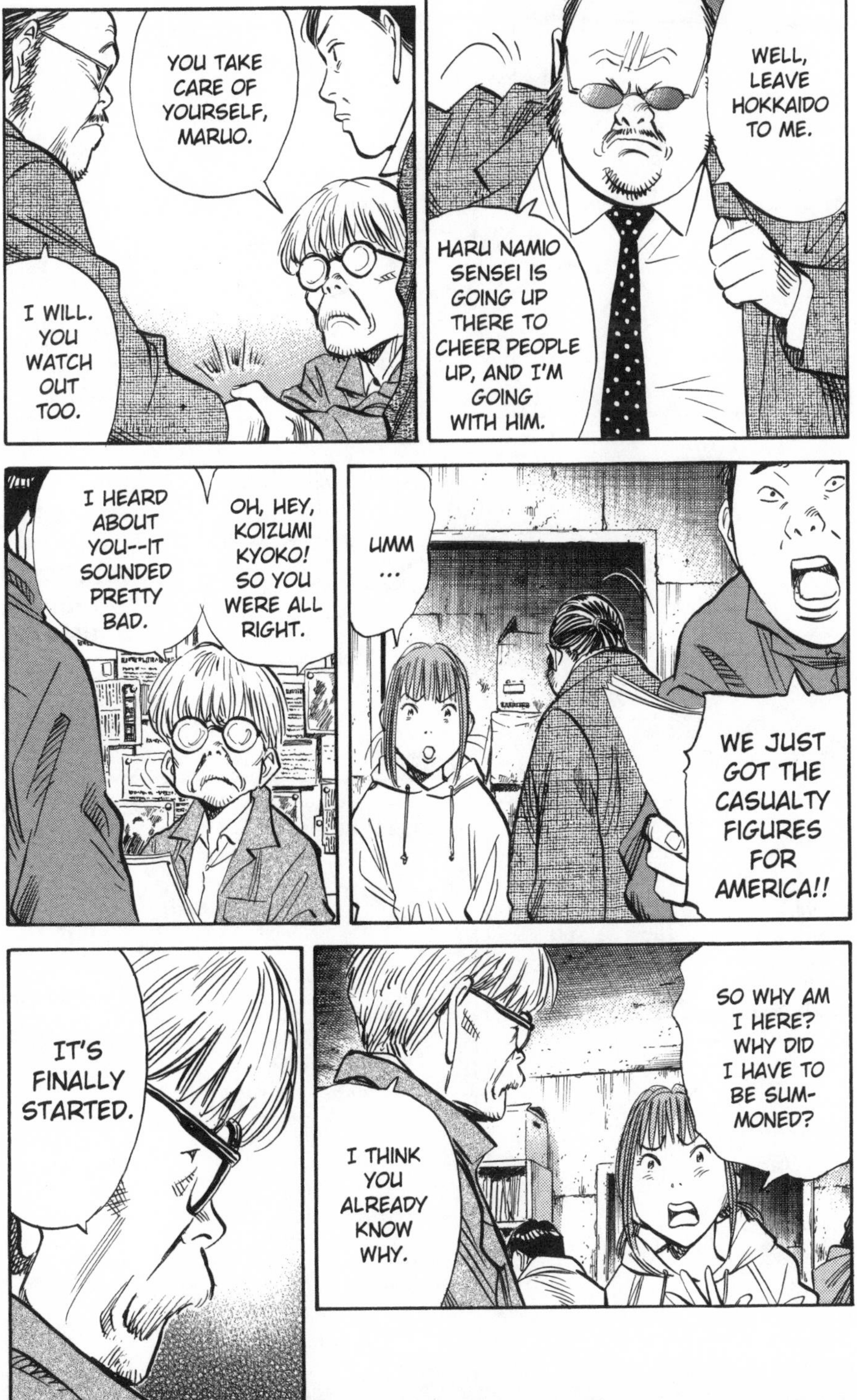
WELL, LEAVE HOKKAIDO TO ME.
HARU NAMIO SENSEI IS GOING UP THERE TO CHEER PEOPLE UP, AND I'M GOING WITH HIM.
YOU TAKE CARE OF YOURSELF, MARUO.
I WILL. YOU WATCH OUT TOO.
WE JUST GOT THE CASUALTY FIGURES FOR AMERICA!!
UMM ...
OH, HEY, KOIZUMI KYOKO! SO YOU WERE ALL RIGHT.
I HEARD ABOUT YOU--IT SOUNDED PRETTY BAD.
SO WHY AM I HERE? WHY DID I HAVE TO BE SUM-MONED?
I THINK YOU ALREADY KNOW WHY.
IT'S FINALLY STARTED.

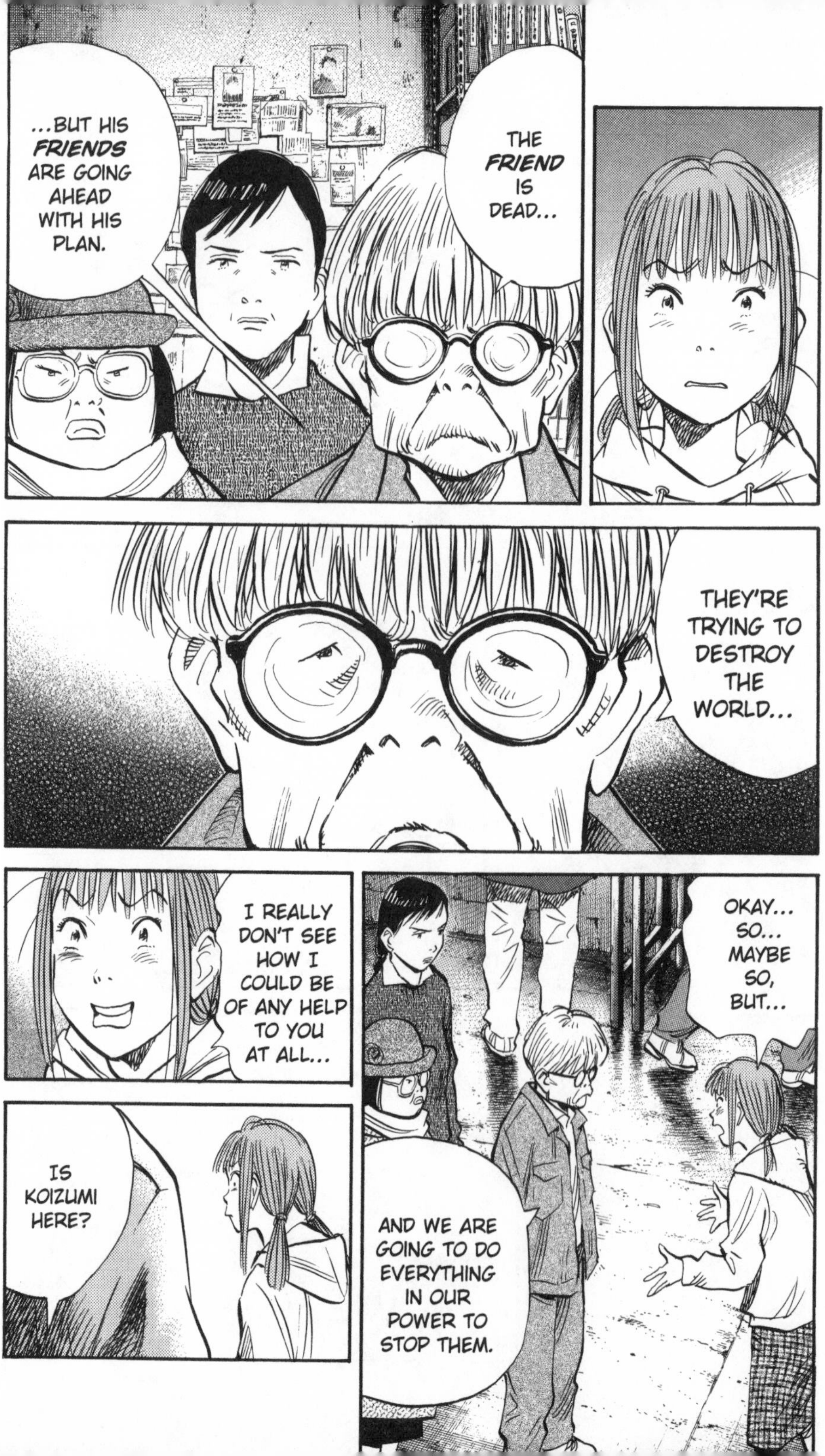
THE ***FRIEND*** IS DEAD...
...BUT HIS ***FRIENDS*** ARE GOING AHEAD WITH HIS PLAN.
THEY'RE TRYING TO DESTROY THE WORLD...
OKAY... SO... MAYBE SO, BUT...
AND WE ARE GOING TO DO EVERYTHING IN OUR POWER TO STOP THEM.
I REALLY DON'T SEE HOW I COULD BE OF ANY HELP TO YOU AT ALL...
IS KOIZUMI HERE?

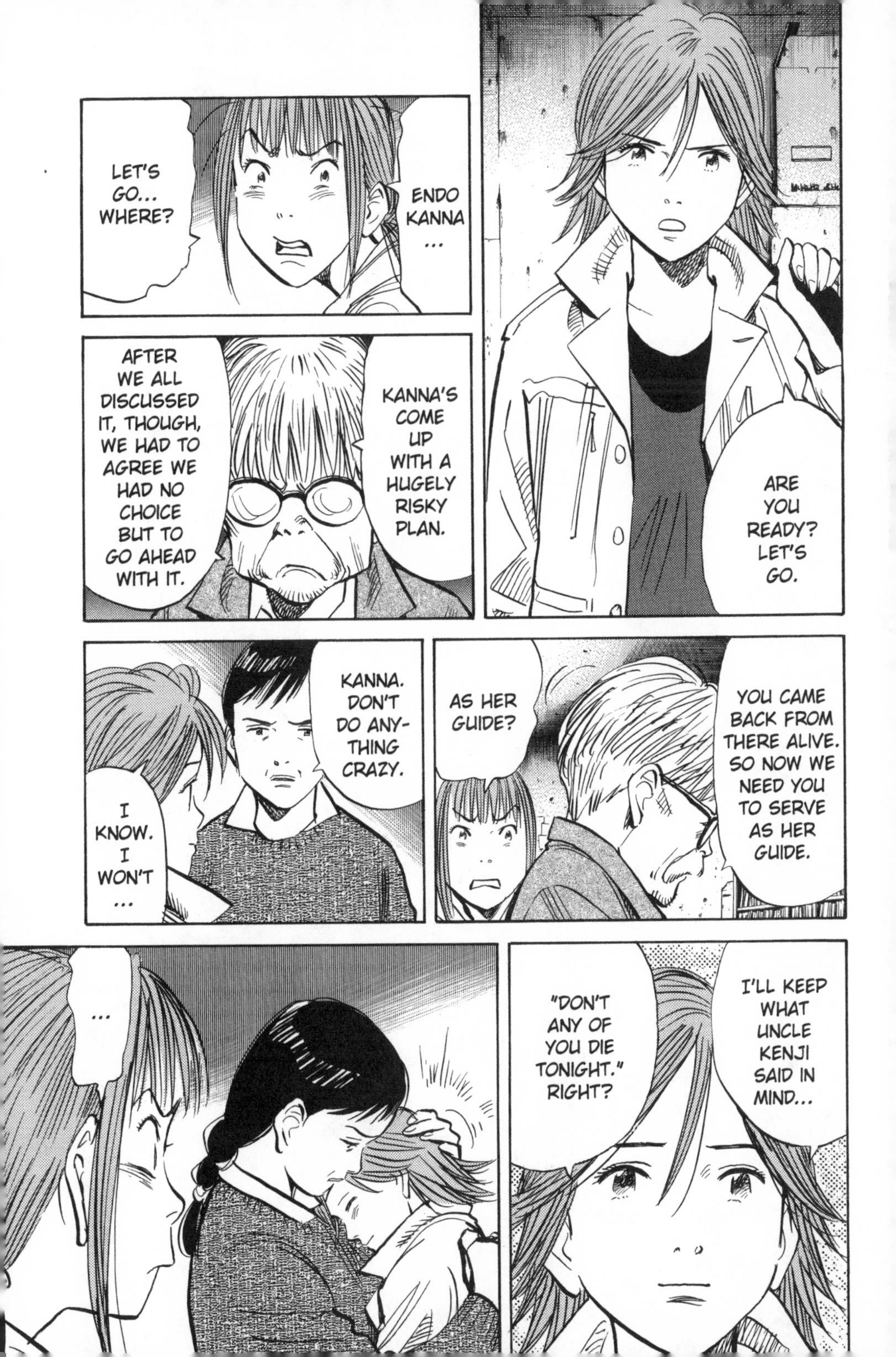
ARE YOU READY? LET'S GO.
ENDO KANNA...
LET'S GO... WHERE?
KANNA'S COME UP WITH A HUGELY RISKY PLAN.
AFTER WE ALL DISCUSSED IT, THOUGH, WE HAD TO AGREE WE HAD NO CHOICE BUT TO GO AHEAD WITH IT.
YOU CAME BACK FROM THERE ALIVE. SO NOW WE NEED YOU TO SERVE AS HER GUIDE.
AS HER GUIDE?
KANNA. DON'T DO ANY-THING CRAZY.
I KNOW. I WON'T...
I'LL KEEP WHAT UNCLE KENJI SAID IN MIND...
"DON'T ANY OF YOU DIE TONIGHT." RIGHT?
...

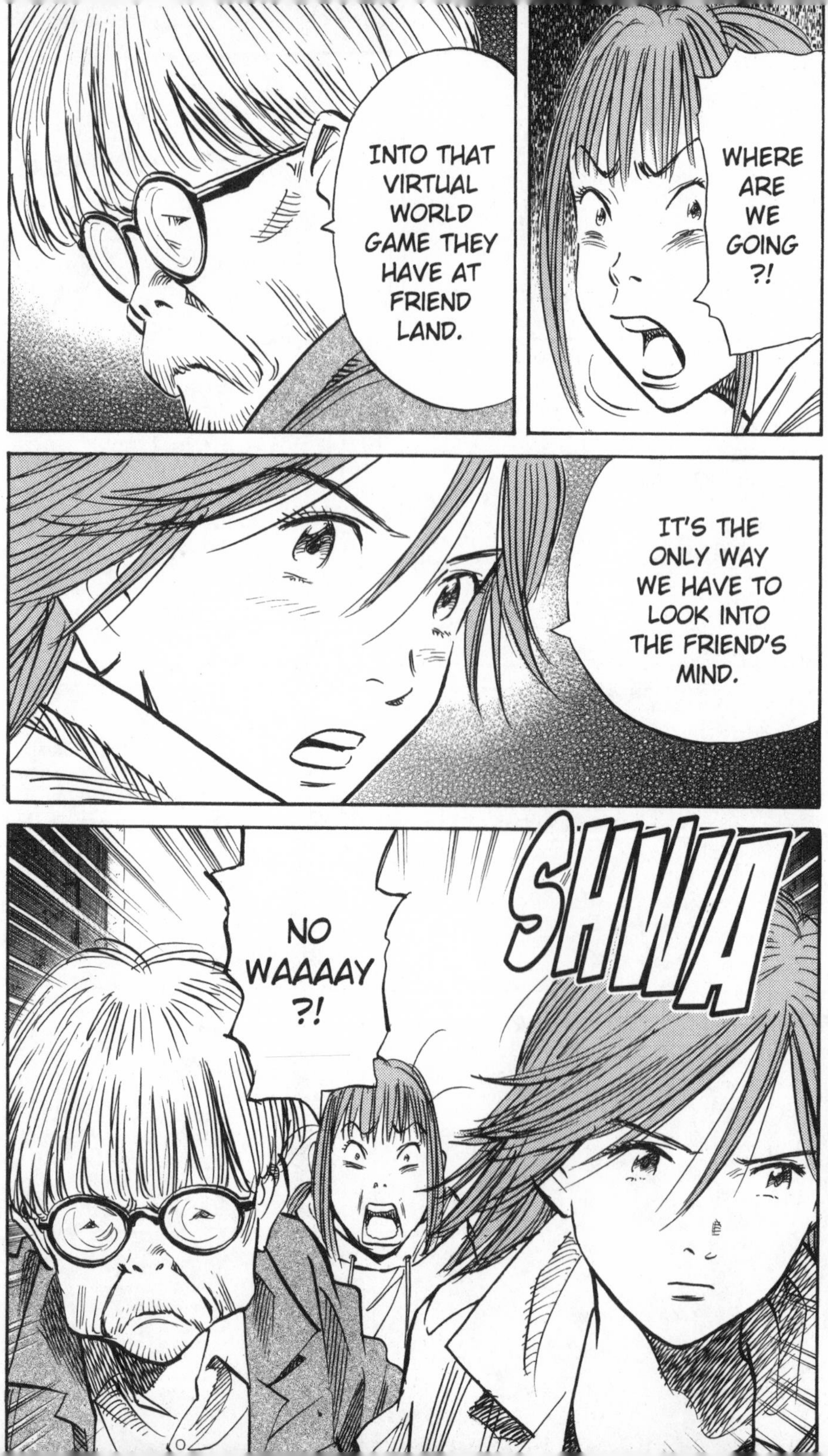
WHERE ARE WE GOING?!
INTO THAT VIRTUAL WORLD GAME THEY HAVE AT FRIEND LAND.
IT'S THE ONLY WAY WE HAVE TO LOOK INTO THE FRIEND'S MIND.
SHWA
NO WAAAAY?!

TO BE CONTINUED

NOTES FROM THE TRANSLATOR

This series follows the Japanese naming convention, with a character's family name followed by their given name. Honorifics such as *-san* and *-kun* are also preserved.

Page 35: Ninja Hattori-kun is a character from a manga by Fujiko Fujio Ⓐ, which was adapted into live-action TV series and anime.

Page 200: Ishikari-nabe is a hotpot dish featuring salmon and vegetables.